Walter W. Wymer, Jr.
Jennifer Lees-Marshment
Editors

Current Issues in Political Marketing

Current Issues in Political Marketing has been co-published simultaneously as *Journal of Nonprofit & Public Sector Marketing*, Volume 14, Numbers 1/2 2005.

Pre-publication REVIEWS, COMMENTARIES, EVALUATIONS . . .

"INTERESTING, CHALLENGING, AND DIVERSE. . . . An up-to-date review of current practice and critical thinking in international political marketing. . . . Examines the relationship between marketing and politics, and in particular the many ethical and practical issues associated with political marketing's implementation. . . . A MUST-READ for academics and practitioners of political marketing."

Declan Bannon, MBA, DipM
*Lecturer in Marketing
and Strategic Marketing Management
University of Paisley, Scotland*

Best Business Books®
An Imprint of The Haworth Press, Inc.

New York • London • Victoria (AU)
www.HaworthPress.com

Current Issues
in Political Marketing

Current Issues in Political Marketing has been co-published simultaneously as *Journal of Nonprofit & Public Sector Marketing*, Volume 14, Numbers 1/2 2005.

Current Issues in Political Marketing, edited by Walter W. Wymer, Jr., DBA, and Jennifer Lees-Marshment, PhD (Vol. 14, No. 1/2, 2005). *"AN EXCELLENT TEXT FOR A NUMBER OF UNDERGRADUATE AND GRADUATE CLASSES in both political science and marketing . . . . Addresses concerns across a wide variety of traditional academic disciplines but is also accessible to non-academics."* Jonathan Knuckey, PhD, Associate Professor of Political Science, University of Central Florida

Social Marketing, edited by Michael T. Ewing, PhD (Vol. 9, No. 4, 2001). *"Stimulating . . . Extremely timely . . . With contributions from eminent academics from diverse parts of the world, this book covers a wide range of ideas, research methods, and philosophical concepts."* (Barry Howcroft, ACIB, MSc, BA, Professor of Retail Banking, Banking Centre, Longhborough University, United Kingdom)

Marketing Communications for Local Nonprofit Organizations: Targets and Tools, edited by Donald R. Self, DBA, Walter W. Wymer, Jr., DBA, and Teri Kline Henley, MBA (Vol. 9, No. 1/2, 2001). *"Excellent . . . a test that is of great relevance to practitioners and academics alike. The authors have successfully produced a comprehensive review of the marketing needs of non-profit professionals/organizations and offer relevant sets of tools."* (Ram Cnaan, PhD, Associate Professor, School of Social Work, University of Pennsylvania, Philadelphia)

Volunteerism Marketing: New Vistas for Nonprofit and Public Sector Management, edited by Donald R. Self, DBA, and Walter W. Wymer, Jr., DBA (Vol. 6, No. 2/3, 1999). *"Offers the volunteer coordinator in these organizations the information needed to better understand where, and how, to effectively recruit and mobilize these increasingly important 'customers.'"* (Michael J. Tullier, East Alabama Community Blood Bank, LifeSouth Community Blood Centers)

Marketing University Outreach Programs, edited by Ralph S. Foster, Jr., BS, William I. Sauser, Jr., PhD, and Donald R. Self, DBA (Vol. 2, No. 2/3, 1995). *"Should be required reading . . . The authors not only know marketing but they also reflect a deep understanding of outreach and its place in the 21st century university."* (James C. Vortruba, Vice Provost for University Outreach, Michigan State University)

Public Mental Health Marketing: Developing a Consumer Attitude, edited by Donald R. Self, DBA (Vol. 1, No. 2/3, 1993). *"Provides a balance of theoretical and practical information on marketing local, state, and national mental health agencies."* (Reference and Research Book News)

Current Issues
in Political Marketing

Walter W. Wymer, Jr., DBA
Jennifer Lees-Marshment, PhD
Editors

Current Issues in Political Marketing has been co-published simultaneously as *Journal of Nonprofit & Public Sector Marketing*, Volume 14, Numbers 1/2 2005.

Best Business Books®
An Imprint of The Haworth Press, Inc.

New York • London • Victoria (AU)
www.HaworthPress.com

Published by

Best Business Books®, 10 Alice Street, Binghamton, NY 13904-1580 USA

Best Business Books® is an imprint of The Haworth Press, Inc., 10 Alice Street, Binghamton, NY 13904-1580 USA.

Current Issues in Political Marketing has been co-published simultaneously as *Journal of Nonprofit & Public Sector Marketing*, Volume 14, Numbers 1/2 2005.

Cover design by Wendy Baker

Library of Congress Cataloging-in-Publication Data

Current issues in political marketing / Walter W. Wymer, Jr., Jennifer Lees-Marshment, editors.
    p. cm.
    "Co-published simultaneously as Journal of nonprofit & public sector marketing, volume 14, numbers 1/2 2005."
    Includes bibliographical references and index.
    ISBN: 13: 978-0-7890-2437-4 (hard cover : alk. paper)
    ISBN: 10: 0-7890-2437-3 (hard cover : alk. paper)
    ISBN: 13: 978-0-7890-2438-1 (soft cover : alk. paper)
    ISBN: 10: 0-7890-2438-1 (soft cover : alk. paper)
    1. Campaign management. 2. Political campaigns. 3. Marketing–Political aspects. I. Wymer, Walter W. II. Lees-Marshment, Jennifer. III. Journal of nonprofit & public sector marketing.

JF2112.C3C87 2005
324.7'3–dc22
                                                   2005004146

Indexing, Abstracting & Website/Internet Coverage

This section provides you with a list of major indexing & abstracting services and other tools for bibliographic access. That is to say, each service began covering this periodical during the year noted in the right column. Most Websites which are listed below have indicated that they will either post, disseminate, compile, archive, cite or alert their own Website users with research-based content from this work. (This list is as current as the copyright date of this publication.)

Abstracting, Website/Indexing Coverage . . . . Year When Coverage Began

- *ABI/INFORM. Contents of this publication are indexed and abstracted in the ABI/INFORM database, available on ProQuest Information & Learning @ http://www.proquest.com.* **2001**

- *ABI/INFORM Global. Contents of this publication are indexed and abstracted in the ABI/INFORM Global database, available on ProQuest Information & Learning @ http://www.proquest.com* . . . **2001**

- *ABI/INFORM Research. Contents of this publication are indexed and abstracted in the ABI/INFORM Research database, available on ProQuest Information & Learning @ http://www.proquest.com* . . . **2001**

- *Business Source Corporate: coverage of nearly 3,350 quality magazines and journals; designed to meet the diverse information needs of corporations; EBSCO Publishing <http://www.epnet.com/corporate/bsourcecorp.asp>* **1999**

- *Business Source Elite: coverage of scholarly business, management and economics journals; EBSCO Publishing <http://www.epnet.com/academic/bussourceelite.asp>* **2000**

(continued)

(continued)

Special Bibliographic Notes related to special journal issues (separates) and indexing/abstracting:

- indexing/abstracting services in this list will also cover material in any "separate" that is co-published simultaneously with Haworth's special thematic journal issue or DocuSerial. Indexing/abstracting usually covers material at the article/chapter level.
- monographic co-editions are intended for either non-subscribers or libraries which intend to purchase a second copy for their circulating collections.
- monographic co-editions are reported to all jobbers/wholesalers/approval plans. The source journal is listed as the "series" to assist the prevention of duplicate purchasing in the same manner utilized for books-in-series.
- to facilitate user/access services all indexing/abstracting services are encouraged to utilize the co-indexing entry note indicated at the bottom of the first page of each article/chapter/contribution.
- this is intended to assist a library user of any reference tool (whether print, electronic, online, or CD-ROM) to locate the monographic version if the library has purchased this version but not a subscription to the source journal.
- individual articles/chapters in any Haworth publication are also available through The Haworth Document Delivery Service (HDDS).

Current Issues in Political Marketing

CONTENTS

ABOUT THE EDITORS

Walter W. Wymer, Jr., DBA, is Associate Professor of Marketing at Christopher Newport University in Newport News, Virginia. Dr. Wymer's research has focused on marketing in nonprofit organizations. His work has been published in several academic journals and presented at numerous academic conferences. Dr. Wymer is the editor of *Journal of Nonprofit & Public Sector Marketing*. He also serves on the editorial boards of *International Journal of Nonprofit & Voluntary Sector Marketing*, *Health Marketing Quarterly*, and *Journal of Ministry Marketing & Management*.

Jennifer Lees-Marshment, PhD, is a specialist in Political Marketing and is Director of the Centre for Political Marketing at Keele University (www.keele.ac.uk/depts/mn/cpm). She holds a BA in American Studies and History from the University of Keele, an MA (Econ.) in European Politics and Policy from the University of Manchester and a PhD in Political parties and political marketing from Keele. Her publications include the book *Political Marketing and British Political Parties* (MUP 2001) which analysed the marketing of the Labour and Conservative Parties in the UK, and *The Political Marketing Revolution* (MUP 2004), which broadens the scope of political marketing and applies marketing to health and education, the media, parliament, the monarchy, interest groups, and local/devolved government, as well as party politics. Jennifer was organiser of the 2002 Political Marketing Conference and edited special issues of *Journal of Public Affairs* and *International Journal of Non Profit and Voluntary Sector Marketing*, both published in the UK in 2003.

Introduction

Political marketing is an area of growing interest and importance. Marketing is now used by a wide range of institutions within the political arena, including not just parties but presidents, individual politicians and parliaments, worldwide. Politics would seem to be being transformed from a leadership-run system to that dictated by public needs and demands. Marketing has permeated all political organizations: as people act increasingly like consumers in the marketplace, the rise of political consumer puts pressure on all public institutions to become more responsive to the demands of those they serve. Political parties, the media, universities, local government, charities and legislatures are adopting the tools of market intelligence to understand their market needs and demands. Politicians, professors and even princes are using marketing to design their political product in the hope it will satisfy the ever-critical political consumer.

There are, however, many ethical and practical difficulties associated with implementing an approach originating from business into the political and public world. It is the duty of academics to discuss such issues, such as whether marketing is good for democracy, can students and voters act like consumers, the problems of following public opinion in every sphere of politics. In the UK but also elsewhere there is a perceived crisis due to the lack of interest in voting or politics itself, which both politicians and commentators are attempting to address. The range of political marketing activity is broad and complex, encouraging academics to play a significant role in exploring and debating the consequences of increased use of marketing within the political arena.

Political marketing scholarship has developed in quality, quantity and scope tremendously in the last 2-3 years, helped by a growing group of aca-

[Haworth co-indexing entry note]: "Introduction." Lees-Marshment, Jennifer. Co-published simultaneously in *Journal of Nonprofit & Public Sector Marketing* (Best Business Books, an imprint of The Haworth Press, Inc.) Vol. 14, No. 1/2, 2005, pp. 1-3; and: *Current Issues in Political Marketing* (eds: Walter W. Wymer, Jr., and Jennifer Lees-Marshment) Best Business Books, an imprint of The Haworth Press, Inc., 2005, pp. 1-3. Single or multiple copies of this article are available for a fee from The Haworth Document Delivery Service [1-800-HAWORTH, 9:00 a.m. - 5:00 p.m. (EST). E-mail address: getinfo@haworthpressinc.com].

Available online at http://www.haworthpress.com/web/JNPSM
doi:10.1300/J054v14n01_01

demics from different disciplines working together in the UK. The international political marketing conference is run every year in the UK. There is a specialist group within both the marketing and political science discipline which draws together scholars from that area interested in this exciting new topic. This special issue came about during discussions between myself and Walter Wymer when I was organising the 2002 political marketing conference in Aberdeen. The 2002 Political Marketing Conference called for papers from practitioners as well as academics, from scholars around the globe, to come together to debate the practice as well as the theory of political marketing. Contributions were made by academics in political science, advertising and management studies, but also by those who have attempted to practice political marketing 'on the ground.'

That conference, together with political marketing panels run at the UK Political Studies Association Conference in 2003, helped to forge new links between colleagues from different backgrounds, stimulate further thoughts and develop new research. The development of these networks has enabled the creation of improved dialogue, feedback and review. This, together with the work attracted within the USA and other countries by Walter Wymer, has resulted in a highly-developed and critical set of articles which illustrates the current issues in political marketing.

All articles submitted for this special issue were subject to a double-blind peer-review from specialists in the field. It was not possible to publish all of them, despite the high quality of submissions, and those published here represent those that were rated most highly by the review system. The majority deal with British politics because this is where the current locus of academic energy in political marketing lies, but such articles are relevant for all western liberal democratic countries. It is hoped they will also stimulate further work and comparison by scholars in the USA as well as countries such as New Zealand and Australia. Read as a whole, the special issue offers a critical reflection on the consequences of political marketing for democracy, offering a timely contribution to an issue at the heart and minds of politicians and political commentators of all kinds.

One of the obstacles faced by the political marketing field is that such people lie in an array of departments, disciplines and institutions and we therefore need such events and arenas to bring us all together. Only then can research really progress. I hope this special issue will play a role in stimulating new debates and international connections. I would like to thank Walter Wymer for providing this opportunity and serving as a very supportive, patient and co-operative co-editor. I would also like to thank all the reviewers for their time spent making constructive comments which not only checked, but served to improve, the quality of the final articles selected for publication. If anyone has any comments, thoughts or questions please do email me or the author(s) individually. I would hope that the issue will not only prove of interest in itself, but will stimulate thoughts and further research by its readers.

Dr. Jennifer Lees-Marshment
Founding Director of the Centre for Political Marketing
www.keele.ac.uk/depts/mn/cpm
Keele University
Keele, Staffs, ST5 5BG UK
E-mail: j.lees-marshment@keele.ac.uk

Political Marketing:
The Cause of an Emerging
Democratic Deficit in Britain?

Darren G. Lilleker

SUMMARY. Political marketing, as a set of techniques for policy design and development, was welcomed as a route towards a more participatory form of democracy. However, as New Labour attempted to rebrand itself to suit key segments of the electorate, we find that voters are not participating to any greater extent. In fact sections of the electorate are rejecting the democratic process, feeling that parties have little care for those outside their target segment. This paper questions the way New Labour employed marketing and, drawing on primary data, relates this to the dramatic fall in turnout in 2001. *[Article copies available for a fee from The Haworth Document Delivery Service: 1-800-HAWORTH. E-mail address: <docdelivery@haworthpress.com> Website: <http://www.HaworthPress. com> © 2005 by The Haworth Press, Inc. All rights reserved.]*

Dr. Darren G. Lilleker is Senior Lecturer of Political Communication, Bournemouth Media School, Bournemouth University, Fern Barrow, Poole, Dorset, UK BH12 5BB (E-mail: dlilleker@bournemouth.ac.uk).

The author would like to thank the focus group members and Labour Party workers who agreed to participate in the research project. He would also like to thank colleagues at Bournemouth University and delegates to the Political Studies Association Annual Conference, Leicester 2003, for their comments on earlier drafts, as well as the three anonymous reviewers.

[Haworth co-indexing entry note]: "Political Marketing: The Cause of an Emerging Democratic Deficit in Britain?" Lilleker, Darren G. Co-published simultaneously in *Journal of Nonprofit & Public Sector Marketing* (Best Business Books, an imprint of The Haworth Press, Inc.) Vol. 14, No. 1/2, 2005, pp. 5-26; and: *Current Issues in Political Marketing* (eds: Walter W. Wymer, Jr., and Jennifer Lees-Marshment) Best Business Books, an imprint of The Haworth Press, Inc., 2005, pp. 5-26. Single or multiple copies of this article are available for a fee from The Haworth Document Delivery Service [1-800-HAWORTH, 9:00 a.m. - 5:00 p.m. (EST). E-mail address: getinfo@haworthpressinc.com].

KEYWORDS. Political marketing, branding, party politics, voter disengagement

Political marketing is about much more than propaganda, rhetoric and advertising (Lees-Marshment 2001; Maarek 1995). While these are clearly aspects of the marketing paradigm, reducing political marketing to just encompass political communication means we overlook the key shifts in the behaviour of modern British political parties. The important development of the last five years is the introduction of techniques that borrow from corporate marketing, in particular corporate-style branding and market segmentation. The fact that a British political party has re-positioned itself following extensive marketing research, and has designed its manifesto, public image and communication as a result of interacting with the market, has been hailed as moving democracy towards a more consultative future. The theory is that political parties that adopt a market orientation are more attuned to public needs and desires and so can be described as organic to the society they seek to represent. However, marketers usually focus on a strategic section of the population: the target market; a concept that appears anathema to politics. If political parties talk to certain groups, other sectors of the electorate may feel disenfranchised, and indeed evidence from recent elections does not substantiate the position that politics and the people have become more connected. If anything, the UK General Election of 2001 indicates that the reverse has taken place. This article discusses the role of political marketing as the cause of an emerging democratic deficit in UK politics, rather than it creating a more Periclean or super-democratic form of parliamentary government.

When speaking of a democratic deficit we seldom think of this as a feature of domestic politics in democratic nations; usually we refer to a lack of democratic accountability in a supranational context, the European Union, or at sub-governmental level, the so-called Quangos. However the result of the 2001 General Election, showing the lowest turnout for over a century, has led some commentators to comment on an increasing disenfranchisement and the disconnection of the electorate from their political representatives, in other words democracy seemed to be privileging sections of society and ignoring others. Much of the blame for this has been placed upon two factors; firstly that politics is perceived as a dishonest business that deceives the public through the use of propaganda and media control; (Mandelson 2002, pp. xliii-xlv; Wring 2001) secondly that political parties, and New Labour in particular, lack any significant body of ideas and therefore no longer appeal to their traditional voters. (Brivati and Bale 1997, pp. 195-7; see also Marquand 1988. On the 2001 General Election see Whiteley, Clarke, Sanders, and Stewart 2001) These causal factors are connected, this article argues, by the application of marketing by political parties.

POLITICAL MARKETING:
AN OVERVIEW

Marketing strategies have become a central feature within the campaigns of all of the political parties in the UK, however the Labour Party adheres most closely to the model of a market-oriented party. Philip Gould shows how re-naming the party 'New Labour' was not simply a rhetorical ploy but an attempt to introduce a rebranded product into the political marketplace. Through a process that identified what the electorate disliked about the Labour Party, aspects of the party were redesigned to counter negative public perceptions and introduce a 'new' party to the electorate (Lees-Marshment 2001, pp. 181-210). The rebranding of Labour was founded around voter desires, just as consumer desires drive product development, allowing New Labour to emerge as the ultimate market-oriented paradigm.

The market-oriented paradigm was initially heralded as reconnecting political parties with public opinion. Bowler and Farrell argued: "Part of the use of polls is not only that parties learn about the issues and concerns of the voters whom they seek to represent, but also that parties can be responsive . . . to public preferences and concerns" (Bowler and Farrell 1992, p. 231). The result, a landslide victory at the 1997 General Election, was highlighted as evidence that the market-oriented paradigm was successful and would require emulation if opponents were to regain the balance of political power: "Major political parties seeking to win elections need to become market-oriented. A market-oriented party designs its behaviour to provide voter satisfaction . . . It does not attempt to change what people think, but to deliver what they need and want" (Lees-Marshment and Lilleker 2001, p. 207).

However, evidence from the 2001 General Election refutes these comments. Through an examination of the marketing process undertaken by New Labour, it is possible to show why such a project has significant flaws. The 1997 General Election landslide is shown to be a result of a range of factors, which marketing clearly had input into but was not the deciding factor. Finally studying the perception of New Labour around the time of the 2001 General Election we find that the strategy adopted by New Labour had limited attraction and that the second landslide was more to do with careful targeting of resources, than with the widescale appeal of the New Labour product. This argument will allow us to reassess the utility of the market-oriented paradigm and whether political marketing, in its present guise, has a future.

THE MARKET-ORIENTED PARADIGM–
FORGING NEW LABOUR

While it would be wrong to argue that the Labour Party could become a new party, abandoning its traditions and ethos (Lees-Marshment and Lilleker 2001), the period from 1987 onwards saw concerted attempts to redesign the party in line with public opinion. These largely failed, therefore the 1992 defeat saw the party more determined than ever to regain the reins of government. Discussions over democratisation of the party followed the change in leadership, from Neil Kinnock to John Smith, in 1992 and continued after Tony Blair became leader in 1994. The Labour party had to, as Gould explained, reclaim the support of people like him: "Labour had failed to understand that the old working class was becoming a new middle class: aspiring, consuming, choosing what was best for themselves and their families. They had outgrown crude collectivism and left it behind in the supermarket car park" (Gould 1998, p. 4).

The route to reclaiming 'Labour's lost voters,' Gould argued, was to convince the electorate that the party had changed. Various internal discussion documents, speeches by Blair and the post-1994 party leadership and, in particular, the definitive strategy, 'Partnership with the People,' all characterised the party as a market-oriented paradigm. Gould's role was primarily to inform the party what the public perception was; Blair increasingly took charge of positioning the party in terms of internal organisation, policy and image. Gould quotes a note, written by him in 1996 at the heart of the Partnership with the People period, "We must definitely be New Labour, not old. A further raft of internal reform, if necessary, should be put together . . . We must be in the centre ground: the real one-nation party" (Gould 1998, p. 264.).

This re-positioning was, at the same time being informed theoretically. Beginning with *Beyond Left and Right* (Giddens 1994), Anthony Giddens put forward his formula for creating a new social democratic settlement relevant to the changing, globalised, environment. Blair's speeches discussed similar topics. However the image of 'newness' was not simply to appear dynamic in a changing world order, but to appear different from that which had gone before. To put clear distance between the donkey jacket of Michael Foot and the working class oratory of Neil Kinnock, Tony Blair's image as party leader was above all, business-like and in-touch.

Such notions of recasting and repositioning borrow heavily from ideas common to corporate enterprise, in particular product branding or rebranding and brand positioning. Most readers will be familiar with the concept of branding. One simple definition is provided by Aaker who argues a brand is: "A distinguishing name and/or symbol (such as a logo, trademark or package design) intended to identify the goods or services of either one seller or a group of sellers, and to differentiate those goods or services from those of competitors" (Aaker 1991, p. 2). A brand is a signifier, an iconic image, an entity that is recognised by the consumer as representing a range of connotations. Successful brands are signifiers for quality, value or prestige. The problem for the 'Old' Labour Party was that the brand had negative connotations. It was high taxes, economic incompetence and Trade Union control that the public identified with the Labour Party, therefore the party had to relaunch its product.

BRANDING POLITICAL PARTIES: EVALUATING THE MARKET FOR THE NEW LABOUR BRAND

Terminology such as branding is often argued to be antithetical to the world of politics. Political parties must be seen to stand for 'ideas,' have an ethos and a set of traditions and it should be these factors that are significant to public consciousness. There is, however, little difference with the traditional model of brand equity. Kapferer's pyramid model of brand identity identifies three layers to a brand: kernel, codes and promises (Kapferer 1997, pp. 173-7). At the heart of the brand is the kernel, the source of brand identity, an entity which Kapferer argues is invisible, or that becomes invisible over time, but "must nevertheless be known because it imparts coherence and consistency" (Kapferer 1997, p. 174). The next layer would be the codes: the concepts which govern communication and define positioning, these constrain the brand within parameters demarcated by its kernel. The final layer, the base of Kapferer's pyramid, are the promises; this represents the style of the brand, that which leaves a mark upon the consumer or potential consumer, see Table 1.

While Kapferer's pyramid, and the language he uses, can be appropriated to represent a political party's equity, three spheres perhaps better illustrate the concept of a political party brand. The inner sphere represents the kernel of the political party; its roots and history. Surrounding the heart are the core concepts; those policy constraints that cannot be altered. Finally the outer sphere is the public representation of the other two spheres, how the kernel and core concepts are communicated to the potential consumer in order for the brand, or party, to appeal. Table 2 illustrates this alternative.

With the creation of New Labour there were few fundamental changes to the kernel or core concepts; despite the rhetorical appearance of newness encapsulated in the Third Way, much of New Labour's political programme had historical precedent (Desai 1994; White 2001). The only significant changes were the alteration of Clause IV, which had huge symbolic significance, but little practical role over policy. Structural changes were made to the way pol-

TABLE 1. Kapferer's Pyramid Model of Identity (Kapferer 1997, p. 173)

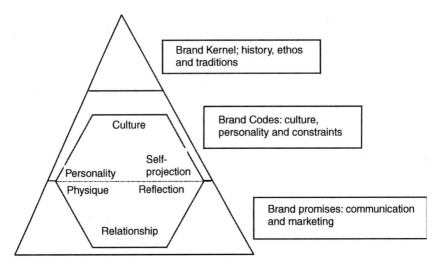

Taken from Strategic Brand Management by Jean-Noel Kapferer 1997 published by Kogan Page.

TABLE 2. The Lilleker Three Sphere Model of a Political Party Brand

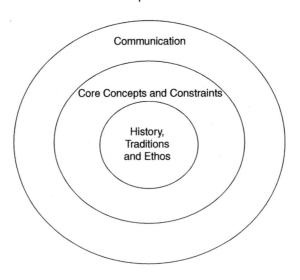

icy was debated and formulated, in particular the increased influence of the leader-centred National Policy Forum, but these were largely to avoid a repeat of left-wing domination that damaged the party during the early 1980s. Therefore the changes that took place were largely within the area denoted as 'promises' by Kapferer. That which the party claims it will do if elected and how it will achieve these aims. To many on the left these changes did denote a drastic shift towards the centre ground of British politics (Barrat-Brown, and Coates 1996; Allender 2001), however it was arguably a rebranding, an updating of the party's logo, imagery and objectives, and not a redefinition of its ethos. Underpinning the rebranding was a belief that society had changed since the party's constitution was originally drawn up, the party had to reflect society and the needs of the electorate in 1997 (Mandelson, and Liddle 1996).

The point at which our understanding of political parties and our perception of branding diverges is over appeal to the market and attracting a market share. Parties have traditionally viewed their loyal customers in class terms, a not totally accurate perception but one that did allow the electorate to be segmented as 'partisan to this party' or 'partisan to the opposition' (Lilleker 2002, pp. 67-73). The erosion of class alignment has meant that parties increasingly have to broaden their appeal and target those who may vote for them but currently do not. Identifying these so called 'switchers' and targeting them, again supports the assessment of New Labour as a brand attempting to broaden its market share.

As is the case with the market for consumable products, we can identify sections of the market that political parties compete over. The simplest model would be a three tier market: supporters competed for and lost, supporters competed for and won and supporters not competed for but who offer support due to an ideological partisan attachment. These correspond to Ohmae's groups C, D and E (Ohmae 1982). Ohmae also identifies two other groups; A and B, these represent areas of the market the brand do not attempt to attract or to areas not covered by the supply network. These are applicable to a very minor extent within the political context.

De Chernatony and McDonald (1992) develop Ohmae's breakdown of the market by segregating section D into a further four categories: loyalists, swingers, apathetics and doubters (see Table 3). Loyalists fit more accurately into category E, those who the brand no longer has to compete for. Swingers are arguably the most important section of the market, their loyalty is fragile and their decisions weighed carefully in relation to personal circumstances and economic conditions. Apathetics can be turned into loyal consumers, but need direct appeals. Doubters similarly require convincing, but it is difficult to convert these to loyalists; they will retain a degree of scepticism about the brand and only 'buy in' under certain circumstances.

TABLE 3. The Strategic Meaning of Market Share

Brand type not offered: Section A	Brand type not offered: Section A	Loyal Conservatives in safe seats
Customers not covered by campaign: Section B	Customers not covered by campaign: Section B	Loyal Conservatives in marginal seats
Customers competed for and lost: Section C	Customers competed for and lost: Section C	Non-Labour voters 1987 & 1992; possible swingers
Customers competed for and won: Section D	D1: Loyalists; D2: Swingers; D3: Apathetics; D4: Doubters	Weak Labour supporters; definite swingers
Loyal Customers not competed for: Section E	Loyal Customers not competed for: Section E	Heartland supporters in safe Labour seats

Ohmae's scale	**De Chernatony & McDonald variation**	**New Labour's simplification**

⇐ ⇐ **LABOUR'S TARGET GROUPS**

The political market can be similarly demarcated. The Labour party has always had its loyalists. There are also swingers; those who currently favour Labour, but if Labour appears to become too radical or to lack economic competence they may choose an alternative. In the modern age many voters are said to show apathy towards politics, they need convincing of the importance of voting, not to mention convincing that one party or another is the most capable of forming a government. In terms of Labour's market share, there are equally those apathetic to Labour who need convincing of Labour's specific suitability. Finally there are also doubters; those who doubt Labour has changed and would perhaps prefer another party to be in government. Labour's strategists identified that swingers, apathetics and doubters existed in the market, and a variety of ways were developed for targeting those individuals. Labour's process of rebranding itself as New Labour was intended to position the party as corresponding to these voters' needs and demands.

Philip Gould, senior adviser to the Labour party campaigns and communications strategists from 1986 onwards, described the target market thus: "Not disadvantaged, not privileged, not quite working-class, not really middle-class–they don't even have a name" (Gould 1998, p. 17). Drawing on his experiences working on Bill Clinton's New Democrat campaign in the United States in 1992, Gould argued the party: "need[ed] to reassert their claim to represent the majority of working [people]. The working middle-class needs to figure at least as centrally in the party's identity as the traditional blue-collar imagery" (Gould 1998, p. 173).

Focus groups concentrated on discovering what the ideal party would be among those identified as swingers. The questions underpinning discussions were designed to extrapolate what factors would convince these people to vote Labour. The information gathered was fed into party strategy and the concept of 'Partnership with the People' was developed. The process of rebranding has been well-documented elsewhere (see for example Lees-Marshment 2001) this article argues that the problem for the party, in the long term, was that 'the people' who New Labour were in partnership with were actually a fairly narrow section of the British electorate. These people may be strategically important within a number of key constituencies–such as Gloucester Woman and Basildon Man–however they excluded large sections of voters in the Labour heartlands. However, as Ohmae argues is necessary, the strategists had identified the section of the market that was most ripe for conversion. It is to these sections that New Labour appealed directly in the run up to the 1997 General Election.

The important question is whether Labour, when it became New Labour and adopted a market orientation, began a process that would lose the party unequivocal support among its loyalists as a consequence of rebranding the party towards the swingers? If this is correct then the application of such techniques in politics appear far from beneficial to the efficacy of parliamentary democracy. Though many argue that politics is for the powerful, that politicians are a self-serving elite and that the political process grinds on regardless of the outcome of elections, the mass electorate seem even less inspired when politics is supposedly being driven by their concerns. New Labour offered this, in 1997 it seems to have earned them the support of the majority of UK voters; however, and as 2001 shows, this should not be seen as vindication for the market-oriented paradigm.

THE 1997 VICTORY–
GIVING WHAT EVERYONE WANTS?

New Labour's 1997 landslide victory has been argued to have been a victory for the people. The voter had enjoyed substantial input into designing the 'product' and it was elected on the back of a national consensus. We can also say that Labour's parliamentary majority was secured by gaining a majority of support across the nation, it was not due to the vagaries of the first past the post electoral system. Therefore those who argued marketing could reconnect politics to society appeared vindicated. However was the support New Labour gained the product of rebranding, or could it have been achieved by relying on a broader appeal while highlighting the negative qualities of the Conservative Party. In fact it is fair to ask the question, could Labour have lost in 1997 without the party moving in to the realms of political extremism.

Determining the extent to which Labour's rebranding influenced the 1997 General Election result has numerous difficulties. The only accurate source of information is opinion polls, from which we can infer whether Blair's adjustments to the party had any significant effect in terms of support. Looking at long term fluctuations in support for Labour can allow us to draw some conclusions with regards to Blair's impact on party support. One indicator of the public attitude is the fact that Labour and the Conservatives were about equal in terms of support during the 1992 General Election campaign, suggesting the Conservatives did not have the overall lead throughout Labour's period in the political wilderness. However, it is also clear that Labour were not trusted to form a government. As the media played up the notion that Labour would win, support drifted back towards the Conservative Party. Data from opinion polls is sketchy for the period between the Election and the end of 1992, however by 1993 Labour had a clear lead in the polls.

What had occurred in the period between the Election and February 1993 to cause this dramatic change in Labour's fortunes? Firstly Labour had elected a new leader. On 18 July 1992 John Smith had replaced Neil Kinnock as party leader, however little had yet occurred to suggest rebranding, only reclaiming Labour's traditional position on the centre left. The dramatic event that altered Labour's electoral fortunes was exogenous to Labour's reform process. That event was Black Wednesday; Britain's forced exit from the European Exchange Rate Mechanism on 16 September 1992, the subsequent recession and ongoing recriminations between Prime Minister John Major and his Chancellor Norman Lamont. This event broke the Conservatives' image for economic competence and party cohesion (Stephens 1996, pp. 193-260). It was following the events of September 1992 that Labour seemed to regain public confidence. Conservative MPs' sexual indiscretions and cash for questions, which dogged John Major's term of office 1992-7, compounded with bitter splits over the issue of European integration, caused the Conservatives to remain in second place throughout the period. Though the party re-established control over the British economy, the Conservative government lost the confidence of the voters.

Blair himself made a negligible impact on the polls, as indicated in Figure 1. While Blair's campaign coincided with a peak in Labour's fortunes, his victory also coincided with a dip. The introduction of one member one vote, removing the Trade Union control over Conference decisions, did see popularity rise again–indicated by the peak in October 1994 the closest poll to the 1994 Conference–Blair's Summer tour of 1994 also saw party popularity increase. However these alone do not indicate that Blair's personality or image, or the brand equity he possessed, had a profound effect on public opinion. While Figure 1 makes it appear that a sharp drop took place between 1994 and 1997, it was actually a steady decline. This indicates that the public may have responded well to Blair initially, but that his honeymoon was short lived. The 1997 General Election campaign saw a wobble, when the Labour/Conservative gap narrowed dramatically. It is difficult to make definitive conclusions regarding this data, however it is equally difficult to construct an argument that Blair's rebranding was the key factor that led to the landslide victory of 1997.

Blair's image was also not a deciding factor. Despite his personal image management strategies, personal efficacy was no higher for Blair than for Ma-

FIGURE 1. Support for the Three Major UK Parties 1992-2001

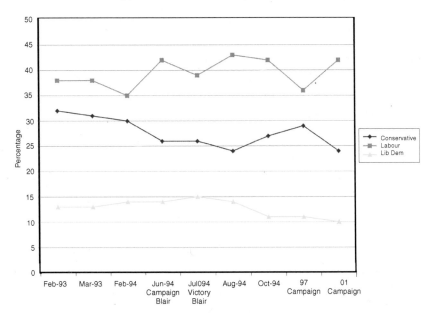

jor. Major received an average of 30% responding he was 'more honest' 1991-2, however by July 1993 this had fallen to 20% (http://www.mori.com/polls/trends/trust.shtml). Despite the images of sleaze that surrounded his party he maintained this level. Blair's honesty rating fared little better, on the eve of the 1997 General Election his was only 20%, just below that of Major who scored 22%. Therefore, it appears Blair was seen to be a leader who was capable of doing the best job, but his personal standing was actually below that of Major, the Prime Minister charged with leading incompetently. Therefore it appears that 'trust to govern effectively' was key and personality played little part. The Conservatives had lost the confidence of the electorate; arguably any Labour party, beyond the divided version which Michael Foot led 1980-83, would have had a good chance of election given the political climate.

Labour were also in a good position because their ideological kernel was compatible with societal desires. Opinion polls from 1996/7 show the public's chief concern was public services, a natural political terrain for the Labour Party. The public perception of the Conservatives was that they had little care for the Welfare State. In contrast Labour, as its creators and defenders, were seen as the natural trustees. Therefore, once again, it is hard to say that Labour's branding had the profound effect some claim it had in 1997. Labour's theme song; D:Ream's 'Things Can Only Get Better' encapsulated the mood of the electorate succinctly. The part played by marketing is important. Labour were listening while the Conservatives were not. Labour was modern, forward-looking; the Conservatives out of touch and inwardly focussed. But, Labour was also largely free from stigma, even if trust was lacking from the start; the Conservatives were tarred with sexual and financial indiscretions. Importantly, the Conservatives were seen as unfit for government, all Labour's campaign strategists had to do was to present the party as a credible if untested alternative. The party did not have to focus messages purely at swingers, polls indicate they had won this group over as a result of the Conservative's demise. Therefore were the rebranding and ruthless targeting necessary, and in the long-term did they create greater problems?

ASSESSING THE IMPACT

Gauging the effects of a communication strategy is difficult if not impossible. The various influences that impact upon the electorate are impossible to isolate and no experimental methodology can effectively determine the cause of something like political disaffection. The research design was therefore exploratory within one sector of the disaffected non-voting group. Twelve focus groups, each consisting of an average of 15 individuals (a total of 214 non-voting Labour supporters) were held in Barnsley, South Yorkshire. Each was designed to find out the following: why these voters chose not to vote, what they think of politics and politicians in general, what they think about the Labour Party and what they would advise Tony Blair should do in the future. The focus groups were held between September 2001 and March 2002.

Interviews were also carried out with a number of Labour Party workers, mainly those who had been active during the 2001 Election in the two constituencies Labour lost: Norfolk North West and Upminster. However, due to contacts made during a previous research project, additional Labour Party members also contributed in various ways, many of whom wished to remain anonymous and unidentifiable. The majority of interviews were carried out during the summer of 2002, though further data was gained during November 2002 and March 2003.

The results from these focus groups and interviews were correlated with data from the British Election Panel Study [BEPS]. From the data, those who recorded themselves as 'Labour supporters' and 'working class' were extracted for analysis, as well as those who recorded having not voted in 2001. this data was used to present evidence of perceptions of New Labour held by those that are the party's natural constituency.

The aim is to build up a general picture of how those who should feel most closely aligned to the Labour Party feel about the party and its current position in the political market. While not being a national study of all non-voters, or all working-class Labour supporters; the data from the focus groups, the observations of party activists and the BEPS data present indications of the mood among what we can describe as heartland supporters.

NEW LABOUR IN 2001–
WHOSE PARTY IS IT ANYWAY?

From 1997 onwards Labour's goal became a full second term, allowing Blair to achieve something none of his predecessors had. Once again, the tactics seem tremendously sophisticated considering the chances of a Conservative win. However, what did happen was that the public switched off from politics. Turnout at the 2001 General Election reached an all-time low, particularly in Labour's heartland constituencies. This gives the impression that the election campaign and its context had turned voters away from the polling booth.

As in 1997, a Labour win was inevitable. The public perception of the Conservatives changed little from 1997 to the General Election of 2001. William Hague, who replaced John Major as party leader, attempted to rebuild party cohesion. This involved listening to opinion within the party, not the electorate (Lees-Marshment and Quayle 2001), this strategy retained the party its heartland support, and was sufficient to reclaim Norfolk North West, Romford and Upminster. Largely however the policies of 'Keep the Pound' and tougher preventative measures against asylum seekers entering the UK did not reflect the broader public mood. Despite advice from special advisors within the party to engage with the voters (Interview, Feb 2002), Hague pursued what can be described as a sectional manifesto. In the light of the second defeat, party academics Seldon and Snowden (2001) recommended the party adopt similar tactics to Labour. However does rebranding the party in response to polling and focus group data actually equate to increasing support, or just narrowing the market share to swingers?

It could be argued, based upon the size of New Labour's second landslide victory at the 2001 General Election alone, that the rebranding of the party was a tremendous success. However two factors need to be considered. Firstly, the Conservatives failed to win back public confidence. More importantly Labour's victory was based on the lowest turnout for a century, in their heartland constituencies their victory was based on an average of 24% of those eligible to vote. This seems to indicate that the link between elector and elected had broken down, not become more synergistic.

The focus group members offered these perceptions of the campaign:

> The Labour guy seemed not to be bothered, Scargill's mob are all nutters, the Conservatives talked about keeping a pound note I don't give a stuff about. No I didn't vote; I went down [to] the club instead.

> Labour are only bothered about the business types who live around London in the big posh houses, they've forgotten who was leafleting for them in the 80s when they needed people. I'd have voted for the Liberal, she was interested in us on the council estates, she had no chance though.

Across all the participants, the perception was very similar. Labour was perceived to be targeting a small section of society and ignoring its heartland. This strategy can work effectively in the world of commerce, but it appears that such tactics lead to severe disaffection within the context of political campaigns.

Data from the BEPS records an increasingly mixed perception of New Labour, perhaps proving that loyal Labour voters are no longer certain what 'their' party represents. While it is impossible to identify respondents from heartland constituencies such as the Barnsley wards, self-reporting working class members who identify themselves as loyal Labour voters are indicative of opinion among those we would describe as loyalists. The data throws up some very interesting results.

The key conclusion is that these people are confused. When answering the question 'Is the Labour party good for only one class now?' the overwhelming majority replied the party was 'good for all classes.' However when asked if New Labour could be most closely identified with the working class, 89% replied very closely or fairly closely. When asked if the party identified with the middle class 81% responded very or fairly closely. The fact that these conflicting responses came from the same respondents' answers to adjoining questions on the same survey indicates some confusion as to New Labour's position within the political market place. Similar conflicting responses can be found regarding questions covering the Trade Unions or big business dichotomy. Expectedly, 81% agreed New Labour looked after Trade Union interests, however 68% said the party was 'closest' to big business. 72% also argued New Labour looked after those on benefit, yet 44% said the party looked after the rich. Equally indicative, 53% disagreed that under New Labour 'working people get a fair share of the national wealth,' a less creditable 28% agreed with the premise. Perhaps most important, in terms of the central theme of this article, 61% of the loyalists said they agreed that 'people like me have no say in government actions,' only 17% thought they did.

The results paint a very confusing picture of how loyalists perceive New Labour as a brand. The same ambiguity can be seen in the responses of those asked to place New Labour on a left-right scale. With zero indicating far left, and ten far right, comparing the results obtained from loyalists and those from respondents identifying themselves as middle class voters with no strong party identifications, the swingers, we get an interesting perspective of the way the party is viewed (see Figure 2).

We can see that the majority of loyalists see New Labour as largely centrist, few position the party on the left wing. In contrast swingers place the party on the centre left, in line with New Labour's positioning strategy. Again, this indicates that loyalists are confused when thinking about the party, its ideology and who it represents. The swingers, in contrast, have responded positively to Labour's communication. Thus we see the rebranding process causing a gulf between the party and its loyalists.

Further evidence for this lies in the pattern of turnout across the UK in 2001. The constituencies that witnessed the lowest turnout, on average, were safe Labour seats in those areas regarded as the party's heartland. Though no surveys have specifically looked at a large enough number within these constituencies to enable us to draw definite conclusions, the BEPS provides some indications. Using the same cohort of loyalists: 358 respondents declared they had not voted; 148 gave practical reasons–out of the country, too busy, etc.–the remainder declared more instrumentalist reasons for not voting. The actual figures are listed in Table 4. The focus groups members argued that they

FIGURE 2. Perceptions of the New Labour Brand on the Left-Right Political Spectrum

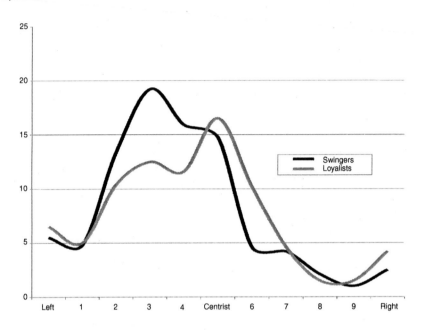

TABLE 4. Reasons Given for Non-Voting: Working Class Labour Loyalists

	Number	Percentage
All parties/candidates seemed the same	45	21.4%
Didn't like any parties or candidates	42	20
Didn't care who won	48	22.6
Not interested in politics	40	19
Vote would have made no difference	35	17

N = 210, Source: BEPS data.

saw their local contest as a procession: the candidates marched out and they were expected to vote in their traditional way. These people saw their vote making little difference, they often 'didn't care who won,' and felt discouraged from taking an interest. A further group: 'didn't like any parties or candidates' or who felt 'the parties and candidates seemed the same.' Though these are only snapshots taken from a very small group of respondents they appear indicative of a trend that seemed to engulf the Labour heartlands during the 2001 General Election campaign.

Non-voting should not just be taken as evidence of political apathy; it was described as a positive democratic action. When exploring their feelings and motivations in focus groups, non-voting loyalists talked about deliberately withdrawing their support. This attitude is displayed succinctly in the following quote:

> It is a message isn't it. If Labour could have lost I would have walked over hot coals to vote for them. But they couldn't. Me not going out was a kick up the arse to the party. I was saying in the only way I could, I'm not happy with you, I didn't elect you so you could ignore me and pander to them in the London suburbs. Start bloody listening or else!

The scale of apathy is worth recording. Across the seats where Labour enjoyed a 20% majority or more at the 1997 General Election, 81% saw a swing against Labour. Within those seats, on average, the turnout was 56.8%–though the low point was 36%. On average, 18.2% of those who voted Labour in 1997 did not turnout. This figure compares with only 9.2% that did not turn out to vote Conservative and 2.7% that failed to vote for an incumbent Liberal Democrat. The latter could easily be a result of the various practical factors highlighted in examinations of turnout in 2001 (Whiteley et al. 2001), the loss of Labour voters was clearly the result of a break in the link between the party and its supporters.

POLITICAL MARKETING:
BAD IDEA OR BAD APPLICATION?

Academics who pioneered the field of political marketing declared that democracy was being remoulded. This argument hinged on the notion that a party that used marketing would necessarily link directly to the desires of the public so ensuring government by the people. However, this premise clearly depends on the definition of the public. Saul Rae, democratic theorist turned pollster, argued that any activity that explicitly linked public sentiment to governance was a positive move away from the age when "the common people . . . [were] dominated by a small ruling clique" (Rae 1939, p. 24).

But, despite talk of participation with the people, the party had a narrow definition of 'the people.' Labour had little reason to talk directly to heartland supporters, the target market were those with a propensity to vote Labour but who required convincing that the party was a credible party of government. These people were reached successfully and, in both 1997 and 2001, turned out and voted Labour.

The reason that the loyalists disengaged from the party is due to the way New Labour is perceived by that section of the electorate. Although the ethos, traditions and core concepts remain largely identical to those that underpinned Labour policy throughout its century of existence, the fact that the party's promises are now more oriented towards the middle-class swingers, rejecting working-class based politics, means many feel the party has changed radically. This is a failure in the communication process. New Labour interacts with one section of the electorate, those of greatest strategic importance, thus they have failed to carry their loyal consumers along.

Largely this had little effect on the overall outcome, it did however depress the average turnout. In some constituencies, however, there was a tangible negative effect. Interviews within the Upminster Constituency Labour Party revealed that Labour had retained those identified in 1997 as swingers, the fact that the Labour MP lost was because those who lived in the council estates, the loyalists, did not bother voting (Interview, March 2002). A similar picture was painted by the results in Norfolk North West, Labour lost by 7%, a figure that can be attributed to those Labour supporters who could not be convinced of the importance of turning out on election day. As a Labour activist in King's Lynn stated: "The middle class, as I would call them, those who never voted for us before, all came out. You go onto the . . . [council] estate and people would say what's Tony Blair done for me, why should I. The rural vote was always Tory, it was the town vote we needed, we just couldn't get them out what ever we did" (Interview, November 2001).

This highlights the problem of Labour's rebranding strategy. Those who Labour were relying on for unequivocal support felt the brand was no longer for them and so rejected the product entirely. One activist put her perception of New Labour's political marketing well: "Well it's like selling cars [by] only using nude women draped across them, women would say well stuff you I'm not buying a car. Labour did the same, well that's the story on the doorsteps" (Interview, December 2001).

The targeting, however, reaped successes in most constituencies. Table 5 represents data collected by party activists in a Labour held target seat and illustrates the gains the party made among the target group. The result is clearly satisfactory to the party, however it is based on winning the majority of swing voters over. Few gains were made among loyal Conservatives, while a large proportion of those identified as loyal Labour supporters failed to engage with the campaign and largely did not turn out. As Maarek argued, the most likely outcome of a targeted campaign was disengagement: "The candidate's communication procedure should not limit itself to one or more specific target categories . . . Ignoring the rest of the voting population . . . [can create] the impression that it has been abandoned, and can produce a negative effect that

TABLE 5. Results from One Labour Held Target Constituency Showing the Voting Patterns of Segments of the Electorate

	Loyal Conservative		Swing Voters		Loyal Labour	
	%	Votes	%	Votes	%	Votes
Vote Con	74	14,047	12	2,645	14	2,829
Vote Lab	3	569	70	15,431	43	8,689
Vote Other	6	1,139	7	1,543	8	1,617
Not voted	17	3,228	11	2,425	35	7,072
Total	31	18,983	36	22,044	33	20,207

Results 2001

	%	Votes
Con	32	19,521
Lab	40	24,689
All Others	7	4,299
Did not vote	21	12,725
Total	100	61,234

could annul the potential gain of a few voters (Maarek, 1995, p. 39). In 2001 New Labour gained more than just a few voters from among its target groups, but this was under specific circumstances. Had the Conservatives performed better and only 50% of the swing voters been won, while the same proportion of Labour loyalists had abandoned the party, it would not have been sufficient to win the constituency which Table 5 reflects. Linking this argument to those put forward by some forward-looking party strategists, and the comments made by disillusioned loyalists, it appears that the modern techniques of segmentation of the market and targeting of communication are to some extent responsible for causing a division in society: those to whom politics belongs and those whom politics has abandoned.

This article does not wish to offer solutions, but to merely highlight the problem with the move towards building catch-all, electoral professional parties (Kirchheimer, 1966; Panebianco, 1988). That problem is how to create and maintain a wide base of support that include voters with disparate ideas and concerns. With a demoralised opposition the only issue for Labour was ensuring sufficient numbers turned out. The next election may be very different. If the Blair government cannot prove it has delivered on its promises to all sections of the British electoral market, and at the same time the Conservatives are able to position themselves as a credible potential government, the Conservatives could steal large sections of Labour's vote. Furthermore the Liberal Democrats, using their unique pavement politics strategy, could undermine Labour's position in heartland constituencies.

While all this is hypothetical, clearly there are problems with the process of applying marketing strategies in a political context. Marketing implicitly suggests a segment of society that is to be targeted, in contrast politics is about inclusion. Clearly no party can be totally inclusive, however they must also decide how large a section they dare exclude. New Labour were confident that the heartlanders, a key section of their electorate, would support them unequivocally. In this they were wrong.

All the UK political parties are assessing what electoral advantage marketing can offer. Perhaps it is natural that marketing is seen to offer so much potential within the post-modern era of capitalist triumphalism. The Conservatives, once pioneers of marketing, appear to be lagging behind in terms of innovation and direction. Under Ian Duncan-Smith, they are concentrating on reforming the public services and offering themselves as 'compassionate Conservatives.' The Liberal Democrats, who formerly eschewed all things market-oriented, are equally seeking ways of expanding their market share. In an expansion to their successful tactic of targeting seats, party strategists are discussing plans to segment the electorate and target specific types of voter. Using the complicated descriptors of 'innovators,' 'self-actualisers' and 'contented conformers,' the party plans to discover the concerns of these target voters, design policies and then road test them in focus groups of target voters (Ward 2002). New Labour are, perhaps, refocusing on a more working-class agenda of higher taxation to create social equality. Does this indicate a new marketing direction?

New Labour is again looking to building partnerships. The party has launched a new centre for policy research: Forethought. Party General Secretary David Triesman, in his launch speech, argued the party needed a "period of critical research and serious investigation" that would provide a manifesto "in tune with the nation's needs and the concerns of the majority of British people" (Triesman 2002). As with any service supplier, the aim is to develop a brand that is relevant, credible and desirable. Whether such a strategy is tenable, whether such forums need to be publicly discussed and audited and whether the electorate will feel even more excluded are all moot points. What this development may see is less of a focus on those swing voters in Basildon or Gloucester, and at least some interest shown in Barnsley woman and Huddersfield man. While neither of the latter were required to ensure Labour's victories in 1997 and 2001, if they are lost to the party they could be instrumental in its defeat in 2006 or 2010.

REFERENCES

Aaker, David A. (1991), *Managing Brand Equity*, New York: Macmillan.

Allender, Paul (2001) *What's wrong with New Labour*, London: Verso.

Barratt-Brown, Michael, and Ken Coates (1996), *The Blair Revelation: Deliverance from Whom?*, Nottingham, UK: Spokesman.

De Chernatony, Leslie. and Malcolm H.B. McDonald (1996), *Creating Powerful Brands*, Oxford: Butterworth-Heinemann.

De Chernatony, Leslie (2001) *From Brand Vision to Brand Evaluation: strategically building and sustaining brands*, Oxford: Butterworth-Heinemann.

Desai, Radhika (1994) *Intellectuals and Socialism: Social Democrats and the Labour Party*, London: Lawrence & Wishart.

Giddens, Antony (1994), *Beyond Left and Right: The future of radical politics*, Cambridge: Polity.

Gould, Philip (1998), *The Unfinished Revolution: how the modernisers saved the Labour Party*, London: Little Brown and Co.

Kapferer, Jean-Noel (1997), *Strategic Brand Management*, London: Kogan Page.

Kirchheimer, Otto. (1966) "The Transformation of Western European Party Systems" in *Political Parties and Political Development*, eds Myron Weiner and Joseph LaPalombra, Princeton: Princeton University Press, p-p.

Lees-Marshment, Jennifer (2001), *Political marketing and British political parties: The party's just begun*, Manchester, UK: Manchester University Press.

Lees-Marshment, Jennifer. and Darren Lilleker (2001), "Political marketing and traditional values: Old Labour for new times," *Contemporary Politics*, 7 (3), 205-216.

Lees-Marshment, Jennifer. and Stuart Quayle (2001), "Empowering the Members or Marketing the Party? The Conservative Reforms of 1998," *Political Quarterly*, 5, 204-212.

Lilleker, Darren G (2002), "Whose Left? Working class political allegiances in post-industrial Britain," *International Review of Social History*, 47, 65-85.

Maarek, Phillippe (1995), *Political Marketing and Communication*, London: John Libbey.

Mandelson, Peter (2002), *The Blair Revolution Revisited*, London: Politicos.

Mandelson, Peter, and Roger Liddle (1996), *The Blair Revolution: Can New Labour Deliver?*, Boston, MA: Faber & Faber.

Marquand, David (1988), *The Unprincipled Society*, London: Jonathan Cape.

Ohmae, Kenneth (1982), *The Mind of the Strategist*, Harmondsworth, UK: Penguin.

Palmer, Jerry 2002, "Smoke and mirrors: is that the way it is? Themes in political Marketing," *Media, Culture and Society*, 24 (3), 345-363.

Panebianco, Angelo. (1988) Political Parties: Organisation and Power, Cambridge: Cambridge University Press.

Rae, Saul Forbes (1939), "The Oxford By-election: a study in the straw vote," *Political Quarterly*, 10(2), 15-28.

Seldon, Antony. and Peter Snowdon (2001), *A New Conservative Century*, London: Centre for Policy Studies.

Stephens, Philip (1996), *Politics and the Pound: the Conservative's struggle with sterling*, London: Macmillan.

Shaw, Eric (1994), *The Labour Party since 1979: Crisis and Transformation*, London: Routledge.

Triesman, David (2002), "Speech at launch of Forethought," 9 July 2002. *www.labour.org.uk/forethought*

Ward, Lucy (2002) "Lib Dems look to marketing techniques" *The Guardian*, 4 December *http://www.guardian.co.uk/guardianpolitics/story/0,3605,855483,00.html*

White, Stuart (2001), *New Labour: The progressive future?*, London: Palgrave.

Whiteley, Paul, Harold Clarke, David Sanders, and Marianne Stewart (2001), "Turnout," *Parliamentary Affairs*, 54, 775-788.

Square Peg, Round Hole?
Can Marketing-Based Concepts
Such as the 'Product'
and the 'Marketing Mix'
Have a Useful Role
in the Political Arena?

Jenny Lloyd

SUMMARY. Over recent years, whilst there has been increasing acceptance of the existence and role of marketing in the political arena, there
has also been much discussion as to the applicability of its concepts and
models. This paper focuses upon issues surrounding definition of the
'product' and the 'marketing mix.' It examines the varying definitions of
the political 'product' and, from the perspective of elector as 'consumer,' offers its own. In addition it suggests that political marketers
should follow the lead of their counterparts in the fields of service and
social marketing and modify the marketing mix to suit the political environment in which they function. Finally, based upon existing definitions

Jenny Lloyd is affiliated with the University of the West of England, Bristol Business School, Frenchay Campus, Coldharbour Lane, Bristol, BS16 1QY, UK (E-mail:
jenny.lloyd@uwe.ac.uk).

[Haworth co-indexing entry note]: "Square Peg, Round Hole? Can Marketing-Based Concepts Such as
the 'Product' and the 'Marketing Mix' Have a Useful Role in the Political Arena?" Lloyd, Jenny. Co-pub-
lished simultaneously in *Journal of Nonprofit & Public Sector Marketing* (Best Business Books, an imprint of
The Haworth Press, Inc.) Vol. 14, No. 1/2, 2005, pp. 27-46; and: *Current Issues in Political Marketing* (eds:
Walter W. Wymer, Jr., and Jennifer Lees-Marshment) Best Business Books, an imprint of The Haworth
Press, Inc., 2005, pp. 27-46. Single or multiple copies of this article are available for a fee from The Haworth
Document Delivery Service [1-800-HAWORTH, 9:00 a.m. - 5:00 p.m. (EST). E-mail address:
getinfo@haworthpressinc.com].

of the political 'product' and the criticisms of the current marketing mix frameworks, initial suggestions are made for the provision of a new political marketing mix. *[Article copies available for a fee from The Haworth Document Delivery Service: 1-800-HAWORTH. E-mail address: <docdelivery@ haworthpress.com> Website: <http://www.HaworthPress.com> © 2005 by The Haworth Press, Inc. All rights reserved.]*

KEYWORDS. Political marketing, marketing mix, product, product anatomy

INTRODUCTION

It is symptomatic of the newness of the field of Political Marketing that there are a number of basic but contentious issues that are yet to be resolved. Indeed, there is still much discussion as to what political marketing actually is. Scammell (1999) highlights the lack of consensus concerning the precise definition of 'political marketing,' whilst elsewhere debates rage as to whether 'the marketing concept' is either applicable, appropriate or even desirable (Lock and Harris 1996; Palmer 2002) as a framework upon which to model political processes. The aim of this paper is to focus upon two aspects central to the concept of marketing, that of the 'product' and the 'marketing mix,' and examine the extent to which they are applicable to the political arena.

Lees-Marshment (2001a) suggests that there has been a move towards the adoption of a 'marketing orientation' by political parties with significant electoral success. She submits that the adoption of a 'marketing orientation' is one in which political parties 'use[s] market intelligence to identify voter demands, then design[s] the product to suit them' (p. 30). Therefore, having accumulated an understanding of the demands of the elector as consumer, the next logical area for analysis is that of the political 'product' and its construction, the 'marketing mix.'

A LOSS OF IDEOLOGY?

Scammell (1999) in her influential review of political marketing literature identifies the fact that a systematic investigation as to what constitutes the political 'product' has yet to take place. However, despite this lack of precise definition, a number of distinct themes have emerged in the course of recent political marketing papers.

One of the first of these themes involves the discussion of the complexity of the political 'product' and the components of which it is comprised. Interestingly, in their discussion of the political marketing 'product,' the majority of scholars of political marketing do not appear to identify 'ideology' as central to the political 'product.' This is despite the fact that, historically, it has been the most basic differentiating feature between the main political parties. To Butler and Collins (1994) 'ideology' is only part of the multi-component nature of the political 'product' offering and is usually indivisible from factors such as 'people' and 'party.' Rather than 'ideology,' O'Shaughnessey (2001) identifies 'policy' and Harris (2001) 'policy commitments' as central to the political product. This may be due to the fact that the terms are sometimes used, however incorrectly, interchangeably. Alternatively, 'policies' and 'policy commitments' may be seen to provide a more tangible manifestation upon which electors evaluate the relative merits of the political parties than purely through ideological standpoint. Whatever the case, like Butler and Collins (1994), both O'Shaughnessey (2001) and Harris (2001) highlight the fact that the political 'product' is a highly complex concept and encompasses a variety of elements. Interestingly, at first glance, Lees-Marshment (2001b) appears to simplify the 'product' definition in her use of the term 'party behaviour.' However, such a broad generalisation actually emphasises the complexity and variety of factors that potentially exist under the single 'umbrella' term.

GETTING PERSONAL

The second and strongest theme to emerge was the importance of personal characteristics of individual candidates although, within this theme, opinions vary widely. Posner (1982) and O'Cass (1996) propose that the politicians themselves central to the party 'product.' Niffenegger (1989) identifies the candidate as a political 'product' but broadens his definition to include other aspects such as the party platform he or she supports, the candidate's past records of achievement and his or her personal characteristics. Plasser, Scheucher and Senft (1999) suggest that this single-person emphasis may well be the result of the candidate-centred culture that pervades US political activity. This candidate-based view of the political product may be sharply contrasted with the views put forward by academics from the UK whose political system is more party-based. Instead of the image of the individual candidates proving central, Foley (1993), Crew and King (1994), O'Shaughnessey (2001) and Harris (2001) cite the image of the party leader as crucial to the political product.

According to Newman and Sheth (1985) this importance of an individual's image stems from the need by the electorate to simplify the complex bundles of stimuli associated with political parties, campaigns and the electoral system. They cite Sears (1969) who suggested that, based upon such a complex scenario, voters tended to form opinions not on the basis of campaign issues, but on the basis of candidates' images. This stance is supported by Nimmo (1975) who, according to Newman and Sheth (1985) was one of the first to draw a line between political science and the elector as 'consumer.' He defined 'political image' as the voters' subjective appraisal of the candidate. However, although Kotler and Kotler (1999) suggest that "Clothes, manner, statements and actions shape the impressions made on people," Scammell (1995) argues those key elements such as credibility, reputation and trustworthiness are far more influential.

PAST, PRESENT AND FUTURE

The third theme centres upon the elector's personal and cultural experience of the political system in the past, present and future. Niffenegger (1989) highlights the past record of a candidate in terms of his or her ability to fulfil policy commitments as a key component. Similarly, O'Shaughnessey (2001) suggests that the acceptance or rejection of a party's political product at election time may also be seen as a "referendum on past performance"(p. 1048). Less tangibly, he goes on to suggest that 'inherited memory' is also intrinsic to the way that the electoral consumer perceives the political 'product.' The extent to which electors' past lives and cultural contexts impact upon their political choices is also highlighted by Inglehart (1990, p. 422) when he claims that "people live in the past much more than they realise." Jackman and Miller (1998, p. 82) expand upon this point when they explain that "the impact of experience on behaviour is affected by norms passed across generations through early socialization." Therefore, it might be concluded that the historical and cultural context in which the elector exists undoubtedly colours their understanding of the political 'product.'

In terms of the 'present,' Dermody and Scullion (2000) identify the consumption experience as an intrinsic part of the political product's 'value.' They cite Heilbrunn's (1996) argument that individuals attribute value to a product through a constructive and evaluative process of consumption. Therefore, they continue, the attribution of value to the political product extends to the non-tangible experience of voting itself.

Finally, the futuristic idea of 'promise' and potential future benefits are observed as aspects of the political 'product' by both O'Shaughnessey (2001) and Niffenegger (1989). Indeed, Niffenegger suggests that the political product is:

> ... really a complex blend of many potential benefits voters believe will result if the candidate is elected. (p. 47)

It is somewhat surprising therefore that despite the often-cited exchange-based nature of political marketing (Henneberg 1996) the issue of consumer benefit has received such slight consideration. However, Dermody and Scullion (2001) identify the fact that "the electorate have learnt to be much more discerning customers looking for obvious benefits to themselves" (p. 1086) and that if such 'customers' conclude that there is no benefit in political participation, they will choose not to do so. They go on to suggest that such "self-centred" political attitudes have actually lead to the detachment of many from the political process, a situation in which any consideration of the political 'product' on their part may be seen to be unnecessary.

POLITICAL PARTIES–
A PRODUCT OR A SERVICE?

Another theme that runs through much of recent literature suggests significant agreement that political marketing has more in common with service and not-for-profit marketing than product marketing. There can be no doubt that there are strong similarities. Butler and Collins (1994) cite Shostack (1997) in their characterisation of the political product within the context of a service by highlighting the fact that the service sector and the political arena share such features as intangibility, perishability, heterogeneity and inseparability. Cowell (1984) highlights a fifth service characteristic that also relates well to the field of politics; that of lack of ownership.

Lock and Harris (1996) cite Kotler and Andreasen (1991) and Lovelock and Weinberg (1984) when they suggest that the existence of multiple audiences within the field of politics lend a greater likeness to public and non-profit organisations than consumer product-based companies. Scammell (1999) highlights the fact that the scope of marketing theory has been broadened to encompass the service and non-profit sectors but does not discuss in any detail how such parallels can be drawn.

However, it is through Gronroos (1998) and his conceptualisation of service provision within the paradigm of relationship marketing that the true similarities emerge. He states that consumer satisfaction stems not only from the final outcome of the service, but also by the quality of the process of the production of that outcome. This has become apparent over recent months with the field of politics, with growing public concern over issues such as 'stealth taxes,' the effectiveness of public/private partnerships and the overall influence of 'spin.'

In addition, Gronroos (1998) concurs with Calonius (1980) in his proposition that the 'promise concept' (p. 324) is central to the conceptualisation of the marketing concept within the service sector. This concept is no stranger to the political arena as the giving and fulfilling of promises has always been the central tenet of the giving and fulfillment of manifesto promises. In addition Gronroos (1994) highlights the importance of trust in the inter-relationship between service provider and consumer. Once promises are made, consumers must have confidence in the ability of the service provider to maintain their word or the relationship can be irrevocably damaged.

Finally, Gronroos (1998) highlights the fact that within the service industry, only preparations for a service process can be made beforehand and partly prepared services can exist. This mirrors the practice of political parties preparing manifestos and policy statements before an election but only being able to put them into practice following an electoral mandate.

It is therefore unclear as to why, when the similarities between service marketing and political marketing have been alluded to, there has been so little detailed discussion as to how and why this might prove to be the case. One possible reason for this lack of discussion might be the difficulty in finding a direct comparison with any other 'service.' However, Brassington and Pettitt (1997) highlight the fact that 'service'-type products are not homogenous but vary widely in terms of the degree of service involved and the type of service offered. As a result, direct comparison of any 'services' would be difficult. Another suggestion stems from Levitt's (1972) contention that connotations relating to servitude and low status continue to affect thinking about the service sector. Literature pertaining to 'product'-based marketing strategy can often appear much more attractive and accessible, particularly when the focus is largely upon communication.

Further, it has often been suggested that the 'personalisation' of politics (Harris 2001) has lead to situation in which 'the party leader is at the centre of its brand image' (Lock and Harris 1996, p. 17). This focus on the individual, either in the form of candidate or party leader, creates an apparent contradiction between the tangibility of a human being and the intangibility of the services that human beings can offer. In the face of such difficulties, the temptation has often been to dismiss marketing models as inappropriate to the political field.

PRODUCT COMPLEXITY AND THE ANATOMY OF A PRODUCT

There are three main criticisms that run throughout political marketing literature in the discussion of the applicability of marketing theory to the field of politics. The first of these involve the complexity of the nature of the political 'product' is a theme that runs throughout most political marketing literature. It is on this basis of complexity that some commentators on the existence of political marketing suggest that the marketing concept and models such as the 'Marketing Mix' might be deemed inappropriate (Lock and Harris 1996).

In the field of marketing, this issue is countered by simplifying the structure of the product. By breaking the product down and understanding each of the product components and their inter-relationships, marketers might generate a more acute awareness of the implications of various actions, for example, a change in policy direction or the election of a new leader.

According to Brassington and Pettitt (1997), most products, however intangible, may be broken down into bundles of benefits that mean different things to different 'consumers.' These 'bundles' may then be further divided according to the function they fulfil within the construct of a given product's anatomy. They depict the basic anatomy of the product as a series of four concentric rings.

The first and central ring is seen as the 'core product' and is described by Brassington and Pettitt (1997 p. 254) as 'the heart of the product, the main reason for its existence . . .' In terms of political marketing, this may be viewed as the basic ideology upon which all aspects of a political party are grounded and is central to its very being. It is therefore no surprise that when changes to the 'core product' are proposed, they shake the very foundations of a party. A good example of such a case is that of the reform of Clause IV of the Labour Party constitution. Not only did the proposal of reform prompt thirty-two Labour MEPs to take out an advert against its reform in The Guardian in January '95, but as Fielding (1995) reported, provoked Tony Benn's comparison of the proposal to that of an attempt to revise the Ten Commandments. Despite the popularity of the idea that individual personalities are of greatest importance in the formulation of the political product, it is hard to imagine a change of personnel creating such tensions within a party.

The next ring is that of the 'tangible product.' This is the aspect of the political 'product' that the elector sees and is embodied by all aspects of the marketing mix. There has been much criticism over the use of such marketing tools as a tactic to gain votes at the expense of principle. Dermody and Scullion (2001) suggest that 'Politicians have become magpies seeking out tactical marketing techniques in order to gain the benefits of re-election' (p. 1086). However, unless the adoption of a specific product mix appears a logical extension of the core product, such a cynical approach may backfire. The lack of apparent continuity between traditional Labour Party ideology (perceived as the core product) and the position adopted by New Labour resulted in much criticism of Tony Blair for his lack of principle; a fact that he himself acknowledged in his election broadcast of the 27th of May 2001. Indeed, Lees-Marshment and Lilliker (2001) highlight the fact that Blair had received significant criticism that he had 'overridden his Party's traditional values in order to lead it to electoral success in 1997' (p. 205). It is not the role of this paper to pass judgement on a political party's principles, or lack of them. Instead, it should suffice to say that such criticism arose from an incongruity between core and tangible products that can only be remedied through an adjustment of one or the other. Should the incongruity continue to persist, a credibility gap will remain with the associated cynicism on the part of the electorate and the media.

The third ring is that of the 'augmented product.' This consists of factors that may not in themselves form an intrinsic part of the product but add to the product's overall attractiveness. Within the field of political marketing these factors may be perceived as the less tangible aspects such as those 'hedonistic, experiential aspects' recognised by Dermody and Scullion (2001, p. 1087) that are often ignored. They highlight the fact contemporary marketing thinking has moved towards an understanding of the 'centrality of consumption in the construction of meaning and significance in peoples' lives' (p. 1087). Therefore, intangible experiences associated with the political 'product' such as the experience of voting, the feeling of belonging and the satisfaction of election promises fulfilled may all be seen as aspects of the 'augmented product.'

The outer ring is that of the 'potential product.' According to Brassington and Pettitt (1997), this final ring acknowledges the 'dynamic and strategic nature of the product' (p. 255). Whilst the other components focus upon the current make-up of the political 'product,' the 'potential product' focuses upon what might happen in the future. Harris and Lock (1996) suggest that the complexity and intangibility of the political product means that voters make their electoral choices based upon an 'overall packaged concept or message.' It would therefore not be unreasonable to suppose that, without specific policy commitments, electors may make their party selection on the basis of similar political, ethical or moral standpoints in the hope that they might be persuaded in future. For example, a voter with a specific commitment to animal rights may choose to vote for a political party with a strong ecological bias (albeit no specific animal rights policies). This might be done in the hope that they would be more likely to move in that direction than any of the other competing parties. Therefore voters may be seen to be gambling their vote on the potential for future satisfaction.

Therefore, taking a view of the product anatomy as a whole, it is possible to see that, as many have stated, the political product is a complex one. However, it is not complexity without reason but layer upon layer of interdependent aspects of party existence. Indeed, because of the experiential nature of the service-type product, the links between the product components are more highly interdependent than for a manufactured product. Consequently, the use of concentric circles allows the various components of the political product to be analysed individually whilst at the same time underscoring that relationship.

DEFINING AND REFINING

Having reviewed recent literature, difficulty in ascribing a precise definition to the political 'product' appears to have arisen as a result of a lack of consensus over its precise nature, the misuse of marketing terminology and some misunderstandings pertaining to the marketing mix.

As we have seen, there have been numerous and varied attempts to define the political marketing 'product' with the only point of over-riding agreement being that there are distinct similarities between the political 'product' and services. Indeed, O'Shaughnessy (2001) submits that analogies may be drawn with the promise-based offers found in the insurance or finance industries. However, it is with Harrop's (1990) suggestion that the central tenet of political marketing is the projection of belief in a party's ability to govern that we get the first proposition that the 'product' within the sphere of politics is not an 'output' but an 'outcome.' This, together with the premise provided by Gronroos (1998) that consumer satisfaction is dependent upon both the outcome and the processes by which it is reached, provides some further insight into the precise nature of the political product. Therefore, on this basis, the political 'product' may be defined as the processes and outcome associated with the management of national security, social stability and economic growth on behalf of the electorate.

In this light, the political 'product' may be more akin to that of management consultants and project managers. Adapting the analytical framework created by Gronroos (1998), the rationale for such a conclusion is as follows:

a. Political parties do not, in themselves, produce anything tangible. Instead, like project managers and management consultants, they co-ordinate activity across a variety of functions, managing those who undertake the production activity.
b. From the perspective of the elector/consumer, the service offered by political parties has two dimensions; the outcome (i.e., decrease in the number of patients on hospital waiting lists) and the process (the way in

which it is achieved). The relative success of the political 'product' will depend upon the extent to which the electors believe a political party can deliver the desired outcome in the desired fashion. For a party in power, this is likely to have a historical perspective as they are judged by past performance, whilst the party challenging for power (assuming it does not have a recent track record) will be judged on credibility and future potential.

c. Whilst the leadership of a political party can formulate its strategic direction and objectives (in the role as 'management consultants'), the development of the processes required to deliver the 'product' is much more complicated. It requires the co-ordination of a vast array of different departments and disciplines in order that they all work towards the same set of objectives (project management). This requires significant levels of internal marketing together with investment in support systems, equipment and personnel in order to facilitate the smooth delivery of the political 'service' offered by the party.

Ultimately, a political party is judged on its ability (either proven or potential) to successfully run Great Britain plc. Increasingly, it is also being judged on the way that it chooses to run it. Therefore, this is the basis of the political 'product' offered by the main political parties.

CHARACTERISTICS OF POLITICAL MARKETING

The political product now re-defined, the next step before the formulation of the marketing mix is the attainment of a greater understanding of the 'product' characteristics. Only then is it possible to formulate a product mix that responds to the expectations of the electorate.

As we have seen, there appears to be general agreement that there are some basic similarities between the characteristics of the service and political fields of study. Kearsey and Varey (1998), in their summary of the characteristics of 'services' identify five key areas; intangibility, inseparability, heterogeneity, perishability, and lack of ownership. However, Beaven and Scotti (1990) cite the fact that these descriptors were formulated using the characteristics associated with 'goods' production as the standard point of reference. As a consequence, they propose that, in order to truly understand the nature of service marketing, it is first necessary to move away from the manufacturing-based definitions and terminology that have been used to describe service-type organisations. They suggest that a cognitive bias has distorted the way that services are perceived and has thus 'circumvented appropriate conceptualisation of services marketing theory and practice' (p. 5).

Such a proposition is particularly pertinent for political marketing at this moment on three counts. Firstly, the consumer-based perspective proposed by Beaven and Scotti (1990) coincides nicely with the growing call for political marketing to become more 'market-oriented' (O'Cass 1996, Lees-Marshment 2001a). Secondly, it acknowledges the difficulties and pitfalls associated with the practice of trying to fit political marketing concepts into the straitjacket afforded by traditional marketing models. Finally, it proposes a way forward in the characterisation of the political product and the conceptualisation of political marketing theory.

Table 1, columns (a) and (b) summarise the four main differences highlighted by Beaven and Scotti (1990) between manufacturing-oriented thinking and service-oriented thinking in consideration of a service-type product. Rather than using manufacturing-oriented thinking as a counterpoint to ascertain what services are not, they focus upon what they are. Discussion of points 1 to 4 largely centres upon the fact that, as outcomes, services are both able to change the recipient's status in some way and may also be viewed as experiences in themselves. Consumers are not seen as passive receivers of a service but actively process and store their experiences in the form of a 'script.' However, Beaven and Scotti (1990) fail to address the fifth difference identified by Kearsey and Varey (1998), that of lack of ownership. Nevertheless, following the premise established by Beaven and Scotti (1990), by focussing upon the service offering, the lack of ownership may be seen to afford greater flexibility and efficiency of resources as they are only ' rented' for the duration of the provision of the service.

From the perspective of political marketing, whilst political outcomes share significant service characteristics with those identified by Beaven and Scotti (1990), there are also significant differences. The characteristics of political outcomes have been outlined in Table 1, column (c), and they differ from services in three key areas. Firstly, political outcomes are standardised at the point of production. Variation arises from the way that an elector's life experience, values and expectations affect the way that he or she perceives the outcome. For example, the recent move to ban hunting has been viewed quite differently by The Countryside Alliance, who see it as an attack upon their way of life, and Animal Rights activists, who see it as a moral imperative in the prevention of animal cruelty.

Another way in which political outcomes differ from service outcomes centres upon how they are received. Assuming that the individual elector has spent the whole of his or her life within a culture that is governed, he or she has been subject to political outcomes from the moment of conception. Pre and post-natal care, the provision of hospitals and health care, education and levels of child support (or lack of it) are all the result of political outcomes. The indi-

TABLE 1. Contrasting Manufacturing-Oriented, Service-Oriented and Political Outcome-Oriented Perspectives

MANUFACTURING VS. SERVICE-ORIENTED THINKING (ADAPTED FROM KEARSEY AND VAREY (1998), BEAVEN AND SCOTTI (1990))		
MANUFACTURING-ORIENTED THINKING **(A)**	**SERVICE-ORIENTED THINKING** **(B)**	**POLITICAL OUTCOME-ORIENTED THINKING** **(C)**
1. Services are abstract and intangible products. 2. Services are non-standardised heterogeneous outputs. 3. Services are instantly perishable and cannot be produced in advance or stored for future sale. 4. Services are simultaneously produced and consumed; customer involvement often interrupts operations and interferes with efficiency. 5. Services cannot be 'owned' following payment as no physical product is exchanged and the service is instantly perishable. Facilities used in the provision of the service remain the property of the provider and the customer only has access for the duration of the service.	1. Services are processes with outcomes that can be perceived directly and indirectly leaving concrete impressions. 2. Services are personal experiences that can be uniquely tailored to meet individual needs and expectations. 3. Services are processes that are created and experienced with outcomes that are often distinct, direct and imperishable. 4. Services are encounters that afford opportunities for greater satisfaction through participation, shared responsibility, and timely feedback. 5. Services offer greater efficiency and flexibility in terms of resources because they are effectively 'rented' only for the period of the provision of the service.	1. Politics involves a series of outcomes, processed, and perceived both directly and indirectly leaving concrete impressions. 2. Political outcomes are standardised at the point of production. Variations arise from the way they are perceived, based upon electors' experience or expectations. 3. Political outcomes may work singly, or cumulatively, affecting a change in the status quo for individuals or groups of electors. 4. Political outcomes are encounters that afford opportunities for greater satisfaction through participation, shared responsibility, and timely feedback. 5. Whilst the political outcomes are not owned directly by the electors, the public goods used to generate them are likely to have been purchased through taxation. There is therefore a greater degree of accountability as to how the resources are used. 6. In general, electors have been receivers of political outcomes, either actively or passively for the whole of their lives.

vidual and cumulative effect of these outcomes become part of electors personal biographies that will colour their perspective for the whole of their lives.

Finally, unlike most services, electors are stakeholders in the resources that create political outcomes. Most public goods and services are financed through public taxation, as are the salaries of public servants. Therefore, as a result, many electors take an active interest in the way that public money is used, an interest often fuelled by the media. Subsequently, their understanding of the effectiveness with which resources are employed will colour their perception of political parties and the associated political 'product.'

WHICH MIX?

Having re-conceptualised the characteristics of the political product in terms of both 'process' and 'outcome,' the next logical step is to review the applicability of the classic marketing tool, 'the marketing mix.' The concept of 'The Four Ps' (product, promotion, place, price) first introduced by Borden (1962) and then popularised by McCarthy (1964), was an insightful tool that provided the organising framework for the integration of diverse marketing tasks. However, over recent years there has been growing discussion as to its applicability to other sectors. In an attempt to reflect the different nature of service provision, Booms and Bitner (1981) expanded the marketing mix to encompass a further three 'Ps.' The additional 'Ps' involved the inclusion of 'process' (the efficiency of service delivery), 'people' (the image, skills and ability of the people delivering the service) and 'physical evidence' (the evidence that a service has been performed).

Despite this modification, some discontent still rankled. Beaven and Scotti (1990) proposed that, having re-conceptualised the characteristics of service marketing the associated marketing mix required further adaptation. Using an alternative acronym, Beaven and Scotti (1990) suggested the use of SOAR; Service scripts, Outlay, Accommodation and Representation as a more appropriate analytical framework.

However, despite this, there appears little doubt that the political 'product' struggles to fit neatly with any of these incarnations of the marketing mix. Nevertheless, despite the general consensus that it is possible to draw parallels between political marketing and service marketing, there is still an ongoing tendency to employ the product rather than the service marketing mix (Harris 2001, Lees-Marshment 2001a). This is despite the fact that severe weaknesses were highlighted in terms of the political 'price' and 'place' (Lees-Marshment 2001b).

At first glance, Booms and Bitner's '7ps' appears a more appropriate framework with which to analyse the political marketing mix than Borden's (1962) '4ps.' The inclusion of 'people' took into account the increased 'personalisation' (Harris 2001) of politics, whilst the 'physical evidence' relates to factors highlighted by Lees-Marshment (2001b) such as symbols, the party constitution, and party conferences. Finally, with regard to 'process,' the efficiency, effectiveness and integrity with which the political 'product' is delivered has never had such a high profile, following the Millennium Dome and Picket's Lock affair. Indeed, Lees-Marshment (2001b) remarked that an ICM exit pole indicated that Tory voters failed to return to the party in 2001 because of a lack of confidence in the Tory ability to improve public services. This supports a previous statement made by Lees-Marshment (2001) that the delivery of the political 'product' could only increase in importance.

However, as with Borden's (1962) product marketing mix and Booms and Bitner's (1981) service marketing mix also failed to respond to the concerns voiced over the relevance of the 'price' and 'place' to the political arena (Lees-Marshment 2001b). In contrast, Beaven and Scotti's (1990) 'outlay' addresses the 'economic costs' such as taxes, interest rate changes and alterations in government benefits highlighted by Niffenegger (1989), together with physical costs to the elector (in terms of time and effort). Yet, despite the fact that they include discussion on the inclusion of social and interpersonal 'outlay,' they do not include any mention of emotional 'outlay.' Finally, having premised the development of a new conceptual framework for the service marketing mix on the need to break away from the cognitive bias of the 'product' marketing mix, it is curious that they felt the need to relate SOAR to each of the components of the '4ps.'

According to Lock and Harris (1996) 'the assumption that there is a direct transferability of marketing theory and applications seems [to them] questionable' (p.16), a sentiment echoed by both Butler and Collins (1994) and O'Cass (1996). However, as we have seen with Beaven and Scotti (1990), there is no real need for direct transference. Indeed, direct transference of theory from one field to another only serves to impose a bias that circumvents appropriate conceptualisation of marketing theory. Instead, whilst the concept of a marketing mix may be seen as a constructive analytical tool within the political arena, in order for it to be truly useful, it needs to be developed as a result of consideration of the characteristics of the political market. On this basis the following is proposed as an initial step in the creation of a "political marketing mix."

THE COMPONENTS FOR A POLITICAL 'MIX'

We suggest that the following five components should be key to the development of a political marketing mix. Whilst some exhibit similarities to those proposed by Borden (1962), Booms and Bitner (1981) and Beaven and Scotti (1990), also included are aspects that take into account the unique nature of the political market.

The first of the components involves the 'services offering' afforded by the political party. At the broadest level this includes policy on the management of national security, social stability and economic growth. However, in cases where the party of government takes on a visible management role, the Millennium Dome being a case in point, they also acquire specialist project management roles. Electors judge the suitability of a party not only on their electoral policies, but also as to whether they feel they have the ability to fulfil their responsibilities. Consequently, political parties must ensure that they have appropriate management skills and expertise.

The second component is that of 'representation.' This involves the way that all aspects of the political party, its policies and its members are represented to the electorate. This goes further than purely 'communication' or 'promotion' because it takes into account both the controllable aspects of political activity such as policy statements and briefings, public appearances and political advertising and PR, and the uncontrollable elements such as media coverage. Electors consult their mental 'scripts' to match expectation to representation. If a match occurs, the representation will serve to reinforce the existing perception of the political 'product.' In contrast, a mismatch will result in dissonance and a resulting alteration of the mental 'script.'

The implications of 'representation' for the political product are three-fold. Firstly, in light of recent allegations of 'sleaze' within the political sphere, any dubious activity observed on the part of a politician is likely to be viewed with distrust on the part of the electorate. Therefore, politicians must not only maintain their integrity, they must be *seen* to display integrity if electors' 'scripts' are ever to be modified. Secondly, all aspects of the party must be represented in a realistic way. If electors are allowed to acquire unrealistic expectations on the basis of representation, the inability to deliver will only result in disappointment and distrust. Finally, in the event that the political 'product' is misrepresented in the media, the way that it is seen to respond through controllable elements can not only minimise the damage, but actually enhance the image of the 'political product.'

Accommodation is the third component to be taken into account in the formulation of the political marketing mix. It highlights the requirement on the part of political parties to understand the needs of the electorate and be able to respond to them appropriately. This does not mean, however, that political parties should simply become 'focus-group lead.' Instead, parties should attain an understanding of public priorities and public interest and be prepared to address these topics on the basis of their 'core product' or ideology. During the 2001 election, there was much criticism of the strategy adopted by the Conservative Party and their decision to focus upon Europe, perceived as a Labour Party weakness, rather than deal in detail with issues such as the NHS and education. According to one caller to a BBC Radio 5 phone-in, they had simply "lost the plot."

In addition, Beaven and Scotti (1990) also cite Webster's Dictionary definition of 'accommodation' as 'something supplied for convenience.' In terms of the political market, electors must be able to access it and ideally participate within it with some degree of ease. Members of parties, MPs and members of the Government should be seen as accessible and open, whilst participation at all levels should be both encouraged, and seen to be encouraged, across all sections of the community. Central to this notion is the requirement that those participating should feel that they have (and be seen to have) some degree of influence. Without this, potential participants will question the point of expending time and effort doing so. At a time when we are looking at an ever more presidential-style system of government, the need for accommodation becomes all the more acute.

'Investment,' the fourth component, can take a number of forms. Unlike the term 'outlay' (Beaven and Scotti 1990) or 'price' (Borden 1962, Booms and Bitner 1981), the term 'investment' relates more directly with the stakeholder-type relationship that the electorate has with its political representatives. 'Investment' can be a direct financial payment in the form of subscriptions or donations to a political party or candidate. However, it can also take the form of a delayed financial 'investment,' for example, likely changes in tax or welfare benefits or changes in the standard of living. Alternatively, 'investment' can also take the form of less financially based factors such as the time and effort to participate (Beaven and Scotti 1990) and the emotional and experiential aspects (Dermody and Scullion 2001) attached to participation within the political process. Whatever the form, electors expect to see a return, either tangible or intangible.

The final component of the political marketing mix is that of 'outcome.' The ability to deliver upon policy issues and election promises is one of the most tangible ways by which electors judge the performance of political parties. However, it is not just the final outcome that counts, but also how that outcome is achieved. For example, according to a BBC Online report (Health Doubts Raised over Hospital Waiting Lists, 1/9/99) patients were being dropped from hospital waiting lists in order to meet government targets.

Therefore, political parties should be seen to deliver upon their promises effectively, efficiently and ethically.

CONCLUSION

There is no doubt that marketing concepts developed from and based upon the market for manufactured goods have only limited applicability to the political arena if left unmodified. As such, it certainly appears that we are looking at a case of trying to fit a 'square peg into a round hole.' However, as those within the fields of social and service marketing have demonstrated, it is possible to embrace the concept of a product mix in principle, but modify it according to the context in which the 'market' exists.

In attempting to ascertain whether the marketing concepts of the 'product' and the 'marketing mix' have any validity in the political arena, we have tried to re-conceptualise the key aspects of the political 'product' into a framework that both facilitates theoretical development in this area. Also, from a practical perspective, it enables practitioners to adopt a structured approach in their 'product' development. However, whilst the political 'mix' differs significantly from the 'mixes' proposed for the areas of manufactured products and of services, there are certain similarities in the way that these frameworks are employed.

The political 'product' is the sum total of its components. As a result, individual components are inter-related and should not be considered in isolation, nor should they be dismissed as irrelevant. Each and every component has an impact upon the way that the others are perceived and any inconsistencies, either through mistake or neglect, will create dissonance on the part of the elector.

In addition, each component of the marketing mix should be considered in relation to each aspect of product anatomy. Continuity is essential that the tangible and the augmented products are seen to logical extensions of the core product in order for a party to maintain its ideological credibility. The potential product therefore provides the ideal vehicle for longer-term strategic party development.

At first glance it might appear presumptuous to attempt to revise concepts that are the marketing equivalent of The Ten Commandments. And it must be remembered that this is only an initial attempt to move discussion on this point on. However it is pointless for the political marketing community to continue to use the traditional framework of the marketing mix when it readily admits its unsuitability. Beaven and Scotti (1990) highlighted the fact that adhesion to unsuitable frameworks only serve to restrict valuable conceptual development. Certainly in the case of political marketing, the use of the '4ps' not only restricts development; it puts it in a conceptual straitjacket.

AREAS FOR FURTHER RESEARCH

The intention of this discussion of the definition of the political 'product' and its associated marketing mix has been to initiate the development of a dialogue in this area. Most of the definitions and analysis to date have come from the perspective of academics and political commentators. However, much more research has to be undertaken from the perspective of the elector as 'consumer.' In addition, further research should examine the extent to which the 'consumer' perception of the political 'product' affects voting action and the extent to which it can be modified in a repositioning exercise.

REFERENCES

Beaven, M.H. and Scotti, D.J. (1990) Service-Oriented Thinking and its Implications for the Marketing Mix. *The Journal of Services Marketing 4*, 5-19.

Booms, B.H. and Bitner, M.J. (1981) Marketing strategies and organisation structures for service firms. In Donnelly, J and George, W.R. (Eds), *Marketing of Services* (American Marketing Association, Chicago).

Borden, N. (1965) 'The Concept of the Marketing Mix' in *Science in Marketing*, ed. George Schwartz, NY: Wiley and Sons. 386-397.

Brassington, F. and Stephen Pettitt (1997) *Principles of Marketing*, Pitman Publishing, London.

Butler, P. and Collins, N. (1994) Political Marketing: Structure and Process. *European Journal of Marketing 28*, 19-34.

Cowell, D. (1984) *The Marketing of Services*, Heinemann Professional Publishing, Oxford.

Crew, I. and King, A. (1994) Did Major win? Did Kinnock Lose? Leadership effects in the 1992 British General Election. In A. Heath (Ed). *Labour's last chance*? London: Dartmouth.

Dermody, J. and Scullion, R. (2001) Delusions of Grandeur? Marketing's contribution to 'meaningful' Western political consumption. *European Journal of Marketing 35*, 1085-1098.

Fielding, S. (1995) Labour: Decline and Renewal. *Baseline* 106.

Foley, M. The rise of the British presidency. Manchester University Press, Manchester.

Gosschalk, B., Marshall, B. and Kaur-Ballagan, K. (2002) Non-Voters, Political Disconnection and Parliamentary Democracy. *Parliamentary Affairs 55*, 715-730.

Gronroos, C. (1994) From Marketing Mix to Relationship Marketing: Towards a Paradigm Shift in Marketing. *Management Decision, 32*, 4-20.

Gronroos, C. (1998) Marketing services: the case of a missing product. *Journal of Business & Industrial Marketing, 13*, 322-338.

Harris, P. (2001) To Spin or not to Spin, that is the Question: The Emergence of Modern Political Marketing. *The Marketing Review 2*, 35-53.

Harrop, M. (1990) Political Marketing. *Parliamentary Affairs 43*.

Heilbrun, B. (1996) "In search of the hidden go(o)d: a philosophical deconstruction and narratological revisitation of the eschatological maetaphor in marketing" in Brown, Bell and Carson (Eds.), *Marketing Apocalypse. Eschatology, Escapology and the Illusion of the End*, Routledge, London.

Henneberg, S. (1996) "Second conference on political marketing." *Journal of Marketing Management 12*, 777-783.

Inglehart, R. (1990) *Culture Shift in Advanced Industrial Society*, Princeton, NJ, Princeton University Press.

Jackman, R.W. and Miller, R.A. (1998) Social Capital and Politics. *Annual Review of Political Science 1*, 47-73.

Kearsey, A. and Varey, R.J. (1998) Managerialist Thinking on Marketing for Public Services. *Public Money and Management* January-March.

Kotler, P. and Andreasin, A.R. (1991) *Strategic Marketing for Nonprofit Organisations*, Prentice-Hall, Englewood Cliffs, NJ.

Kotler, P. and Kotler, N. (1999) Generating effective Candidates, Campaigns and Causes. In *Handbook of Political Marketing*, Ed. Bruce I. Newman, Sage Publications Inc, California, USA.

Lees-Marshment, J. (2001a) The Marriage of Politics and Marketing. *Political Studies 49*, 692-713.

Lees-Marshment, J. (2001b) '*Political marketing and British political parties–The party's just begun*,' Manchester University Press, Manchester.

_____ and Lilleker, D. (2001) Political Marketing and Traditional Values: 'Old Labour' for 'new times'? *Contemporary Politics 7*, 205-216.(Abstract).

Levitt, T. (1972) Product-line Approach to Service. *Harvard Business Review 50*, 41-52.

Lock, A. and Harris, P. (1996) Political Marketing–Vive la Difference! *European Journal of Marketing 30*, 14-24.

Lovelock, C.H. and Weinburg, C.B. (1984) *Marketing for Public and Non-profit Managers*, Wiley, New York, NY.

McCarthy, E.J. (1964) *Basic Marketing: A Managerial Approach*, Homewood, Ill. 38-40.

Newman, B.I. and Sheth, J.N. (1984) The 'Gender Gap' in Voter Attitudes and Behaviour: Some Advertising Implications. *Journal of Advertising 13*, 4-16.

Newman, B.I. and Sheth, J.N. (1985) A Model of Primary Voter Behaviour. *Journal of Consumer Research 12*, 178-187.

Niffenegger, P.B. (1989) Strategies for success from the political marketers. *The Journal of Consumer Marketing 6*, 45-51.

Nimmo, D.I. (1975) "Images and Voters' Decision-Making Processes," in *Advances in Consumer Research*, ed. Mary Jane Schlinger, Ann Arbor, Association for Consumer Research , MI. 2, 771-781.

O'Cass, A. (1996) Political Marketing and the Marketing Concept. *European Journal of Marketing 30*, 37-53.

O'Shaughnessy, N. (2001) The marketing of political marketing. *European Journal of Marketing 35*, 1047-1057.

Plasser, F., Scheucher, C. and Senft, C. (1999) Is there a European Style of political Marketing? A survey of political Managers and Consultants. In *Handbook of Political Marketing*, Ed. Bruce I. Newman, Sage Publications Inc, California, USA, 89-112.

Posner, M. (1992) Repositioning the Right Honorable. *Canadian Business*.

Scammell, M. (1995) *Designer Politics: How Elections are Won*. Basingstoke, Macmillan.

Scammell, M. (1999) Political Marketing: Lessons for Political Science. *Political Studies XLVII*, 718-739.

Sears, D.O. (1969) 'Political Behavior,' in *The Handbook of Social Psychology*, eds. Gardner Lindzey and Elliot Aronson, Addison Wesley, Reading MA. 5, 315-458.

Seawright, D. (2001) Landslide II or Trauma II? The National Results. *The Journal of Marketing Management 17*, 1019-1033.

Shostack, G.L. (1977) Breaking Free From Product Marketing. *Journal of Marketing 41*.

Weinreich, N.K. (1999) *Hands on Social Marketing–A Step by Step Guide.*

A Conceptual Model
of Political Market Orientation

Robert P. Ormrod

SUMMARY. This article proposes eight constructs of a conceptual model of political market orientation, taking inspiration from the business and political marketing literature. Four of the constructs are 'behavioural' in that they aim to describe the process of how information flows through the organisation. The remaining four constructs are attitudinal, designed to capture the awareness of members to the activities and importance of stakeholder groups in society, both internal and external to the organisation. The model not only allows the level of a party's political market orientation to be assessed, but also aids the party in making a context-specific decision with regard to the reallocation–or not–of party resources in order to attain the party's long-term objectives. *[Article copies available for a fee from The Haworth Document Delivery Service: 1-800-HAWORTH. E-mail address: <docdelivery@haworthpress.com> Website: <http://www.HaworthPress.com> © 2005 by The Haworth Press, Inc. All rights reserved.]*

KEYWORDS. Political market orientation, political marketing, market orientation

Robert P. Ormrod is Research Assistant, Business Research Academy, Langvangen 8, Building 108, 8900 Randers, Denmark (E-mail: ropo@erfak.dk).

The author would like to thank Assistant Professor Joachim Scholderer at the Aarhus School of Business and two anonymous *Journal of Nonprofit & Public Sector Marketing* reviewers for helpful comments on previous drafts of this article.

[Haworth co-indexing entry note]: "A Conceptual Model of Political Market Orientation." Ormrod, Robert P. Co-published simultaneously in *Journal of Nonprofit & Public Sector Marketing* (Best Business Books, an imprint of The Haworth Press, Inc.) Vol. 14, No. 1/2, 2005, pp. 47-64; and: *Current Issues in Political Marketing* (eds: Walter W. Wymer, Jr., and Jennifer Lees-Marshment) Best Business Books, an imprint of The Haworth Press, Inc., 2005, pp. 47-64. Single or multiple copies of this article are available for a fee from The Haworth Document Delivery Service [1-800-HAWORTH, 9:00 a.m. - 5:00 p.m. (EST). E-mail address: getinfo@haworthpressinc.com].

Available online at http://www.haworthpress.com/web/JNPSM
doi:10.1300/J054v14n01_04

The term 'market orientation' has existed in the business marketing literature for many years, but has only since around the beginning of the 1990's been conceptualised in a way that has facilitated testing in a scientific manner (Harrison-Walker 2001), beginning with Narver and Slater (1990) and Kohli and Jaworski (1990). There has since, however, been much work dealing with various alternative conceptualisations of the constructs that make up a market orientation, varying from Deshpandé, Farley and Webster's (1993) view that a market orientation should be considered as synonymous with a customer orientation, to Harrison-Walker's (2001) behavioural/cultural conceptualisation, where Narver and Slater's (1990) 'Customer Orientation' and 'Competitor Orientation' are matched with Kohli and Jaworski's (1990) 'Intelligence Generation,' 'Intelligence Dissemination,' and 'Responsiveness' constructs, and expanded by the addition of a fourth behavioural construct, a 'Shared Interpretation of Information,' inspired by Daft and Weick (1984) and located between the dissemination and responsiveness to information.

This article introduces a conceptual model of political market orientation that is developed from business and political marketing literature. It will begin with a short review of the research to date into the concept in both the business and political marketing literature, then continue to discuss the conceptualisation of the behavioural and cultural constructs proposed by Harrison-Walker (2001) and show the way in which they can be used in the political context. The importance of an 'Internal Orientation,' loosely based on Narver and Slater's (1990) 'Interfunctional Coordination' construct will be demonstrated, and a further construct, an 'External Orientation,' will be developed and that is argued to enhance the sensitivity of the model to the political arena. The implications of Ormrod's (2003) research lead to the final two constructs of Harrison-Walker's (2001) conceptual model being redefined, again in order to reflect the nature of the political marketplace, labelled 'Member Participation' and 'Consistent External Communication.'

THE NATURE OF A MARKET ORIENTATION

A market orientation is normally conceptualised as a point on a continuum rather than as an either/or construct (Kohli and Jaworski 1990; Kohli, Jaworski, and Kumar 1993), and this characteristic enables the firm to determine the existing level of market orientation. Several authors (e.g., Harrison-Walker 2001; Narver and Slater 1990; Slater and Narver 1994) treat a Customer and a Competitor Orientation as separate constructs, and this enables the firm to measure the relative amount of resources allocated to understanding and serving each stakeholder group, which in turn can be adjusted and used to maximise the return on investment of these resources via a "balanced external orientation" strategy (Slater and Narver 1994). An investigation into the level of a firm's market orientation is not prescriptive in the sense that it provides hard and fast guidelines for success, but rather allows the organisation to make context-specific decisions in order to maximise the return on resources employed.

A related point is made by Kohli and Jaworski (1990), that "The orientation is useful only if the benefits it affords exceeds the cost of these resources," that is, there is an opportunity cost of resources employed. They also note that the implementation of market orientation does not automatically result in an increased performance, as "simply engaging in market-oriented activities does not ensure the *quality* of those activities" (Kohli and Jaworski 1990); in some circumstances it is conceivable that, for example, a product or sales orientation would be more profitable to the firm due to the nature of the competitive environment (e.g., Noble, Sinha, and Kumar 2002; Gray et al. 1998; Slater and Narver 1994; Kohli and Jaworski 1990). Whilst it is beyond the scope of this article to discuss this issue, it is proposed to be an important area for future research into the implications of adopting a political market orientation.

It is also important to note that a market orientation is not a market*ing* orientation. Until recently there has been some discussion in the business marketing literature as to the difference between a 'market' and a 'marketing' orientation, and as such it is important to clarify the position taken in this article with regard to the two concepts. The view accepted by the majority of business market orientation authors (e.g., Kohli and Jaworski 1990; Narver and Slater 1990; Harrison-Walker 2001; Lafferty and Hult 2001) is that the term 'market orientation' concerns the holistic, organisation-wide nature of the concept's emphasis on both internal and external stakeholder relationships, whilst a 'marketing orientation' is mainly the preserve of the marketing function and is primarily concerned with "marketing's functional role in coordinating and managing the 4P's to make companies more responsive to meeting customer needs" (Gray et al. 1998). A 'political marketing orientation' would therefore be primarily concerned with investigating the discrete exchanges that occur as a result of, for example, election campaigns, whilst the emphasis on building and maintaining stakeholder relationships by the entire organisation makes the term 'political market orientation' more appropriate to the conceptual model proposed in this article.

PREVIOUS WORK ON POLITICAL MARKET ORIENTATION

O'Cass (1996, 2001a, 2001b) proposes a semantic redefinition of the marketing management paradigm for the political context as "the analysis, planning, implementation and control of political and electoral programs" (O'Cass 1996), but does not really discuss the differences between the business and political marketplaces. Despite the fact that various stakeholder groups' influence on political parties is acknowledged, as "significant pressures are being placed on political parties and politicians by voters, business and lobby groups" (O'Cass 2001a), only the party/voter exchange process is investigated with the emphasis of his research being on the use of traditional marketing tools to attain party objectives. The success criteria he lays down does concern satisfying "voter needs and wants . . . within ideological bounds and parliamentary numbers rather than the percentage of the vote" (O'Cass 2001a), but his research concentrates mainly on the effects of a marketing orientation on campaign activities (O'Cass 1996, 2001a, 2001b). Although noting that a market orientation is not a marketing orientation, in O'Cass (2001b) he considers it possible to use them to supplement each other in an investigation rather than acknowledging that they rest upon different paradigms, each with its own assumptions.

Lees-Marshment (2001a, 2001b, 2001c) describes the process that a market oriented party goes through during an electoral cycle, beginning with the generation of formal and informal market intelligence by party members and professionals alike. Lees-Marshment (2001a) takes the view that political marketing is concerned with "the relationship between a political organisation's 'product' and the demands of the market," and that "the basic argument of a market orientation is to follow, rather than lead, voter demands."

Internal stakeholders are also considered to be of prime importance when developing and marketing the market oriented party's political product, especially grassroots party members, as their inclusion can "promote a feeling of involvement, value and worth amongst those within the party" (Lees-Marshment 2001a). The information that is generated on, for example, voter opinions should then be disseminated to all members and used to assist in the joint formulation of party policy by members and party professionals, as this will "increase co-operation and understanding between them and help to reduce the chances of an 'outsider/insider' (professional/party member) distinction arising" (Lees-Marshment 2001a).

In short, the party which adopts a market oriented approach first generates market intelligence into voter needs and wants, disseminates this intelligence throughout the party, and then "designs a product that will actually satisfy voters' demands: that meets their needs and wants, is supported and implemented by the internal organisation, and is deliverable in government" (Lees-Marshment 2001a). The political product is then communicated out to voters at all points on the electoral cycle so that come election time, "The actual election campaign is then almost superfluous to requirements but provides the last chance to convey to voters what is on offer" (Lees-Marshment 2001a). The final stage is that of delivery: should the party gain enough support to form a government then it will be able to put its policies into practice, and it is this stage that "is crucial to the ultimate success of marketing and therefore political marketing" (Lees-Marshment 2001a).

Whilst it could be argued that Lees-Marshment's (2001a, 2001b, 2001c) process model of how a market oriented party should act is in fact closer to a marketing orientation rather than a market orientation, it is however similar to Kohli and Jaworski's (1990) conceptualisation of a market orientation as behaviour. There is an emphasis on generating information, disseminating it to all party members and including all internal stakeholders–to the extent possible–in the marketing and strategy formulation process as a prerequisite for party success. Lees-Marshment (2001a) also advocates an awareness of competitor actions in that it is recommended that a SWOT analysis (Strengths and Weaknesses, Opportunities and Threats) be carried out, but fostering an attitude in the party to the possibility of cooperating with competitors, an important consideration in some political systems (Bowler and Farrell 1992), is not so apparent; nor is an explicit reference to the importance of generating information directly from other external stakeholder groups.

The conceptual model of political market orientation proposed in this article has obvious parallels to Lees-Marshment's (e.g., 2001a) work, but differs in that the possibility of cooperating with competing parties is acknowledged, as is the importance of all stakeholder groups in society. Therefore, it is proposed that a political market orientation exists when all members of a party are sensitive to internal and external stakeholders' attitudes, needs and wants, and synthesize these within a framework of constraints imposed by all stakeholders to develop policies and programmes with which to reach the party's objectives.

POLITICAL MARKET ORIENTATION AS BEHAVIOUR

Many of the previous conceptualisations of a market orientation have consisted of exclusively behavioural constructs, which is reflected in the definition of the concept as "the physical actions of [actors] that can be directly observed and measured by others" (Peter, Olsen, and Grunert 1999). The behavioural constructs of the conceptual model of political market orientation presented in this work follow closely those first proposed by Kohli and Jaworski (1990), in that the Information Generation and Information Dissemination constructs are linked with Ormrod's (2003) 'Member Participation' and 'Consistent External Communication' constructs.

Lafferty and Hult's (2001) article, a synthesis of previous work on market orientation that resulted in four dimensions, shows Kohli and Jaworski's (1990) conceptualisation to have the most utility in explaining the behavioural constructs of the business market orientation model, as other authors have restricted it to focusing on a particular external stakeholder group (e.g., Ruekert 1992–the generation of customer information) or to the managerial level at which the information is disseminated in the firm (e.g., Shapiro 1988–upper management). Despite the fact that Kohli and Jaworski (1990) also emphasise upper management as the key facilitating group amongst employees, their conceptual model is on a more general level and stresses the 'importance of information' and of 'taking action,' two of Lafferty and Hult's (2001) dimensions; as such it is not only applicable across a broader spectrum of industries, but also more applicable to political parties.

The use of the term 'information' instead of Kohli and Jaworski's (1990) 'intelligence' is more than merely a semantic preference–'intelligence' can be said to refer to the generation of pieces of information pertaining to sources external to the organisation, which then pass through the three remaining behavioural constructs of the conceptual model of political market orientation proposed in this article. The term 'information,' on the other hand, is broader in scope as it can also apply to the Internal Orientation construct of the political market orientation recognition of the ability of individual party members, independent of position in the party, to generate ideas and information and to participate in policy and political program development.

Finally, it must be noted that a central assumption of the conceptual model of political market orientation is that the four behavioural constructs are consecutive, as information has to be generated before it can be disseminated, disseminated before it can be interpreted, and so on. This behavioural chain (Figure 1) demonstrates the direction of information flow through the party, and should not be interpreted as indicating capability dependence; it is conceivable that a party could generate a large amount of both formal and informal information, yet not have the organisational structure necessary to disseminate this information. A final defining characteristic of the behavioural chain is its application, as a whole, to each of the attitudinal constructs (Harrison-Walker 2001; Kohli and Jaworski 1990).

This conceptualisation enables the model to discern the extent to which the party is oriented to the individual stakeholder markets, and to aid the party in optimising the resource allocation to each stakeholder group in order to achieve the agreed-upon party objectives. This characteristic of the conceptual model also enables it to be used in different electoral systems and by different party structures in that it is not prescriptive in the sense that it gives answers to

FIGURE 1. The Behavioural Chain

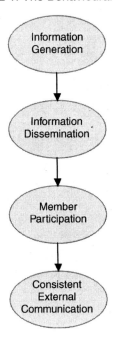

the resource allocation question, but rather aids the party as a whole in adjusting–or not–the emphasis placed on different stakeholder groups.

INFORMATION GENERATION

Kohli et al. (1993) define their concept of Intelligence Generation as being "the collection and assessment of *both* customer needs/preferences and the forces (i.e., task and macro environments) that influence the development and refinement of those needs," i.e., both customers and external stakeholders. They also stress the necessity of this occurring in all departments in the business, as "each has a unique market lens"; whilst political parties are generally organised as hierarchies (Dean and Croft 2001) rather than as functions, each party member has a particular perspective on society and is, to a certain extent, capable of generating information about stakeholder opinions.

The importance of the generation of information emphasised in the business market orientation literature is mirrored in the political market orientation literature, with both Lees-Marshment (2001a, 2001b, 2001c) and O'Cass

(1996, 2001a, 2001b) regarding it as a necessary activity in order to explicate voter needs and wants. Lees-Marshment (2001a) goes further and proposes that the generation of information occurs formally (i.e., traditional market research at the party level) and informally (i.e., social exchanges at the individual level), and suggests that research should also be carried out by the party leadership on internal stakeholder opinions, as "The party leadership needs to understand the views of all within the organisation and alter the product accordingly to ensure that it will gain the necessary level of acceptance." This formal/informal conceptualisation is considered to have some explanatory power, and therefore Information Generation is defined as the party-wide generation of formal and informal information regarding all internal and external stakeholders.

INFORMATION DISSEMINATION

The second stage in Kohli and Jaworski's (1990) market orientation construct is concerned with the dissemination of information throughout the organisation. Kohli and Jaworski (1990) argue that "market intelligence need not always be disseminated by the marketing department to other departments. Intelligence may flow in the opposite direction, depending on where it is generated," that is, all individuals in the organisation are capable of generating intelligence. Kohli et al. (1993) elaborate on this conceptualisation by explicitly stating that "the dissemination of intelligence occurs both formally and informally."

This emphasis on the importance of horizontal and vertical dissemination of information is also accepted in the political market orientation research to date, in that Lees-Marshment (2001a) argues that "The results of professional research should be made fully available to them [MP's and members]," and O'Cass (2001a) considers the Kohli and Jaworski (1990) typology as being the most applicable to the study of political marketing phenomena. In the context of the conceptual model of political market orientation presented in this article, Information Dissemination is defined to be the party-wide communication and reception of information through formal and informal channels.

MEMBER PARTICIPATION

In addition to the Kohli and Jaworski (1990) Generation-Dissemination-Responsiveness typology, Harrison-Walker (2001) argued for the inclusion of a fourth behavioural construct concerning the 'Shared Interpretation of Information,' occurring between dissemination and responsiveness, a conceptualisation inspired by Daft and Weick (1984, in Harrison-Walker 2001). Whilst Harrison-Walker (2001) places the organisational interpretation of information as occurring after the dissemination of information and being the responsibility of upper management, Kohli and Jaworski (1990) see this as occurring as part of the Information Generation stage at the individual level rather than a separate process at the collective level, although they do see the dissemination stage as providing "a shared basis for concerted actions by different departments."

Ormrod (2003) found that there was evidence to suggest that the internal and external aspects of the behavioural chain should be separated, where the internally focussed construct would consist of behaviours relating to the inclusion of all members in both making sense of the disseminated information and creating a coherent strategy from it. It must be remembered that whilst the actual result of this process of making sense of information may not be agreed upon by all members, the fact that there is an awareness of the collective interpretation facilitates a consistent message to be communicated out of the party. An example of this could be the discussions inside of a party surrounding the periodic development of a policy program; although many different views are likely to exist concerning the exact formulation of the text, there is (in most cases) only one, final document. In the conceptual model of political market orientation, the inclusive nature of political parties is captured in the definition of the Member Participation construct as the process of including all members in creating a coherent party strategy; this facilitates consistent responses which are agreed upon by all party members.

CONSISTENT EXTERNAL COMMUNICATION

An element that occurs explicitly in all three of the behavioural conceptualisations of market orientation surveyed by Lafferty and Hult (2001) is that of the importance of a Responsiveness to Information. Several authors (e.g., Harrison-Walker 2001; Kohli et al. 1993) note that the responsiveness construct consists of two parts, the planning and implementation of a response strategy, and Shapiro (1988) considers this to be essential to a market orientation, in that "When the implementers also do the planning, the commitment will be strong and clear."

However, as noted above under 'Member Participation,' Ormrod (2003) found that the conceptualisation of a Responsiveness to Information as both having internal and external foci may not be appropriate to the political context, as whilst only the elected politicians can actually pass laws, all party members can act as 'part-time marketers' (Johansen 2002) and provide an enthusiastic base of representatives with which to build up individual relationships with external stakeholders in order to achieve the party's long-term objectives. This conceptualisation may also help combat the negative effects of "the arbitration of an independent communications power centre, the mass or 'free' media which they [parties] may be able to influence but cannot control" (O'Shaughnessy 2001). Therefore, a Consistent External Communication can be defined as the process of communicating a consistent, agreed-upon strategy to external stakeholder groups.

POLITICAL MARKET ORIENTATION AS ATTITUDES

Several business market orientation authors (e.g., Harrison-Walker 2001; Griffiths and Grover 1998) have conceptualised a market orientation as consisting of behavioural and cultural constructs, but whilst behaviours can be observed, a 'culture' can be defined as including "the beliefs, attitudes, goals and values held by most people in a society, as well as the meanings of characteristic behaviours, rules, customs, and norms that most people follow" (Peter et al. 1999). This definition demonstrates that a 'culture' contains many diverse elements, making an operationalisation of a cultural conceptualisation extremely difficult, if not impossible. In order to increase the utility of the conceptual model of political market orientation as a statistical tool for use in real situations, it is more constructive to analyse the attitudes party members have towards the different stakeholder groups in society. An attitude is defined as "a person's overall evaluation of a concept," consisting of "favourable and unfavourable feelings towards an object" (Peter et al. 1999), and this enables the attitude object to be made explicit and measured with comparatively more precision.

The attitudinal constructs of the conceptual model of political market orientation are not as easy to deduce from the business market orientation literature as the behavioural components outlined above, as only the Customer and Competitor Orientation constructs have been directly proposed (e.g., Narver and Slater 1990; Harrison-Walker 2001). The Internal Orientation construct proposed in this article is conceptually similar to Narver and Slater's (1990) 'Interfunctional Coordination' construct, but the construct has been contextually redefined and relabelled. The inclusion of an explicit External Orientation construct expands the various conceptualisations of a business market orientation, focussing on stakeholder groups outside of the party that are not voters or competitors. The four stakeholder groups are presented in Figure 2.

FIGURE 2. The Four Stakeholder Orientations

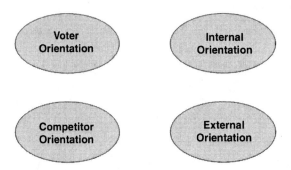

It is important to note that Lafferty and Hult (2001) class Narver and Slater's (1990) concepts of Customer Orientation, Competitor Orientation and Interfunctional Coordination as "culturally-based behaviours," emphasising that the concepts focus on an organisational understanding of the need to collect information about customers' present and future needs and wants, and competitors' actions. However, Slater and Narver (1995) redefined their concept of market orientation and separate the culture from the behaviour, stating that the culture "provides norms for behaviour regarding the organizational development of and responsiveness to market information."

VOTER ORIENTATION

Of the five general approaches discussed by Lafferty and Hult (2001), the focus present in all conceptualisations of a business market orientation was that of a Customer Orientation. A large amount of research in political marketing has concentrated on the effects of electoral tactics and strategy on voter behaviour, and it is generally accepted in the literature that the political consumer is the voter. It is of course true that there are certain characteristics of voters which set them apart from consumers in the business sense, such as the existence of the 'counter-consumer' (Butler and Collins 1999, 1996), but there are, however, characteristics that voters and customers have in common, such as the suitability of traditional market research tools for uncovering voter opinions (e.g., Lees-Marshment 2001a; Sparrow and Turner 2001) and of marketing communication strategies (e.g., Kaid 1999; Scammell 1996), together with the conceptualisation of voting as an exchange process (e.g., O'Cass 1996).

The Voter Orientation construct is defined such that an emphasis is placed upon social exchanges between individual actors complementing the utilisation of traditional marketing management tools. As such, the Voter Orientation construct can be seen as the attitudes of all party members towards being aware of voter needs and wants at the individual level through a willingness to enter into social exchanges with these voters, and an acknowledgement of the usefulness of traditional marketing tools' place in uncovering voter opinions at the party level; in short, the party-wide awareness of voter needs and wants and an acknowledgement of the importance of knowing these.

COMPETITOR ORIENTATION

A competitor orientation is considered by several authors (e.g., Harrison-Walker 2001; Narver and Slater 1990) to be essential to the business market orientation concept, and by Lees-Marshment (e.g., 2001a) to the activities involved in a political market orientation. Bowler and Farrell (1992) discuss the behaviour of parties in different electoral systems at election time, stating that "in multi-party systems the parties have to make allowances for possible coalition partners and so temper their campaign messages," and Butler and Collins (1996) describe four market positions for political parties (market leader, challenger, follower and nicher), based on those discussed in marketing textbooks such as Kotler (1997), that can affect the strategic direction pursued by the individual party vis-à-vis other parties in the political marketplace. Interestingly, Dean and Croft (2001) do not include competing political parties in their Multiple Markets model of important stakeholder groups, although an explanation that they themselves give is that the model is based upon the British party system where coalition governments are uncommon.

A separate Competitor Orientation construct is considered necessary in a political market orientation, and that it must be conceptualised so as to take into account the nature of political competition in that it is essential in some systems to create alliances with other parties in order to pass legislation. A Competitor Orientation is therefore defined as the party-wide awareness of other parties' attitudes and behaviours, and an acknowledgement that cooperation with other parties may be necessary to attain the party's long-term objectives.

INTERNAL ORIENTATION

Narver and Slater (1990) define the concept of an Interfunctional Coordination as "the coordinated utilization of company resources in creating superior value for target customers." Lafferty and Hult (2001) find that this construct is to a greater or lesser extent present in all of the approaches to market orientation that they identify, and that the emphasis is placed more on the 'Interfunctional' nature of the concept. The very precise definition proposed by Narver and Slater (1990) makes it difficult to apply directly to the political marketing context, and the horizontal emphasis risks overlooking the hierarchical structure of parties, in that political parties tend not to be organised as functions that contribute to the day-to-day running of the organisation, but as vertical hierarchies (Dean and Croft 2001). In a political marketing context, Narver and Slater's (1990) focus on 'company resources' should be seen as all party members, and as such it is considered to be necessary to re-label 'Interfunctional Coordination' to reflect these differences, hence 'Internal Orientation.'

The importance of party members to the functioning of political parties has been emphasised by several authors (e.g., Johansen 2002; Butler and Collins 1999; Lees-Marshment 2001b), and Lees-Marshment (2001a) states that "Parties can get ideas about what voters want by 'keeping an ear to the ground' or talking to party activists," and underlines the importance of including grassroots members and their opinions in the formulation of party policy. This emphasis on the inclusion of all party members is reflected in the definition of an Internal Orientation, in that it is the party-wide awareness and acceptance of the value of other members' opinions, irrespective of position in the party.

EXTERNAL ORIENTATION

Selnes, Jaworski, and Kohli (1996) note that little research has explicitly addressed the nature of the exogenous environment's moderating effects on the results of a market orientation, and few authors have noted the importance of being aware of external stakeholders (e.g., Slater and Narver 1995). This is also true of the political marketing literature to date, in that whilst acknowledging the importance of the exogenous environment to political parties, research has mainly concentrated on the effects of the media (e.g., Kraus 1999; Róka 1999; O'Shaughnessy 1990) and lobby groups (Harris, Gardner, and Vetter 1999; Harris and Lock 1996).

There are few articles in the political marketing literature that explicitly list the important external stakeholder groups. The most notable example is that of Dean and Croft (2001), who adapt Christopher, Payne, and Ballantine's (1991) Six Markets model to the British electoral system, and define the external stakeholder groups to be trade unions and business associations, pressure groups, peer groups, and civil servants. Dean and Croft (2001) acknowledge that the inclusion of this last category "is, perhaps, a surprising one," but base its inclusion on the fact that it is the civil service (to be understood as public sector employees) that is responsible for the implementation of policy, a point that has also been made by Lees-Marshment and Laing (2002). It can be said that there is a growing focus in the political marketing literature on the influence of all external groups that have an interest in or affect the outcome of political decisions, and this is reflected in the final attitudinal construct of the conceptual model of political market orientation, an External Orientation, defined as the party-wide acknowledgement of the existence and importance of stakeholders in society that are not voters or competitors.

CONCLUSION

The four behavioural constructs of the conceptual model of political market orientation proposed in this article are Information Generation, Information Dissemination, Member Participation and Consistent External Communication. The four behavioural constructs are consecutive, in that information has to be generated before it can be disseminated, disseminated before it can be made sense of by members participating in strategy formulation, and so on. Another defining characteristic of this 'behavioural chain' is its application, as a whole, to each of the attitudinal orientation (Harrison-Walker 2001; Kohli and Jaworski 1990). The first two attitudinal constructs, a Voter and Competitor Orientation, are similar to those that already exist in the business, and to a certain extent, political marketing literature, whilst the third construct, an Internal Orientation, is a development of Narver and Slater's (1990) Interfunctional Coordination construct in order to take into account the idiosyncrasies of the political context. The fourth attitudinal construct, an External Orientation, has been proposed in order to reflect the importance of stakeholder groups in society that are external to the party and not voters or competing parties. The complete conceptual model of political market orientation is presented in Figure 3.

The conceptual model presented in this article is designed to be used by all types of political parties regardless of ideological persuasion or electoral system, and to be used independently of the position in the electoral cycle. As an analytic tool it can discern the level of a party's political market orientation with regard to different stakeholder groups in society, thus enabling the party as a whole to decide whether or not resources have to be reallocated in order to achieve the party's long-term objectives, within a framework of constraints imposed by all of society. Future research into the concept of a political market orientation should investigate implementation issues, tak-

FIGURE 3. A Conceptual Model of Political Market Orientation

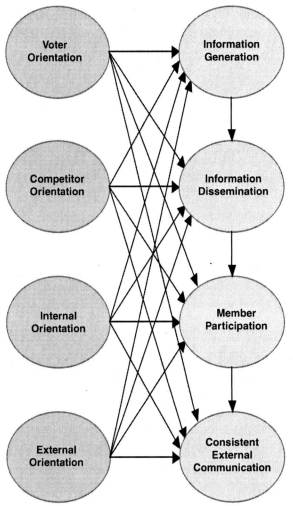

ing into consideration the national idiosyncrasies of political markets and political party structures, and in general it is necessary for research in this field to
continue in order to generate a deeper understanding of how the concept of a
business market orientation can be tailored–rather than indiscriminately applied–to have utility in the political marketplace.

The conceptual model of political market orientation presented in this article is a contribution to the field of Political Marketing that can provide an interesting perspective from which to understand political parties, their behaviours, and the attitudes of their members towards stakeholder groups in society.

BIBLIOGRAPHY

Bowler, S. and Farrell, D. M. (eds.) (1992), *Electoral Strategies and Political Marketing*, London: The Macmillan Press, Ltd.

Butler, Patrick and Neil Collins (1999), "A Conceptual Framework for Political Marketing," in *Handbook of Political Marketing*, ed. Bruce I. Newman, Thousand Oaks, CA: SAGE Publications, Inc., 55-72.

Butler, Patrick and Neil Collins (1996), "Strategic Analysis in Political Markets," *European Journal of Marketing*, Vol. 30 (10/11), 25-36.

Christopher, Martin G., Adrian Payne, and Ballantyne, D. (1991), *Relationship Marketing*, Oxford: Butterworth-Heinemann.

Daft, R. L. and Weick, K. E. (1984), "Toward a Model of Organization as Interpretations System," *Academy of Management Review*, Vol. 9, 284-295.

Dean, Dianne and Robin Croft (2001), "Friends and Relations: Long-Term Approaches to Political Campaigning," *European Journal of Marketing*, Vol. 35 (11/12), 1197-1216.

Deshpandé, Rohit, John U. Farley, and Frederick E. Jnr Webster (1993), "Corporate Culture, Customer Orientation and Innovativeness," *Journal of Marketing*, Vol. 57 (1), 23-27.

Gray, Brendan, Sheelagh Matear, Christo Boshoff, and Phil Matheson (1998), "Developing a Better Measure of Market Orientation," *European Journal of Marketing*, Vol. 32 (9/10), 884-903.

Griffiths, Janice C. and Rajiv Grover (1998), "*A Framework for Understanding Market Orientation: The Behavior and the Culture*," 1998 AMA Winter Educator's Conference, American Marketing Association.

Harris, Phil, Hanne Gardner, and Nadja Vetter (1999), " 'Goods Over God': Lobbying and Political Marketing–A Case Study of the Campaign by the Shopping Hours Reform Council to Change Sunday Trading Laws in the United Kingdom," in *Handbook of Political Marketing*, ed. Bruce I. Newman, Thousand Oaks, CA: SAGE Publications, Inc., 607-626.

Harris, Phil and Andrew R. Lock (1996), "Machiavellian Marketing: The Development of Political Lobbying in the UK," *Journal of Marketing Management*, Vol. 12 (4), 313-328.

Harrison-Walker, L. Jean (2001), "The Measurement of a Market Orientation and its Impact on Business Performance," *Journal of Quality Management*, Vol. 6, 139-172.

Johansen, Helene P. M. (2002), *"Political Marketing: More than Persuasive Techniques. An Organisational Perspective,"* Paper presented at the Political Marketing Conference, Aberdeen, 19th-21st September 2002.

Kaid, Lynda Lee (1999), "Political Advertising: Summary of Research Findings," in *Handbook of Political Marketing*, ed. Bruce I. Newman, Thousand Oaks, CA: SAGE Publications, Inc., 423-438.

Kohli, Ajay K. and Bernard J. Jaworski (1990), "Market Orientation: The Construct, Research Propositions and Managerial Implications," *Journal of Marketing*, Vol. 54 (April), 1-18.

Kohli, Ajay K., Bernard J. Jaworski, and Ajith Kumar (1993), "MARKOR: A Measure of Market Orientation," *Journal of Marketing Research*, Vol. 30 (November), 467-477.

Kotler, Philip (1997), *Marketing Management: Analysis, Planning, Implementation and Control*, New Jersey: Prentice-Hall, Inc.

Kraus, Sidney (1999), "Televised Debates: Marketing Presidential Candidates," in *Handbook of Political Marketing*, ed. Bruce I. Newman, Thousand Oaks, CA: SAGE Publications, Inc., 389-401.

Lafferty, Barbara A. and G. Tomas M. Hult (2001), "A Synthesis of Contemporary Market Orientation Perspectives," *European Journal of Marketing*, Vol. 35 (1/2), 92-109.

Lees-Marshment, Jennifer (2001a), *Political Marketing and British Political Parties: The* Party's Just Begun, Manchester: Manchester University Press.

_____ (2001b), "The Marriage of Politics and Marketing," *Political Studies*, Vol. 49, 692-713.

_____ (2001c), "The Product, Sales and Market-Oriented Party: How Labour Learnt to Market the Product, Not Just the Presentation," *European Journal of Marketing*, Vol. 35 (9/10), 1074-1084.

Lees-Marshment, Jennifer and Angus Laing (2002), *"Time to Deliver: Why Political Marketing Needs to Move Beyond the Campaign,"* Paper Presented at the Political Marketing Conference, Aberdeen, 19th-21st September 2002.

Narver, John C. and Stanley F. Slater (1990), "The Effect of a Market Orientation on Business Profitability," *Journal of Marketing*, Vol. 54 (October), 20-35.

Noble, Charles H., Rajiv K. Sinha, and Ajith Kumar (2002), "Market Orientation and Alternative Strategic Orientations: A Longitudinal Assessment of Performance Implications," *Journal of Marketing*, Vol. 66 (4), 25-39.

O'Cass, Aron (1996), "Political Marketing and the Marketing Concept," *European Journal of Marketing*, Vol. 30 (10/11), 37-53.

O'Cass, Aron (2001a), "Political Marketing: An Investigation of the Political Marketing Concept and Political Market Orientation in Australian Politics," *European Journal of Marketing*, Vol. 35 (9/10), 1003-1025.

_____ (2001b), "The Internal-External Marketing Orientation of a Political Party: Social Implications of Political Party Marketing Orientation," *Journal of Public Affairs*, Vol. 1 (2), 136-152.

Ormrod, Robert P. (2003), "Qualitative and Quantitative Investigations into the Utility of a Conceptual Model of Political Market Orientation," unpublished dissertation, Institute for Marketing, Aarhus School of Business, 8210 Aarhus V, Denmark.

O'Shaughnessy, Nicholas J. (1990), *The Phenomenon of Political Marketing*, London: The Macmillan Press, Ltd.

O'Shaughnessy, Nicholas J. (2001), "The Marketing of Political Marketing," *European Journal of Marketing*, Vol. 35 (9/10), 1047-1057.

Peter, J. Paul, Jerry C. Olsen, and Klaus G. Grunert (1999), *Consumer Behaviour and Marketing Strategy*, Maidenhead: McGraw-Hill International, Ltd.

Reukert, Robert. W. (1992), "Developing a Market Orientation: An Organisational Strategy Perspective," *International Journal of Research in Marketing*, Vol. 9, 225-245.

Róka, Jolán (1999), "Do the Media Reflect or Shape Public Opinion?," in *Handbook of Political Marketing*, ed. Bruce I. Newman, Thousand Oaks, CA: SAGE Publications, Inc, 505-518.

Scammell, Margaret (1996), "The Odd Couple: Marketing and Maggie," *European Journal of Marketing*, Vol. 30 (10/11), 114-126.

Scammell, Margaret (1999), "Political Marketing: Lessons for Political Science," *Political Studies*, Vol. XLVII, 718-739.

Selnes, Fred, Bernard J. Jaworski, and Ajay K. Kohli (1996) "Market Orientation in United States and Scandinavian Companies. A Cross-Cultural Study," *Scandinavian Journal of Management*, Vol. 12 (2), 139-157.

Shapiro, Benson P. (1988), "What the Hell is 'Market Oriented'?" *Harvard Business Review*, November-December 1988, 119-125.

Slater, Stanley F. and John C. Narver (1994), "Does Competitive Environment Moderate the Market Orientation–Performance Relationship?" *Journal of Marketing*, Vol. 58 (January), 46-55.

Slater, Stanley F. and John C. Narver (1995), "Market Orientation and the Learning Organization," *Journal of Marketing*, Vol. 59 (July), 63-74.

Sparrow, Nick and John J. Turner (2001), "The Permanent Campaign: The Integration of Market Research Techniques in Developing Strategies in a More Uncertain Political Climate," *European Journal of Marketing*, Vol. 35 (9/10), 984-1002.

Membership Benefits, Membership Action: Why Incentives for Activism Are What Members Want

Sue Granik

SUMMARY. This article identifies the benefits of political party membership and which of these benefits also operate as incentives for participation. This exploration is conducted in the context of competing relationship marketing hypotheses, and frameworks from other relevant academic disciplines.

Exploratory empirical research identifies two purposive and three solidary benefits of membership. Values functional motivations, socialization and job satisfaction are identified as having statistically significant relationships with participation. Frequency of agreement with party policies and enhancement functional motivations do not appear to have any relationship with participation.

The article concludes that members using their membership as a vehicle for realizing solidary benefits are more likely to respond to incen-

Sue Granik is a doctoral candidate, Department of Industrial Relations, London School of Economics, Houghton Street, London WC2A 2AE, UK (E-mail: S.D. GRANIK@lse.ac.uk).

The financial assistance of the Economic and Social Research Council (Postgraduate Training Award R00429934169) is gratefully acknowledged.

[Haworth co-indexing entry note]: "Membership Benefits, Membership Action: Why Incentives for Activism Are What Members Want." Granik, Sue. Co-published simultaneously in *Journal of Nonprofit & Public Sector Marketing* (Best Business Books, an imprint of The Haworth Press, Inc.) Vol. 14, No. 1/2, 2005, pp. 65-89; and: *Current Issues in Political Marketing* (eds: Walter W. Wymer, Jr., and Jennifer Lees-Marshment) Best Business Books, an imprint of The Haworth Press, Inc., 2005, pp. 65-89. Single or multiple copies of this article are available for a fee from The Haworth Document Delivery Service [1-800-HAWORTH, 9:00 a.m. - 5:00 p.m. (EST). E-mail address: getinfo@haworthpressinc.com].

tives for participation, whilst those merely seeking a relationship with their party are more likely be inactive. *[Article copies available for a fee from The Haworth Document Delivery Service: 1-800-HAWORTH. E-mail address: <docdelivery@haworthpress.com> Website: <http://www.HaworthPress. com> © 2005 by The Haworth Press, Inc. All rights reserved.]*

KEYWORDS. Political parties, membership, relationship marketing, participation

INTRODUCTION

This article explores which benefits political party members perceive they gain from their membership and whether it is worthwhile for political parties to provide members with these benefits. The first avenue of exploration might seem somewhat strange to political scientists who may consider that the benefits of party membership are obvious and documented elsewhere. However, this article will argue that existing research into the benefits of political party membership is inadequately theorised and *ad hoc* rather than systematic. The second avenue of exploration may appear a little strange to marketers who are likely to wonder why should political parties not provide their members with the benefits they seek. The response to this point is that it may not necessarily be in parties' best organizational interests to provide all the benefits sought by members, as some benefits do not have relationships with desirable membership behaviors.

The empirical evidence presented in this article indicates that only some of the solidary benefits arising from party membership also operate as incentives for participation in party activities, but members who value purposive benefits may not be responsive to incentives for participation. The article will also argue that avenues of enquiry prompted by marketing theory and analytical frameworks from the disciplines of organizational behavior and nonprofit studies provide appropriate, methodologically robust and easily replicable means of analyzing grassroots membership behavior.

LITERATURE REVIEW

There is a substantial body of thought which assumes that motivation arises out of what is essentially individual selfishness; although there are conflicting ideas as to the ends to which that selfishness is directed. The desired outcome can be to fill individual needs in a hierarchical order (Maslow 1954), or along a series of discrete dimensions (McClelland 1961). In the context of joining a group, Olson (1965) suggests altruism as motivation for joining is exceptionally rare. He argues that "rational, self-interested individuals will not act to achieve their common or group interests" without either coercion or "some separate incentive" (p. 5). That incentive can be economic, or less tangible; but the group has to offer that benefit to each individual member separately and selectively. Vroom's (1964) expectancy theory is a variation on these themes. This theory argues that motivation is determined by whether an individual considers that using ability and effort will produce the anticipated satisfaction from an outcome.

If motivation is essentially selfish, incentives theory (Clark and Wilson 1961) argues that organizations seeking to motivate individuals to work for them must provide incentives for those individuals to do so. Indeed, the incentive system may be regarded as the principal variable affecting organizational behaviour. Incentives may be material, solidary or purposive. Material incentives are tangible; they have a monetary value or a monetary value can be easily placed on them. Solidary incentives are defined as those which are essentially intangible, e.g., socializing and congeniality. A financial value cannot easily be placed on them. These incentives may vary considerably between individual members. They are derived from the act of belonging to an organization, but are generally independent of organizational aims. Purposive incentives, conversely, are those deriving from the aims of the organization itself and not from the act of association. These benefits are also intangible, without financial value, but are easier to identify as their origin lies in the goals of the organization.

Historically, political scientists have attempted to explain why party members work for their party by linking the incentives for activism almost exclusively to belief in party ideology. For the past three decades, the theory generally known as May's Law (May 1973) has provided the underpinning for this studies into membership participation. May argued that a special law of curvilinear disparity applied to the opinion structure of party leaders, activists and voters. He argued that activists had more extreme opinions than either party voters or party leaders. Those operating along purely ideological considerations had more freedom to be active without the constraints of having to appeal to electorates in order to retain elected office. Their belief in ideology led to aspirations of shaping candidate selections and party policies in order to promote their particular point of view. This argument was based on historical data, and not subjected to empirical testing by its originator.

Empirical work across Western European parties and party systems has failed to demonstrate that it is generally applicable. Seyd and Whiteley (1992) claimed that their study of British Labour Party activists demonstrated some support for May's Law. However, this finding was not repeated in their subsequent study of the Conservative Party (Whiteley, Seyd and Richardson 1994), nor was it tested for in a subsequent study of the Labour Party (Seyd and Whiteley 2002). Norris (1995) suggested that only those who are the most committed to party principles will be motivated to become involved in "the humdrum tedium of local party politics" (p. 31). But her study, using data from the 1992 British Candidate Survey and British General Election Study concluded that party leaders tended to be more radical than their followers. Narud and Skare (1999) also cast doubts on the robustness of May's theory. Their study of differences in opinion between Norwegian voters, party activists and leaders on a number of different issues showed that only one party out of six, the Conservatives, demonstrated curvilinear disparity of opinion structure over a majority of those issues. Unfortunately, this latter study cannot be dealt with in more detail here because its authors did not provide any mechanism for linking opinion structure to participation.

A contrasting theory used by political scientists to analyse participation is rational choice theory. This model is associated with Downs (1957) who suggested that individuals can make a decision from a range of alternatives by ranking these alternatives in order of preference and choosing the alternative which is ranked highest. Olson (1965), who dealt more specifically on the applications of rational choice theory to participation, identified a key phenomenon of participation in an organization working to provide collective goals, resulting in collective goods. Collective goods, by their very nature, are available to everyone, whether or not they participate in the organizations' efforts to realize these collective goods. Therefore if individuals realize that they will reap the benefits of success whether or not they participate in the organization, they will generally choose not to participate–the phenomenon of free-riding.

British political scientists have interpreted Olson's line of argument as presenting a paradox of participation (Seyd and Whiteley 1992, Whiteley, Seyd and Richardson 1994). Why should anyone participate at all, if, by free-riding they can get the collective goods they seek without having to incur any of the costs of participation? This question assumes that participation is atypical in some way. It assumes that there must be something that distinguishes the participants from the free-riders, and the purpose of research into participation is to find out what makes participants different from others.

British political science research has suggested three selective incentives for participation (Seyd and Whiteley 1992, Whiteley, Seyd and Richardson 1994) although no theoretical underpinning for any of these suggestions is presented in either of these studies. This body of research suggests that selective incentives are either outcome-oriented, concerned with achieving private goals through the political process, or process incentives, deriving from the process of participation itself. Only one outcome-oriented incentive was identified, that of political ambition. But no theoretical justification was provided to explain why this should be the only outcome-oriented incentive potentially available to political party members. Process incentives were measured by "the individual's attitude to political activism in general" (Seyd and Whiteley 1992, p. 106), a statement which assumes that attitudes lead to participation. But there are two flaws in this line of reasoning. Firstly, a simple psychological definition of attitude–"an . . . evaluative reaction toward something or someone, exhibited in one's beliefs, feelings or intended behavior" (Myers 1999, p. 631) indicates that attitude does not necessarily constitute an incentive for actual behavior. Indeed, there is a considerable body of psychological evidence suggesting that behavior determines attitudes (e.g., Bem 1972; Myers 1999). Secondly, if attitudes precede participation, how can they be a direct incentive for it?

Indeed, the discussion of incentives theory presented at the beginning of this article suggests that an alternative question is relevant in the context of rational choice theory. Which selective incentives are so valued by individuals that they choose to participate in organizations working for collective goals in order to receive them? This question suggests an analytical framework where participation is not a 'paradox,' but entirely rational: individuals who value the selective incentives offered by participation must participate in order to get them. Additionally, in this scenario, there is no such thing as free-riding. Those who do not participate simply do not value the selective incentives offered by the organization enough to be motivated by these incentives. Whether or not they want the collective goods on offer may simply not be relevant. This is not a line of enquiry that has been pursued methodically by political scientists.

Incentives for Participation: The Marketing Literature

However, research in the fields of marketing and nonprofit studies is based on the implicit assumption that rational choice underlies all participation and, accordingly, that the selective incentives for participation are of crucial importance for understanding why it occurs. The explicitly financial relationship between individual and party involved in membership of British political parties indicates that marketing frameworks are appropriate for an exploration of membership behaviour. Indeed, research in the field of political marketing is beginning to provide evidence to suggest that party members demonstrate consumer behaviors when deciding whether or not to renew their political party dues (Bauer, Huber and Herrman 1996; Granik 2001). Specifically, these behaviors include post-purchase evaluation of membership, confirmation and disconfirmation and co-production and, possibly, price sensitivity (Granik 2001). Exploratory research amongst new British party members suggests that their self-reported experience of membership bears similarities to behavioral characteristics noted amongst customers of extraordinary service experiences (Granik 1997).

Historically, marketing was viewed as a process of exchange: money in return for access to products and services (Bagozzi 1975). This view came under sustained criticism, and by the early 1990s a new paradigm emerged: relationship marketing, defined as "establishing, developing and maintaining successful relational exchanges" between organization and customer (Morgan and Hunt 1994, p. 20). In 1995 a landmark article in the relationship marketing literature by Sheth and Parvatiyar claimed that consumers engaged in relational market behaviour primarily to reduce their available choice. They put forward the suggestion that consumers engage in relational market behaviour to "achieve greater efficiency in their decision making, to reduce the task of information processing, to achieve more cognitive consistency in their decisions, and to reduce the perceived risks associated with future choices" (p. 256). Alongside their choice reduction argument, Sheth and Parvatiyar also suggested that consumers engaged in relational market behavior because of family and social norms, peer group pressures, government mandates, religious tenets, employer influences and marketer policies. Responding to their article, Bagozzi (1995) suggested that "another motive for entering a marketing relationship in other (rare) instances might be to be part of the relationship . . . and not necessarily for what the relationship might lead to in an instrumental sense. In other words, a marketing relationship may be an end in and of itself for some customers" (p. 273).

Although these articles kick-started a lively academic interest in relationship marketing, the debate largely by-passed the unique features of relationship marketing applying in non-profit contexts. An early lacuna in the literature identified by Mitchell and Taylor (1997) was that of connecting relationship marketing with internal marketing in the context of organizational culture. They concluded that the organization whose culture was compatible with the personal value systems and self-images of volunteer members would be more effective in competing with other organizations for the time, energy and monetary contributions of potential donors. Gruen (2000) noted a number of distinguishing features of membership organizations–the specific contractual period of membership, the amount of co-production required of members by the organization, the role of social identification in membership relationships and high levels of interdependence amongst members–which suggested that relationship marketing techniques associated with profit-making organizations would not be successful in these environments if applied wholesale. As recently as 2003, Arnett, German and Hunt observed: "the importance of particular relationship characteristics in producing relationship marketing success may be more context specific than heretofore thought" (p. 89).

Indeed, it should be noted that not all of the elements identified by Sheth and Parvatiyar are relevant in the context of British political party membership. For example, political party membership is not mandatory in Britain, and there is no documented evidence that employers influence their workers to join. Therefore it is difficult to test responses to the 'government mandates' and 'employer influences' elements of the argument. Political party membership as a response to religious tenets is certainly a salient issue in some parts of the United Kingdom, but not necessarily in Wales, where the fieldwork for this research was conducted. Nevertheless, the remaining 'reductionist strategy' and 'social approval' elements of the Sheth and Parvatiyar argument, are still germane to an exploration of the relationship between benefits and participation in British political parties. If political party members are buying a relationship in order to receive these benefits, it could be expected that members would participate in activities for two reasons. The first would be as a means of expressing and reinforcing their beliefs, and preventing exposure to conflicting ideas and ideologies that might expose them to doubt their current values. The second reason would be as a vehicle for realizing solidary benefits, including, perhaps, social approval. Both rational choice theory and psychological theories of motivation suggest strongly that if certain benefits are sufficiently valued by members, and if these benefits can be obtained via a relationship with the organization, it is in parties' interests to ensure that members get what they value. This argument indicates that it is not sufficient to be casual about defining the various purposive and solidary incentives available to party members. If members perceive specific incentives for participation as benefits of that relationship, delivering others is a waste of organizational resources.

Additionally, it can be hypothesized that Bagozzi's suggestion that entering into a relationship with an organization for the relationship's sake would be far less rare in the context of a political party than it would be in the context of a relationship with a profit-making organization. For example, it is quite plausible that an individual joins a political party to "nail their colors to the mast," and, having made this public declaration, feels no need to do anything more. Members falling into this category will be fairly resistant to incentives to encourage them to participate, because all they want is a passive relationship with the party of their choice. The hypothesized differences between the likely outcomes of the differing membership motivations suggested by the competing suggestions of Sheth and Parvatiyar and Bagozzi are summarized in Figure 1.

Incentives for Participation:
The Organizational Behaviour and Nonprofit Literature

It was noted above that existing attempts in the political science literature to identify the selective incentives for participation are characterized by a lack of appropriate theorization and a somewhat *ad hoc* approach. Literature to be found in two further disciplines, organizational behavior and nonprofit studies, also focuses on incentives for participation in varying types of organizations whilst avoiding some of the shortcomings in existing political science literature. The organizational behavior literature has, to date, largely been by-passed by political scientists, but marketers have been somewhat more receptive to the opportunities for analysis provided by organizational behavior frameworks (e.g., Kelley 1992). Two concepts from the organizational behaviour literature are particularly germane to the task of identifying the incentives for participation within political parties: socialization and job satisfaction.

Socialization is described as the process by which individuals acquire the skills, social knowledge and behaviors needed to participate as an organizational member (Van Maanen and Schein 1979). Workplace studies have found that successful employee socialization also has links with job satisfaction, intent to stay in the organization and job performance (Bauer and Green 1998; Chao et al. 1994; Kelley 1992; Wanburg and Kammeyer-Mueller 2000). In trade unions, socialization is associated with member loyalty, and with an increased likelihood of attendance at union meetings and participation in strikes (Gordon 1980; McShane 1986). The purpose of measuring socialization in the context of party members is, firstly, to investigate whether it has the relationship with activity suggested by studies in other organizational settings, and,

FIGURE 1. Alternative Membership Motivations and Likely Behavioural Outcomes

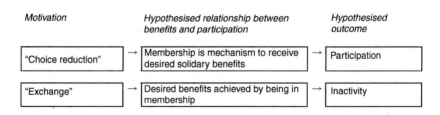

secondly, to investigate whether members perceive that socialization within the party is a benefit of their membership.

Job satisfaction is also hypothesized to constitute a solidary benefit for political party members. Parties have very few options to coerce their members into working: if members do not receive some kind of benefit from participation, there is no reason for them to do so. Simply defined, job satisfaction is how people feel about their jobs and different aspects of their jobs (Spector 1997). It can be considered as an overall feeling about a job, or as a related set of attitudes about various aspects of the job. In this paper, job satisfaction is treated as an overall feeling about the work which respondents do for their party.

Strands of the literature of the management of nonprofit organizations have gone to considerable lengths to identify which incentives underlie voluntary participatory behaviors. The implicit assumption in much of this literature is an acceptance of rational choice theory: those who work ostensibly for nothing do so because they want something, even if their motivation is not for material gain (e.g., Widmer 1985; Clary and Snyder 1991). One scholar with practitioner experience of managing volunteers Francies 1983) examined the concept of the fulfillment of psychological needs as motivation for volunteering. In a conclusion which implicitly supports later arguments for the importance of internal marketing, he concluded that the degree of match between need and work assignment had positive relationships with volunteer satisfaction, and with retention.

Psychologists with an interest in volunteering identified a series of motivations for volunteering by noting, from empirical studies conducted in a number of different settings, which motivations for volunteering respondents cited most clearly and consistently (Clary and Snyder 1991; Clary, Snyder and Ridge 1992). This exercise resulted in an analytical framework–the Volunteer Functions Inventory (VFI)–measuring six distinct functional motivations underlying volunteering. The VFI has been tested, in laboratory studies and in the field, on six documented occasions (Clary et al. 1998). Findings from these tests have led the authors to conclude that those subjects who chose: "service opportunities that provided benefits matching their initial motivations more strongly believed that they would make volunteerism a continuing part of their lives than individuals who chose opportunities that did not provide functionally relevant benefits or that provided functionally irrelevant benefits" (p. 1526).

The VFI brings to the study of party behavior a rigorous and appropriate analytical framework for identifying incentives for volunteering within a membership context. It identifies one potential purposive incentive and five potential solidary incentives for participation. The purposive incentive identified in this framework is the values functional benefit: the desire of individuals to be able to act on their beliefs, to express their own values in a meaningful way, and to serve a cause which has some personal meaning for them. The five potential solidary incentives are career, enhancement, protective, social and understanding functional benefits. Career benefits refer to the use of volunteering to benefit one's professional life by acquiring new skills or making new contacts. Enhancement benefits accrue when volunteering can make the individual appear needed and important; protective benefits refer to the use of volunteering as a means of relief or escape from negative feelings about oneself. Volunteering may also be used to gain social approval from others, or as a vehicle for learning more about the cause or organization which the volunteer decides to serve.

METHODOLOGY

The research on which this paper is based was carried out in a left-of-center nationalist political party based in Wales. At the time of the study the party, Plaid Cymru, had seats on local government authorities throughout Wales, formed the official opposition in the Welsh Assembly, had four MPs in the UK House of Commons, and two MEPs in the European Parliament. At the time of the study the party had slightly over 15,000 members registered on its database.

The research instrument comprised a ten-page questionnaire for self-administration sent unsolicited through the mail to party members. The questionnaire was produced bilingually in Welsh and English in line with the party's language policy. A copy of the questionnaire, in either language, is available from the author on request.

Respondents were asked for information about their background regarding Plaid Cymru membership, and memberships of other organizations in order to establish baseline measures of motivation for joining and other affiliations. The questions measuring the frequency of agreement with party policy and the respondents' self-perceived political position on the ideological spectrum, as described above, were also used in the opening section of the questionnaire. Members were asked about their participation in party activities during the 12 months prior to the survey. They indicated what they had done out of a range of routine, election-specific and internal party activities that would have been on offer during that period. The total number of activities in each category were summed together to provide an overall activity score for each survey respondent, activity measurements were not weighted for the purposes of data analysis.

Members were asked about their satisfaction with the experience of Plaid Cymru membership. A series of open-ended questions asked respondents what they had expected when they joined the party, whether these expectations had been fulfilled, and whether they felt membership had done anything for them in any way. The responses to these open-ended questions were categorized into relevant groups and each group was given a separate coding for the purposes of data analysis. A seven point satisfaction scale allowed respondents to categorize their overall feelings about membership (Westbrook 1980).

The solidary benefits of membership hypothesized by the organizational behavior and nonprofit management literatures were measured by relevant batteries of questions. Socialization was measured by an adapted version of the Organizational Socialization Scale (OSS) devised by Kelley (1992). This scale, which measures the extent to which individuals feel they "belong" to the party is one of the few measures of socialization which also attempts to identify the dimensions along which "belonging" is experienced. In the context of political party membership, the relationship between individuals and their local branch was the focus of investigation, as this is the unit of the party with which most members will have the most contact. Responses to ten scale items were recorded on a 7-point Likert scale. The other hypothesized solidary benefit of membership, job satisfaction, was measured by the short Michigan Organizational Assessment Questionnaire (MOAQ) which also uses a 7-point Likert scale (Camman et al. 1983). An amended version of the VFI was used in this survey: two statements were used to measure each functional benefit instead of the five used in the original VFI, and some wording was slightly amended to be more acceptable to members' sensibilities. Responses were recorded on a 7-point Likert scale.

Other variables measured in the survey included: respondents' perceptions of their own political efficacy measured by five statements using a 7-point Likert scale, and respondents' psychological attachment to the party, measured by the Organizational Commitment Questionnaire (OCQ), which was scored by the same method (Allen and Meyer 1990). Respondents rated the efficacy of their local party branch via a tick-box question. The survey concluded with requests for basic demographic information.

One in eight party members were randomly selected to receive questionnaires, which were mailed with a covering letter explaining the purpose of the survey, and a reply-paid envelope for return. A total of 1,849 questionnaires were sent out, and 472 useable questionnaires were returned, giving an overall response level of 25.5%. A demographic breakdown of the survey sample appears at Table 1.

RESULTS

The relative importance of the various purposive and solidary incentives to the party membership as a whole was obtained by summing the total score for

TABLE 1. Characteristics of Survey Sample (n = 472)

Characteristic	N	%	Characteristic	N	%
Gender			*Language of response*		
Male	256	54.2	Welsh	311	65.9
Female	204	43.2	English	161	34.1
Age			*Household income*		
16-24	14	3	Up to £8,000	70	14.8
25-34	29	6.1	£8,000 - £15,000	82	17.3
35-44	68	14.4	£15,001 - £25,000	104	22.0
45-54	122	25.8	£25,001 - £40,000	96	20.3
55-64	98	20.8	£40,001 - £60,000	46	9.7
65-74	83	17.6	£60,001+	23	4.9
75+	52	11	Missing	51	10.8
Missing	6	1.2			
			Joining date		
Education level			1999-2000	29	6.1
None	64	13.5	1994-98	63	13.3
CSE/GCE/GCSE	27	5.7	1989-93	36	7.6
A/S level or technical	37	7.8	1979-88	59	12.5
Professional	74	15.7	1969-78	81	17.2
University degree/diploma	228	48.3	1968 or earlier	156	33.1
Missing	20	4.2	Missing	48	10.2

each incentive and calculating the mean. However, it was not possible to compare all eight incentives in this way. Two purposive incentives, frequency of agreement and ideological position, were not measured by Likert scale, and socialization was measured by more statements than were used to measure job satisfaction and each functional benefit. However, the incentives which could be compared, ranked in descending order of importance to party members were: values benefits (M = 10.51, SD = 2.77), job satisfaction (M = 10.43, SD = 2.72), understanding benefits (M = 9.60, SD = 3.27), social benefits (M = 7.72, SD = 3.69), enhancement benefits (M = 7.47, SD = 3.35), protective benefits (M = 4.32, SD = 2.98) and career benefits (M = 3.41, SD = 2.31). Whilst these results are incomplete, one distinguishing feature of ranking these potential incentives is that the solidary incentives of job satisfaction and understanding benefits are very nearly as important to members as the purposive incentive of values benefits.

The next stage was to explore which, if any, of these incentives were considered by members to be benefits of their membership. It was hypothesized that if members perceived an incentive to be a benefit, there would be a statistically significant positive relationship between each incentive and overall feelings about the experience of membership. These relationships were measured by a series of bivariate regressions using the summed total score for each incentive. The predicted relationship was found for five of the eight incentives. The strongest relationships with overall feelings about the experience of membership were found for two of the purposive incentives, values benefits and frequency of agreement. However, one solidary incentive, socialization, had a relationship of the same strength. This finding indicates that a sense of belonging to a political party is considered just as much a benefit of membership as is agreeing with its policies or sharing and acting on its values. The three incentives that did not fit the predicted pattern were ideological position, social benefits and career benefits. Although all three incentives had a positive relationship with overall satisfaction, the relationships were weak and not statistically significant. These results are summarized in Table 2.

It was further hypothesized that if an incentive was perceived by members to be a benefit, members would be unlikely to think that membership had given them no benefits at all. A statistically significant negative relationship was predicted between each incentive and a measure of whether respondents considered that membership had done nothing for them. These relationships were measured by a series of bivariate regressions. The predicted relationship was found for six of the eight incentives. The strongest relationship in this context was, as before, values benefits. This indicates that the ability to act on one's own values is perceived as a greater benefit than agreeing specifically with policies. The two incentives not showing the predicted relationship were ideological position and career benefits. These relationships with no membership benefits were positive, weak, and statistically insignificant. Neither test used in this study suggests that members do not perceive that ideological position or career benefits accrue as benefits from party membership. However, the position regarding social benefits is not as clear. In contrast to the regression with overall satisfaction, the predicted relationship between social benefits and the perception of no benefits was found to exist. These results are also summarized in Table 2. It was further predicted that, if members perceived any one variable to be a benefit of their membership, mean scores on that variable would be higher amongst members who were satisfied with their membership than amongst those who were not. The responses to the satisfaction scale were coded as a high/low dichotomous variable, and the summed score for each in-

TABLE 2. Correlations and Bivariate Regressions Between Incentive Variables, Overall Satisfaction and No Benefits

		Overall satisfaction	No benefits
Purposive incentives	Frequency of agreement	.30**	−.15**
	Ideological position	.05	.02
	Values functional benefits	.34**	−.37**
Solidary incentives	Career functional benefits	.03	.01
	Enhancement functional benefits	.16**	−.18**
	Social functional benefits	.08	−.15**
	Protective functional benefits	.12**	−.16**
	Understanding functional benefits	.18**	−.26**
	Socialization	.30**	−.23**
	Job satisfaction	.24**	−.22**

**denotes coefficient significant at the $p < .01$ level or above, *denotes coefficient significant at the $p < .05$ level or above.

centive was used as before. The purposive incentives considered by members to be benefits–frequency of agreement and values functional benefits–were measured first, and mean scores for both incentives showed the predicted statistically significant differences (Table 3). However, the results for frequency of agreement were unreliable because of evidence of statistically significant differences within groups. This could have been an artefact of the low number of respondents in the low satisfaction category ($n = 36$) and the relatively large standard deviation (.69) in that category. Nevertheless, the evidence that frequency of agreement is a purposive benefit of political party membership is somewhat mixed, due to this measure. There were no differences within groups for the mean scores for values functional benefits. This finding provides additional preliminary evidence that the opportunity to act on one's values is perceived as a functional benefit of political party membership.

The same method of analysis was carried out for each of the solidary variables, to test the hypothesis, as before, that mean scores on each benefit would be higher amongst members who were satisfied with their membership than amongst those who were not. Although all the solidary benefits showed the hypothesized differences in mean variable scores (Table 4), these differences were not statistically significant in respect of potential social benefits. The results for social benefits are, therefore, unreliable, in this test. When added to the mixed evidence about members' perceptions of social benefits of membership, there must be considerable doubt as to whether political party member-

TABLE 3. Means, Standard Deviations and Contrast Effects of Purposive Benefit Scores and Overall Satisfaction

	Mean scores			
	Frequency of agreement		Values motivations	
	M	SD	M	SD
High satisfaction	2.9	.33	10.8	2.5
Low satisfaction	2.5	.69	7.8	3.0
Contrast F	42.275** (1,412)		50.525** (1,341)	
Levene statistic	92.912**		1.639	

**p < .05 level

TABLE 4. Means, Standard Deviations and Contrast Effects of Solidary Benefit Scores and Overall Satisfaction

	Mean scores					
	Job satisfaction		Socialization		Enhancement	
	M	SD	M	SD	M	SD
High satisfaction	10.6	2.6	55.1	9.9	7.6	3.3
Low satisfaction	8.2	2.4	44.7	11.6	6.0	3.0
Contrast F	15.968**(1,256)		24.869**(1,248)		9.374** (1,372)	
Levene statistic	.739		.169		.641	

	Mean scores					
	Protective		Social		Understanding	
	M	SD	M	SD	M	SD
High satisfaction	4.4	3.0	7.8	3.6	9.8	3.1
Low satisfaction	3.2	2.2	6.9	3.7	7.8	3.9
Contrast F	5.794**(1,368)		2.335(1,365)		13.573**(1,373)	
Levene statistic	8.0**		.029		6.7**	

**p < .05 level

ship really is a vehicle for gaining social approval from others. Additionally, the results for protective benefits and understanding benefits were unreliable because of evidence of statistically significant differences within groups. In both cases, these differences within groups could have been an artefact of the low number of members falling into the low satisfaction category combined with relatively large standard deviations.

The next stage of analysis was to investigate whether any of these benefits of members were also related to participation within the party. Five indicators of activism were used in the study: whether respondents took part in any one activity or were completely inactive, the average amount of time spent weekly on activities, and the numbers of routine, election time and internal party activities undertaken by each of the respondents. Variables with a statistically significant relationship with each indicator of activism were identified by a series of regressions. All the measures used in the wider survey were clustered into groups, and the various groups were regressed against each indicator. Variables retaining their significance were placed into subsequent composite models, and regressions continued until all variables in the model retained their significance with the relevant indicator.

The three variables retaining statistical significance in the final model of participation in any one activity were protective motivations, values motivations and the 55-64 age group (Table 5). Members scoring above the party mean on protective motivations were nearly three times as likely to participate in at least one activity than those scoring below. Those scoring above the party mean on values motivations were just over twice as likely to participate than those scoring below. This finding indicates that, in the political party context, solidary incentives may be stronger in motivating participation than purposive incentives. The finding that members aged between 55-64 are the most active group within the party is congruent with findings from other British parties (Seyd and Whiteley 1992). A Hosmer-Lemeshow test indicates that the model is a good fit of available data.

Only one variable was found to retain significance with the decision to spend a substantial amount of time on party activities, and this was the purposive incentive of values motivations. Members scoring above the party mean on values benefits were twice as likely to spend more than five hours a week on activities than those scoring below (Table 6). With only one statistically sig-

TABLE 5. Participation in Any One Activity

Variable	B	S.E.	Wald	df	Sig	R	Exp(B)
PROTECTIVE	1.0061	.3129	10.3382	1	.0013	.1532	2.7348
VALUES	.8002	.3191	6.2892	1	.0121	.1099	2.2259
AGE 55-64	.9670	.4095	5.5757	1	.0182	.1003	2.6301
Constant	.6228	.1878	10.9984	1	.0009		

Hosmer-Lemeshow Goodness-of-fit test Sig = .3926

nificant variable remaining, a Hosmer-Lemeshow test for goodness of fit was not appropriate.

However, whilst one specific purposive incentive appears to predict whether a member will be active or not, and how much time will be devoted to party activities, there is no evidence to suggest that any purposive incentive is an antecedent of the type of party activity undertaken. Only the solidary incentives of socialization and job satisfaction were found to have any statistically significant relationship with the various types of activity available to party members. In the case of routine activities (e.g., attending party meetings, delivering leaflets), the incentives of socialization and job satisfaction retained statistical significance, alongside the highest quartile scores on political efficacy (Table 7). The interesting feature of this finding is that the level of socialization retaining significance is quite low–only the lowest quartile of socialization scores failed to display any relationship with participation in routine activities. The resulting model is statistically significant and explains 30% of the variance in the decision to participate in routine party activities.

In a final model of election time activities (e.g., canvassing for a candidate, helping on polling day) the combination of job satisfaction and socialization are found to be statistically significant again (Table 8). On this occasion, how-

TABLE 6. More Than Five Hours a Week on Party Activities

Variable	B	S.E.	Wald	df	Sig	R	Exp(B)
VALUES	.7121	.3158	5.0839	1	.0241	.1118	2.0383
Constant	−1.1575	.2444	22.4253	1	.0000		

TABLE 7. Routine Party Activities–Regression Coefficients

	B	S.E	Beta	T	Sig
(constant)	−.112	.582		−.191	.848
Medium low socialization	1.138	.457	.198	2.493	.014
Medium high socialization	1.273	.441	.258	2.889	.004
High socialization	2.294	.474	.469	4.842	.000
Total - job satisfaction	.191	.064	.232	2.989	.003
High political efficacy	.600	.300	.130	2.004	.047

Model summary:
$R = .567$, $R^2 = .322$, Adjusted $R^2 = .301$, F ratio = 15.736, Sig = .000

TABLE 8. Election Activities–Regression Coefficients

	B	S.E	Beta	T	Sig
(constant)	−.029	.422		−.232	.817
Total–job satisfaction	.182	.042	.315	4.313	.000
High socialization	.681	.247	.201	2.761	.006
Model summary:					

$R = .437$, $R^2 = .191$, Adjusted $R^2 = .182$, F ratio = 21.508, Sig = .000

ever, the levels of socialization retaining significance with election activities appears to be much higher, as only the top quartile scores retain their significance. Whilst the model itself is statistically significant, it explains only 18% of the variance in participation in election time activities.

Job satisfaction is the only incentive found to have a statistically significant relationship with participation in internal party activities such as standing for local or national party office (Table 9). Other variables in this participation model are highest quartile scores on political efficacy and the total amount of donations made to the party over a 12-month period. This last variable may be explained by significant positive relationships between amount of donations and household income found in a previous study of British political parties (Granik 2001), and widely documented positive relationships between high incomes and personal efficacy. Nevertheless, the model itself is significant, and explains 16% of the variance in the decision to take part in internal party activities.

The one drawback of this method of analysis is that, although these models specify the significance of the relationships between the various incentives and activity indicators, they do not necessarily specify the direction of the relationships, i.e., whether incentives are antecedents or outcomes of participation. However, it is reasonable to infer these relationships with reference to other published studies. In the case of the items drawn from the VFI, there is evidence that functional motivations for activity pre-date the actual activity undertaken (Clary et al. 1998). Therefore it is reasonable to assume that values and protective motivations operate as incentives for activism. But there is no documented evidence linking any of the functional motivations with the amount of activity that, in practice, is undertaken. Socialization is likely to be an antecedent of participation, as the trade union studies cited earlier in this article (McShane 1986, Kelley 1992) indicated. However, job satisfaction can be considered either an outcome of activity rather than an antecedent, or as a factor motivating continued and better performance (Hackman and Lawler

TABLE 9. Internal Party Activities–Regression Coefficients

	B	S.E	Beta	T	Sig
(constant)	−1.180	.419		−2.819	.005
Total of donations	.207	.069	.210	3.000	.003
High political efficacy	.564	.185	.213	3.040	.003
Total–job satisfaction	.125	.035	.247	3.609	.000
Model summary					

$R = .418$, $R^2 = .175$, Adjusted $R^2 = .161$, F ratio = 12.449, Sig = .000

1971). It would be reasonable to assume that, although, in the first instance, job satisfaction must be an outcome of work, in a voluntary context it may well be an incentive for subsequent and sustained participation.

DISCUSSION

So, to return to the opening question of this article, what do these results tell us about what party members want from their membership and the relationship between benefits and participation? Is political party membership a vehicle for political "choice reduction" and for gaining social approval from others as Sheth and Parvatiyar would suggest, and is there any support for the further hypothesis that these members are likely to be the most active in the party? Or is political party membership one of the rare instances which Bagozzi identified in which the motivation for entering into a marketing relationship with an organization is specifically to have a relationship with it, with the corollary that such members might not be receptive to incentives for participation.

The evidence from this research supporting Sheth and Parvatiyar's hypothesis appears to be somewhat mixed. It is notable that the opportunity to express one's values and act on them is seen as a benefit of membership. This implies that members perceive this opportunity accrues to them by virtue of their remaining in the party. Yet this can be countered by the argument that, if individuals had not held these values in the first place, they might not have decided to join. Therefore continuation of membership constitutes a continued reduction of their political options. It may also constitute a mechanism for avoiding any cognitive dissonance that might result from a shift in their political values. The evidence that members perceive frequency of agreement with the party as a whole as a benefit of membership throws as much doubt on the validity of the Sheth and Parvatiyar paradigm as it lends support. It is not clear whether members stay in membership in order not to be receptive to policies from other parties, or whether they enjoy being in the company of politically like-minded people. Additionally, the statistical evidence supporting the social approval argument as a benefit of membership is unreliable, and not all of this unreliability can be explained away by statistical artefact.

The most serious challenge to the applicability of Sheth and Parvatiyar's hypothesis to political party membership appears to come from the model achieved for time spent on activities described in Table 6 where those scoring highest on values motivations spend the most time working for Plaid Cymru. Surely this constitutes evidence that the most active members are those who are highly motivated by purposive incentives? In fact, it is entirely possible that this model is demonstrating the opposite relationship: the values motivations are an outcome of participation. There is no published evidence linking values motivations to any quantified amount of participation. Some of the members who are the most responsive to solidary incentives may also be the most likely to believe that they genuinely share party values because behaviours predict attitudes (Myers 1999). Individuals are likely to infer their own attitudes by observing what they do. Self-perception theory (Bem 1972) suggests that Plaid Cymru members who are highly active in order to receive solidary benefits are likely to assume that they share party values to a substantial extent. This will help them rationalize their decision to spend such a great amount of time on party matters. In this scenario, values motivations are not an incentive for activism, but arise from it. Participation in a political party, motivated by the incentives of having enjoyable work to do and a sense of belonging to the organization, functions as a mechanism for political choice reduction.

In support of Bagozzi's hypothesis, it is clear that values motivations and frequency of agreement with policies are considered to be benefits by members. But whilst values motivations have some kind of relationship with the decision whether to participate or not, these motivations lose significance in relation to activity type, and frequency of agreement with policies has no statistically significant relationship with any indicator of participation. The identification of values motivations and frequency of agreement with policies as benefits of membership indicate that for some members, membership is a mechanism for having a relationship with Plaid Cymru. But this is a relationship defined by the payment of membership dues, valid for a fixed period of time, rather than by participation. If what a member wants is a relationship with their party of choice, all they need do is maintain their dues in order to be able to claim this relationship.

The analysis presented in this article suggests that, in the context of political party membership, the two hypotheses may be complementary rather than mutually exclusive. There appear to be two groups of political party members; those who are highly responsive to the solidary benefits of socialization and job satisfaction and reduce their political choice in so being, and those who are somewhat more committed to the party in terms of attitude but who are less likely actively to participate in their party's affairs. An unfortunate implicit assumption of pre-existing studies of British political party memberships is that if members' political views are, broadly speaking, reasonably homogeneous, then their motivations for participation and actual behaviors ought also to be roughly similar. This is an assumption that should not persist unchallenged.

It was noted earlier in this article that another weakness of pre-existing studies of British political parties lies in the rather *ad hoc* "identification" of benefits of membership. The data in this article suggest that only one benefit theorized by political scientists, frequency of policy agreement, is also a salient benefit from the perspective of political party members. This indicates that frameworks grounded in appropriate theory from the fields of nonprofit studies and organizational behavior are far more helpful in the analysis of membership behavior than the rather casual approach towards identifying membership benefits and incentives that has, to date, prevailed. In particular, this study adds to the body of evidence that May's Law does not withstand empirical scrutiny. There is no evidence that position on an ideological spectrum is either perceived by members as a salient benefit of membership, or that it provides an incentive to become active within the party. In general, this study indicates that political scientists would find reference to literatures from other disciplines extremely helpful in understanding what members themselves perceive constitutes a benefit of belonging to a party.

The use of the VFI in a political party context has the potential to make a substantial contribution to our understanding of the motivations of political party members. It provides an opportunity to identify a range of potential purposive and solidary benefits and incentives available to party members, and for party practitioners to devise methods of ensuring that salient incentives for activism are delivered to its members. The VFI also provides a mechanism for direct comparison of the functional benefits and motivations of political party members between and across parties, and with members of other organizations such as trade unions, advocacy groups and voluntary organizations. This has the potential to increase our understanding of the differences, if any, underlying participation between parties, and between types of participatory organization.

A serious limitation of this study is, of course, that it has only been carried out in one political party. A replication study in another party would be highly desirable to see which variables retain their significance between parties and which, if any, are specific to Plaid Cymru members. This, of course, highlights the value of using analytical frameworks grounded in other disciplines in a political party context. Just as, noted above, the VFI can be used across parties so that the same constructs are measured in the same way across organizations, the other major scales used in this study–the amended OSS and the MOAQ– are equally transferable. Using the same measures across parties is the only means of discovering which perceptions and behaviors are generic amongst all political party members, and which are party-specific.

One further limitation of this study was apparent in the statistical analysis presented in Tables 3 and 4. It is not possible to identify whether the unreliable statistical evidence generated due to statistically significant differences within groups reflects the perceptions of members, or is an artefact of statistical analysis. The obvious solution to this problem is that, in further research, larger numbers of respondents should be sought (and, indeed, with 472 respondents, the sample size in this study is modest compared to those achieved in the British Labour and Conservative studies). However, this response might be slightly too simplistic. The reality is that, in an environment where membership is entirely voluntary, members who are dissatisfied with their membership leave (Granik 2001). Therefore, a disproportionately large sample would need to be generated in order to be reasonably certain of enough responses from dissatisfied members (who are likely to form a very small percentage of the total membership) to avoid running the risk of this kind of statistical distortion.

CONCLUSIONS

In summary, the findings of this paper suggest that members consider two purposive benefits and three solidary benefits accrue to them by virtue of their party membership. The purposive benefits are values functional benefits–the ability to express and act on their personal values–and being in an organization in which they are in agreement with their fellow members. There is reliable statistical evidence which indicates that members realize three solidary benefits of membership. These are socialization into the party, the extent to which members feel they "belong"; satisfaction with the work they do; and enhancement functional benefits, a sense of feeling needed and important. There is less reliable evidence of other solidary benefits of membership: namely, protective functional benefits, an opportunity to escape from the pressures of everyday life; and understanding functional benefits, the opportunity to learn more about the party and the political process.

The findings of this paper also suggest that the benefits of membership which it is in parties' interests to deliver comprise one purposive benefit–values benefits–and two solidary benefits–socialization and job satisfaction–because these are the antecedents of participation in party activities. But it should be noted that not all members are likely to be responsive to incentives for participation, those members who want only a relationship with the party for its own sake are likely not to be motivated into participation by even the most relevant solidary benefits.

This study provides preliminary evidence that there is considerable common ground between what motivates members to participate in the party, and what at least some members want from their membership. These members want a relationship with the party that provides them with a sense of belonging and activities that they enjoy doing. The party that can deliver this to its members is the party that is likely to have a productive and loyal membership base. In summary, many, but not all party members consider that incentives for participation are also the benefits they value from their membership.

REFERENCES

Allen, Natalie J. and John P. Meyer (1990) 'The Measurement and Antecedents of Affective, Continuance and Normative Commitment to the Organization,' *Journal of Occupational Psychology*, 63, pp. 1-18.

Arnett, Dennis B, Steve D. German and Shelby D. Hunt (2003) "The Identity Salience Model of Relationship Marketing Success: The Case of Nonprofit Marketing," *Journal of Marketing*, 67, pp. 89-105.

Bagozzi, Richard P. (1975) "Marketing as exchange" *Journal of Marketing*, 39, pp. 32-9.

(1995) "Reflections on Relationship Marketing in Consumer Markets," *Journal of the Academy of Marketing Science*, 23 (4), pp. 272-277.

Bauer, Hans H., Frank Huber and Andreas Herrman (1996) "Political Marketing: an information-economic analysis," *European Journal of Marketing*, 30, pp. 159-172.

Bauer, Talya N. and Stephen G. Green (1998) 'Testing the Combined Effects of Newcomer Information Seeking and Manager Behavior on Socialization,' *Journal of Applied Psychology*, 83, (1), pp. 72-83.

Bem, Daryl J. (1972) 'Self-perception theory.' In L. Berkowitz (Ed.) *Advances in experimental social psychology*, 6, New York: Academic Press.

Cammann, Cordtland, Mark Fichman, David Jenkins and John R. Klesh (1983) "Assessing the attitudes and perceptions of organizational members." In Stanley E. Seashore, Edward E. Lawler III, Philip H. Mirvis and Cordtland Cammann (Eds) *Assessing organizational change: A guide to methods, measures, and practices.* New York, Wiley pp. 71-138.

Chao, Georgia.T., Anne M. O'Leary-Kelly, Samantha Wolf, Howard J. Klein and Philip D. Gardner (1994) "Organizational Socialization: Its Content and Consequences," *Journal of Applied Psychology*, 79, (5) pp. 730-743.

Clark, Peter B. and James Q. Wilson (1961) "Incentive Systems: A Theory of Organizations," *Administrative Science Quarterly*, 6, pp. 129-166.

Clary, E.Gil, Mark Snyder, and Robert D. Ridge (1992) "Volunteers' Motivations: A Functional Strategy for the Recruitment, Placement and Retention of Volunteers," *Nonprofit Management and Leadership*, 2, pp. 333-350.

Clary, E.Gil, Mark Snyder, Robert D. Ridge, John Copeland, Arthur A. Stukas, Julie Haugen, and Peter Miene (1998) "Understanding and Assessing the Motivations of Volunteers: A Functional Approach," *Journal of Personality and Social Psychology*, 74, pp. 1516-1530.

Downs, Anthony (1956), *An Economic Theory of Democracy*, Harper and Row.

Francies, George Ray (1983) "The Volunteer Needs Profile: A Tool for Reducing Turnover," *Journal of Volunteer Administration* (Summer), pp. 17-33.

Hackman J. Richard and Edward E. Lawler (1971) 'Employee Reactions to Job Characteristics,' *Journal of Applied Psychology*, 55 (3), pp. 259-286.

Granik, Sue (1997) "Beyond Belief: the consumer behaviour of political party members," M.A. dissertation, University of Westminster (unpublished).

_____ (2001) "Should I stay or should I go?" *Proceedings of the Fourth International Political Marketing Conference*: Dublin City University.

Gruen, Thomas W. (2000) "Membership Customers and Relationship Marketing." In Jagdish N. Sheth and Atul Parvatiyar (Eds) *Handbook of Relationship Marketing*, Thousand Oaks: Sage pp. 355-380.

Gordon, Michael E., John W. Philpot, Robert E. Burt, Cynthia A. Thompson, and William E. Spiller (1980) "Commitment to the union: development of a measure and an examination of its correlates," *Journal of Applied Psychology*, 65, pp. 479-499.

Hoffman, K. Douglas, and John E.G. Bateson (1997) *Essentials of Services Marketing*, Fort Worth: The Dryden Press.

Kelly, Caroline and Sara Breinlinger (1996) *The Social Psychology of Collective Action*, London: Taylor and Francis.

Kelley, Scott W. (1992) "Developing Customer Orientation Among Service Employees," *Journal of the Academy of Marketing Science*, 20, pp. 27-36.

Maslow, Abraham (1954) *Motivation and Personality*, New York: Harper and Row.

May, John D. (1973) "Opinion Structure of Political Parties: The Special Law of Curvilinear Disparity," *Political Studies*, 21, pp. 135-51.

McClelland, David C. (1961), *The Achieving Society*, New Jersey: D Van Norstrand.

McShane, Steven L. (1986) 'The multidimensionality of union participation,' *Journal of Occupational Psychology* 22, pp. 177-187.

Mitchell, Mark A and Susan L. Taylor (1997) "Adapting Internal Marketing to a Volunteer System," *Journal of Nonprofit and Public Sector Marketing*, 5 (2), pp. 29-41.

Morgan, Robert M. and Shelby D. Hunt (1994) "The Commitment-Trust Theory of Relationship Marketing," *Journal of Marketing*, 58 (July), pp. 20-38.

Myers, David G. (1999) *Social Psychology* (6th ed), Boston: McGraw-Hill.

Narud, Hanne M. and Audun Skare (1999) 'Are Party Activists the Party Extremists? The Structure of Opinion in Political Parties,' *Scandinavian Political Studies*, 22, pp. 45-65.

Norris, Pippa (1995) 'May's Law of Curvilinear Disparity Revisited,' *Party Politics*, 1, pp. 29-47.

Olson, Mancur (1965) *The Logic of Collective Action*, 2nd ed, Massachusetts: Harvard University Press.

Seyd, Patrick and Paul F. Whiteley (1992) *Labour's Grass Roots*, Oxford: Clarendon.

Seyd Patrick and Paul F. Whiteley (2002) *New Labour's Grassroots: The Transformation of the Labour Party Membership*, Basingstoke: Palgrave Macmillan.

Sheth, Jagdish N. and Atul Parvatiyar (1995) 'Relationship Marketing in Consumer Markets: Antecedents and Consequences,' *Journal of the Academy of Marketing Science*, 23, pp. 255-271.

Spector, Paul E. (1997) *Job Satisfaction: Application, assessment, causes and consequences*. Thousand Oaks: Sage.

Van Maanen, John and Edgar H Schein (1979) "Toward a theory of organizational socialization," *Research in Organizational Behavior*, 1, pp. 209-264.

Vroom, Victor H. (1964) *Work and Motivation*, New York: Wiley

Wanburg, Connie R. and John D. Kammeyer-Mueller (2000) 'Predictors and Outcomes of Proactivity in the Socialization Process' *Journal of Applied Psychology*, 83 (3) pp. 373-385.

Westbrook, Robert A. (1980). "A Rating Scale for Measuring Product/Service Satisfaction." *Journal of Marketing*, 44, pp. 68-72.

Whiteley, Paul F., Patrick Seyd and Jon Richardson (1994) *True Blues: the politics of Conservative party membership*, Oxford: OUP.

Widmer, Candace (1985) "Why Board Members Participate" *Journal of Voluntary Action Research*, 14, pp. 8-23.

Vote Winner or a Nuisance: Email and Elected Politicians' Relationship with Their Constituents

Nigel Jackson

SUMMARY. MPs have traditionally relied on the organisation and image of their national Party for the bulk of their voter support, but constituency service is probably more relevant for electoral success than at any other time in history. So far, however, new technology has had a very limited impact on the constituency role of MPs. The emergence of email represents potentially a 'killer app' which might revolutionize the way MPs approach re-election. One of the main effects of email is to encourage MPs to consider techniques and terms in common business usage, such as direct marketing and segmentation of their key audiences. By looking at how MPs use email to support their constituency role, this article assesses whether MPs use email as part of a relationship marketing strategy, a traditional transitory marketing approach or ignore marketing altogether. The marketing approach taken, combined with the resources available, will determine whether MPs use email only because they

---

Nigel Jackson is Senior Lecturer in Public Relations, University of Bournemouth, Bournemouth Media School, Weymouth House, Talbot Campus, Bournemouth University, Fern Barrow, Poole, BH12 5BB, UK (E-mail: njackson@bournemouth.ac.uk).

The author would like to acknowledge the help and advice of Professor Michael Rush.

[Haworth co-indexing entry note]: "Vote Winner or a Nuisance: Email and Elected Politicians' Relationship with Their Constituents." Jackson, Nigel. Co-published simultaneously in *Journal of Nonprofit & Public Sector Marketing* (Best Business Books, an imprint of The Haworth Press, Inc.) Vol. 14, No. 1/2, 2005, pp. 91-108; and: *Current Issues in Political Marketing* (eds: Walter W. Wymer, Jr., and Jennifer Lees-Marshment) Best Business Books, an imprint of The Haworth Press, Inc., 2005, pp. 91-108. Single or multiple copies of this article are available for a fee from The Haworth Document Delivery Service [1-800-HAWORTH, 9:00 a.m. - 5:00 p.m. (EST). E-mail address: getinfo@haworthpressinc.com].

think they should or because they have grasped the campaigning opportunities it represents. *[Article copies available for a fee from The Haworth
Document Delivery Service: 1-800-HAWORTH. E-mail address: <docdelivery@
haworthpress.com> Website: <http://www.HaworthPress.com> © 2005 by The
Haworth Press, Inc. All rights reserved.]*

KEYWORDS. MPs, email, relationship marketing, politics

A number of commentators (Scammell 1995, Margetts, 2000 and Kavanagh 1997) have predicted that technology will transform political communication. Within the wider framework of the Internet, email represents a
potentially revolutionary force in British politics that could fundamentally alter how MPs seek re-election and change the nature of their relationship with
constituents.

Email is an easy and convenient means for electors to contact their MPs.'
Being cheaper than posting letters email may encourage greater dialogue between constituents and their MP. But email is not restricted to making casework easier for the constituent. Email can radically enhance the campaigning
ability of MPs to conduct political marketing by quickly and cheaply sending
tailored messages to individual constituents.

There is a belief in parts of the business world that email might be a 'killer
app' (Downes & Mui 2000), namely a technological development that has
far-reaching effects on society, business and politics. Downs and Mui cite the
introduction of the humble stirrup in the 8th Century. Technologically this just
allowed a man on horseback to use a spear without falling off when he hit an
opponent. But Downes and Mui believe it ultimately created the Holy Roman
Empire which dominated medieval Europe because it directly led to a Knighted
class. Whether they are right is almost irrelevant, the significance is in the concept of a 'killer app.' If email, and it is a huge if, is indeed a technology that
dominates all others, then it sends into disarray pre-Internet political relationships. As an electoral Holy Grail the government, party or politician which
first controls email will dominate the political market. However, content analysis of candidates' and MPs' websites by Ward and Gibson (2001), Johnson
(2002, p. 213) and Jackson (2003) suggest that websites are not, and may
never be, the 'killer app.' But limited research by Cain et al. (2001) implies
that email is on the cusp of becoming the political 'killer app.' If there is a difference between the impact of websites and email, it may be explained by the
fact that the demand for websites has primarily come from the politicians
themselves. The pressure for greater use of email has in part come from con-

stituents. As Tom Steinberg (2001) comments "An MP in the new parliament who cannot use email will seem to at least half the population as anachronistic as one that cannot use the telephone."

Email as a technology dovetails with the view that 'constituency service' (Butler and Collins 2001) is a means of increasing an individual MP's re-election chances. Traditionally it was felt that 'a good constituency MP' might be worth only 500 votes, but since the 1970s MPs have been aware of the possible growing electoral impact of their casework (Barker and Rush 1970). By 1987 Cain et al. (1987) suggested that the personal vote may have been 1,500-2000 votes. As a consequence the concept of incumbency, well-understood in American elections, is becoming more relevant to the UK.

THE IMPORTANCE OF RELATIONSHIP MARKETING

Although a concept derived from political science, constituency service is linked to a marketing idea, relationship marketing. Healy et al. (2001) point out that relationship marketing has been developing since the 1970s. Coined by Berry (1983) it is perhaps best associated with, on the practical side, Mckenna (1986) and on the academic the Nordic School (Gummerson 2002, Gronroos 1997).

Traditional marketing was based on the four Ps approach which emphasises, according to Tapp (2000), brand, market share and product. Each sale is viewed as a transient one-off based on applying the appropriate marketing mix. As a result communications is a mass tool with the same message being sent to a wide number of consumers (O' Malley et al. 1999). Relationship marketing developed as an alternative to this approach. It gained support not because it was felt there had to be a better way, rather it was primarily due to changes in the business environment (O'Malley et al. 1999). The recession of 1990 and technological changes, such as the database capabilities of computers, enabled a more targeted communications strategy (Chaffey, 2003).

In 1986 McKenna stated that personal relationships were often more permanent than those based on product based loyalties alone. Clearly as the recession of the late 1980s/early 1990s took hold, more and more businesses recognised that the locus of the marketing effort had to switch from customer acquisition to customer retention. For example, Reichheld and Sasser (1990) found that by retaining only 5% more customers, profits could increase by up to 100%. For MPs this implies that the nature of the relationship with voters may be as important to their re-election as their Party's overall brand image, policies and leadership.

Relationship marketing is based on what Gummersson (2002) refers to as 'relationships, networks and interaction,' so that any history of contact between producers and consumers has to be recognised and acted upon by marketers. Therefore, communication strategies are tailored with the emphasis on one-to-one marketing. Building a relationship between the producer and the individual consumer is considered key, so that marketers are looking for a lifetime association, not just a one-off sale. As a result Dwyer et al. (1987) suggests that there is a 'marriage' between buyer and seller. Therefore, MPs need to persuade constituents to vote for them not just for the next election but for all remaining elections throughout their life. When in the 1950s high partisanship meant that people could proclaim that they were either a "Labour man" or a "Conservative man," now with relationship marketing the implication is that they have a similar level of loyalty, but that it is with the individual person and not necessarily their Party.

Technology has played a significant role in the development of relationship management by, as Chaffey (2003) points out, allowing for greater profiling of consumers. Indeed Zineldin (2000) believes that relationship marketing is only effective with the appropriate use of technology. Therefore, the use of email may link the concepts of the 'killer app,' constituency service and relationship marketing.

It is within the context of a more volatile electorate, and the opportunities presented by new technologies, that political marketing has developed. However, political marketing so far has predominantly taken a traditional marketing mix, 4 P's approach (Mauser 1983, Lees-Marshment 2001, Wring 2001) where a vote is comparable to a transitory sale. Reichheld and Sasser (1990) point out that in the commercial world customers who purchase a transient product then join the 'customer scrap heap.' After an election voters join the 'voters scrap heap.' This approach tends to emphasise the election campaign and the role of party elites who control it. Dean and Croft (2001) counter that conventional marketing is inappropriate in politics. With a relationship marketing approach MPs seek to build long-term relationships with their constituents outwith election campaigns. Constituency service, therefore, can be seen as an attempt by MPs to build personal relations with voters.

Political parties, pressure groups and individual politicians have increasingly adopted marketing approaches common to business. Although referring to the American experience, Sherman and Schiffman (2002), suggest that in the last 10 years direct marketing has altered the political marketing landscape. It is possible to draw parallels with business and politics. The increased use of targeting by businesses via direct marketing was driven by the rising cost of marketing and consumer fragmentation (O' Malley et al. 1999). With the cost of running national elections increasing and voting behaviour becoming more difficult to predict, cheaper and more tailored communication with voters is required. The low turnout of the 2001 UK General Election has alerted politicians towards the importance of voter retention.

EMAIL AND RELATIONSHIP MARKETING

Unlike most traditional marketing techniques, email is both an inbound and outbound channel (Tapp, 2000). If MPs want to use it as a campaigning tool to build long-term relationships, they have to accept that it will also be used as an inbound route. Individuals and groups will want to establish relationships with MPs for their own purposes, not necessarily the ones MPs want to encourage. There is, then, a potential cost to online relationship marketing.

Given that it appears inevitable that MPs will face growing numbers of inbound email, there are a number of positive purposes for which they might use outbound email. First, to help them win votes. As a cheap, easy to use and asynchronous technology it could be used as an improved campaign tool. Sir George Young (Conservative) has suggested that used properly email could increase votes by 5% (Wearden 2001). Second, email by informing MPs what constituents think and want could help them better represent their constituents, irrespective of how they voted. Third, as an unmediated communication tool email helps MPs have far greater control of their outbound channels by speaking directly to constituents. Fourth, as a source of market research email helps MPs develop their political campaigns and policy stances. Therefore, email can enhance the building of relationships by facilitating effective two-way communication between elector and elected.

MPs have been accused of contacting constituents only during election campaigns when they need their votes. Whilst this is surely a simplification, email can challenge this perception by providing a regular reminder of a MPs local presence. Moreover, unlike most political communication tools email is potentially two-way. In addition, the nature of email allows for a more chatty and informal style of communication from MP to constituent and from constituent to MP in return. However, email will not automatically lead to a dramatic change in a MPs' political fortunes, MPs have to use it effectively as an outbound communication.

This article will identify whether email has led to a relationship marketing approach by MPs by assessing the following criteria:

1. Regularly used outwith of an election campaign.
2. Communication is tailored to the requirements of the receiver.
3. Communication is two-way and not just one-way.
4. Builds 'networks' between an MP and their constituents.

Conversely, if email represents a marketing mix approach we would expect that it will be:

1. One-way in nature from MP to constituent.
2. Primarily an election campaign communication tool.
3. Promoting Party product and brand.
4. A mass communication tool.

METHODOLOGY

Carried out in June/July 2002 the research is based on an email survey of 100 Members of Parliament (MPs), plus follow up interviews. It is worth noting that some 10% of respondents had initial difficulty with the technology in terms of returning their completed questionnaire. Although all MPs are issued with an email address, the survey was limited to only those politicians (412 out of 658) whose email address was publicly available (accessed via www.parliament.uk), as it was assumed these had decided to encourage email. This suggests that a third of MPs do not want to encourage email contact with constituents. MPs are notoriously poor questionnaire responders and the response rate of just under 25% was considered sufficient to allow meaningful statistical analysis. Indeed several MPs commented that as a normal policy they did not respond to questionnaires, but given the subject matter they made an exception.

Analysis is based on frequency and cross-tabulation of the fourteen questions using SPSS11. Respondents were categorised by constituency characteristics (geography), personal characteristics (age, gender, seniority) and political characteristics (marginality of seat).

The article seeks to answer three key questions. First, how is email being used as part of the MP-constituent relationship, Second, what is the impact of email on this relationship. Third, is email encouraging a relationship marketing approach to constituents by MPs?

THE GROWTH OF MPs EMAIL

Although MPs have had access to email in their offices since 1995 its use for constituency work has only recently reached critical mass. The are three possible barriers put forward by MPs to justify why their email addresses are not publicly available. First, it might open the floodgates of communication from organised pressure groups. Certainly, the House of Commons Information Committee commented "The ease with which constituents and others can send email is seen by Members as both an opportunity . . . and as a threat, in that it could generate a demand that Members cannot meet with existing structures and resources" (HC Information Committee July 2002: 18). Second, some MPs argue that email is not relevant to constituencies of lower socioeconomic background (Campbell et al. 1999). Third, email does not add anything which the postbag and physical surgeries already offer constituents.

For constituents to contact their MP they need an email address. From slow beginnings there has been very rapid growth recently in the public availability of MPs email addresses on www.parliament.uk. This suggests that there is a 'head of steam' which technophobic MPs will find increasingly harder to resist. In 1996 White identified nearly 50 MPs with email (White 1996). The general election of June 2001 acted as a catalyst with the number rising to 187 Gardner (2001). By March 2002 this number had risen to 296 but by June 2002 the number dramatically increased to 412.

Downes and Mui's (2000) Law of Disruption suggests that politics is always slower than society and business at responding to new technologies. Certainly Coleman (1999) points out that MPs tend to initially resist new technological developments, but then eventually they come to accept and adapt them for their own purposes. Certainly the dramatic growth rates suggest that email is a clear example of what may be called the parliamentary herd instinct. There may be a number of motives, from the identification of positive benefits through to a desire to avoid being thought of as behind the times, but the total effect is the same. At some point in 2002 email reached critical mass for MPs with less and less MPs willing to be left behind.

Tables 1 and 2 show that the two main Parties have significantly increased the number of their MPs whose email address is publicly available. Although the Liberal Democrats are still the most likely to take this step, in fact their

TABLE 1. Percentage of MPs Whose Email Address Was Publicly Available May 2001

Party	Percentage
Conservatives	24.4%
Labour	23.4%
Liberal Democrats	81.5%
Others	24.1%

TABLE 2. Percentage of MPs Whose Email Address Was Publicly Available June 2002

Party	Percentage
Conservatives	58.5%
Labour	60.8%
Liberal Democrats	77.7%
Others	41.4%

number has slightly decreased suggesting a small number of their MPs either question the value of em
ail or have been overwhelmed by it.

ARE MPS BEING SWAMPED BY CONSTITUENCY EMAIL?

MPs do not appear to be overwhelmed by the amount of email they receive from constituents. The vast majority, 86%, receive less than 100 emails a week from constituents. For example, one Conservative MP representing a rural area receives only one or two emails a week from constituents. Others suggest that the number is currently low but has been steadily growing. Only 5% receive more than 200 a week, however, one MP (Interview 2003) stated that he expects his modest number of constituency emails to double every six months.

There are, however, individual MPs who report significant numbers of emails from constituents. For example, Brian White (Labour) claims that between a quarter and a third of his constituency work is now carried out online (Wearden 2001). Labour MPs seem the more likely to receive more than 101 emails from constituents representing 17% of their respondents, with the Liberal Democrats least likely with 6.7% of their MPs. If party is only a minor predictor, so is marginality (as defined by Finer et al. 1961). For example, collectively marginals and near marginals provide 20% of respondents but only 15% of those receiving the higher email returns from constituents. This suggests a potentially tighter electoral contest does not necessarily encourage more email contact from constituents.

There is an inconsistent approach from MPs, for example, the office of one Welsh MP discourages casework by email because it takes extra time (Interview 2002). A Scottish MP, however, deliberately promotes his email address to constituents (Interview 2002). Both MPs represent geographically spread rural constituencies but take different approaches to email. Whilst both are computer literate with laptops and the ability to use email themselves, the nature of their staff are very different. The former is from a traditional office background, whereas the staff of the latter have IT degrees. Anecdotally, there is a suggestion that the background of a MPs staff is a significant factor in determining how an MP uses email.

The real danger to MPs appears to be from non-constituents with spam, unrequested junk mail, a real problem. Some 90% of MPs have received co-ordinated campaign materials via email from pressure groups. Table 3 demonstrates that there is a serious concern that many are being plagued by emails from non-constituents. For a clear majority, 55%, over half of emails they receive come from non-constituents. Indeed, one urban Labour MP from Scotland claims that at least 98% of his emails are from non-constituents. E-lobbying as an inbound channel of communication appears to be a fact of life for many MPs.

Given the concern that email opens up the floodgates to non-constituents, it would be logical to expect that many MPs would feel they were not coping. The reality does not yet support this. Table 4 shows that only a small number of MPs, 12%, appear not to be coping. Some MPs are quite clear that this is

TABLE 3. Average Percentage of Emails from Non-Constituents

Amount	MPs
Less than 10%	15%
11-20%	6%
21-30%	10%
31-40%	4%
41-50%	10%
51%=	55%

TABLE 4. How Well Are MPs Coping with the Volume of Email?

How well	MPs
Very well	26%
Reasonably well	35%
Adequately	27%
Not very well	5%
Badly	7%

due to the amount of junk mail, rather than what one Labour suburban MP refers to as " 'real' constituency email."

Given that MPs do not appear swamped by email we would expect that they have sufficient training, skills and resources, but this does not appear to be the case. For example, 35% stated they do not have the necessary resources and skills. If many do not have the required support, why are not more struggling? The most obvious answer is that amount of inbound email has not yet reached critical mass for most MPs.

THE IMPACT OF EMAIL
ON THE RELATIONSHIP WITH CONSTITUENTS

For 64% of MPs, email is perceived as helping them provide a better service for their constituents. However, this means there is a significant minority, 30%, for whom email has not helped provide a better service. One MP's office does not accept emails for constituency work because the bulk of their casework is social security based, and they do not know who is using the computer. Therefore, they ask people who email them to send their case by post (Interview 2002). But another MP's office points out that for one constituent who cannot speak "email has become a lifeline for them" (Interview 2002).

There is also evidence that some MPs view email as only benefiting certain constituents or constituencies. For example, one Labour MP representing a fairly deprived north east constituency said that email did not help with what he called "the verbally disenfranchised," those who do not have access to the Internet. In comparison to this he went on to say that "it does serve the middle classes and obsessed brilliantly" (Correspondence 2002). From a completely different perspective, one Liberal Democrat representing a primarily rural, though not considered prosperous constituency, commented "Generally email has opened up the sport of 'MP baiting' to an entirely new group of constituents: mainly younger, intelligent, often professional types, who just would not have contemplated writing a letter, or would have never found time to" (Correspondence 2002). Whilst only anecdotal these two quotes suggest that certain constituencies or constituents might be more likely, at present, to use email. The last quote, in particular, suggests that a new type of constituent is engaging with their MP.

If email does indeed help improve the service a constituent receives, it comes at a cost to the MP. An overwhelming majority of respondents, 90% believed that, compared to posted letters, email creates an expectation among constituents of a speedier reply. For example, the Liberal Democrat mentioned above comments "The new emailers certainly expect a reply quicker, and, are far more argumentative about what I say in response: both because of the immediacy of email, and because they are more informed and articulate (and less deferential) than letter writers" (Correspondence 2002). This suggests that greater expectation of a speedier reply is not just a factor of technology itself, but also probably the profile of those using that technology. In order to build successful relationships, MPs will need to understand the needs of their e-constituents.

EMAIL AND POLITICAL CAMPAIGNING

Whilst MPs are generally coping with inbound email traffic it is clear that very few are managing to fully utilise the outbound use of email. Except for a very small number it is quite clear that email is a one-way communication tool, from constituents and non-constituents to MPs. It is not being used, except by a few pioneers, as either a one-way or a two-way communications channel from MPs to their constituents. Email is not yet a widely used tool for building relationships with constituents.

Promotional signature files at the bottom of an email are a simple device extensively used by commercial companies (Ollier 1998, Haig 2001). They can be used to highlight, for instance, a MPs' website, key campaigns or request feedback. Signature files are a useful marketing tool which can help reinforce key messages. However, only 12% of MPs use promotional signature files, a very low figure for a technique which takes minutes to set up and update. This suggests that an opportunity is being missed. One Labour MP freely admitted that they did not know how to set up a signature file. MPs either are not aware of the possible usage of signature files or they do not yet have the mindset to fully utilise email for campaigning purposes.

MPs are much better at actively collecting constituents email addresses for later campaign purposes, with 33% doing so. But this still means that two thirds of MPs will find it difficult to build up a relationship with constituents by email if they have not taken the first step of collecting addresses. One Midlands based Labour MP claimed that he did not receive enough emails from constituents to make it worth while collecting their email addresses. Therefore, he viewed the development of the web and the use of email as something for the future for his primarily deprived area. Even an enthusiastic supporter of email has only built up a list of 1,000 constituents' email addresses (Correspondence September 2002).

The logic of relationship marketing is that it takes time to build up relationships with constituents. If, and it is a big if, e-campaigning techniques plays a significant role in the next General Election, the Conservatives are currently far behind the race, and the Liberal Democrats way ahead. Only 13% of Conservative MPs undertake this key first stage of building relationships online, as opposed to 53.3% of Liberal Democrats. Labour are close to the overall average at 35.6%.

Although a third of respondents currently collect constituent email addresses, they appear to be saving them for a political rainy day–presumably an election campaign. But by then it may be too late as any database needs to be kept up to date to be of use (Chaffey et al. 2000, Haig 2001). Table 5 shows that currently very few elected politicians are proactively sending emails to constituents. In part this may be because of the sheer amount of time and effort it takes to properly handle these lists. The enthusiastic MP mentioned above states that it takes "1-2 hours a day to service, including all the responses . . . this is what puts off my colleagues from doing it."

Emailing a newsletter is believed by many commentators to be the most effective outbound use of email (Chaffey et al. 2000, Collin 2000, McManus 2001). By meeting the four stated criteria referred to earlier e-newsletters represent the clearest indication of a relationship marketing approach. First, e-newsletters can be used at any time, not just during elections. Second, messages can be tailored, indeed there can be a number of e-newsletters. Third, because they are interactive (Haig 2000) e-newsletters encourage feedback. Fourth, they represent a new means by which MPs develop networks of interested people. Emailed newsletters have a major role to play in developing long-term relationships between MPs and their constituents. Such newsletters are not a hard sell like a hand-delivered leaflet during an election, rather their aim is to build relationships. However, if e-newsletters are the clearest indication of a relationship marketing approach, the fact that only 4% of respondents provide such a communications tool suggests that at present very few at pres-

TABLE 5. Use of Emails Proactively to Constituents

Activity	MPs
Changes to website	7%
Details of speeches/press releases	5%
Details of your campaigns	8%
A regular newsletter	4%
Party policies	2%
Election campaigns	8%
Appeals for help	10%

ent are engaging in a relationship marketing strategy. If respondents are typical of all 412 with a publicly available email address this suggests that less than twenty MPs have endorsed relationship marketing through email.

Although the numbers are low, there is a clear party bias, with all the newsletters being Labour MPs. None of the respondents from other parties seems interested in using a technique which is now common in the commercial marketing world. Nor are they being viewed as a means to win votes, with only one near marginal seat providing a newsletter and the rest in safe seats.

The enthusiastic MP sees benefits to him in providing his constituents with a regular e-newsletter low on partisan material but high on balance and information. "I try to make them feel that they are unusually well-informed and consulted. This helps defuse tabloid nonsense–if they're heard from me why we want to set up refugee centres, for instance, they are less likely to freak out when they hear one is being built nearby. Conversely, they put me right when I get things wrong–so for instance when I wrote an email about an EU ban on battery cages, various misunderstandings on my part were corrected by someone on the list who happens to be an inspector of chicken cages. Last but not least, I use the list to organise swift help for local people in trouble, so it becomes an extended village–in a number of cases, people who were really desperate have had a dozen strangers rallying round as a result." This MP is clearly following a relationship marketing approach, one which he hopes will secure more votes, or at the very least retain existing support.

The researcher for one MP suggested that email has a different psychological impact on constituents. He believes that *"A leaflet goes from the letter box to the bin. They are perhaps more likely to read an email."* However, having identified this possible strength of email their MP has not yet tried e-campaigning because they are concerned about whether it incurs an election expense (Interview 2002).

There are two obstacles that need to be overcome before MPs are likely to make much use of newsletters to build relationships with constituents. First, a concern over how complex and difficult it is to produce and manage an e-newsletter. In fact one of the key benefits for the political marketer is that these newsletters are in fact easy to construct (Holtz 1999). Second, the potential resources they may require. This second barrier is more serious than the first.

The most critical resource for MPs is not likely to be the financial cost or the technical issues of sending out a newsletter by email. An e-newsletter is far cheaper to produce and distribute than a printed publication, and with the appropriate software is not technically difficult to achieve (Holtz 1999, McManus 2001, Haig 2001). What will be critical for MPs is the human resources and knowing how to best use the technology. As the enthusiastic MP above notes it takes a significant amount of almost daily effort to manage the database, send out regular newsletters and then respond to replies. It is quite likely that this acts as a disincentive to many MPs. But it is not just a case of lacking the time and human resources, but also a fear of mis-using the technology. In a short space of time a netiquette has built up governing the use of e-newsletters which for the unwary is easy to break. For example, an MP who sends out what is considered spam, that is unrequested mail, is likely to receive a backlash. Moreover, for MPs there is a particular question, namely can they use email from their Parliamentary email address for what may be considered campaigning activity. Clearly MPs have come to a range of different answers to this question.

If only approximately 4-5% of MPs are using outbound email as part of relationship marketing, this does not mean that the remaining 95% are automatically using email for transient marketing. The figures in Table 5 for details of campaigns, appeals for help, details of speeches/press releases and as part of election campaigns suggest that at best 10-20% are using outbound email for transient marketing. If respondents are typical of the 412 MPs with a publicly available email address this equates to probably 40-80 MPs using transient e-marketing through email.

Marginality does not appear to be a factor in determining the use of transient marketing. For example, not one of the marginal seat MPs uses proactive emails to tell constituents of their campaigns, and only 9% of near-marginals as opposed to safe seats. Whilst it might be expected that those MPs in the closest electoral contests have greatest need for new volunteer helpers, it is safe seats that appeals are made. . Not one marginal made such an appeal, with only 9% of near marginals as opposed to 11% of safe seats.

If the results of Table 5 can be generalised approximately 60-100 MPs (out of 658) conduct any form of e-marketing though the outbound use of email. This suggests that over 500 do not use email as a marketing tool at all, that it is purely an inbound communication tool.

WHAT NEEDS TO BE DONE?

Table 6 demonstrates that there is a lack of clarity as to what technical help MPs require to make better use of email. The single, most popular idea was improved filtering software, a point which the Hansard Society and Parliamentary authorities grappled with after the survey was conducted. It is interesting that when this filtering software was indeed introduced it faced a number of teething problems. The appropriate staff and training do not appear to be significant factors for most MPs, though several make reference to the

TABLE 6. What Would Help You Better Serve Your Constituents?

What would help	MPs
Training	27%
Better equipment	11%
Filtering software	46%
Specialist staff	23%
Online surgeries	11%
Sending out regular e-mailings	33%

need for their own staff to have more time, or for them just to have more staff to take on this new workload. Direct online communication via cyber surgeries does not appear that popular, although a significant number, 33%, were favourable to sending regular emails to constituents.

If we accept that collecting email addresses and then sending out regular e-mailings equates to some form of e-marketing, whether it be relationship or transient, then at present there appears to be a cap of 33% willing, at present, to consider this approach. If typical of all 412 MPs with a publicly available email this equates to approximately 120 MPs prepared to endorse some form of email marketing at present. However, a note of caution is raised by one MP (Interview 2003) who states that two of his colleagues who are keen uses of e-newsletters are beginning to consider whether the amount of work it generates is worth the hassle.

CONCLUSION–
THE IMPACT OF EMAIL ON MPs?

The research shows that so far email has not stimulated a relationship marketing approach. There are probably less than twenty MPs who are using email as part of a relationship marketing approach, and, in addition there may be another forty to eighty MPs practicing some form of traditional transient email marketing. These figures could be viewed as either a promising start to a new and different approach using an unfamiliar technology, or they might be considered very disappointing. Certainly given the amount of time and effort it takes to build up effective relationships the research suggests that email relationship marketing will only be a factor in a small number of seats at the next General Election contest. In part, this can be explained by the concerns that politicians have of marketing in general, but there are four specific factors.

First, the spectacular growth in the public availability of MPs email has been driven by a parliamentary herd instinct and constituent demand. Generally MPs view email as a fact of life rather than as an opportunity. Most are reacting to the technology and the demands placed on them by constituents. The research suggests that the use of email is being driven by constituents, and is not, generally, the result of a planned, deliberative and strategic approach by MPs.

Second, the research shows that there is a clear imbalance between whether email is inbound or outbound. The impact of the former has been far greater than that of the latter. Email has had a detrimental impact on the ability of an individual MP to control the messages they receive, both in terms of volume and content. But this has not yet been offset by an increase in the control of the outbound communication process. For most MPs email has led to a communication imbalance, which can only add to the stresses and strains they endure.

Third, the lack of resources, primarily staff time to handle the amount of email and the appropriate skills to make best use of the campaigning opportunities email presents. Despite concerns to the contrary, most MPs do not appear to be swamped by constituency email, but if non-constituency email continues to grow this may change in the future. So resourcing the inbound and outbound use of email by MPs may become an ever-growing issue.

Fourth, email does not appear to be considered a vote winner. Only a small number of pioneers appear to be using email to establish and build online relationships to help them win votes.

However, email does appear to be encouraging a number of interesting developments. First, there is anecdotal evidence that different types of constituents are using email to contact their MP, perhaps for the first time. Second, nearly two-thirds of respondents felt that email was helping them provide a better service for their constituents. This in turn may help develop constituency service as a local electoral factor. Third, there is a slight difference in the approach of the Party's towards the campaigning aspects of email. Labour and Liberal Democrat MPs are slightly more likely to make proactive use of email than the Conservatives.

For MPs email is here to stay, and its use is likely to grow, but it is not a political 'killer app.' It is a useful, but at present underused campaigning tool and an ever-growing link between constituents and their MPs. It's impact, therefore, is likely to be more and more relevant to a politician's representative role. This will require a significant increase in the resources available to MPs to use email. There is also a need for greater clarity and transparency of how MPs are allowed (or are not) to use email as a campaigning tool. These changes should help MPs take greater control of both the inbound and outbound use of email, only then might it become less of a nuisance and instead help them win votes.

REFERENCES

Barker, A and Rush, M., (1970) *The Member of Parliament and his Information*, London: Allen & Unwin.

Berry, L., (1983) 'Relationship marketing' in Berry, L., Shostack, G., Upak, G (eds.) *Perspectives on services marketing* American Marketing Association.

Butler, P., and Collins, N., (2001), 'Payment on Delivery–recognising constituency service as political marketing,' *European Journal of Marketing* Volume 35 (9-10) pp. 1026-1037.

Cain, B., Ferejohn, J., Fiorina, M., (1987) *The personal vote–constituency service and electoral independence* London: Harvard University Press.

Cain, P., Crabtree, J., Jellniel, D,. Steinberg, T., (April 2001) *How to use the Internet effectively, securely and legally in election campaigns*. Hansard Society.

Campbell, A., Harrop, A., Thompson, B., (1999) 'Towards the virtual Parliament–what computers can do for MPs,' in *Parliamentary Affairs*, 52 (3), pp. 388-403.

Chaffey, D., Mayer, R., Johnston, K., Ellis-Chadwick, F., (2000) *Internet Marketing*, Harlow: Pearson Education.

Coleman, S., (1999) 'Westminster in the Information Age,' *Parliamentary Affairs*, 52 (3), pp. 371-387.

Dean, D, and Croft (2001) 'Friends and relations: long-term approaches to political campaigning' *European Journal of Marketing*, 35 (11/12), pp. 1197-1216.

Downes, L. and Mui, C. (2000) *'Unleashing the Killer App,'* Boston, MA: Harvard University Press.

Dwyer,R,. Schurr P. and Oh S., (1987), 'Developing Buyer-Seller Relationships' *Journal of Marketing*, 51 (April), pp. 11-27.

Finer, S, Berrington, H, Bartholowmew H,. (1961) *Backbench opinion in the House of Commons 1955-59* New York: Pergamon.

Gardner, S., online at http://www.ukpolitics.org.uk/cgi?category=9&keyword=email& page=4 accessed on 19/6/02.

Gronroos, C., (1997) 'From marketing mix to relationship marketing–towards a paradigm shift in marketing' in *Management Decision*, 35 (4), pp. 322-339.

Gummesson, E., (2002) *Total Relationship Marketing*. Oxford: Butterworth Heinemann.

Haig, M., (2001) *E-pr–the essential guide to public relations on the Internet*. London: Kogan Page.

House of Commons Information Committee 'Digital Report: Working for Parliament and the Public' HC1065, 15 July 2002 online at http://www.parliament.the-stationary-office.co.uk/pa/cm200102/cmselect/cminform/1065, accessed on 13/3/03.

Hansard Society, (2002) *Technology: Enhancing Representative Democracy in the UK?* London: Hansard Society.

Holtz, S., (1999) *Public relations on the net* New York: AMACOM.

Jackson, N., (2003), 'Web technologies–an untapped opportunity' *Journal of Public Affairs*, 3 (2), pp. 124-137.

Johnson, D., (2002) 'Campaign website: another tool, but no killer app,' *Journal of Political Marketing*, 1(1), pp. 213-215.

Kavanagh, D,. (1997) *Election campaigning–the new marketing of politics*. Blackwell.

Lees-Marshment, J (2001) *Political Marketing and British Political Parties*. Manchester: Manchester University Press.

McManus, S., (2001) *Small business websites that work*. Harlow: Pearson Education.

Mauser, G., (1983) *Political marketing: an approach to campaign strategy*. New York: Praeger.

Margetts, H (2000) 'Political Participation and Protest' in Dunleavy, P, Gamble, A, Holliday I, and Peele G, *Developments in British Politics*, 6. Macmillan.

Ollier, A (1998) *The web factory guide to marketing on the Internet*. London: Aurialian Information Limited.

O'Malley, L,. Petterson, M., Evans, M., (1999) *Exploring Direct Marketing*. International Thomson Business Press.

Reichheld, F., and Sasser, W., (1990) 'Zero defects: Quality comes to service,' *Harvard Business Review*, September/October.

Scammell, M, (1995) *Designer Politics–how elections are won*. Macmillan.

Sherman, E and Schiffman, L (2002) 'Trends and issues in Political marketing strategies.' *Journal of Political Marketing*, 1(1).

Steinberg, T, (2001) A Strategic Guide for Online MPs, Hansard Society.

Tapp, A (2000) *Principles of Direct and Database Marketing*, 2nd edition. Pearson Education.

Vavra, T (1992) *Aftermarketing*. Irwin.

Ward, S., & Gibson, R., (2001) 'Online and on message? Candidate websites in the 2001 General Election,' paper to the PSA/BSA Media Group Conference, 10th September 2001, University of Loughborough.

Watts, D (1997) *Political Communication Today*. Manchester: University Press.

Wearden, G., 'MPs turn to Web for votes, 30/10/01 online at http://www.zdnet.co.uk/story/0,,t2098280,00.html, accessed on 26/5/02.

White (1996) online at http://keele.ac.uk/depts/po/table/brit/brit.htm, accessed on 11/3/03.

Wring, D., (2001) 'Labouring the point: operation victory and the battle for a second term,' *Journal of Marketing Management*, 17 (9-10).

Zineldin, M., (2000) 'Beyond relationship marketing: technologicalship marketing,' in *Marketing Intelligence and Planning*, 18 (1), pp. 9-23.

Electoral Participation
and Non-Voter Segmentation

Declan P. Bannon

SUMMARY. This article examines some of the issues and debates surrounding electoral participation in the UK from a political marketing perspective. In particular, this article reviews the current literature and details some of the output of primary research into non-voter behaviour and investigates the opinions and motivations of the electorate. The role of the Electoral Commission and the effects of all-postal voting are analysed. This article both challenges and supports previously presented arguments regarding political issues and voting. In addition, electoral turnout and voter participation is reviewed and the consequences for democracy discussed. *[Article copies available for a fee from The Haworth Document Delivery Service: 1-800-HAWORTH. E-mail address: <docdelivery@haworthpress.com> Website: <http://www.HaworthPress.com> © 2005 by The Haworth Press, Inc. All rights reserved.]*

KEYWORDS. Political marketing, non-voting, turnout, party identification, electoral participation, electoral commission

Declan P. Bannon is affiliated with Paisley Business School, University of Paisley, High Street, Paisley, PA1 2BE, UK (E-mail: declan.bannon@paisley.ac.uk).

[Haworth co-indexing entry note]: "Electoral Participation and Non-Voter Segmentation." Bannon, Declan P. Co-published simultaneously in *Journal of Nonprofit & Public Sector Marketing* (Best Business Books, an imprint of The Haworth Press, Inc.) Vol. 14, No. 1/2, 2005, pp. 109-127; and: *Current Issues in Political Marketing* (eds: Walter W. Wymer, Jr., and Jennifer Lees-Marshment) Best Business Books, an imprint of The Haworth Press, Inc., 2005, pp. 109-127. Single or multiple copies of this article are available for a fee from The Haworth Document Delivery Service [1-800-HAWORTH, 9:00 a.m. - 5:00 p.m. (EST). E-mail address: getinfo@haworthpressinc.com].

INTRODUCTION

Electoral participation varies quite considerably in democratic societies. Democracy is a process within which the electorate is permitted (sometimes forced) to make a choice. Engagement with the process tends to be higher in political volatile democracies and constituencies were the strength of preference is high, e.g., West Belfast. There seems to be a general assumption that democracy is good for democracy's sake and participation within the process is needed to show support for the process. Is democracy, in the words of Thomas Jefferson "the worst system apart from all the others"? The varieties and application of different democratic systems (STV, PR, FPTP, AMS) may affect the nature of participation as well as the variety of voting procedures. However non-participation may be a reflection of a relatively stable democracy and demonstrates a general contentment among the electorate. On the other hand, non-participation may be a reflection of growing voter apathy, distrust of politicians, frustration in the system and decreased awareness of politics in general.

The 2001 general election was the lowest turnout since 1918 (Table 1). Electoral non-participation is of increased interest to the Government, European Union, the Electoral Commission, the media, political parties, researchers and of course different groups of the general public (Berry, 2001; Birmingham, 2001; Black, 2001; Butler, 2001; Gott, 2001; Hertz, 2001; Marquis, 2001; Nucifora, 2001; Pare, 2001; Taylor Nelson, 2001; Urken, 2001; White, 2001; Young, 2001; Younge, 2001). If the increasing trend of non-voting is to be stemmed or reversed, a greater understanding of electoral behaviour is needed. Some authors believe that postal voting, e-voting or supermarket voting will solve the problem, i.e., it's all to do with the ease of access and availability of the transaction event (Berry, 2001; Birmingham, 2001; Fedder, 2001; Mote, 2001; Nucifora, 2001; Reed, 2001; Urken, 2001). But will these quick fix solutions address a complex range of issues not fully explored or understood? Research in the field of non-voter motivation is not extensive.

Although voter participation is in decline in the whole of Western democracies, the UK picture of non-participation and accelerated erosion in the per-

TABLE 1. UK General Election Turnout 1950-2001

1950	84.0	1964	77.1	1979	76.0	1997	71.4
1951	82.5	1966	75.8	1983	72.7	2001	59.4
1955	76.8	1970	72.0	1987	75.3		
1959	78.7	1974	72.8	1992	77.7		

centage of those voting is particularly acute. The UK now has the lowest turnouts to European elections, 36.5% in 1994 and a staggering 24% in 1999.

Local government elections are even more poorly supported–29.6% in England and Wales in 2000. In Scotland, the Scottish parliamentary elections of 1999 turnout was 58.1% which coincided with the local elections. The effect was to increase voter participation with turnouts ranging from 5.03% in Aberdeen up to 55.23% in N Lanarkshire (Hassan & Lynch, 2001:369). The Scottish Executive combined local Scottish Council elections with the Scottish parliamentary election on 1st of May 2003 to specifically increase turnout.

The global average turnout is 64%. The UK came in 65th in terms of turnout in a list of 163 countries for the 1990s (Electoral Commission, 2001). In fact it could be argued that in a relatively stable country politically, socially and economically, it's surprising that the majority of the electorate spend the time and effort in an activity were the outcome is usually decided before the exchange.

RESEARCH OBJECTIVES

The purpose of this article is to review the current literature regarding participation and non-participation in the UK from a political marketing perspective. In particular, this article reviews the current literature and details some of the output of primary research into the opinions and motivations of the electorate.

Specific issues dealt with include:

- turnout and party identification
- the role and opinions of the Electoral Commission
- all-postal voting and its effects and limitations
- multi-channel and electronic voting
- voting and non-voting behaviour
- the electorate's views on politicians, political parties and the political process

THE ELECTORAL COMMISSION

The Electoral Commission is an independent body set up in November 2000 by the Westminster parliament to encourage participation in the democratic process. Their brief is to:

- modernise the electoral system
- educate the electorate
- act as a regulator of political parties and the political process
- manage referendums
- advise on matters relating to political broadcasting

The Commission has consistently stated that changing the method of voting, whilst it may indeed increase participation, will not in itself address the underlying cause of falling turnouts. The factors influencing turnout are complex and multifaceted, however, the Commission blames politicians and political parties for the demise in participation. Politicians and political parties are the obvious scapegoats; however, other environmental factors may also contribute to the phenomena of non-voting:

- better (or worse) education
- media effects, particularly negative coverage
- an increasingly hedonistic society
- the lack of time in peoples' lives to engage
- increased apathy, disillusionment, lack of trust and scepticism among voters
- inability of voters to differentiate the products on offer (even if they are different)
- lack of reform of outdated electoral methods and systems
- alternative forms of entertainment
- a relatively stable democratic society
- decreasing strength of political alignment
- decrease in voting seen as a civic duty, particularly among the young

The Electoral Commission in their Report on the 2001 General Election said 'on the issues of voter turnout and engagement, it is above all the quality and persuasiveness of the policies put forward by the political parties and their ability to motivate voters that will determine future trends.'

The political parties failed to motivate the electorate.

Does the electorate engage with political policy? Political Marketing and Political Scientist authors don't believe that the majority of those who do vote actually engage with manifestos and political policy (Curtice et al., 1985; Pattie & Johnston, 2001; Wring, 1996; Egan et al., 2001; Bannon, 2001). What this situation creates is an uncertainty about the motives and actions of the electorate.

If political parties accept that it's not just about policy why do they persist in making comments like 'this election will be fought and won on the issues'?

Suggested reasons for political parties' failure to accept that voting is more than political policies are listed below:

- parties and politicians are steeped in policy, it's what they know, they don't know any other way
- the electorate expect to hear politicians talking policy
- politicians by nature want to involve themselves in policy making
- the alternative electoral motivators to policy are not generally their field of expertise, e.g., marketing, communications, media management, etc.
- alternative motivators are somehow unworthy, marketing is a dirty word and consumer psychology is even dirtier
- even if they accept that it's not about policy any more, they do not or cannot be seen to be embracing slick presentation, PR, spin doctors and marketing (even if they do)
- politicians and political parties have very strong cultures, they have ways of doing things and change comes slowly

In fact, in a way, it should be reassuring to the electorate that someone is concerned and interested in all those 'boring policy issues,' so they can get on with their lives. 'This election will be won or lost on spin doctoring or marketing strategy' does not have the same re-assuring tone. Tony Blair, Jack McConnell, Ian Duncan Smith, Charles Kennedy and John Swinney all have publicly denounced spin-doctors; all continue to use them.

In fact, does the current electoral system call into question the validity and mandate of those elected? In a letter to the Electoral Reform Society, George Reid, the Deputy Presiding Officer of the Scottish Parliament, stated that the system of electing MPs is failing electors and parties:

> *The fact that more than half of those who voted might just as well have stayed at home, must be a major reason for apathy. . . . their votes did not elect a single MP nor have any effect on the makeup of the commons . . . half of Scotland's MPs are now minority members. More people voted against them than for them in their constituencies.*

- *Labour took 78% of the seats with only 44% of the votes (32 MPs)*
- *The second party, the SNP took only 5 seats*
- *The third party, the Lib Dems took 10 seats*
- *The fourth party, the Conservatives, took only one seat, but had nearly as many votes as the Lib Dems*

The real losers are the people of Scotland. They did not get the representatives for whom they voted (Reid, 2001).

Voters will be less motivated if the system continues not to deliver the products and services that voters request. The counter argument may be that

- the current system is perceived as fair
- all candidates/parties choose to participate
- all are subject to the same rules

Two key questions need to be addressed

1. Is the electorate less interested in political matters?
2. Does the electorate identify less with traditional political parties?

The British Social Attitudes report of 2001 argues that political interest has remained stable over the period 1986 to 1999. Whilst political party identification has weakened, there has also been a small but significant increase in the percentage of the electorate who admit to having no party identification. The numerical values *have* changed from 8% in 1983 to 13% in 1999.

This complex area of study will be the focus of media, public, political and academic interest for many years to come.

ALL-POSTAL VOTING

All-postal voting in Scottish local government by-elections of 2002 recorded some impressive turnout figures. The Teith by-election on 18th April 2002 had a turnout of 63.2%, compared with 67.3% at the last local elections that coincided with the Scottish Parliamentary elections. Two other ward elections occurred on the same day, East Ayrshire, 44.8% and in Fife, 37.2%. In both of these by-elections the turnouts dropped 16% and 17% respectively. Whilst turnout in a ward by-election in the Banff and Buchan Constituency was 66%. These were high turnouts relative to all local authority elections in May 2002, where the average turnout was 32.8%. The average all-postal pilot elections were 47.5%, 15% higher than the average for conventional ballots. Turnout doubled in South Tyneside and almost doubled in Chorley, Gateshead and the pilot wards of Crawley. In 6 out of 10 pilot elections, costs were increased and sometimes quite substantially (Electoral Commission, 2002).

Firstly, you can no longer compare Scottish local government figures with English ones, as Scottish elections occur simultaneously with Scottish Parliamentary elections. This alignment of local elections with the greater participation in Scottish Parliamentary election, was specifically designed to increase turnout. Secondly, a ward by-election is not a normal local election.

Political parties will spend considerably more money and effort in enhancing their position. Thirdly, because the postal votes were available for completion 2 weeks before the day of the election, most of the political parties instigated a 2-week knock-up of the electorate. This is unlikely to happen under normal circumstances. The increased participation due to all-postal voting in local council by-elections could be due to a combination of eight effects:

- all-postal voting itself was more popular with the electorate than traditional polling station voting (in Teith 91% of the electorate were quite happy with all-postal voting: Stirling Council report for the Electoral Commission 18th April 2002)
- all-postal voting over a 2 week period, allowed voters more time to complete the ballot paper
- lower transaction costs in voting, i.e., ease of access to vote
- the effects of a high profile by-election campaign
- political parties conducted a 2 week knock-up; in some cases this was aided by the provision of daily marked-up electoral registers by local councils
- political parties assisted supporters to complete their voting papers and acted as witnesses
- political parties collected and returned postal votes
- local authorities publicised the all-postal ballot, e.g., Chorley council sent a reminder letter; 3 councils used a large thermometer outside their town halls to publicise daily how many votes had been returned

Three of these effects are directly attributable to the all-postal voting system and four are driven by political parties' activities due to an all-postal election. If postal voting is so popular amongst the electorate, then why was there such a poor take-up rate? Only 3.9% used a postal vote in the General Election of 2001. For the first time, anyone who wished a postal vote could apply without restrictions; most of the electorate didn't. Could issuing postal votes automatically to everyone whilst not making it the only method of voting, affect turnout? Applying for a postal vote was not considered by many of the electorate and filling in more forms was not deemed an attractive activity.

There are additional benefits of postal-only elections:

- no requirement for polling stations or staff
- no requirement for political parties to man polling stations
- lower transaction costs for everyone
- counting can be spread over a long period of time
- lost papers can be re-issued up to 5 pm on the final day for receipt of papers

Questions over fraud and equity have been aired. Most all-postal pilots used a declaration of identity form that may discriminate or put off the electorate from voting:

- single people living alone will find it more difficult to get a witness
- illiterate individuals will need help or avoid voting
- ethnic minorities or ESL may be less comfortable with the paperwork
- in some of the pilots, up to 5% of papers were rejected due to incomplete paperwork
- multiple occupancy houses, institutional care homes or apartments where there are communal mail areas, may allow access to voting papers that may be stolen or forged
- postal deliverers are not 100% perfect and seeking a re-issued paper will be inconvenient
- re-issue of post ballot papers ceases before the close of the election submission period
- some pilot wards used drop off delivery points, that were not evenly distributed and were not secure
- the transparency of the return envelopes may allow abuse
- validation of the declaration of identity cannot be achieved (anyone can sign), and thus its benefit is questionable (Interview 27.10.02)
- the declaration form breached confidentially (not that a secret ballot ever takes place)
- in some wards the ballet papers could easily be forged (Interview 28.10.02)
- in Teith, 22% of the electorate thought that all-postal voting was not secure (Stirling Council Report, 2002)

Source: Interviews (2002) & Electoral Commission Reports (2002)

MULTI-CHANNEL AND ELECTRONIC VOTING

A diverse range of methods of voting have been piloted:

- internet
- telephone
- text messages
- touch screen kiosks
- digital television

There is growing support among the electorate for alternative forms of voting being made available (KPMG, 2001). This is not to say that there is a demand from the electorate to use alternative methods, just that there is no strong wave of public opinion in favour of preserving the traditional election methodology. Uptake of alternative methods (apart from all-postal) in pilots was not huge. However they could grow rapidly as public confidence and awareness increases. Concerns over security and privacy were highlighted. There is a general misconception that traditional voting is a secret ballot. Interviewees were appalled to hear that their papers carried their voting number and that their vote could be traced back to them. Whilst historically the vast majority of voters were unaware of the potential for 'big brother to electorally spy,' there is concern over ensuring electoral integrity. Local Government Association research (2002) has identified various issues:

- the electorate's ability to accurately key in long pin numbers
- the stigmatisation of uses of traditional methods
- public confidence in electronic methods
- secrecy
- the greater suspicion of e-voting as compared with postal voting
- reliability of e-voting, e.g., service availability, viruses, hacking, power cuts, the system's capacity to cope, systems crash, confirmation of acceptance
- training to use new methods

Introducing new methods before public confidence is established could lead to undermining the integrity of the whole system and add to the catalogue of reasons for not voting. No one wants to participate in a system that is inherently unsound.

NON-VOTING BEHAVIOUR

There are 2 categories of non-voters, voluntary and involuntary abstainers (Johnston & Pattie, 1997). As the nomenclature suggests, involuntary is when a member of the electorate cannot vote for whatever reason and voluntary is when there is no obstacle to voting except the individual's motivation to so do.

Individuals may hold more than one reason for not voting and the strength of this motivation will vary. Further research is needed to identify and validate non-voting segments (NVS). Where possible the size of these segments and areas of overlap need to be quantified.

Non-participation may be caused by a variety of factors:

1. The electorate is relatively content and therefore is not motivated by the need for change.
2. The electorate is relatively content and does not see the need to defend the status quo.
3. The products on offer are perceived as being similar and a rational choice is not needed as all outcomes are acceptable. If a choice is not made, a product is still received.
4. None of the products on offer match the requirement of the vote, so the exchange of the vote is withheld (disillusionment, lack of trust).
5. Transaction costs are too high.
6. Non-voting occurs, not by choice, but by circumstance.
7. The voter may genuinely not be interested.
8. Literacy difficulties will obstruct participation.
9. Voting is perceived as not being able to influence the outcome, i.e., same party always wins or one vote doesn't matter.
10. Systemic failure prevents voting or indicates non-voting.
11. Not registered to vote

Source: Adapted from Bannon (2003).

The author rejects viewing the voting event as an unconnected, discrete transaction. Not all voters have a relationship with a political party or a candidate, however, to transact, a voter must possess some element of trust and/or commitment with whom they transact (Bannon, 2000; Bannon 2001; Franzio, 2000; Marquis 2001).

The process of choosing who to vote for occurs over a much longer period of time–in most cases over many years. The decision of whom to vote for (or not) and subsequent evaluation of that decision is a mystical process that political scientists have pondered for many generations.

The identification of psychographically developed segments would allow a prioritising of segments for marketing communication. In other words, instead of regarding non-voters as a homogeneous group, segments more susceptible to voting can be targeted with the intention of motivating this group to vote. Different non-voting segments (NVS) will probably require communication specifically designed and delivered for their requirements. For a psychographically developed NVS, the message, mode of delivery and style of communication is important if the objective is to successfully minimise and reduce non-voting behaviour. Is it possible to categorise non-voters into segments of similar motivation? Could segments judged to be easier to influence, be selected for intensive social marketing campaigns? If segments can be targeted to motivate buying behaviour, logically this could also be done for NVS:

Most conventional accounts of voting behaviour fit single models to the entire electorate, implicitly assuming that all voters respond to the same sets of influences, and do so in similar ways. However, a growing body of research suggests that this approach may be misleading and that distinct groups of voter approach politics and the electoral decision from different perspectives. (Pattie & Johnston &, 2001)

VOTING

Voting is a process as well as an event. A form of relationship usually exists between the process and each member of the electoral system. This relationship in the case of non-voters may be poor, inconsequential or non-existent. As Gronroos (1994) argues from a Relationship Marketing perspective, there exists a spectrum of strengths of relationships. There are several theories on voter behaviour. Like all motivational theory this remains a complex and difficult area to fully understand, however each theory allows a different insight into the behaviours and subsequent actions of voters. There are 6 major theories of voter choice, 3 deriving from political science and 3 from consumer buying behaviour (Denver, 1994; Kavanagh, 1997; Foxall, 1997; Smith et al. 1990).

1. The party identification theory
2. The social determinism theory
3. Issue voting
4. Expressive theory
5. Instrument theory
6. Interactionist theory

In viewing voter behaviour from a political science and marketing perspective we can identify considerable overlap and agreement. An important factor to highlight is that having a political preference is different from who you actually vote for, if you actually voted. In election campaign canvassing returns, only a small percentage of the electorate identify themselves as 'non-voters' or voice their intention not to vote (Interviews). Even if all identified 'don't knows' don't vote, this still does not represent the actual percentage of the electorate who actually don't vote, i.e., voters with a political preference also don't vote. 80% of voters identify with a political party (Kavanagh, 1997: 130), whilst only 60% vote. Whilst the percentage of the electorate who identify with a party remains high the strength of this party identification is reducing and voters are becoming more volatile, particularly the young (Denver, 1994; Kavanagh, 1997).

This identification means that aligned voters view everything a party does from a supporter's perspective, not an objective by-stander's position. Surveys have indicated that party allegiance tends to harden over time, even if their party is performing badly (Kavanagh, 1997:130).

There is also the issue of tactical voting. A voter may identify with a party but vote for their next preference party for tactical reasons or decide not to vote at all.

The *party identification theory* is easy to describe but not so easy to explain. A voter identifies with a party, *'I been Labour all me days'* or *'of course I always vote Tory'* (Interviews).

The concept of party identification derives from the 1950s and was first comprehensively covered in a classic book on Presidential elections, *The American Voter Today* (Campbell et al., 1960).

The concept argues that a voter will loosely, but potentially strongly, attach themselves to a political party depending on the 2 specific influencing factors, group membership and family influence. Party identification affects the voter by influencing the attitudes towards a party even without evaluation, analysis or rational judgement. These attitudes are developed based on the individual's perception of 3 factors:

1. The Candidate
2. The Policies
3. The links between parties and social groups (Harrop and Miller, 1987: 132).

Having aligned with a party the individual will believe that this chosen party will best represent their social interest group, even if there is no information on which to base this belief (Harrop and Miller, 1987).

If this is true, then what parties do or don't do becomes less relevant. It's like supporting a football team, win or lose; play well or badly you still support them. Without taking the analogy too far, teams who are playing badly have smaller turnouts. Their supporters don't change sides, they just turnout in lesser numbers. The role of Marketing in this instance is focused less on political persuasion and policy arguments and more encouraging and discouraging the individual voter from actually casting a vote. The interesting question is why do people support who they support? The Michigan model (1960) was the basis of this theory and suggests that long-term factors are at play.

The determinants of party identification are social in nature and long lasting. Factors such as interactions with family, friends, communities and organisations we belong to. The longer a party identification is held, the stronger it becomes (Harrop and Miller, 1987:133). As a consequence it is difficult to change allegiance. Party identification is not necessarily a logic-based decision and varies in intensity.

Children develop a basic party allegiance. This is predominately due to parental loyalty and this family influence continues throughout their life, weakening as the individual gets older. According to the Michigan theory this party identification makes it easy for the voter. Firstly the initial buying decision is copying people we trust and any subsequent buying decision is an automatic repeat purchase.

'The fact that party loyalty develops before policy preferences was a strong argument against the rational choice view that partisanship is a consequence of policy agreement between voter and party' (Harrop and Miller, 1987:136), i.e., voter's party loyalty occurs before any policy evaluation. Politicians reluctantly have to admit that it's the process that aligned the parents and grandparents that's delivering the support, not their current policy proposals.

It is arguable that an individual who is strongly aligned can be influenced to vote against their chosen party. They certainly, under normal circumstances, would not vote against their preferred party. Could demarketing influence their actions? For example, if they were persuaded that their preferred party was almost certainly going to win or lose they may be encouraged not to vote, i.e., 'inertia marketing' (Egan, 1999).

Party identification continues even under circumstances where a person votes for another party. A single issue or short-term influence may persuade the voter to vote against their usual party, however at subsequent elections the voter returns to voting in their traditional way. This is called the homing tendency (Harrop and Miller, 1987).

Whilst party identification remains high, the strength of the identification is rapidly reducing and thus the potential for persuasion increases with the potential number of less strongly committed voters increasing (Denver, 1994:54; Lees-Marshment, 2001:20). In fact party identification was relatively consistent from 1964-1992, both in overall percentage of the populace who identify with a party and the party they support as an aggregate (Table 2). However 1997 changed this situation and questions the validity of the view that party identification is long term in development and supports the view that the strength of party identification is reducing and voters are acting more like consumers.

Voter identification parallels and reflects closely the actual election result (exceptions in 1987 & 1992 possibly due to sampling error). 'The close tracking of changes in vote and party identification prompts acute suspicions about the validity of the standard questions about party identification. Do they measure long-term attachments or are they, for many respondents, simply an alternatively phased question about their immediate voting preferences? Does the very distinction between party identification and voting have any meaning for most voters?' (Evans & Norris, 1999).

Research in the States into monthly variations in the change of party identification, concluded that the responses in the survey were questionable as to their validity in reflecting long held political affiliation (Brynin & Sanders, 1993).

Parentage has a major influence on voter identification as demonstrated by Butler and Stokes (1974). Seventy-five percent of voters with both parents Conservative supporters, vote Conservative. This decreases to 37% if only one parent is a Conservative supporter. Similarly, 81% of voters with both parents Labour supporters, vote Labour. This decreases to 49% if one parent is a supporter. However more recent research suggests that voters are less likely to offer support to one particular party simply because their parents did (Lees-Marshment, 2001:21). This is supported by research conducted by Mori in 2003 that indicates a 67% and 62% support for Conservatives and Labour respectively if both parents support the same party (Mortimore & Tyrrel, 2003). As Sanders (1998:221) explains, 'variables closer to the voter may now have a greater impact on party preference than the sort of deep-seated factors such as class and party identification that lie further back in causal sequence.' As a consequence it might be argued that 'real issues' may influence voters' decisions in a more rational basis (Lees-Marshment, 2001:20). The counter argument is, of course, that this reduction in the importance of social class and party identification is also contributing to the electorate voting less and not necessarily causing or being caused by a greater awareness of political issues.

METHODOLOGY

Constructivism is based on induction, i.e., individual facts are pulled together in clusters to form manageable sets of generalisations which act as theories. A constructivist approach to research in most cases is more appropriate when studying behaviour from a phenomenological perspective. Qualitative research stresses the validity of multiple meaning structures and holistic analysis, as opposed to the criteria of reliability and statistical compartmentalisation of quantitative research (Burns, 2000).

The constructivist approach adopts an ontology and epistemology that does three things:

1. it puts weight and values the individuals view of the world and how they interpret events in their environment

2. it avoids searches for 'the truth' and instead focuses on socially agreed understanding. The onus is shifted to the researcher to be convincing as to the accuracy and value of their understanding, and knowledge proceeds by consensus
3. the approach 'facilitates the constant conscientious and careful monitoring of the person, social and situational factors which experience in the field under study suggest, may lead to a consensus which is likely to turn out to be unhelpful, biased, unreliable or tendentious' (Jankowicz, 2000: 118).

Research was conducted in the period May 2001 to February 2002 as a pilot study into voting and non-voting. The objective of the research was to build an overview of the electorate's views on politicians, political parties and the political process.

Various focus groups were established, some with participants who were experienced discussing political opinions and voting intentions with the electorate.

Four focus groups and 82 in-depth interviews form the basis of the following results.

Focus Group Composition

- 2 focus groups were students (1 undergraduate, 1 postgraduate)
- 1 focus group consisted of senior political campaign managers
- the final focus group was made up of political activists, local Councillors, an MSP and an MP

The interviews were conducted with politicians, political activists, political journalists, a political scientist and some members of the general public. The objective was not to select a representative sample of the Scottish public, but to take a constructivist approach to developing an overview of opinions.

RESEARCH RESULTS

Primary research conducted by the author allows insights into the electorates' views of politicians and political parties.

Overall they portray an unattractive image of politics, politicians and political parties:

- inability to differentiate the perceived products on offer (even if they are different)

- doing it the same old way
- lack of innovation which adds value
- failure to convey the importance of the process
- untrustworthy
- failure to create exciting enjoyable campaigns
- lack of on-going engagement with the electorate for the campaign
- failing to communicate to the ordinary voter
- being patronising and authoritative
- not doing things that are relevant
- perceptions of not delivering and not delivering
- viewed as 'self interested,' 'power crazy,' 'egotistical,' 'self opinionated toffs,' 'who play a game that is out of date' (Interviews)

Source: Interviews and Focus Groups (2002, 2003), Hansard Society (2002) & Electoral Commission Reports (2002)

The limitations of the research are 4 fold:

- qualitative in nature
- sample selected was not representative
- the sample may be responding in a manner which is socially desirable, posturing or rationally articulating irrational feelings
- the sample may be voicing an opinion based on little or no experience

CONCLUSIONS

Politicians are not marketers, but they may engage in a form of pseudo marketing or spin doctoring. However politics does need proper marketing, not just the cherry picking of tools from Marketing Communications Theory for Machiavellian purposes. Politics is in somewhat of a crisis, as demonstrated by the views of the electorate. Whilst interest in politics and party identification remains high, strength of identification and turnouts are down. Respect and trust of the process and politicians is decreasing. If politics were a commercial product, the Marketing Director would be replaced. According to the Electoral Commission only 10% of 18-25 year olds are very interested or interested in politics. This crisis is not a new malaise, however by its very nature, it is a dynamic and complex phenomena which requires a variety of research approaches. Increasing voting short term by increasing the choices available to potential voters as to how, where and when they vote is an honourable and decent initial first step, but it is not addressing the core causes of decreased engagement, only the symptoms of it.

REFERENCES

Bannon, D. (2000) 'Political Marketing: Plotting the development of political activity into an evolutionary framework.' In Proceedings of the UK Political Studies Association Media and Political Group in conjunction with the UK Academy of Marketing Special interest group on Political Marketing, Loughborough University, 2000.

Bannon, D. (2001) 'Political Marketing as Social Marketing: if the cap fits.' In. Proceedings of the 4th annual conference of the Political Marketing Group of the UK. Academy of Marketing, Dublin City University, 6-8th September.

Bannon, D. (2003) 'Voting, Non-Voting and Consumer Buying Behaviour: non-voter segmentation and the underlining causes of electoral inactivity' *Journal of Public Affairs*, Volume 3, Number 2, pp. 138-155.

Barnes, L. B. (1981) 'Managing a paradox of organisational trust' *Harvard Business Review*, March/April, 107-116.

Barnes, J. (1994) 'Close to the customer: but is it a relationship?' *Journal of Marketing Management*, 10, 561-570.

Barnes, J. G. (1995) 'Establishing Relationships–getting closer to the customer may be more difficult than you think' *Irish Marketing Review*, V8, pp. 107-116.

Berry, L. (2001) 'Voting via internet may be on its way,' *Denver Business Review·*9th February.

Birmingham Business Journal (2001) 'Voter turnout is the real issue,' 20th April.

Black, A. (2001) 'Non-voting is partly fuelled by the new generation of hedonism.' *Financial Times*, 14th June 2001.

Bromley, C.; Curtice, J.& Seyd, B. (2001) 'Political engagement, trust and constitutional reform' *British Social Attitudes*, 18th Report, pp. 199-223.

Brynin, M. & Sanders, D.1993 'Party identification, political preferences and material conditions,' *Party Politics*, 3: 53-77.

Butler, D. (2001) 'Tactical voting and turnout,' *Financial Times*, 28th May.

Butler, D. (1996) 'Elections in Britain Today,' *Dick Leonard*, pp. ix.

Butler, D. and Stokes, D. (1974) *Political Change in Britain*: 2nd edn, MacMillan.

Campbell, A.; Converse, P.; Miller, W. E. and Stokes, D. (1960) *The American Voter*, New York: Wiley.

Crewe, I. (1981) Why the Conservatives Won, In *Britain at the Polls* 1979 ed. Howard Penniman. Washington, DC: American Enterprise Institute.

Crewe, I. (1985) Great Britain. In *Electoral change in Western Democracies*, eds. Ivor Crewe and David Denver, London: Croom.

Crewe, I. (1992) 'Changing votes and unchanging voters.' *Electoral Studies*, 11: 33-45.

Crewe, I. & Thomson, K. (1999) Party Loyalties: dealignment or realignment? in *Critical Elections*, London: Sage.

Curtice, J. (2001) 'Repeat or Revolution,' *Politics Review*, Vol. 11, No. 1, pp. 2-5.

Denver, D. (1994) *Elections and Voting Behaviour in Britain*, 2nd edition, Sussex: Harvester-Wheatsheaf.

Denver, D. (2003) *Elections and Voters in Britain*, Palgrave, Basingstoke.

Downs, A. (1952) *An economic theory of democracy*, New York: Harper and Row.

Dwyer, F. ; Schurr, P. & Oh, S. (1987) ' Developing Buyer-Seller Relationships,' *Journal of Marketing*, Vol. 51, pp. 11-27.

Egan, J. (1999), 'Political Marketing: Lessons from the mainstream,' *Journal of Marketing Management* 1999: 15, 495 -503.

Egan, J.; Lynch. R. & Baines, P. (2001) 'Competitive Advantage, Strategic Resources and Political Campaigning: A Resource-Based perspective. In Proceedings of the 4th annual conference of the Political Marketing Group of the UK Academy of Marketing, Dublin City University, 6-8th September.

Election Commission Report (2001) *'Election 2001 The Official Results,'* Politico's Publishing.

Election Commission Report (2002) *'Modernising Elections: A strategic evaluation of the 2002 electoral pilot schemes,* Aug.

Festinger, L. (1957) *'A theory of cognitive dissonance.'* Stanford, CA: Stanford University Press.

Franzio, S. (2000) ' *Social Psychology'* 2nd ed. McGraw-Hill.

Franklin, M. (1985) *'The Decline of Class Voting in Britain.'* Oxford Press.

Gott, R. (2001) ' I shall not vote,' *Guardian*, 7th June.

Grayson, K. & Ambler, T. (1999) 'The dark side of Long-Term Relationships in Services Marketing,' *Journal of Marketing Research*, Vol. XXXV1, 132-141.

Gronroos, C. (1994) 'From the marketing mix to relationship marketing,' *Management Decision*, 32(2), 1994, pp. 4-20.

Gummesson, E. (1995) 'Broadening and specifying Relationship Marketing,' *Asia-Australian Marketing Journal*, Vol. 2, No. 1, pp. 31-43.

Gummesson, E. (1997) 'In search of Marketing Equilibrium: Relationship Marketing versus Hypercompetition,' *Journal of Marketing Management*, 13, pp. 421-430.

Gummesson, E. (1997) 'Relationship Marketing–The Emperor's new clothes or a paradigm shift? *Marketing and Research Today*, Feb. pp. 53-60.

Gummesson, E. (1998) 'Implementation requires a Relational Marketing Paradigm' *Journal of the Academy of Marketing Science*, Vol. 26, pp. 242-249.

Hansard Society Briefing (2002) *'None of the Above: Non-voters and the 2001 election.*

Harker, M. (1999) 'Relationship Marketing defined? an examination of current relationship marketing definitions' *Marketing Intelligence and Planning*, Vol. 17, Issue 1.

Harrop, M. and Miller, W.L. (1987) *'Elections and voters. A comparative introduction'* Basingstoke: MacMillan.

Heath, A.; Jowell, R. and Curtice, S. (1985) *'How Britain votes,'* London: Pergamam.

Hertz, N. (2001) 'Why consumer power is not enough,' *New Statesman* 30th April.

Himmelweit, H. et al. (1978) 'Memory for past vote,' *British Journal of Political Science*, 8, 8, 365-384.

Himmelweit, H. ; Humpheys & Jaeger (1985) *'How voters decide,'* O.U. Press 1985.

Hunt, S. (1997) 'Competing through Relationships: Grounding Relationship Marketing in Resource-Advantage Theory,' *Journal of Marketing Management*, 13, pp. 431-445.

Jackson, B. B. (1985) 'Building customer relationships that last,' *Harvard Business Review*, Vol. 63, pp. 120-128.

Kavanagh, D. (1995) *'Election Campaigning–the new marketing of politics,'* pp. 11, Blackwell.

Kavanagh, D. (1997) 'The Labour Campaign,' Vol. 50, *Parliamentary Affairs*, pp. 533.

Lees-Marshnent, J. (2001) *'Political Marketing and British political parties,'* Manchester University Press.

Marquis, S. (2001) 'UK political apathy reveals an important lesson for marketers,' *Marketing*, 14th June.

Morgan, R. M. & Hunt, S. (1994) 'The commitment-trust theory of Relationship Marketing, *Journal of Marketing*, Vol. 58, pp. 20-38.

Mote. D. (2000) *New Scientist*, 17th March, pp. 19.

Nucifora, A. (2001) 'Let Marketers run the voting system and polling procedures,' *Capital District Business Review*, 26th February.

Palmer, A. (2000) *'Marketing,'* Oxford, pp. 11-14.

Pare, M. (2001) 'Getting out the vote worked here; elsewhere? *Providence Business News*, 29th January.

Pattie, C. & Johnston, R. (2001) 'A Low Turnout Landslide: Abstention at the British General Election of 1997,' *Political Studies*, Vol. 49, 286-305.

Reed Elsevier Business Publishing, Ltd. (2001) 'E-voting–yes please,' *Computer Weekly*, 10th May.

Reid, G. (2001) ' Failing the Voters' Bridge of Allan, *SNP Newsletter*, July.

Rose, R. and McAllister (1986) *'Voters begin to choose,'* London: Sage.

Rose, R. and McAllister (1990) *'The loyalty of voters,'* London: Sage.

Smith, G. & Saunders, J. (1990) 'The application of Marketing to British Politics.' *Journal of Marketing Management*, No. 3, pp. 295-306.

Taylor Nelson Sofres (2001) 'Voters pledge to turn out in force at polling booths,' *Marketing*, June 7th, pp. 1.

Tomer, J. (1998) 'Beyond transaction markets, towards relationship marketing in the human firm: a socio-economic model,' *Journal of Socio-Economics*, March-April 1998.

Urken, A. (2001) 'Technology alone can't fix voting problems,' *Computerworld*, 5th March.

White, D. (2001) 'First past the post poll system,' *Financial Times*, 7th June.

Wolfe, D. (1998) 'Developmental relationship marketing (connecting messages with mind: an emphatic marketing system)' *Journal of Consumer Marketing*, Vol. 15, Issue 5.

Young, H. (2001) 'Politicians treat voters as idiots,' *Guardian*, 25th May.

Younge, G. (2001) 'Vanishing voters,' *Guardian*, 5th February.

Young People's Attitudes
Towards British Political Advertising:
Nurturing or Impeding Voter Engagement?

Janine Dermody
Richard Scullion

SUMMARY. This article presents findings from a national survey of 'potential' first time voters at the 2001 British General Election–specifically their attitudes towards the print advertising used by the main political parties during this election. In analysing the data, the authors were particularly interested in examining the claim that political advertising contributes to a sense of malaise–most acutely apparent among young people. While we found high levels of claimed advertising awareness, this was coupled with largely unfavourable attitudes towards most of the print advertising used in the election. Despite these judgements, most young people considered the advertising to be at least as persuasive as its commercial cousins. Not surprisingly the evidence provides a mixed picture in terms of the role political advertising plays in the political dis-

Janine Dermody is Senior Lecturer in Marketing, Business School, University of Gloucestershire, Park Campus, The Park, Cheltenham, Gloucestershire, GL50 2QF, UK (E-mail: jdermody@glos.ac.uk).

Richard Scullion is Senior Lecturer of Marketing Communications, The Media School, Bournemouth University, Talbot Campus, Fern Barrow, Poole, Dorset, BH12 5BB, UK (E-mail: rscullio@bournemouth.ac.uk).

[Haworth co-indexing entry note]: "Young People's Attitudes Towards British Political Advertising: Nurturing or Impeding Voter Engagement?." Dermody, Janine, and Richard Scullion. Co-published simultaneously in *Journal of Nonprofit & Public Sector Marketing* (Best Business Books, an imprint of The Haworth Press, Inc.) Vol. 14, No. 1/2, 2005, pp. 129-149; and: *Current Issues in Political Marketing* (eds: Walter W. Wymer, Jr., and Jennifer Lees-Marshment) Best Business Books, an imprint of The Haworth Press, Inc., 2005, pp. 129-149. Single or multiple copies of this article are available for a fee from The Haworth Document Delivery Service [1-800-HAWORTH, 9:00 a.m. - 5:00 p.m. (EST). E-mail address: getinfo@haworthpressinc.com].

129

positions of young people. As a familiar discourse advertising offers the political classes an entry point to establish a dialogue with young sections of the electorate. However, for many young people, political advertising appears to help reinforce their predilection about politics being something one naturally distrusts. *[Article copies available for a fee from The Haworth Document Delivery Service: 1-800-HAWORTH. E-mail address: <docdelivery@haworthpress.com> Website: <http://www.HaworthPress.com> © 2005 by The Haworth Press, Inc. All rights reserved.]*

KEYWORDS. Election campaigns, electoral malaise, liberal democracy, negative political advertising, political advertising, political attitudes, political cynicism, political distrust, voter engagement, youth voting

INTRODUCTION

Increasingly, politicians appear to be encountering greater difficulties in communicating with the British electorate through mass advertising (Bromley et al. 2001; Bromley and Curtice 2002). Electoral malaise seems to be on the increase–manifest in low voter turnout at recent elections–coupled with a growing sense of cynicism towards political actors and disengagement with political systems and institutions. The apparent rise in young people's awareness of and cynicism towards advertising activity compounds the difficulties facing election campaigners. This challenge was further magnified by the events leading up to the 2001 British general election–creating a exigent environment for the advertising agencies tasked with creating the ad campaigns (Table 1).

The advertising campaigns we are discussing here are outlined in detail in Dermody and Scullion (2001a). In essence a confident Labour party were quite innovative with an up-beat advertising strategy reminding people how things were improving. They used humour in the best remembered ad of the campaign showing William Hague wearing a Margaret Thatcher hairstyle 'wiggy' and a pastiche of a blockbuster film in others. The Conservatives started by attacking the incumbent's policies in public services delivery, but them seemed to move onto narrower ground with ads focusing on saving the pound and asylum. They ended up accepting defeat in their last ad that simply called for voters to reduce the expected Labour majority. The Liberal Democrats used their advertising to promote awareness of their then new leader–

TABLE 1. Characterising the 2001 British General Election

The Macro Climate	The Micro Climate
A strong economy	Ad spending regulated for first time
Relatively new incumbent government	Ad content unregulated for first time–only requirement was for the ad sponsor to be shown
A main opposition party widely reported as weak	Party attachment and identification weakening
Election delay from foot and mouth crisis–led to additional month of ad spending on poster sites	Low public trust in political parties
	Public apathy–obvious election outcome
	A non-event–low levels of emotional interest, perceived importance and salience among the electorate

Source: adapted from Dermody, J. and Scullion, R., (2001), An Exploration of the Advertising Ambitions and strategies of the 2001 British General Election, Journal of Marketing Management, Vol.17, No. 9-10, 969-987.

Charles Kennedy. Near the end of the campaign they switched focus, calling for more spending on public services, more in the style of a pressure group than a party hoping to gain power.

In this paper, we analyse the election advertising as a form of direct, unmediated, sponsor- biased communications–a type of communication that has, in the past, been shown to exert a powerful influence (Kaid 1999, Hall Jamieson 1992).

We begin by examining key facets of the literature pertinent to this area, before moving on to discuss the design, findings and implications of our empirical research.

EXPLORING POLITICAL ADVERTISING AND VOTER ENGAGEMENT: AN OVERVIEW OF THE EVIDENCE

Marketing reported, just prior to the 2001 General Election, that both younger voters and women were the most likely sections of the electorate to agree that advertising might sway their voting intentions (Marketing front cover, May 17 2001). It would therefore appear that political advertising campaigns have the potential to engage young voters. Studies looking at young peoples attitudes towards advertising in general indicate that they hold more favourable attitudes towards it than older people (O'Donohoe 1997; Shavitt et al. 1998). Additionally literature suggests young people appoint a central role for advertising–ranging from helping them to make choices to aiding social interaction, (Nava and Nava 1990; O'Donohoe 1994). There is also widespread evidence of attitudes towards the advertising (Aad) influencing attitudes towards the sponsoring brand and purchase intentions (see Alwitt and Mitchell 1992). Within a political context, young peoples' attitudes towards the advertising may well be influencing their perceptions of politicians and parties, thereby influencing their voting intentions. Consequently investigating their attitudes towards political advertising will provide some insight into the future role advertising might play within campaign strategy.

However western political advertising, particularly those ads that personally attack political candidates, has been charged with of contributing to political disengagement–an increasing societal trend among western democratic publics, culminating in non-voting behaviour. This trend is most apparent in the US, (Boylan 1991; Miron 1999; Teixeira 1992), but it is also becoming increasingly visible in the UK. This is not surprising given attack advertising is widely used in US and UK campaigning (Butler and Kavanagh 1997; Hall Jamieson 1992).

Commenting on the 1996 presidential campaign, which witnessed the lowest voter turnout for 72 years, Curtice Gans states, categorically, attack advertising was the major culprit:

> The trouble . . . was not with the candidates but with their greater-than-ever dependence on the negative advertising that was flooding the airwaves. The mudslinging disgusted the public to a point where more than half of the eligible voters simply washed their hands of the whole business and stayed at home on election day. (Curtice Gans [American Political Consultant], cited in Germond and Witcover, 1996, 2562)

The 2001 British general election witnessed the lowest voter turnout ever recorded in the UK–at 59.4%. The overall turnout in 2001 was approximately 12% below that of 1997 (71.2%), which in turn was 6.5% below 1992 turnout (77.7%), which, in turn, was the lowest since 1935 (Butler and Kavanagh 1997/). Non-voting therefore seems to have accelerated in the UK in recent years.

Focusing on young members of the electorate, this emerging trend is particularly worrying for campaign strategists, where potentially a whole lifetime of voting and political participation could be lost from younger generations. There is already evidence of this from the 2001 voting figures–where according to MORI's most senior pollsters–Robert Worcester and Roger Mortimore–only 39% of 18-24 year olds voted (Worcester and Mortimore 2001; Electoral Commission 2001; King 2002). The MORI results also confirm that 18-24 year olds are much more likely to opt out of the electoral process than other age groups. Research by Gallup on the day of the 1997 British General Election reported that only 57% of 18-24 year olds said they would definitely vote, compared with 86% of 45-64 year olds. While findings from the 1999 British Social Attitude Survey reported that 44% of 18-24 year olds said they voted in the 1997 election, compared with 64% of 25-34 year olds (Park 1999). This indicates a decline in voting among this age group between the period 1997 and 2001. In addition the evidence suggests that young people are more politically alienated than older adults (Mulgan and Wilkinson 1997); that a widening gap in political interest exists between 18-24 year olds and older adults (25+ years) (Park 1999); and significantly fewer young adults view voting as a civic duty compared with older adults (based on MORI data from the Hansard society; Bromley and Curtice 2002; Park 1999).

Given that voting is essentially at the core of political participation in a democracy, this steady decline in turnout is perturbing. Non-voting destabilizes democracy because it undermines the legitimacy of elected political leaders, (Miron 1999). This threat is compounded by an international millennium survey by Gallup International, where western publics expressed some very pessimistic attitudes towards the well-being of democracy, particularly among those aged under 30 (Spogard and James 2000). Clearly the reasons for this feeling of 'democratic drift' are manifold, so why has so much blame been attributed to negative political advertising?

The inherent nature of negative advertising does little to portray the act of political consumption in a positive light, instead it creates a climate of public apprehension and suspicion where malicious attacks on political candidates reputation are the norm (Dermody and Scullion 2001). Ansolabehere et al. (1994, 829) stress these ads are designed to 'criticize, discredit, or belittle their opponents rather than promoting their own ideas and programs.' James and Hensel (1991, 55) argue negative political ads 'Impute inferiority, denigrate or destroy the competitions image; they are malicious, vicious and violate 'fair play'.

Portrayal of candidates in this way may well be signalling to a non-partisan electorate that all the candidates lack the integrity needed to govern, they therefore reject them. Or it may cause partisan voters to feel uncomfortable with the behaviour of their candidates. Having the failings of all competing parties and candidates highlighted to them in this aggressive manner, it isn't surprising that some of the electorate believe they are behaving responsibly in not voting for any of them.

Critics of negative advertising therefore maintain it demobilises voters by creating voter cynicism and apathy, in turn eroding public confidence in political institutions and the process of western political democracy itself, (Ansolabehere et al. 1999; Ansolabehere and Iyengar 1995; Banker 1992; Germond and Witcover 1996; Kahn and Kenney 1999; Kates 1998; Taylor

1990). Research into UK youth indicates the strength of this disaffection among this age group, (see Park 1999; Pirie and Worcester 2000; Russell et al. 2002; Mulgan and Wilkinson 1997). The consequences are an increasing sector of the electorate who distrust all political candidates and parties, and who have lost faith in the process of democracy, (expressed through their non-voting), not necessarily the ideal of it. Without trust, it is unlikely that voter participation will increase, instead it will continue to decline, in time making a mockery of the very process by which we elect governments. There is certainly evidence of this in the research of Pirie and Worcester (2000), Spogard and James (2000), and White et al. (2000). These views are also echoed in a study of British attitudes towards the advertising used in the 1997 British General Election, which was essentially negative in tone. Highly informed and involved respondents, (typically political party members), found the ads irritating and patronizing, there was very little communication they felt was targeting them, (Dermody and Scullion, 2000). As Hall Jamieson (1992, 237) states, 'how we elect is as important as who we elect,' a healthy process facilitates public participation, it successfully communicates the "who," "what" and "how" of governance, thereby allowing the electorate to take responsibility for and ratify their own futures.

However not all analysis of negative political advertising suggests it has such damaging consequences, it also appears to have some potential benefits. These include the added weight it is accorded by audiences (Pinkleton 1997), the higher levels of memorability it elicits (Carlston 1980), and the greater accessibility it provides to the content of the message (Fazio and Williams 1986). Further, the younger electorate are very familiar with advertising (Wernick 1991), avoid it less (Danaher 1995), and appreciate its multiple uses (O'Donohoe 1997). Finally a study of the 1997 British General Election found that those with low involvement in politics tended to judge the advertising as informative and useful (Dermody and Scullion 2000).

In conclusion, given the somewhat contradictory evidence on the impact of advertising on voter engagement, this study sought to outline first time voters attitudes towards the political advertising used during the 2001 General Election, thereby attempting to establish some kind of 'base line' of young people's attitudes towards political advertising in order to aid evaluation of the claims and counter claims made about it.

RESEARCH DESIGN

Specifically, this empirical study aimed to examine some of the issues surrounding electoral malaise and cynicism amongst young British adults, set against a backdrop of the advertising campaigns employed in the 2001 British General Election campaign. This involved a multi-method approach involving a content analysis of the national advertising campaigns, depth interviews with the advertising agencies responsible for the ad campaigns, and a survey and focus group interviews with 18-22 year old British citizens. This paper presents some of the findings from the survey research–specifically young people's attitudes towards the styles of advertising in the Labour, Conservative and Liberal Democrat campaigns.[1] Accounts of young people's awareness of the advertising can be found in Dermody and Scullion (2003), advertising strategies (Dermody and Scullion 2001), and a content analysis of the party election broadcasts in Scullion and Dermody (2003).

A quasi-random sampling approach was adopted for the survey. A filtering system was used to ensure all respondents were British Citizens aged between 18-22–the interview was terminated if they did not conform to this criterion. The survey involved street intercept interviews–using an interviewer-administered questionnaire. The survey took place in principle towns in geographic regions throughout the UK, during the three-week period following the general election in June 2001. Once this time period ended all survey data collection ceased, giving a total of 867 useable questionnaires.

The survey questions were based on key issues arising from the literature and previous research, and primary qualitative research. Two exploratory focus groups were carried out to examine these emerging issues more deeply and to highlight any further issues that had been overlooked. The questionnaire was fully piloted and revised prior to the survey commencing. The question style essentially consisted of attitudinal scales (Likert and semantic differential) aiming to provide general and ad specific judgments, print ad awareness questions, and classification questions. SPSS was used to analyse the survey data.

Finally in order to aid understanding of the survey findings, a profile of our respondents is presented in appendix 1, alongside corresponding national average profiles. In essence our sample was equally mixed in terms of gender; contained a mix of students, employed and unemployed respondents; approximately half of the respondents were aged 21-22 years; over half of our respondents claimed they voted; the majority classified themselves as 'White British,' and were educated to GCSE standard, with a large cluster also holding A/AS qualifications. The majority of students in the sample were reading for their first degree. Comparing our sample against the national profile–there is a marginal bias towards students, young people who claimed they voted and alleged Labour supporters–overall, our respondent "fit" is reasonably tight, confirming the robustness of findings from our reasonably large sample of 867 respondents.

ATTITUDES TOWARDS THE PRINT ADVERTISING:
FINDINGS AND ANALYSIS

Before presenting our attitudinal findings, it is first necessary to give an overview of the degree of ad awareness upon which these judgments are based. Clearly if our respondents had seen very little of the advertising, our attitudinal findings would have to be treated with caution. However, our respondents' unprompted, claimed awareness of the print advertising was high–84.5% maintained they seen the poster advertising and 69% the newspaper advertising. Overall more respondents had seen more of the poster ads than newspaper ads–not surprising when we consider there was significantly more poster advertising in the 2001 election, and a much smaller amount of newspaper advertising compared with previous elections. Having established that the ads did appear to penetrate young people's awareness thresholds, our attitudinal results will now be presented.

Overall Perceptions: Personality or Policy?

Asked whether they considered the advertising was mainly about the policies, candidates' personalities or a mixture of the two, 36.6% of our respondent's maintained personalities and 38.4% considered them to be a balance between personality and policy. Only 7.9% maintained they were mostly about policies (Figure 1).

Given that advertising content analysis of both previous elections (Hodess et al. 2000) and the 2001 election (Dermody and Scullion 2001a) show an actual bias towards a policy orientation in the party advertising, these findings might appear peculiar. MORI's findings (2001) give us some clues as to why this might be when they talk of a public who want both more candidate *and* policy information not just policy information. These overall judgements in terms of policy/personality dimensions do indicate a degree of perceived *'personalisation'* of politics, but the figures indicate that many young members of the electorate do not consider the advertising to be as heavily skewed as many political commentators suggest (Gould 1998; Jones 1997)–with nearly 40% thinking they were 'balanced.' Whether these assessments come purely from the ads themselves, is debatable, since media coverage of the election itself may well have influenced our respondents judgements. However given the bias of media coverage towards "spin" during the election campaign, (Dermody and Scullion, 2001; 2003), it is perhaps surprising that more of our respondents did not judge the ads to be more about personality than policy. This suggests that while the media may have been influential, other factors were probably at work too at both a conscious and subconscious level.

FIGURE 1. Overall Perceptions of the Election Print Advertising

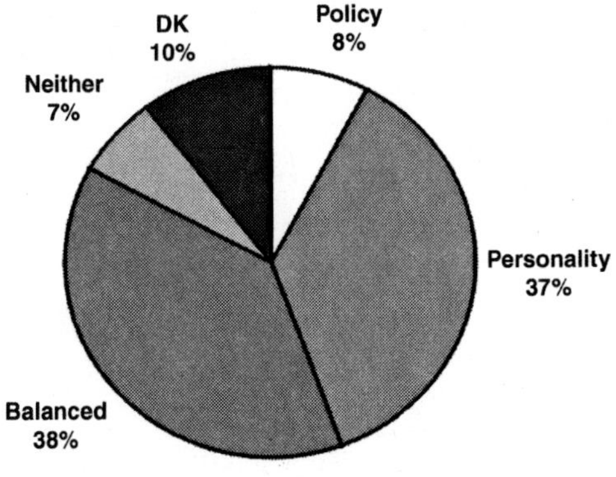

Judging the "Worthiness" of the Print Advertising

Respondents who maintained they had seen the print advertising were also asked to give their overall impressions of it from a list of ten adjectives ranging from helpful to persuasive (Figure 2).

While some of their judgements of the advertising were mixed–boring, irritating, patronising, hypocritical and irrelevant particularly, overall the judgment of the advertising was negative. A large majority of the sample regarded them as unhelpful (78.6%), untrustworthy (84.4%), dishonest (79.8%) and unpersuasive (75.6%).

Of particular importance here is the fact that so few respondents regarded the advertising as *honest* or *trustworthy*. These attributes may well act as gatekeepers as suggested in the literature on advertising (Mittal 1994; Shavitt et al. 1998), relationship marketing (Morgan and Hunt 1994) and source credibility (Hovland et al. 1953; Miller 1987). Messages audiences believe to be dishonest and untrustworthy are unlikely to be fully attended to, (Pollay and Mittal 1993), and the message sources treated with suspicion (Hovland et al. 1953; Miller 1987; Perloff 1994). Evidence from studies on the attitudes of young people towards advertising in general, which presents a more positive picture than that indicated in Figure 2, indicate clear contextual effects taking place. Given the widespread media coverage of politics as sleazy and lacking conviction, (Oborne 1999; Parris 2001; Tempest 2001), perhaps this backdrop causes part of this interpretation of the ad–a stance of: "they are politicians, it must be deceitful." It is therefore to be expected that young voters did not generally find the ads particularly helpful. Nevertheless, the severity of their judgements

FIGURE 2. Overall Judgements of the Print Advertising

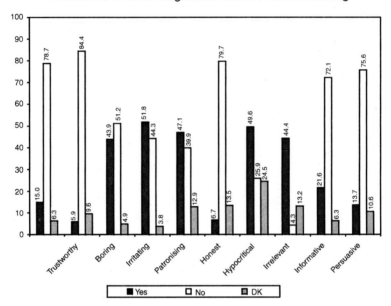

is noteworthy. Perceived trustworthiness and honesty are critical elements of promotional communication, and indeed all facets of marketing, without them the ads are likely to have a minimal role in aiding young voters decision-making, thereby making them seem pointless. It is therefore not surprising that the majority of our respondents–66.3%–maintained the print advertising did not influence their voting behaviour at all.

These judgements may, as outlined above, simply mirror a wider distrust of political parties, but they may also be reinforcing and fuelling negative evaluations, thus contributing to more negative attitudes towards party politics and participation among young people. There was some evidence of this 'fuelling effect' in our qualitative research. Prior research also supports this proposition (Ansolabehere and Iyengar 1995; Kline 1997; West 1997). These unintended consequences need to be considered by both political parties and their ad agencies, since this 'cycle of cynicism' necessitates communication that highlights the value of elections and political participation in liberal democracies; and it perhaps needs to be done outside political party campaigns to prevent the messages becoming tangled within party agendas. The "Rock the Vote" event in 1997 and the 'votes are power' campaign (Electoral Commission) are examples attempting to engage young people with politics.

What might the consequences have been of a party-neutral campaign, prior to the 2001 election, which actively promoted the benefits of the electorate paying close attention to the political advertising they were about to be exposed to? Would it too have been tarnished with the 'it is politics so it cannot be trusted' syndrome? Although not party neutral, Labour's 2001 election strategy did attempt to address voter apathy, partially through their use of spoof film ads perceived to be "for us" by young people, (Dermody and Scullion 2001a). So here is an example of a political ad that might have gone some way to break the young people's cycle of political cynicism.

The view that the ads were not informative, expressed by 72.1% of our sample, coupled with over 50% saying the ads were not boring, strikes a chord with MORI (2001) findings, which found that the electorate in general, and young people specifically, did not view the election to be as boring as many commentators suggested. However, they wanted more messages that they considered to be informative. This request for more informative political ads may signal that young people are not completed alienated from electoral politics and would welcome more information from a variety of sources. This implies a need by those responsible for political advertising to investigate the precise nature of the information young people require. It may require less obvious political sponsorship of the messages in order to overcome the dishonest/untrustworthy gatekeeper effect discussed earlier. One further observation on these judgements–while 75.6% found the advertising unpersuasive, the fact that 13.7% found it persuasive is actually a robust figure when compared to findings related to advertising in general, which tends to suggest between 10-15% of consumers are willing to admit that advertising has a persuasive effect, (Marketing 2001; Perlof 1993; Shavitt et al. 1998). Balanced against the significantly negative attitudes outlined earlier, it is surprising that any young voters found the advertising persuasive.

The Relationship Between Attitudes Towards the Print Advertising and Ad Awareness

Table 2 illustrates judgement of the advertising in relation to degree of poster ad awareness. Claimed Ad awareness was highest for posters, hence our focus on it here. In many cases Table 2 illustrates that the advertising judgements are more positive with higher claimed awareness and more negative with lower claimed awareness.

The large cluster of respondents, who regarded the advertising as unhelpful, untrustworthy, dishonest, uninformative, and unpersuasive, had a lower degree of claimed awareness of the poster advertising than those who judged the

TABLE 2. Overall Judgements of the General Election Poster Advertising by Ad Awareness

JUDGEMENTS	POSTER ADVERTISING AWARENESS							
POSITIVE	A Lot		Moderate		Few		Total	
	N	%	N	%	N	%	N	%
Helpful*	46	40.7	47	41.5	20	17.7	113	15.0
Trustworthy	16	35.5	18	40.0	11	24.4	45	5.9
Not Boring*	116	30.0	149	38.5	113	29.2	387	51.2
Non-Irritating	101	30.1	124	37.0	96	28.6	335	44.3
Non-Patronising*	83	27.5	100	33.1	103	34.1	302	39.9
Honest*	25	49.0	16	31.3	10	19.6	51	6.7
Not Hypocritical	60	30.6	73	37.2	56	28.5	196	25.9
Relevant	94	29.3	120	37.5	95	29.7	320	42.3
Informative*	55	33.7	58	35.6	48	29.4	163	21.6
Persuasive*	41	39.4	40	38.4	20	19.2	104	13.7
NEGATIVE								
Unhelpful*	139	23.3	229	38.4	204	34.3	595	78.7
Untrustworthy	167	26.1	248	38.9	200	31.3	638	84.4
Boring*	71	21.3	129	38.8	115	34.6	332	43.9
Irritating	89	22.7	158	40.3	134	34.1	392	51.8
Patronising*	95	26.7	155	43.5	99	27.8	356	47.1
Dishonest*	150	24.9	243	40.3	187	31.0	603	79.7
Hypocritical	96	25.6	157	41.9	109	29.1	375	49.6
Irrelevant	84	25.0	129	38.4	112	33.3	336	44.4
Uninformative*	135	24.7	217	39.8	173	31.7	545	72.1
Unpersuasive*	132	23.0	224	39.1	197	34.4	572	75.6
TOTAL AWARENESS	195	22.5	297	34.3	240	27.7	732	84.4

Notes: 135 respondents excluded from this question because they had not seen any of the poster ads. Don't know excluded from table.
Independent variable = Judgment: column % calculated – N divided by row total, i.e. 46/113 = 40.7%.
* = Statistically significant at 0.05% (2-tailed).

ads less harshly. The smaller proportion of respondents, who perceived the advertising to be helpful, trustworthy, honest, informative, and persuasive, had a higher degree of claimed awareness of the poster advertising. Clearly what seems to be emerging here is more positive judgements of the advertising—helpful, trustworthy, honest, informative, persuasive—with higher awareness, and more negative judgements of the advertising—unhelpful, untrustworthy, dishonest, uninformative, unpersuasive—with lower awareness of the advertising. This is illustrated in Figure 3. This relationship also appeared to exist for those who judged the ads as (not) boring, or irrelevant. However for these variables, with their lower chi square values, the relationship is less clear.

Figure 3 illustrates that many young people were engaged in some form of selective perception, with those least disposed to the advertising most likely to avoid it. However, we cannot dismiss the possibility that for some young people, the early advertising they were exposed to stimulated their desire to be exposed to yet more. Certainly there is evidence, from our qualitative research, that young people were attracted Labour's '*Economic Disaster II*' spoof Hollywood movie-style posters because they were novel and seemed to be aimed specifically at them. This may have important implications for future segmentation and timing issues of political advertising campaigns.

Party Specific Attitudinal Judgements of the Print Advertising

Finally, those respondents who had seen the advertising were asked to rate the advertising of the three major British political parties—Labour, Conservative and Liberal Democrats across a very positive to very negative spectrum (Figure 4).

Beginning with Labour, the largest cluster of respondents perceived their advertising as a mixture of positive and negative—39.6%. This rating is complemented by 18.9% who regarded Labour's advertising as positive and 21% who regarded it as negative.

FIGURE 3. The Relationship Between Attitudes and Ad Awareness

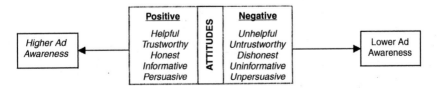

FIGURE 4. Overall Judgements of the Party Advertising

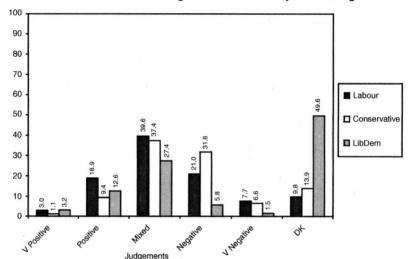

Moving on to the Conservatives, again the largest cluster regarded their advertising as mixed–37.4%. However, unlike Labour, a higher proportion regarded it as negative (31.8%) and a much smaller proportion regarded it as positive (9.4%). Overall this gives a greater skew towards a negative judgment for the Conservative advertising, compared to that of Labour's advertising.

The advertising for the Liberal Democrats appeared to be least easily judged, with nearly half of the respondents not knowing whether their advertising was positive, negative or mixed. Of those who were able to make a judgment, 27.4% maintained the LibDems advertising was a mixture of positive and negative messages, while 15.8% regarded their advertising as positive or very positive. Only 7.3% regarded their advertising as negative or very negative.

Overall the advertising of the Liberal Democrats was judged to be the least negative (7.3%), compared with Labour (28.7%) and the Conservatives (38.4%). Comparing positive responses across the three parties, Labours advertising was judged to be the most positive (21.9%), followed by the Liberal Democrats (15.8), while the Conservatives' advertising was perceived to be the least positive–with only 10.5% judging their advertising to be positive or very positive.

It is interesting to note that these assessments of the parties advertising appear more moderate compared with the much more mordant judgements of the advertising illustrated in Figure 2. This reflects the reality of the advertising strategies employed by the parties that were less negative compared to some previous campaigns (Dermody and Scullion 2001; 2001a). Yet, given some of the extremely negative attitudes expressed by our respondents, it is surprising that a greater proportion did not judge the advertising more negatively. This age group's interpretation of 'negative' may well be different from older age groups, given the increasing use of shocking advertising targeting them and permeating their consumer cultures. It may also be that once our questioning became less general–more party specific–party loyal voters were less willing to judge their party's advertising too severely.

CONCLUSION

We have painted a relatively detailed picture of the attitudes of young people towards the party political advertising for the 2001 British General Election. What emerges is a young electorate aware of the advertising, but with some quite mixed reactions to it, coupled with nearly half who say they voted and who were interested in the election itself. It appears, therefore, that this segment of the electorate is not as totally disengaged from party politics as current thinking suggests.

So how do our findings equate with the claim that negative ads aid voter disengagement? It is probable that the political attitudes of young voters–whether positive or negative–already exist when they come to vote for the first time. Consequently it is difficult to disentangle the role pre-election advertising plays in shaping these attitudes. It is also clear that the relationship between the political attitudes of young people, their attitudes towards political advertising and their political behaviour is a complex one. This is not surprising given the exhaustive scholarship on attitudes and behaviour that has established there is not always a clear link between them. While our research does not assert that political advertising has a direct effect on voting behaviour, it may be influencing intervening variables, e.g., attention levels, given that the ads are being attended to and are a form of communication well understood and used by young people. As Norris et al. (1997, 172) point out "If scholars believe that all the intense activity surrounding political communications does not matter, then they may have been looking for the wrong sort of effect." It should also be recognised that for this generation, socialization of group norms surrounding political attitudes and behaviour are likely to be more dominant than for other generations (Pirie and Worcester 1998; Reed 2002)–this would have influenced their judgements of the advertising and their perceived role for it. Further the political attitudes of this group are still likely to be evolving, creating some degree of insecurity and possibly, therefore, an unacknowledged role for political advertising as a discussion point among peers and a decision-making aid. Applying understanding of advertising's role in the world of commercial branding, our findings support the notion that political advertising influences the attitudes of young people towards politics in general, the election itself, and individual leader and party images.

Our findings demonstrate that young people judged the election adverting far more disparagingly and severely than advertising per se. Yet this did not lead them to deem the ads any less persuasive than ads in general. This rather peculiar combination offers both an optimistic and pessimistic outlook for future political advertising. If political communicators can design ads that are judged more favourably by young people, they may act as a point of '*break though*'–linking politics to this audience and having significant persuasive potential amongst them. On the other hand, these findings might illustrate the strength of '*mindset*' young people bring to this arena called 'mainstream politics' (full of distrust and suspicion), which sets the tone for how they go on to judge all communications attached to it. If the later is the case, there is some evidence that the attributes of honesty and trustworthiness act as gatekeepers, where advertising that scores poorly in these areas has very limited usefulness and indeed fuels the original misgivings of young people.

Finally while we have not set out to 'prove' a direct relationship between negative political attitudes and political participation, it would seem that advertising is likely to reinforce the existing negative political attitudes of those who are already disengaged from politics. Further, as we concluded in our analysis of the general election advertising strategies, the ambitions for the advertising itself appeared to be very limited–what is also required, then, is a re-examination of the role of advertising in general election campaigning. In order to act as a catalyst in engaging the young, they must perceive it to be credible and relevant–this is a major challenge for campaign strategists if they wish to connect with the young electorate through this medium. With voter turnout in the UK steadily in decline, liberal democracy can ill-afford to loose an entire lifetime of voting from these segments of the electorate. Consequently there is a need to appraise the role and consequences of negative advertising in election campaigning, as part of a review to address the electoral malaise of young people, and in so doing, to nurture the future welfare of liberal democracy in contemporary British Society.

NOTE

1. The findings presented here relate to respondents' overall impressions of the electoral advertising–they were non-ad specific at this stage in the questionnaire.

REFERENCES

Alwitt, A. and Mitchell, A., (1992), *Psychological Processes and Advertising Effects*, LEA.

Ansolabehere, S., and Iyengar, S., (1995), *Going Negative: How Political Advertisements Shrink and Polarize the Electorate*, New York: Free Press.

Ansolabehere, S., Iyengar, S., Simon, A., and Valentino, N., (1994), "Does Attack Advertising Demobilize the Electorate?" *American Political Science Review*, Vol. 88 (December), 829-838.

Ansolabehere, S.D., Iyenger, S., and Smith, A., (1999), "Replicating Experiments Using Aggregate and Survey Data: The Case of Negative Advertising and Turnout," *American Political Science Review*, Vol. 93 No. 4 (December).

Banker, S., (1992), "The Ethics of Political Marketing, The Rhetorical Perspective," *Journal of Business Ethics*, Volume 11, Issue 11, 843-849.

Boylan, J. (1991), "Where Have All The People Gone? Reflections on Voter Alienation and the Challenge it Poses to the Press," *Colombia Journalism Review*, Vol. 30, 33-35.

Bromley, C., Curtice, J., and Seyd, B., (2001), "Political Engagement, Trust and Constitutional Reform," in A. Park, J. Curtice, K. Thomson, L. Jarvis, and C. Bromley, (Eds.), *British Social Attitudes. The 18th Report: Public Policy, Social Ties*, Chapter 9, (National Centre for Social Research), London: Sage.

Bromley, C., and Curtice, J., (2002), "Where Have All The Voters Gone?," in A. Park, J. Curtice, K. Thomson, L. Jarvis, and C. Bromley, (Eds.), *British Social Attitudes. The 19th Report*, Chapter 7, (National Centre for Social Research), London: Sage.

Butler, D., and Kavanagh, D., (1997), *The British General Election of 1997*, Basingstoke: Macmillan Press.

Carlston, D., (1980), "The Recall and Uses of Traits and Events in Social Inference Processes," *Journal of Experimental Social Psychology*, Vol. 16, No. 4.

Danaher, P., (1995), "What Happens to Television Ratings During Commercial Breaks?" *Journal of Advertising Research*, Vol. 35 No. 1. (Jan/Feb.), 37-48.

Dermody, J. and Scullion, R., (2000), "Perceptions of Negative Political Advertising: Meaningful or Menacing? An Empirical Study of the 1997 British General Election Campaign," *International Journal of Advertising*, Vol. 19, No. 2, 201-225.

Dermody, J., and Scullion, R., (2001), "Delusions of Grandeur? Marketing's Contribution to 'Meaningful' Western Political Consumption," *European Journal of Marketing* (special edition on Political Marketing), Vol. 35, No. 9/10, 1085-1098.

Dermody, J., and Scullion, R., (2001a), "An Exploration of the Advertising Ambitions and Strategies of the 2001 British General Election," *Journal of Marketing Management* (special edition: The Marketing Campaign: The 2001 British General Election), Vol. 17, No. 9-10, 969-987.

Dermody, J., and Scullion, R., (2003), "Facing the Future: Young People's Awareness of the 2001 British General Election Advertising Campaigns," *Journal of Public Affairs*, Volume 3, No. 2 (May), 152-165.

Electoral Commission web site *www.electoral-commission.govt.uk/* accessed September 10 2001.

Fazio, R., and Williams, C., (1986), "Attitude Accessibility as a Moderator of the Attitude-Perception and Attitude-Behaviour Relations: An Investigation of the 1984 Presidential Election," *Journal of Personality and Social Psychology*, Vol. 51, No. 3. 505-514.

Germond, J.W., and Witcover, J., (1996), "Why Americans Don't Go To The Polls," *National Journal*, Vol. 28, No. 47, 2562-2564.

Gould, P., (1998), *The Unfinished Revolution*, Little Brown and Company.

Hall Jamieson, K., (1992), *Dirty Politics. Deception, Distraction and Democracy*, Oxford: Oxford University Press.

Hovland, C.I., Janis, I.L., and Kelley, H.H., (1953), *Communication and Persuasion*, New Haven, CT: Yale University Press.

James, K., and Hensel, P., (1991), "Negative Advertising: The Malicious Strain of Comparative Advertising," *Journal of Advertising*, Vol. 20, No. 2, 53-70.

Jones, N., (1997), *How the General Election was Won and Lost*, Indigo.

Kahn, K.F. and Kenney, P.J., (1999), "Do Campaigns Mobilize or Suppress Turnout? Clarifying the Relationship Between Negativity and Participation," *American Political Science Review*, Vol. 93, No. 4 (December), 877-89.

Kaid, L.L., (1999), "Political Advertising: A Summary of Research Findings," in Newman, B. (Ed.) *Handbook of Political Marketing*, CA: Sage.

Kates, S., (1998), "A Qualitative Exploration into Voters' Ethical Perceptions of Political Advertising: Discourse, Disinformation, and Moral Boundaries," *Journal of Business Ethics*, Volume 17, No. 16, 1871-1885.

King, A., (Ed.), (2002), *Britain at the Polls 2001*, USA: Chatham House Publishers.

Kline, S., (1997), "Image Politics: Negative Advertising Strategies and the Election Audience," in M. Nava, A. Blake, I. MacRury and B. Richards (Eds.), *Buy this Book*, London: Routledge.

Marketing, (2001), "Party Ads make Little Impact on Voter Intentions," front cover story, May 17.

Miller, G.R., (1987), "Persuasion," in Berger, C.R., & Chaffee, S.H., (Eds.), *Handbook of Communication Science*, 446-483, CA: Sage.

Miron D., (1999), "Grabbing the Nonvoter," in B. Newman (Ed), *Handbook of Political Marketing*, CA: Sage, 321-343.

Mittal, B., (1994), "Public Assessment of TV Advertising; Faint Praise or Harsh Criticism?" *Journal of Advertising Research*, Vol. 34, No. 1, (Jan/Feb), 35-53.

Morgan, R. and Hunt, S., (1994), "The Commitment–Trust Theory of Relationship Marketing," *Journal of Marketing*, Vol. 58, Iss. 3, (July), 20-39.

MORI Survey, (2001), "Attitudes to Voting and the Political Process," *Study conducted for the Electoral Commission*, www.mori.com/polls/ accessed July 3rd 2001.

Mulgan, G., and Wilkinson, H., (1997), "Freedom's Children and the Rise of Generational Politics," in G. Mulgan (Ed), *Life After Politics: New Thinking for the Twenty-First Century*, London: Fontana.

Nava, M. and Nava, O., (1990), "Discriminating or Duped? Young People as Consumers of Adverting/Art," reprinted in *Changing Cultures: Feminism, Youth and Consumerism*, London: Sage.

Norris, P., (1997), *Electoral Change Since 1945*, London: Blackwell.

O' Donohoe, S., (1994), "Advertising Uses and Gratifications," *European Journal of Marketing*, Vol. 28, No. 8/9, 52-76.

O' Donohoe, S., (1997), "Leaky Boundaries. Intertextuality and Young Adults Experiences of Advertising," in M. Nava, A. Blake, I. MacRury and B. Richards (Eds.), *Buy this Book*, London: Routledge.

Oborne, P., (1999), *Alister Campbell, New Labour and the Rise of the Media Classes*, London: Aurum.

Park, A., (1999), "Young People and Political Apathy," in R. Jowell, J. Curtice, A. Park, K. Thomson, L. Jarvis, C. Bromley, and N. Stratford, (Eds.), *British Social Attitudes. The 16th Report. Who Shares New Labour Values?, Chapter 2, (National Centre for Social Research), Aldershot: Ashgate.*

Parris, M., (2001), "A Craven Audience at Court of King Tony"; "General Election 2001," *The Times*, May 19th.

Perloff, R., (1993), *The Dynamics of Persuasion*, Lawrence Erlbaum.

Pinkleton, B., (1997), "The Effects of Negative Comparative Political Advertising on Candidate Evaluations and Advertising Evaluations: An Exploration," *Journal of Advertising*, Vol. 26, No. 1, (Spring), 19-30.

Pirie, M. and Worcester, R.M., (1998), *The Millennial Generation*, Adam Smith Institute, *http://www.adamsmith.org.uk/*

Pirie, M. and Worcester, R.M., (2000), *The Big Turn-Off: Attitudes of Young People to Government, Citizenship and Community*, Adam Smith Institute, http://www.adamsmith.org.uk/

Pollay, R and Mittal, B., (1993), "Here's the Beef: Factors, Determinants and Segments of Consumer Criticism of Advertising," *Journal of Marketing*, Vol. 57, No. 3, 99-114.

Reed, A., (2002), "Social Identity as a Useful Perspective for Self-Concept–based Consumer Research," *Psychology and Marketing*, Vol. 19, No. 3 (March), 235-266.

Russell, A., Fieldhouse, E., Purdam, K., Kalra, V., (2002), *Voter Engagement and Young People*, The Electoral Commission, London, UK. www.electoralcommission.org.uk

Scullion, R., and Dermody, J., (2003), "Positive and Issue Orientated or Personal and Dirty? A Content Analysis of the 2001 British General Election Campaign" (competitive paper), *Academy of Marketing Conference proceedings*, Aston university, 8-10th July.

Shavitt, S. Lowrey, P. and Haefner, J., (1998), "Public Attitudes towards Advertising; More Favourable Than You Might Think," *Journal of Advertising Research*, Vol. 38, No. 4, 7-22.

Spogard, R., and James, M., (2000), *Governance and Democracy–the Peoples View. A Global Opinion Poll*, Address to the United Nations conference, www.gallup-international.com/survey18.htm

Taylor, P., (1990), *See How They Run: Electing the President in an Age of Mediocracy*, New York: Alfred A. Knopf.

Teixeira, R.A., (1992), *The Disappearing American Voter*, Washington DC: Brookings Institution.

Tempest, (2001), *The Guardian*, May 21st 2001.

Wernick, A., (1991), *Promotional Culture: Advertising Ideology and Symbolic Expression*, London: Sage.

West, D., (1997), "Air Wars: Television Advertising in Election Campaigns 1952-1996," *Congressional Quarterly Inc*, Washington.

White, C., Bruce, S., and Ritchie, J., (2000), *Young Peoples Politics. Political Interest and Engagement Amongst 14-24 Year Olds*, Joseph Rowntree Foundation, York Publishing Services.

Worcester, R., and Mortimore, R., (2001), *Explaining Labour's Second Landslide*, London: Politico's.

APPENDIX 1

RESPONDENT PROFILE							
	N	%	NS%		N	%	NS%
Age				**Ethnic Group**			
• 18	122	14.1		• White British	702	80.9	*93.3*
• 19	153	17.7		• British Black African	35	4.0	-
• 20	156	18.0	N/A	• British Black Caribbean	12	1.4	-
• 21	207	23.9		• British Asian	69	8.0	-
• 22	229	26.3		• British Chinese	23	2.7	-
				• Mixed White & Black Caribbean	5	0.6	-
Gender				• Mixed White & Black African	9	1.0	-
• Female	423	48.8	*51.4*	• Mixed White & Asian	5	0.6	-
• Male	444	51.2	*48.6*	• Other	7	0.8	-
Occupation				**Sample Geographic Mix**			
• Employed	330	38.1	*58.9*	• South East & London	202	23.3	*34.3*
• Student	441	50.9	*32.5*	• South West	223	25.7	*8.1*
• Unemployed	72	8.3	*5.6*	• Wales	151	17.4	*5.1*
• Other	23	2.7	*3.0*	• North	190	21.9	*27.3*
				• Midlands	101	11.7	*16.2*
Education				**Voting Behaviour**			
• GCSE's	796	94.3	*97.1*	• Labour	226	27.8	*20.2*
• A/AS Levels	544	64.5	*46.4*	• Conservative	107	13.2	*9.2*
• NVQ Levels 1-3	95	11.3	*9.9*	• Liberal Democrat	77	9.5	*7.4*
• NVQ 4-5, HNC, HND	36	4.3	*	• Other	24	2.9	*2.2*
• First Degree	207	24.5	*20.2*	• (Voter)	(434)	(53.5)	*(39.2)*
• Higher Degree	28	3.3	*3.0*	• Non-Voter	378	46.5	*60.8*
• Professional qualification	19	2.3	*N/A*				

NS%: national statistics (sources: TGI 2002, Office of National Statistics).
*: 9.9% figures relate to all NVQ levels.

Marketing Government Reforms

Dave Gelders

Steven Van De Walle

SUMMARY. This article examines government communication on two large-scale Belgian governmental reforms: the Federal Administration and the police forces. Using Lees-Marshment's typology of marketing processes, we identify the marketing of the changes by the Federal Administration as sales oriented: a finished product or an expert-developed administrative reform project to be sold to the public. Declining enthusiasm for communication and growing product disagreement gradually forced this reform to disappear from the market. The Police reform followed a market-oriented marketing process. It responded to public outrage. The Government merely reacted to external information. This explains why it failed to deal with a changed market situation. A content analysis of articles in both popular and quality newspapers examines the representation of both reforms in the media and seems to confirm our

---

Dave Gelders is Research Assistant, Fund for Scientific Research-Flanders (Belgium), Department of Communication Science, K.U. Leuven, Van Evenstraat 2A, B 3000 Leuven, Belgium (E-mail: dave.gelders@soc.kuleuven.ac.be).

Steven Van De Walle is Researcher, Public Management Institute, K.U. Leuven, Van Evenstraat 2A, B 3000 Leuven, Belgium (E-mail: steven.vandewalle@soc. kuleuven.ac.be).

The authors would like to thank the anonymous reviewers, as well as Professor W. Wymer, Dr. J. Lees-Marshment and Ms. M. Shwimer for their constructive remarks. The authors are also grateful to the undergraduate students in Communication Science (K.U. Leuven) for their help in coding and in designing the coding guidelines.

[Haworth co-indexing entry note]: "Marketing Government Reforms." Gelders, Dave, and Steven Van De Walle. Co-published simultaneously in *Journal of Nonprofit & Public Sector Marketing* (Best Business Books, an imprint of The Haworth Press, Inc.) Vol. 14, No. 1/2, 2005, pp. 151-168; and: *Current Issues in Political Marketing* (eds: Walter W. Wymer, Jr., and Jennifer Lees-Marshment) Best Business Books, an imprint of The Haworth Press, Inc., 2005, pp. 151-168. Single or multiple copies of this article are available for a fee from The Haworth Document Delivery Service [1-800-HAWORTH, 9:00 a.m. - 5:00 p.m. (EST). E-mail address: getinfo@haworthpressinc.com].

observations. This article shows that marketing reforms are extremely difficult when there is no shared understanding of the product to be marketed. *[Article copies available for a fee from The Haworth Document Delivery Service: 1-800-HAWORTH. E-mail address: <docdelivery@haworthpress. com> Website: <http://www.HaworthPress.com> © 2005 by The Haworth Press, Inc. All rights reserved.]*

KEYWORDS. Political marketing, sales-orientation, market-orientation, change management, policy reform, public communication, government communication

INTRODUCTION

The general population usually views governments, specifically public services and civil servants, in a negative light (Goodsell 1985; Van de Walle and Bouckaert 2003). Popular explanations for this distrust point to a lack of communication by the government and to the malfunctioning of the government machinery. However, an in-depth research on the government's image (Ringeling 1993) shows that the negative image has not so much to do with the government's performances, but rather with the way citizens evaluate the government (focusing on negative aspects, unjust comparisons with the business sector, and high expectations). This is linked with the role and the impact of the media. Most citizens have limited encounters with the government, which makes media coverage a main source of information. The media is also often blamed for being a main source sustaining the negative, stereotypical image of the government (Lichter et al. 1999; Council for Excellence in Government 2001).

This article examines government communication on two large-scale Belgian governmental reforms: a wide-ranging reform of the entire Federal Administration (the so-called "Copernicus reform") and the Police reform. First we use Lees-Marshment's typology of marketing processes (2001; product-orientation; sales-orientation; market-orientation) to understand the marketing approaches used for both reforms. Lees-Marshment's typology distinguishes between a product-orientation where a product is designed and subsequently delivered, a sales-orientation where the product design phase is followed by a market intelligence phase used to support delivery or sales, and a market-orientation where collecting market intelligence precedes the product design. We find that in the marketing of the Copernicus reform used a sales-orientated strategy while the Police reform used a market-orientation strategy. The dif-

ferent marketing approaches were determined by differing citizen attitudes towards these two administrations: citizens feel that the police are short-handed
while they feel public administration should be non-existent as it is considered
redundant. After applying Lees-Marshment's model, we analyse the manner
in which the media (two Flemish newspapers) covered the reforms and their
core issues.

Both reforms will be dealt with separately. We start each case by describing
the political context and some key elements, and then apply Lees-Marshment's
model to this reform. Afterwards, we compare the marketing approach of the
two reforms.

THE COPERNICUS REFORM

A Clean Break with History

Following an historic election on June 13, 1999, the new Prime Minister,
Guy Verhofstadt, installed a "purple-green" cabinet composed of the (French-
speaking and Dutch-speaking) liberal, socialist and green parties. The Verhofstadt Government introduced a different style of governing and communicating in Belgian politics. The Prime Minister himself regularly announced a
"clean break with history" by emphasising the decisiveness of his cabinet as
compared with the presumed immobility of the preceding Dehaene cabinet.

The new Federal Government stated that Belgium must become a "model
state" and considered the modernisation of the governmental apparatus a top
priority (http://www.copernicus.be; Depauw and Deweerdt 2002; Fiers and
Deweerdt 2001; Nomden 2002; Van Hemelrijck and Auwers 2001). In a joint
press conference on February 16, 2000, Prime Minister Guy Verhofstadt and
the Minister for Civil Service and Modernisation of Public Administration,
Luc Van den Bossche, presented a plan for the modernisation of the Federal
Belgian administration. They presented it as a radically new project. A journalist from the Flemish newspaper *De Standaard* used the expression "The
Copernicus programme" to label the governmental plan by making an analogy
with Nicolaus Copernicus, who discovered the earth ("administration") turned
around the sun ("citizen") and not vice versa. Political initiators copied this
clear and ambitious product name.

The Copernicus programme was inspired by New Public Management
principles (economy, efficiency, effectiveness) as were many other Western
public sector reforms (Osborne and Gaebler 1993). In order to improve governmental efficiency and the citizen's trust in the Government, the Copernicus
programme worked to redesign the hierarchically structured administration

into a matrix organisation, to introduce modern HRM and staff assessments, and to improve the Federal Government's processes involving internal and external communication.

Sales-Orientation

We argue that the marketing process used for the Copernicus reform is characterised by a "sales-orientation." The stages are: (1) product design; (2) market intelligence; (3) communication; (4) campaign; (5) election; and (6) delivery. Market intelligence was a central feature in the marketing of the Copernicus reform but was not the first stage of the marketing process. The Copernicus program is an all-encompassing reform plan and is largely developed by experts. The "product" had to be sold to the citizens and the civil servants. Therefore, the Copernicus reform does not follow a product or market-orientation.

Stage 1: Product Design. The Federal Government set up the Copernicus programme. The Copernicus programme is a fundamental reform of the entire Belgian Federal Administration, covering approximately 60,000 civil servants and all aspects of public administration. As a result, the designed "product" is heterogeneous and complicated and must target many levels. The process itself should be communicated professionally to gain support from internal and external target groups and to aid in the implementation of the programme.

Stage 2: Market Intelligence. Successful implementation depends on the ability to identify key players (e.g., trade unions and segments of the general public) not currently supporting the reorganisation reform but might support it further down the road. Therefore, the Federal Government used market intelligence for both internal and external target groups.

Market intelligence for internal target groups. The Federal Government commissioned an independent research bureau to examine the opinion of civil servants regarding the Copernicus programme and the communication used to disseminate information. The project was called the "Artemis Project" and was conducted in the autumn of 2000 (http://www.copernicus.be). The Artemis project distributed a questionnaire to 9,949 civil servants; 3,947 or 39.7% responded. The response rates of high and low-ranking civil servants differed significantly. The Artemis project reveals the following conclusions: (1) Due to negative comments by citizens and politicians, many civil servants created a bunker around themselves and often interpret the announced reform as criticism rather than constructive change. Nevertheless, civil servants have a positive self-image. They are convinced it was the system that failed, but not themselves as individuals; (2) Internal communication (specifically, that concerning the Copernicus programme) was impeded by a lack of communication and the bureaucratic characteristics of the organisation; (3) There are few official and objective information sources about Copernicus. As of December 2000, with the exception of one letter from the competent Minister in September 1999, civil servants received most pertinent information from trade unions or the press; (4) The existing communication channels, such as staff magazines and the intranet, might be improved. They might be used to inform civil servants about the Copernicus programme.

Market intelligence for external target groups. Prior to the Artemis project, a large-scale postal survey ("referendum") among the entire Belgian population (all Belgian citizens of 16 years or older) was conducted concerning the Copernicus reform. Through a structured questionnaire, the population was surveyed on whether or not it agreed with the abolition of the ministerial cabinets, the promotion of civil servants on the basis of personal competence, etc. A leaflet was enclosed to describe the modernisation initiatives. Based on the survey results, the responsible ministers argued that the proposed modernisations of the public administration were supported by an overwhelming majority of the population. However, there was a great deal of criticism vis-à-vis the survey. First, the response rate was 9.2%: only 750,000 ballots out of the 8.2 million were sent back. Opponents of the reform interpreted this low response rate as resistance to the modernisation programme of the Federal Government. Second, there were several methodological concerns such as the compulsory and biased way the questions were posed. As a result, the outcome of the survey was not surprising: only 4% of the respondents were opposed to the modernisation of the civil service. Third, the cost of the survey (€1.98 million) and the alleged violation of the respondents' privacy were criticized as well. Last but not least, opposition parties considered the survey to be a popularity poll of the competent ministers and of the Government as a whole and paid for by the citizenry. However, such an initiative can also be seen as an interesting market intelligence tool to foster the necessary support for the planned reforms.

Stage 3: Communication. The Federal Government underwent several internal and external communication initiatives.

Internal communication. In the beginning, the lack of direct, official and unbiased information turned the press and the trade unions into the main communicators. Based on the Artemis project, a communication policy was implemented to inform the civil servants about Copernicus and then to influence their feelings towards the Copernicus programme (Van Hemelrijck and Auwers 2001). During the process, several communication channels were used: leaflets (e.g., "Setting a new course is absolutely necessary"), road shows, newsletters (e.g., "Today Tomorrow"), monthly magazines, a website (with specific sections targeting the civil servant; *http://www.copernicus.be*), national television broadcasts, press briefings, networking, and personal enquiries.

External communication. In several interviews, the competent ministers stressed the fundamental characteristics of this reform and focused on the accomplishments. By means of various news media, they tried to convince the citizenry that a historic project was being realised and they had passed the point of no return. Direct public communication, such as the leaflet accompanying the questionnaire, informed the citizenry about the necessity and the general outline of the reform. The external communication faced fierce resistance. Generally speaking, the question arose to what extent it was the Government's first and principal aim to improve its image rather than to aid in the implementation of the reform programme (Gelders 2002). As the Auditor General of British Columbia (1995) states: "It is a generally-held view that, while it is acceptable for governments to incur expenditures for communicating about government programs, the taxpayers (. . .) should not have to pay for communications that are of partisan political nature." Referring to Safire's New Political Dictionary, "partisan" is defined as "placing party advantage above the public interest." Many governmental communication guidelines, such as the UK basic conventions from 1985, stipulate that "It is entirely proper to present and describe the policies of a Minister, and to put forward the Minister's justification in defence of them, and this may have the effect of advancing the aims of the Political party in Government. (. . .) It is possible that a well-founded publicity campaign can create political credit for the Party in Government. But this must not be the primary or a significant purpose of Government information or publicity activities paid for from public funds."

Stage 4: Campaign. In the build-up leading to the parliamentary elections on May, 18, 2003, the Prime Minister Guy Verhofstadt used the slogan "Our country is back." In several speeches and interviews, he proudly announced that, due to his Government's efforts, Belgium has become an internationally acclaimed "model state." At the same time, he argued that the former Dehaene Government failed to tackle the issue of public sector reform. According to Verhofstadt, this was ultimately demonstrated during the dioxin crisis of May 1999 in which Belgium was portrayed foolishly both nationally and abroad for a lack of coordination between the governmental departments, communicating too late and for taking unclear or confusing measures.

Stages 5 and 6: Election and Delivery. The mere scope of the Copernicus reform meant that implementation could not be completed during one term in office. It is difficult to establish the extent to which the Government's aim, delivering quality products and services and finally regaining public trust, has already been realised. In the time leading up to the 2003 elections, the Prime Minister and the Minister for Civil Service and Modernisation of Public Administration admitted that the reforms did not occur as fast as they had expected. There was growing disagreement within the Government, mainly between Dutch-speaking and French-speaking ministers. Several ministers publicly stated dissatisfaction with the reforms, thereby undermining the general communication strategy and hindering the selling of the "Copernicus product."

We now discuss the Police reform. Before applying Lees-Marshment's model to this reform, we describe the former Belgian police system subject to the changes in the Police reform.

THE POLICE REFORM

A War Between Three Police Forces

The former Belgian police system was composed of three police forces: the Municipal Police, the federal Gendarmerie and the Judicial Police. The Municipal Police was controlled by the individual municipalities (the ultimate authority being the mayor) and had a local role. The federal Gendarmerie (federal police force) was at one time a branch of the military. Like the Municipal Police, the Gendarmerie had a law and order mission (prevention and protection) but also performed judicial tasks (investigations). The Gendarmerie was the largest branch and consisted of local brigades and central offices (such as central investigative units). Its many functions ranged from traffic control to judicial investigations. The Judicial Police was solely an investigative unit (no law and order tasks) ultimately supervised by the Minister of Justice but investigating under the daily guidance of the office of the public prosecutor. The Judicial Police, a relatively small force, often complained that the Gendarmerie encroached on its terrain and that it was often not informed about operations carried out by the Gendarmerie (Couttenier 1997).

Market-Orientation

We argue that the Police reform is characterised by a "market-orientation." The stages are: (1) market intelligence; (2) product design; (3) product adjustment; (4) implementation; (5) communication; (6) campaign; (7) election; (8) delivery.

For decades, there had been unsuccessful attempts to reform the police forces. A product-orientation would therefore not be sufficient. Market pressure actually forced the Federal Government to start designing a new product. The Government had failed to recognise the subtle signs of unhappiness and saw itself suddenly faced with public outrage. Market intelligence, or better, market pressure, thus played a key role in the initiation of the Police reform. In the Police reform, the Federal Government was confronted with the demands from the market before the new product was designed. It is striking that the Federal Government did not take the initiative itself to discover the market demands. As will be shown, it was actually only after the Dutroux scandal that the Police reform began to take shape. The general public put pressure on the policymakers to create a new police product ("The Integrated Police Force").

Stage 1: Market Intelligence. On August 9, 1996, a fourteen year old girl was kidnapped in Bertrix (Belgium). Following testimonies, Marc Dutroux, his wife and a collaborator were arrested. Two days later, the police found the girl, along with a second girl kidnapped more than two months before, alive in a cage in one of Dutruox's houses. In subsequent weeks, the human remains of four other girls kidnapped during the years before were found on his premises.

This scandal shocked the country in an unprecedented way, especially after it emerged that Dutroux had previously been convicted as a sexual predator and that the police had suspected him in this case but failed to find the girls in an earlier search (Maesschalck 2002). The general public experienced a break in trust with everything that represented "the system": politicians, administrators, the police, the judiciary and even the intellectual elite. The public outrage peaked following a controversial verdict of the highest Belgian court of October 14, 1996. The protests following the verdict culminated in the "White March" on Sunday October 20, 1996; the biggest post-war demonstration in Belgium gathering about 300,000 protesters in the streets of Brussels.

Stage 2: Product Design. The Government needed to respond. The first task for Prime Minister Jean-Luc Dehaene was to change the White March from an act of protest into an act of "additional encouragement" for those in power "to deal with the problems" and as such indicate that the message was understood (Maesschalck 2002). The Government also needed to make decisions to show its willingness to deal with the problem. However, with an issue as large as a "lack of trust in public institutions," the focus of the decisions was limited. In the case of the White March, there was no clear organisation and there was no clear list of demands. Instead, there was an enormous group of individuals expressing general discontent with the management of the country as a common characteristic.

Confronted with these unfocused demands, the Prime Minister tried to focus attention on the issue by stressing the police and judicial aspects and by referring the issue to a newly created committee; the "Dutroux" House Committee of Inquiry was set up a few days before under the presidency of Marc Verwilghen, an opposition MP. This Committee investigated the mistakes made during the previous investigations into the kidnappings and to prevent these failures in the future. By explicitly referring the inquiry to the Committee, the Prime Minister not only (re-)focused the "police and justice reform" issue, but also allowed for a restoration of the image of this issue.

The Committee's hearings attracted a large and continuous interest stimulated by live coverage on television. Those hearings revealed problems previously formulated but that now had a higher profile. There were symbolic examples such as the images of an officer of the Gendarmerie and a magistrate giving contradictory accounts of the same events. The constant and intense media coverage of the search for human remains also worked to keep focus on the issue. During the hearings, the Committee's chair, Marc Verwilghen, gradually emerged as a policy entrepreneur, strongly supported by the media. By managing the hearings and the subsequent debate on the policy recommendations, he helped to structure the broad and still somewhat unfocused issue of "police and justice reforms." He split the issue into manageable sections about which agreements were reached between the Committee's members (Maesschalck 2002).

Following the "Dutroux" House Committee recommendations, the Federal Government announced an integration of the three police forces into one unified police force structured at two levels: the "Federal Police" and the "Local Police." At the federal level, the former central offices of the Gendarmerie and the former Judicial Police would have to be merged in order to take care of inquiries, the maintenance of public order and traffic-regulations. At the local level, the former local brigades of the Gendarmerie and the former Municipal Police would have to be merged as well in order to take care of the basic daily police tasks.

Stage 3: Product Adjustment. The internal target groups were insufficiently involved in the reform process. The creation of the new police structure was created under enormous external pressure exerted by the general public, but was not based on the needs or wishes of the internal target groups. Many internal reactions and public discussions followed regarding the new but not yet completed police product. Several institutions such as the Flemish Association of Towns and Municipalities, trade unions of police officers and the "Dutroux" House Committee voiced their opposition and proposed alternatives to the reform plans (Fiers and Deweerdt 1998). During the debates, a central role was played by MP's who were also mayors and thus responsible for the municipal police force. They had an interest in the Police reform as an integration of Municipal Police forces in "inter-police zones" would reduce the mayor's power over the police. The cleavage between the Dutch-speaking and French-speaking mayors-MPs was particularly deep and dominated the debate. The French-speaking parties claimed, and eventually obtained, a larger say for the mayor in leading these new local inter-police zones.

The debate continued during the subsequent months. Given all of this, the actual reforms would have been rather modest without one of the most spectacular events in recent Belgian history: the escape of public enemy number one, Marc Dutroux, on April 23, 1998 (Maesschalck 2002). Again, external pressure forced the Police reform to pick up steam. Although Dutroux was caught within a few hours, the political world felt that quick and decisive action was necessary "to restore trust in the institutions." On May 11, 1998, the leaders of the four governing parties and of the four opposition parties started the so-called "Octopus"-negotiations under the presidency of Prime Minister Dehaene (Fiers and Deweerdt 1999). The pressure on the negotiators was heavy. Particularly, the media demanded action. None of the parties could afford to be responsible for a failure of the negotiations. The Octopus agreement proposed the integration of the police forces both on a national and a local level and was presented to the press on May 24, 1998, one month and one day after Dutroux' escape.

It rapidly became apparent that the reform operation would not be finalised before the parliamentary elections on June 13, 1999. To increase pressure on the Government and on the MPs of the Octopus partners, the trade unions of the police forces organised three protest campaigns between February and May 1999. The elections on June 13, 1999, impeded the process of reforming the police forces until January 31, 2000. Negotiations were difficult and on numerous occasions police officers marched through the streets of Brussels to stress their grievances. On July 2, 2000, a final agreement stipulated the specific measures at a cost of € 198.3 million. Later, the Minister for the Home Department responded to complaints by the mayors and confirmed that none of the costs would be redirected to the budgets of the local authorities, as the Government had budgeted € 458.6 million to support the local authorities in implementing the new structure.

Stage 4: Implementation. In implementing the Octopus Agreement, the Federal Police took off on January 1, 2001, followed by the set up of the Local Police. During the implementation stage, there were still discussions regarding the police personnel's legal position, their disciplinary code, their social security, their retirement statute and their pay. Wage increases followed, making the reforms very expensive.

Stage 5: Communication. Communication about the Police reform process was started during the earlier stages of this process before the overall plan was determined. Many communication channels were used in addition to the official channel from the Home Department. Communication about the Police reform was far from perfect for several reasons. First, the police personnel often had to rely on news media rather than on their own commanders for information; as a result, the principle that good internal communication is required for facilitating good external communication, is violated. Second, the new Minister for the Home Department often gave information to the public first instead of cooperating with his administration. As a result, there were several hasty, incomplete, inconsistent and polemical statements in which the Minister communicated policy intentions as if they were already realised (Gelders forthcoming). Third, negative statements released by several high-ranking police officers cast a shadow on the reform. Fourth, the unified police tried to make its new characteristics visible by means of new uniforms, a new house style (emblem, colours, etc.) and by their presence at public events such as the national holiday parade and at events organised around the popular Flemish television series "Flikken" ("Cops," a fictional series dealing with non-fictional items of everyday police life in the Flemish city of Ghent). But this attempt incurred problems due to the new uniforms being unavailable for the national holiday parade on July 21, 2002, and due to several demonstrations by the staff in which they marched against the governmental reorganisation plans. Various news media outlets reported about protesting Gendarmerie personnel occupying the main roads around Brussels, about drunken and fighting Judicial Police officers, etc.

Stages 6, 7 and 8: Campaign, Election and Delivery. Marginal issues within the reform dominated communication. Because external pressure faded, attention gradually shifted from the general reform plans to the negative side-effects and the imperfect implementation. The Police reform was not an issue in the 2003 elections.

We now compare the main political marketing elements used in the two government reforms as described above.

THE COPERNICUS REFORM VERSUS THE POLICE REFORM

The Copernicus reform and the Police reform are two recent fundamental government reforms. Issues common to both reforms are: (1) their products are heterogeneous; (2) there is a multiplicity and diversity of target groups and messages; (3) the governmental plans and actions affect many people with great consequence; (4) initially little attention was paid to the communication towards internal target groups; (5) there is great politicisation; (6) there is scrutiny from the media, trade unions, and the general public; (7) there is public disagreement among the policymakers themselves about the product both during the product design stage as well as the implementation stage.

The application of Lees-Marshment's typology shows a somewhat different marketing approach for each reform. The Copernicus reform is characterised by a sales-orientation: the reform had been designed by experts and needed to be sold to the public and to the civil servants. The Police reform, on the contrary, is characterised by a market-orientation with an atypical appearance in which the market intelligence did not stem from an anticipative governmental behaviour but from public outrage. In the Police reform, little attention was paid to internal market intelligence which explains the fierce resistance in the product adjustment and implementation stages. The main difference between the two reforms is that the Copernicus reform was not inspired or accelerated by an external crisis such as in the Police reform. Convinced by the necessity and the importance of a fundamental reorganisation of the entire Federal Administration, the Minister for Civil Service and Modernisation of Public Administration, Luc Van den Bossche, had a clearly defined plan in mind. In order to sell the product (the reform) internal and external target groups needed to be convinced these changes were necessary. In the Police reform, it was the general public itself who claimed changes to the system were necessary after experiencing a public scandal. In this case, the external target group did not need to be convinced; the market itself asked safety for children, efficient police services, etc. But, contrary to the Copernicus reform, the internal target groups were not systematically involved in the reform process. There was a clash of interests, competition, and much external communication without the appropriate preceding internal communication.

CONTENT ANALYSIS OF TWO FLEMISH NEWSPAPERS

The Copernicus reform and Police reform are large-scale and unprecedented. They took a prominent role in the political discourse and it can be expected that press attention for the reforms is correspondingly extensive. The Copernicus reforms had to be sold to the general public, while the Police reform had to accommodate public outrage. Successful reform thus implies that media coverage has to be extensive.

In order to compare news coverage on the Copernicus reform and the Police reform, we selected two Flemish newspapers, *De Standaard* and *Het Laatste Nieuws*, for the period of 1999-2002, a period corresponding to the first Verhofstadt Government legislature. For the selection of specific newspaper editions, we used the technique of the constructed week (week 1: Monday, week 2: Tuesday, etc.). Thanks to the constructed week technique, each date has the same chance of being selected for the sample and each day of the week is proportionally represented. Within the selected editions, we analysed all articles on the Copernicus reform and on the Police reform. *Het Laatste Nieuws* is a popular newspaper with a large distribution, while *De Standaard* is the leading quality newspaper. The analytical tool was tested during several training sessions. The tool continued to be refined until an inter-coder reliability of at least 80% had been found. The coding was done by a group of 11 undergraduate students as part of a seminar on communication science research techniques. Two coders coded each article. Though many codings were subjective, inter-coder reliability (number of identical codings/total number of codings) proved to be very high (92%). The final dataset was constructed by randomly selecting one out of the two codes per article.

Our content analysis focused on three issues:

1. *The coverage* of both reform projects in the two newspapers;
2. *The framing of the title and the article body:* the general attitude of the article's writer in the titles as well as in the article (objective, subjective positive or subjective negative framing);
3. *The key topics and stumbling blocks of the reforms:* 9 issue-topics were selected, 8 of which were common to both reforms (laziness of civil servants and police officers, payment, efficiency, corruption, infrastructure, evaluation, flexibility, cost of the reform) and 1 of which is particular for each reform (the civil servant's statute for Copernicus and safety for Police).

Coverage

Our sampling resulted in 216 articles, 132 in *De Standaard* and 84 in *Het Laatste Nieuws* (Table 1).

Seventy-four percent of the 216 articles dealt with the Police reform. More articles were found in the quality newspaper, *De Standaard*, which also published more on the Copernicus reform than *Het Laatste Nieuws*. In *Het Laatste Nieuws*, 17.9% of the articles dealt with the Copernicus reform, which differs significantly from the 31.1% of articles dealing with the Copernicus reform in *De Standaard* ($\chi^2 = 4.660$, $df = 1$, $p = .031$). This trend was confirmed by a quick-scan of the Mediargus newspaper article archive (*http://www.mediargus. be/vowb*): in the period 1999 to 2002 we found 24 articles mentioning the

TABLE 1. Type of Coverage × Newspaper

	De Standaard	Het Laatste Nieuws	Total
Copernicus reform	31.1% (41)	17.9% (15)	25.9% (56)
Police reform	68.9% (91)	82.1% (69)	74.1% (160)
Total	61.1% (132)	38.9% (84)	100% (216)

word Copernicus for *Het Laatste Nieuws*, as compared with 166 in *De Standaard*.

The articles were longer in *De Standaard* than in *Het Laatste Nieuws*. This is surprising given that *Het Laatste Nieuws* tends to publish page-wide articles on certain topical items. The same goes for the illustrations accompanying the articles: the mean size of the illustrations is almost 50% larger in *De Standaard*.

The relatively low number of articles concerning the reforms and the relatively small size of articles and illustrations in *Het Laatste Nieuws* suggest that the reforms are considered to be a less important topic in this popular newspaper. Of our 216 articles, 32 are editorials or opinion articles, three fourths of which are published in *De Standaard*. This is another illustration of the difference in issue salience for the two newspapers.

Citizens are featured more frequently in articles on the Copernicus reform. This should not come as a surprise as the guideline for the Copernicus reform is that the administration ("earth") should rotate around the citizen ("sun") instead of the citizen ("sun") around the administration ("earth"). When politicians are featured in the article, there is a greater chance of the article being placed on the front page.

Framing of the Title and the Article Body

When we look at the content of the title and of the article, no differences can be found between the two newspapers. Thirty-eight percent of the articles in *De Standaard* are categorised as objective/informative, and 45% are said to have a negative undertone. In *Het Laatste Nieuws*, the number of objective/informative articles is 27% with 52% of these articles having a negative undertone. These differences are not significant.

Although a frequency count (Table 2) reveals no difference at the general level, there is a significant difference in the content of title framing and the content of article framing within the individual title-article combinations ($\chi^2 = 92.493$; $df = 4$; $p = .000$). Seventy-four percent of the articles with a subjectively negative title result in a subjectively negative article, while in 52% of the articles objective/informative titles results in a purely objective/informative article. Combinations of titles and articles differ according to the newspaper. In the popular *Het Laatste Nieuws*, a subjectively negative title usually results in an article with a negatively coloured content. This general tendency also holds for *De Standaard*, but in a quarter of the cases in *De Standaard*, a negatively framed title results in an objective article.

TABLE 2. Framing of Title and Article Body

	De Standaard		Het Laatste Nieuws	
	Attitude in title	Attitude in article	Attitude in title	Attitude in article
Objective (Informative)	38%	38%	43%	27%
Subjective positive	13%	17%	9%	20%
Subjective negative	49%	45%	48%	52%
	100%	100%	100%	100%

Topics

The articles were scanned for 9 possible topics to which the actors could refer. Table 3 shows the topics mentioned for both reforms.

The most important topics mentioned in both reforms are: efficiency, the (often failing) infrastructure of the public services, and the payment of civil servants and police officers. The (failing) infrastructure in the Federal Administration and the introduction of a staff evaluation system means that these two items are mentioned more frequently in relation to the Copernicus reform. The most important difference deals with the cost of the reforms. This is clearly a topic in the Police reform while it is not in the Copernicus reform. In *De Standaard*, the actors mention efficiency and staff evaluation more often, while actors in *Het Laatste Nieuws* devote considerably more attention to the cost of the reform.

Apart from this inventory of topics, coders were asked to indicate the general attitude towards the reform of the actors (except for employees) in the newspaper articles. The predominant attitude towards the Police reform is negative for all actors involved. For the Copernicus reform, citizens and politicians tend to be positive, while employees and trade unions are negative. Trade unions are, in both cases, the most negative actors with more than 80% of the articles showing a union spokesperson with a negative attitude. Trade unions protect their members and, as a result, they tend to lean towards a "resistance to change." The attitudes towards Copernicus reflect those generally to be expected from the actors: politicians defend the reforms and citizens support them while unions are hostile. As for the Police reform, the overall negative attitude can be explained by the excessive costs associated with this reform. The overall attitudes of the actors do not differ depending on the newspaper.

TABLE 3. Topics

	Copernicus reform	Police reform
Laziness	2.0%	0.7%
Payment	17.9%	15.6%
Efficiency	21.9%	23.3%
Corruption	1.3%	1.5%
Infrastructure	21.9%	17.8%
Evaluation	10.6%	7.4%
Flexibility	9.9%	9.2%
Cost of reform	4.6%	15.6%
Safety	n.a.	8.9%
Statute	9.9%	n.a.

Note: % of total topics mentioned

CONCLUSIONS

Recently, the Belgian Federal Government embarked on large-scale re-forms of the Federal Administration (Copernicus) and the Police. Using Lees-Marshment's typology of marketing processes, we identified the Copernicus reform as a sales-oriented marketing process: a finished product, an expert-developed administrative reform project had to be sold. Declining enthusiasm for communication and growing disagreement about the product gradually made the issue disappear from the market. The Police reform followed a market-oriented marketing process. The Police reform was designed to cater to the public's fierce demand for profound and fast changes. However, the absence of new scandals and public outcry made it clear that Government was not actively collecting market information by itself. It merely reacted to external information. This explains why it failed to recognise new market signals. An analysis of newspaper coverage of both reform projects seems to confirm this trend.

Apparently, the Government did not manage to control the communication on its ambitious reforms. The Police reform was nothing more than a reaction to a number of shattering events. Communication failed because of growing disagreement among the actors involved. The product (the Police reform) was tailored as a response to the public outrage, but this "market information" was gradually replaced by pressure from police officers, trade unions, and mayors. Because of the sudden change in the "market," politicians and the media shifted their attention from the pressing need for reforms to the dysfunctioning of the reforms themselves. The Government failed to recognise that the market for the reforms had changed.

We presented the Copernicus reform as a product to be sold. This administrative reform was at first accompanied by a large-scale communication offensive that quickly faded. Government-initiated communication failed due to insufficient attention towards internal communication and due to disagreements within the Government on the nature of the reforms making further marketing impossible. This explains why the administrative reforms quickly became a non-issue in the press. The popular press in particular did not pay attention to this administrative reform.

Our analysis of government marketing efforts of two large-scale reforms showed that the marketing of reforms is extremely difficult when there is no shared understanding of the product to be marketed. Marketing reforms becomes even more difficult when the public does not consider the reform to be important. The public supports the Copernicus reform but is at the same time rather indifferent, as it does not consider the public administration as an important factor in their life. This makes it very difficult for the Government to keep the reforms on the agenda. As for the Police reform, the marketing of the reform was designed using outdated market intelligence. The reform and the communication referred to shattering events and public outcry but failed to recognise that the market had changed. The marketing did not focus on the new key players within the market, the police unions and the mayors.

REFERENCES

Auditor General British Columbia (1995-1996), "Public Communications: Distinguishing between Government Program and Partisan Political Communications," *http://www.oag.bc.ca/PUBS/1995-96/report-5/SEC-4.PDF.*

Council for Excellence in Government (2001), *Changing Images of Government in TV Entertainment*, Washington, DC: Council for Excellence in Government.

Couttenier, Ivan (1997), "Belgian Politics in 1996," *Res Publica*, 39 (4), 532-545.

Depauw, Sam and Mark Deweerdt (2002), "Belgian Politics in 2001," *Res Publica*, 44 (2-3), 255-278.

Fiers, Stefaan and Mark Deweerdt (1998), "Belgian Politics in 1997," *Res Publica*, 40 (3-4), 377-396.

_____ and _____ (1999), "Belgian Politics in 1998," *Res Publica*, 41 (2-3), 265-284.

_____ and _____ (2001), "Belgian Politics in 2001," *Res Publica*, 43 (2-3), 317-341.

Gelders, Dave (2002), "The Tension between Party Political and Administrative Executive Communication," paper presented at The European Consortium for Communications Research Doctoral Summer School, University of Westminster, London.

Gelders, Dave (forthcoming), "Public Information Provision about Policy Intentions: the Dutch and Belgian Experience," *Government Information Quarterly.*

Goodsell, Charles T. (1985), *The Case for Bureaucracy: a Public Administration Polemic*, New Jersey: Chatham.

Lees-Marshment, Jennifer (2001), "The Marriage of Politics and Marketing," *Political Studies*, 49 (4), 692-713.

Maesschalck, Jeroen (2002), "When Do Scandals Have an Impact on Policy Making? A Case Study of the Police Reform following the Dutroux Scandal in Belgium," *International Public Management Journal*, 5 (2), 169-193.

Nomden, Koen (2002), "Het Copernicusplan: de Hervorming van de Belgische Federale Overheidsdienst Nader Bekeken," *Bestuurswetenschappen*, 5, 396-414.

Osborne, David and Ted Gaebler (1993), *Reinventing Government: How the Entrepreneurial Spirit is Transforming the Public Sector*, New York: Plume.

Ringeling, Arthur (1993), *Het Imago van de Overheid: De Beoordeling van Prestaties van de Publieke Sector*, 's Gravenhage: VUGA.

Van de Walle, Steven and Geert Bouckaert (2003), "Public Service Performance and Trust in Government: the Problem of Causality," *International Journal of Public Administration*, 26 (8-9), 891-913.

Van Hemelrijck, Marc and Tom Auwers (1999), "Copernicus: Public Management Reform in the Belgian Federal Administration," *http://www.copernicus.be.*

Political Marketing Segmentation–
The Case of UK Local Government

Patricia Rees
Hanne Gardner

SUMMARY. This article considers the nature and use of segmentation in political marketing. The importance of an awareness of political marketing at a more local level will become particularly important with the onset of regional government. The article particularly concerned with segmentation in local government where there has been little empirical research. The results of a survey amongst local government officers are presented. The article concludes that a significant minority of local government officers use segmentation. The key factors facilitating the use of segmentation were found to be education, experience, the role of the chief executive and central government pressure. *[Article copies available for a fee from The Haworth Document Delivery Service: 1-800-HAWORTH. E-mail address: <docdelivery@haworthpress.com> Website: <http://www.HaworthPress. com> © 2005 by The Haworth Press, Inc. All rights reserved.]*

KEYWORDS. Political marketing, local government, segmentation

---

Patricia Rees and Hanne Gardner are affiliated with Manchester Metropolitan University Business School, Aytoun Campus, Manchester M1 3GH, UK (E-mail: p.l. rees@mmu.ac.uk).

[Haworth co-indexing entry note]: "Political Marketing Segmentation–The Case of UK Local Government." Rees, Patricia, and Hanne Gardner. Co-published simultaneously in *Journal of Nonprofit & Public Sector Marketing* (Best Business Books, an imprint of The Haworth Press, Inc.) Vol. 14, No. 1/2, 2005, pp. 169-184; and: *Current Issues in Political Marketing* (eds: Walter W. Wymer, Jr., and Jennifer Lees-Marshment) Best Business Books, an imprint of The Haworth Press, Inc., 2005, pp. 169-184. Single or multiple copies of this article are available for a fee from The Haworth Document Delivery Service [1-800-HAWORTH, 9:00 a.m. - 5:00 p.m. (EST). E-mail address: getinfo@haworthpressinc.com].

Available online at http://www.haworthpress.com/web/JNPSM
doi:10.1300/J054v14n01_10

INTRODUCTION

Political marketing has been largely concerned with the activities of central government and the major political parties. It now needs to be developed further to consider the wider aspects of politics. The Shorter Oxford English Dictionary defines politics as "the science dealing with the form, organization, and the administration of a state or part of one." Local government is part of the administration of the state and thus part of the remit covered by political marketing. The way in which local government carries out its activities has a direct impact on the way in which political parties and their policies are viewed. Just as political parties need to carry out marketing activities and engage in a market orientation (Lees-Marshment 2001), so too does local government. The conceptual framework for Political Marketing characteristics outlined by Butler and Collins (1999) draw attention to not only the structural characteristics but process characteristics 'that define, develop and deliver value' (p. 56). It is at local government level that value delivery occurs. In addition it must be remembered that good government at a local level can ameliorate the 'protest' votes re central government at the time of local elections. A further imperative for considering political marketing at a local government level is the impending development of regional government in the UK.

This article considers the use of segmentation in Local Government. In order to set the tone of this article with regard to the nature of marketing and by association segmentation, the following definition of marketing, (which has been formed from an extensive study of the nature of local government and the issues facing it) is given:

> Marketing is the philosophical position that places the needs of the customer at the heart of the organization. It is an exchange process between the organization and its customers that recognizes the organization's ability (or not) to provide for the customer's need. The marketing philosophy is based on a long-term approach and in the case of local government, survival rather than profit is often the goal. *Not for profit marketing differs from commercial marketing only in the acceptance of the idea that value need not be monetary.* The customers of local government may be any number of different people–for example, the elected member, the citizen and the family members. The customer is often not the actual user of the service as would be the case in respite care. Those who adopt the marketing philosophy have a toolkit of marketing concepts–including segmentation–to operationalize their standpoint. These concepts go far beyond the popular notions of advertizing and promotion.

We argue that local government is already embracing the concept of marketing and its attendant tools and concepts. To illustrate this a brief overview of the context of local government, as well as the development of not for profit marketing, will be given. This is followed by a discussion of one of the major marketing concepts–segmentation and its use in the not for profit sector and local government. The results of some empirical work regarding the use of segmentation in local government are then presented. The article then concludes and suggests directions for further work to ensure the continued development of the field of political marketing, with particular reference to local government.

LOCAL GOVERNMENT

The history of UK local government indicates that it has never been exactly stable. Since the 1800s it has been expanding and contracting in turn and changing the shape of its functions. Burns, Hambleton and Hoggett (1994) summarize the changes made to local government since the arrival of the Conservative government in 1979. Firstly, cuts were made in financial support for local government from central government. Secondly, local government became more politicized and thirdly central government imposed particular forms of management on local government. Some manifestations of these changes have been: Compulsory Competitive Tendering (CCT). This is where departments, who have in the past provided local services (e.g., refuse collection, the cleaning of public buildings, legal and financial services), now have to compete with private companies for the work; Care in the Community (placing people initially cared for in homes back into the community); Local Management of Schools (taking the management of schools out of the hands of local government and giving it to the schools). More recently the introduction of Best Value (which replaces CCT) in local government stipulates that amongst other things, local authorities must consult with their citizens. There seems little doubt that local government is going to remain under continued external pressure from central government to change.

Coupled with these initiatives is the evolving management style of local government. Byrne (1994) considers that local government is very varied both within and between authorities. The roles of the chief executive and the elected members are changing with speculation as to what the strategic thrust is and from where the impetus should originate (Worrall et al. 1996). The management of local government has moved from the bureaucratic through what Pollitt (1993) terms New Managerialism to variants of New Public Management (Ferlie 1999 and Raine and Wilson 1996). New Public Management, which involves the use of tools and concepts formerly deemed exclusively private sector, is seen as a means of bridging the gap between the pre Thatcher Public Administration ethos and the commercialism of succeeding decades. The debate still rages, but meanwhile local government is turning to frameworks used in the private sector concepts such as marketing, for inspiration and help, in the face of a turbulent environment.

NOT FOR PROFIT MARKETING

Not for profit marketing is associated with all those organizations that do not have profit as their main motivating force. Examples of not for profit marketing include, health marketing, arts marketing, charities marketing and political marketing. Interest in not for profit marketing has been encouraged by two main forces. Firstly the recognition amongst academics and practitioners that marketing can be applied to an area with no profit motive. Secondly the pressure on not for profits to become more business-like.

The notion that marketing in a sector with no obvious profit motive could be possible was probably facilitated by the Social Exchange school of thought. Alderson and McInnes are credited by Sheth, Gardner and Garrett (1988) with putting forward this perspective. They see markets being created by the social intercourse of producers of goods and services and users. Marketing is seen as an activity that brings into being a potential market relationship between producers and users. As Wilmott (1999, p. 215) puts it "The discourse of exchange is so beguiling because it suggests that each individual is a customer who is free to pick and choose in the market place." The paper that is generally accepted as being the starting point of NFP marketing is that of Kotler and Levy (1969). They saw marketing as a "pervasive, societal activity" (p. 10) and as "serving and satisfying human needs" (p. 15). Their point was, that non business organizations could benefit from the use of marketing, in the same way as business organizations did. Since then there has been a growing literature around not for profit marketing in both the UK and the USA (Rees 1998). This growth has been further facilitated by a burgeoning Services Marketing literature (for example, Berry and Parasuraman 1993; Knight 1999).

With regard to the public sector becoming more business-like, Kotler and Andreasen (1996) list critical developments in the social and economic environment which have brought further attention to the concept of "nonprofits"; changes in the political environment encouraging increased privatization of public services; changes in the social climate encouraging increased voluntarism and changes in the traditional sources of support for nonprofits. The last section indicated quite clearly the scale of the changes in the political environment affecting UK local government.

The area of local government marketing is now benefiting from the development of the Political Marketing field (See the special editions of the European Journal of Marketing 2001 and the Journal of Marketing Management 2002). This field is cross disciplinary with academic participation from both the marketing and the political science areas. For example the UK Political Studies Association conferences now have a political marketing group.

Meanwhile there has been considerable disquiet expressed about the applicability and appropriateness of marketing in local government (Walsh 1991, Ratcliffe and Kitchen 1995 and Kearsy and Varey 1998) Aside from the emphasis on the very different nature of local government, the transfer of marketing tools from the private to the public sector with little adaptation is an area of concern. The following anonymous review of an earlier article in this area perhaps best sums up the situation:

> Local government is very diverse in its provision and the application of marketing in local government has to take account of very different needs and expectations of the various user groups in relation to the products and services that are being used. Slavish application of marketing tools that are appropriate to the private sector is not appropriate to the public sector. The drives and motives of buyers and users are fundamentally different where public sector provision is concerned. Furthermore there are very many different types of relationship between provider and user, for example in the police force the relationship between one individual and the police will be different where the person is stopped for speeding on the one hand and seeking assistance after a burglary on the other. The marketing issues therefore are very different.

However, segmentation in particular, is a marketing tool that could address such complex relationships (which incidentally are not only to be found in the public sector–a nightclub bouncer has a similar two-sided relationship as that of the policeman, with a customer that needs to be ejected and another that needs protecting). By understanding more critically the nature of the potential market/audience for services/ideas, government at both the national and local level will be able to strategically develop and target their outputs. Surely this is an important goal and one that could be expedited by the more careful use of segmentation analysis. There has, however, been little empirical research into this area and much of the work has been theoretical and speculative. The next section explores the literature on segmentation from its inception to its use in the not for profit sector and political marketing.

SEGMENTATION

The concept of segmentation was developed by Smith (1957). It is a means of defining customers in terms of what they want or will accept from a product, service or idea, at what price (cost) and also the best way of accessing them. Segmentation seeks to make producers of goods/services/ideas better understand their markets/customers/clients. This better understanding in turn leads to the development of goods/services/ideas which relate more closely to the needs of the customers/clients/citizens. Segmentation has been used for decades by manufacturers of consumer goods to increase market share and profits by creating consumer loyalty based on consumer satisfaction and repeat purchases. Segmentation has been proved to be one of the fundamental marketing tools which has allowed marketers to reach their target market based on accurate segmentation. It has become one of the corner stones of the marketing profession.

Textbooks provide information on the ways to segment markets. These range from the reasonably simple (geographic, demographic) through to the complicated (multivariate techniques). In between there are items such as 'lifestyle profiling' and 'benefit segmentation.' These can be summarized as:

Organizational Markets Segmentation Variables	Consumer Markets Segmentation Variables
Organizational Characteristics: Size, Location, Usage Rate	Geographic
Product or Service Application	Demographic
Product	Geodemographic (e.g., Acorn)
Application	Psychographic (Activities, Interests, Opinions)
Technology	Behaviour (Benefits sought, usage rate, Loyalty, Attitude, Buyer readiness stage)
Purchasing Policies	Multivariable (Combination of above)
Decision Making Unit Structure	
Decision Making Process	
Buyer-seller Relationships	

The criteria for successful segmentation are considered to be (Brassington and Pettitt 1997): distinctiveness–a segment must be significantly different from another segment; tangibility–a segment must be of a suitable size (substantial) to make it worthwhile pursuing; accessibility–a segment needs to be accessible both physically and by means of communication such as advertising; defendability–the segment should be one that can be defended against competition and sustainability–the segment should be likely to be around for a reasonable time. These criteria which have been developed for consumer/for profit markets–may not actually be appropriate in not for profit settings. For example, firstly local government has to provide services for the whole community–it cannot pick and choose its segments and secondly segments may not be easily accessible (for example, children in need of protection or drug users). Nevertheless it is still useful to be able to segment not for profit markets–even if only to ensure a more accurate way of identifying the various groups.

The following outlines some of the research into, and comments about, segmentation in the not for profit sector, both in the US and UK. Yavas and Riecken (1993) and Yavas et al. (1993) investigated donor behaviour with regard to the perceived risk involved in giving to charities. A greater understanding of the donor segments–Non donor, sporadic donor and consistent donor–was attempted, facilitating more suitable targeting of each segment. An earlier study by Harvey (1990) investigated why people donated to charity. Benefit segmentation was utilised in this case, to divide the market. Benefit segmentation is where buyers are segmented according to the particular benefits they are seeking. Three core benefit segments are often recognised in markets–those who seek quality, those who seek service and those who seek to minimize costs (Kotler and Andreasen 1996). Benefit segmentation was also used to understand affluent donors (Cermak et al. 1994).

Kotler and Andreasen (1996) address segmentation in the not for profit sector in some detail. They suggest bases for segmenting markets as: Objective General Measures (Geographic, Demographic); Objective Specific Measures (Past Behaviour); Inferred General Measures (Pychographics) and Inferred Specific Measures (Benefits sought). This produces some colourful segmentation criteria. For example, when drawing up benefit segments for a family planning agency, there are segments called: Firefighters–who need an immediate solution to a problem; Desperates–who need relief from feelings of desperation; Married Rationals–who have freedom of choice, control, financial stability and marital harmony. Other areas where segmentation has been addressed in the US include: Outdoor Recreation (Miles, McDonald and Capella 1993); Green Movement (Olsen, Jackson and Granzin 1993); Museums (Todd and Lawson 2001) State Sponsored Lotteries (Miyazaki et al. 2001) and Associations (Levy 1992).

With regard to the UK, Walsh (1989) considered benefit segmentation as particularly important. Local authorities need to ask themselves about the benefits consumers receive from the services provided, as well as the characteristics that provide those benefits. He does, however express concern (Walsh 1991) about the use of segmentation in general, in the public sector, because of the statutory nature of many services that need to be delivered universally.

However, it could be argued that even if services need to be provided to all, some idea about the varying needs of citizens might ensure more efficient provision. Hannagan (1992) raises the issue of the Pareto effect. He says that in charities it is often the case that 80% of the money raised comes from 20% of the donors. He wonders, therefore what many charities should do about segmentation and targeting. Should they bother communicating with the 80%? Bruce (1995) considers that charities do not pay enough attention to segmenting their publics.

Chapman and Cowdell (1998) say that the public sector needs to approach the issue of market segmentation in two contexts. Firstly in the area of non-discretionary demands such as refuse collection and basic health care. Secondly in discretionary areas, for example leisure services. Once these factors are borne in mind it is generally possible to apply segmentation processes developed for the private sector in the public sector. They stress the importance of recognizing user characteristics (geographic, demographic) and user behaviour (what do they actually do and want). By using such categories segments can be thought showered by those in the organization. The above examples would seem to indicate that those involved in/researching nonprofit marketing are already displaying creativity in the way they apply marketing concepts.

Political Marketing has recognized the importance of segmentation (Baines 1999; Baines et al. 2003; Bannon 2003; Dermody and Scullion 2000.) This is because political parties tend to rely on simplistic segmentation–for example–loyal voter/floating vote; male/female or old/middle aged/young (Lilleker 2003)–ignoring the more complex combination of say, age, culture, gender, race and the actual issue under debate.

Two pieces of empirical work have looked at the role of segmentation in UK local government. The first, by Cowell (1979), investigated the use of segmentation in local government. He discovered that like other marketing concepts it was infrequently applied. The second was by Yorke (1984). His article puts forward the view that leisure centre managers in local authorities need to use segmentation variables that are more sophisticated than the geographic one of 'catchment area' (where most of the clients live). He explains the nature of segmentation and shows how it might be used in order to understand a leisure center's market. To do this he constructs a three dimensional model combining the segmentation variables of family life cycle, sex and employment. This model alone produces 60 theoretical segments. The empirical research carried out amongst leisure center managers, leisure center users and members of the community indicated the gap between the needs of the different segments and leisure center managers' knowledge of them. He concludes that the use of segmentation analysis within the catchment area does have validity. Thus allowing leisure centers to concentrate their resources more effectively.

In recent years there has been little or no empirical research into the use of segmentation in UK local government. Reasons for this could be (a) marketing is considered incompatible with the public sector ethic, (b) marketing is viewed by those working in local government as firmly wedded to pricing and thus inappropriate in a not for profit organization, (c) marketing is misunderstood by those involved with the public sector (as purely advertising and promotion) or (d) there is little money to fund such research. The aim of this research is to see how, if at all the, application of segmentation in UK local government has developed and to provide a basis for further research in the area of segmentation within political marketing. To this end a survey was carried out to update the research.

THE SURVEY

One objective of the survey (amongst others) was to discover the extent to which local government officers knew about and/or used market segmentation. Questionnaires were sent out to two local government officers in every authority (812) in England and Wales. The sample was purposive in nature, as the intention was to choose officers from "opposite" types of departments. By this it is meant departments which seemed to have different roles and therefore, perhaps, a different view of marketing. As an example, the most obvious "opposites" are Leisure and Social Services. Questions in the questionnaire related directly to segmentation were: "Have you heard of segmentation?," "Do you use segmentation?" and "The customers you serve have different needs and some are in need of your service more than others." This last question was included as a surrogate to indicate the sub-conscious awareness of segmentation (even if they were unfamiliar with the term).

RESULTS

Of the 812 questionnaires sent out, 374 were completed and sent back (46% response rate). In answer to the question "The customers you serve have different needs and some are in need of your service more than others" 99% of the respondents tended to agree with this statement. In answer to the question "Have you heard of Segmentation?" 69% answered yes. In answer to the question "Do you use Segmentation?" 40% answered yes. Cross Tabulations were then carried out to discover if there were any factors which might influence the use and/or knowledge of the concept of segmentation. These factors were derived from other questions in the questionnaire.

Table 1 indicates that working outside local government and some training in marketing is more likely to mean that an officer has some knowledge of segmentation and may even use it. The Pearson Chi-squared result for whether someone had worked in local government or not and their knowledge or use of segmentation was: 16.585 with 2 degrees of freedom at the .000 level of significance. The Pearson Chi-squared result for whether someone had been on an educational course containing a marketing element was: 23.914 at the 000 level of significance. Agreement with the surrogate statement was not significant in either case indicating knowledge the spirit of the specific marketing concept (segmentation) was not dependant on education or having worked outside local government.

Further cross tabulations were also carried out with regard to the role of the chief executive and the nature of departments. A question was asked about the role of the Chief Executive. Seven possible alternative roles for the Chief Executive were put forward and respondents were allowed to select more than one. These roles were derived from the literature (Kerley 1994; Dargie 1998;

TABLE 1

Heard of Segmentation	WITH	Always worked in LG	68%
Heard of Segmentation	WITH	Not always worked in LG	72%
Use Segmentation	WITH	Always worked in LG	34%
Use Segmentation	WITH	Not always worked in LG	54%
The customers that you serve have different needs and some are more in need of your service than others	WITH	Always worked in LG	97% agreed
The customers that you serve have different needs and some are more in need of your service than others	WITH	Not always worked in LG	100% agreed
Heard of Segmentation	WITH	Attended an educational course containing a marketing module	83%
Use Segmentation	WITH	Attended an educational course containing a marketing module	93%
The customers that you serve have different needs and some are more in need of your service than others	WITH	Attended an educational course containing a marketing module	99%

Hambleton 1998). It was possible to gather the roles into two main groups–one generally positive and one generally negative:

Generally Negative Perspective	Generally Positive Perspective
The CE plays a minor role	The CE has Vision
Unsure about the role of the CE	The CE works closely with the chairs
The CE plays one group off against the other	The CE is the interface between members and officers
The CE devises all the strategy	

Of the officers with a negative view of the Chief Executive only 33% had heard of used segmentation. This rose to 57% where there was a more positive view of the Chief Executive. This would indicate that where a chief executive is considered to maintain a positive role there is more likely to be an acceptance or use of segmentation.

As has been mentioned, officers from different departments were targeted in this survey. The rationale for this had been derived from both the literature and an earlier exploratory survey. Concern had been expressed, for example, that Social Services departments would have a greater difficulty in utilizing marketing concepts such as segmentation. Responses in the survey came from 125 different department titles. For the purposes of this discussion the departments were grouped under five main types: Leisure, General Administration, Community, Planning and Social Services (see Table 2).

From these results we see that leisure services and marketing are the most likely to be engaged in segmentation. Of the rest of the departments, Social Services use segmentation the most–with Planning departments less likely to do so. As with education and whether an officer had worked outside local government–the department worked for was significant in whether segmentation was used. The Pearson Chi-test was 75.3 at 10 degrees of freedom at the 000.

TABLE 2

	Leisure	General Admin.	Mar-keting	Com-munity	Planning	Social Services
Heard of Segmentation	17%	31%	25%	41%	38%	24%
Use Segmentation	70%	26%	75%	22%	10%	37%
The customers that you serve have different needs and some are more in need of your services than others	98%	100%	100%	100%	97%	100%

level. Once again the surrogate for segmentation was not significant. Associated with the nature of the department and the use of segmentation were the results from the question "Do you think marketing is appropriate for your particular service?" This was cross tabulated with whether they had heard of or used segmentation (Table 3). Not surprisingly, a far greater proportion of those who considered marketing to be appropriate had actually used marketing. The Pearson Chi-test at 2 degrees of freedom was 22.3 at the .000 level of significance.

DISCUSSION AND CONCLUSIONS

A significant minority of local government officers is using segmentation. The survey provided some indication of the basic use of segmentation. It did not suggest, however, the segmentation variables being used by local government officers. Consequently it is difficult to make comparisons with the extant literature on segmentation. Nevertheless this is some improvement of the conclusions drawn by Cowell (1979) more than twenty years earlier. The education and experience of officers outside local government increases their acceptance of segmentation, as does a positive view of the Chief Executive. Whilst there needs to be sensitivity about the nature of local government and its various publics/clients/stakeholders–there would appear to be some immediate applicability of segmentation–at least from the local government officers perspective. Departments associated with leisure services were the most pro active in the area of segmentation. This would seem a marked improvement from the situation described by Yorke (1984). However the results from the other departments indicated that others are beginning to see the efficacy of segmentation.

The advice about context given by Chapman and Cowdell (1998) needs to be heeded, as do the calls to keep segmentation user friendly. However some of the

TABLE 3

Heard of segmentation	**WITH**	Marketing appropriate	29%
Use segmentation	**WITH**	Marketing appropriate	43%
Heard segmentation	**WITH**	Marketing not appropriate	27%
Use segmentation	**WITH**	Marketing not appropriate	0%

more complex segmentation variables suggested by Kotler and Andreasen (1996) may be appropriate in the more complex local government services. Market segmentation allows customers/clients to achieve a greater degree of satisfaction. Moreover the more efficient use of resources provides the opportunity for the use of more sophisticated segmentation criteria, thus reaching the target market more effectively and efficiently.

The main result of this piece of research indicated that local government officers were comfortable with the idea of marketing in general. It also showed some movement down the road towards the use of segmentation as a marketing tool. A possible model of the present situation in local government is shown in Figure 1.

This article has provided a more contemporary view of segmentation in UK Local Government. The next stages of the research are; Firstly, to discover how segmentation is being used in UK local government–notably the types of segmentation variables officers are actually using. This would help to understand the extent to which local government is engaging in what was termed at the start of this article–simplistic segmentation. This research could be done in tandem with the work on segmentation in the area of Political Marketing. Secondly ascertain the relationship these variables have to the actual segments in

FIGURE 1

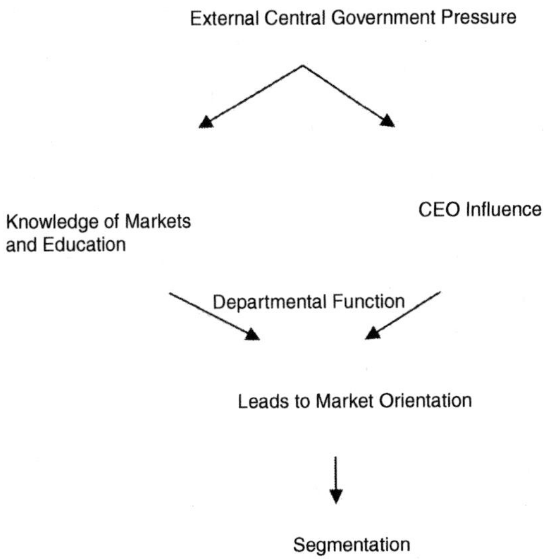

External Central Government Pressure

Knowledge of Markets
and Education

CEO Influence

Departmental Function

Leads to Market Orientation

Segmentation

the local authority population. This could be done by in depth interviews with local government officers and focus groups with citizens.

There is no doubt that the pressure from central government will continue to make Local Government become more business like. Local Government can be aided in this process by a clearer understanding of business practices, tools and concepts adapted to their particular context. Echoing Butler and Collins (1999), it is important to recognize that material from two separate disciplines (Politics and Marketing) may not easily form an integrated model which can be applied to practical situations. What it does achieve however is to highlight the different components of both disciplines and allows researchers to identify those key components in certain situations. Effective implementation is another matter.

REFERENCES

Baines, Paul R. (1999), "Voter Segmentation and Candidate Positioning," in *Handbook of Political Marketing*, ed. Bruce I. Newman, Thousand Oaks, CA: Sage, 73-86.

Baines, Paul R., Robert M. Worcester, David Jarrett and Roger Mortimore (2003), "Market Segmentation and Product Differentiation in Political Campaigns: A Technical Feature Perspective," *Journal of Marketing Management*, Vol. 19, Nos. 1 and 2, 225-249.

Bannon, Declan (2003), "Voting, Non-voting and Consumer Buying Behaviour: Non-Voter segmentation and the underlying causes of electoral inactivity," *Journal of Public Affairs*, Vol. 3, No. 2 Berry, Len and A. Parasuraman (1993), "Building a new Academic Field–The Case of Services Marketing," *Journal of Retailing*, Vol. 69, No. 1, 13-59.

Brassington, Frances and Stephen Pettitt. (1997), *Principles of Marketing*, London: Pitman.

Bruce, Ian (1995), "Do Not-for-Profits Value their Customers and their needs?" *International Marketing Review*, Vol. 12, No. 4, 77-84.

Burns, Danny, Robin Hambleton and Paul Hoggett (1994), *The Politics of Decentralisation–Revitalising Local Democracy*, Basingstoke, England: Macmillan.

Butler, Patrick and Neil Collins (1999) "A Conceptual Framework for Political Marketing," in *Handbook of Political Marketing*, ed. Bruce I. Newman, Thousand Oaks, CA: Sage, 55-72.

Byrne, Anthony (1994), *Local Government in Britain*, 6th Edition, London, England: Penguin.

Cermak, Dianne S.P., Karen M. File and Russ A. Prince (1994), "A Benefit Segmentation of the Major Donor Market," *Journal of Business Research*, 29, 121-130.

Chapman, David and Theo Cowdell (1998), *New Public Sector Marketing*, London: Financial Times/Pitman.

Cowell, Donald (1979), "Marketing in Local Authority Leisure and Recreation Centres," *Local Government Studies*, July/August, 31-41.

Dargie, Charlotte (1998), "The Role of Public Sector Chief Executives," *Public Administration*, Vol. 76, Spring, 161-177.

Dermody, Janine and Richard Scullion (2000), "Perceptions of negative political advertising: meaningful or menacing? An empirical study of the 1997 British Election Campaign," *International Journal of Advertising*, Vol. 19, No. 2, 201-224.

Ferlie, Euan (1999), "The New Public Management and New Labour: An Institutional Perspective," A working paper given at the British Academy of Management Conference, Manchester Metropolitan University, UK, September.

Hambleton, Robin (1998), "Strengthening Political Leadership in UK Local Government," *Public Money and Management*, Jan-March, 41-51.

Hannagan, Tim J. (1992), *Marketing for the Nonprofit Sector*, London: Macmillan Professional.

Harvey, James W. (1990), "Benefit Segmentation for Fund Raisers," *Journal of the Academy of Marketing Science*, Vol. 18, No. 1, 77-86.

Kerley, Richard (1994), *Managing in Local Government*, Basingstoke: Macmillan.

Kearsy, Anthony and Richard J. Varey (1998), "Managerial thinking on marketing for public services," *Public Money and Management*, Vol. 18, No. 2, 51-61.

Knight, G (1999), "International services marketing: review of research 1980-1998," *Journal of Services Marketing*, Vol. 13, No. 4/5, 347-361.

Kotler, Philip and Sidney Levy (1969), "Broadening the Concept of Marketing," *Journal of Marketing*, Vol. 33, No. 1, 10-15.

Kotler, Philip and Alan Andreasen (1991), *Strategic Marketing for Nonprofit Organisations*, 4th Edition, Englewood Cliffs, New Jersey: Prentice Hall.

Lees-Marshment, Jennifer (2001), *Political Marketing and British Political Parties*, Manchester: Manchester University Press.

Levy, Donald R. (1992), "Segment Your Markets," *Association Management*, August, 111-115.

Lilleker, Darren G. (2003), "Political Marketing: the cause of an emerging democratic deficit in Britain?," Paper given at the Political Studies Conference, University of Leicester, April.

Miles, Morgan P., Barbara McDonald, Louis M. Capella and H. Ken Cordell (1993), "A Proposed Segmentation Framework for the outdoor recreation Market," *Journal of Nonprofit and Public Sector Marketing*, Vol. 1, No. 1, 51-69.

Miyazaki, Anthony D., Anne M. Brumbaugh and David E. Sprott (2001), "Promoting and countering consumer misconceptions of random events: the case of perceived control and state sponsored lotteries," *Journal of Public Policy and Marketing*, Vol. 20, No. 2, 254-267.

Olsen James E., Anita L. Jackson and Kent L. Granzin (1993), "Environmental Group Participation: A Focus on the Helping Process," *Journal of Nonprofit and Public Sector Marketing*, Vol. 1, No. 4, 41-65.

Pollitt, Christopher (1993), *Managerialism and the Public Services*, 2nd Edition, Oxford: Blackwells.

Raine John W. and Michael J. Willson (1996), "Managerialism and beyond: the case of criminal justice," *International Journal of Public Sector Management*, Vol. 9, No. 4, 20-34.

Ratcliffe M. and Kitchen P.J. (1995), Theoretical Applicability vs. Environmental Straightjacket: Applying the Marketing Audit to a UK Public Sector Nonprofit Organization, *Journal of Nonprofit and Public Sector Marketing*, Volume 3, Nos. 3/4, pp. 121-146.

Rees P.L. (1998) "Marketing in the UK and US Not-for-Profit Sector: The Import Mirror View," *The Services Industries Journal*, Vol. 18, No. 1, 113-132.

Sheth, Jagdish N., David M. Gardner and Dennis E. Garrett (1988), *Marketing Theory: Evolution and Evaluation*, New York: John Wiley & Sons.

Smith, Wendell R. (1957), "Product Differentiation and Market Segmentation as Alternative Marketing Strategies," *Journal of Marketing*, Vol. 21, July, 3-8.

Todd, Sarah and Rob Lawson (2001), "Lifestyle segmentation and museum/gallery visiting behaviour," *International Journal of Nonprofit and Voluntary Sector Marketing*, Vol. 6, No. 3, 269-277.

Walsh Kieron (1989), *Marketing in Local Government*, London: Longman.

Walsh Kieron (1991), "Citizens and Consumers: Marketing and Public Sector Management," *Public Money and Management*, Vol. 11, No. 2, 9-15.

Willmott, Hugh (1999), "On the Idolization of Markets and the denigration of Marketers: Some Critical Reflections on a Professional Paradox," in Eds. Douglas Brownlie, Mike Saren, Robin Wensley and Richard Whittington, *Rethinking Marketing*, London: Sage.

Worrall Les, Chris Collinge and Tony Bill (1996), "The Strategic Process in Local Government: A discussion Document and Extended Bibliography," Working Paper Series, Wolverhampton Business School Management Research Centre, September.

Yavas Ugur and Glen Riecken (1993), "Socioeconomic and Behavioral Correlates of Donor Segments: An Application to United Way," *Journal of Nonprofit & Public Sector Marketing*, Vol. 1, No. 1, 71-83.

Yorke David A. (1984), "The Definition of Market Segments for Leisure Centre Services: Theory and Practice," *European Journal of Marketing*, Vol. 18, No. 2, 100-113.

The Impact of New Technology
on the Communication
of Parliamentary Information

Rita Marcella
Graeme Baxter
Nick Moore

SUMMARY. This article discusses the results of an exploratory study, funded by the Economic and Social Research Council, which investigated the impact of technology on the communication of parliamentary information to the general public in the United Kingdom. As Stage 1 of the project, interviews were conducted with representatives of the public information services of the UK Parliament, the Scottish Parliament, the National Assembly for Wales and the Northern Ireland Assembly. Stage 2 consisted of interactive, electronically-assisted interviews, delivered in a roadshow environment, where members of the public were given the opportunity to explore, and provide critical feedback on, parliamentary websites. *[Article copies available for a fee from The Haworth Document Delivery Service: 1-800-HAWORTH. E-mail address: <docdelivery@*

Rita Marcella (E-mail: r.c.marcella@rgu.ac.uk) is Professor of Corporate Communications, and Graeme Baxter (E-mail: g.baxter@rgu.ac.uk) is Research Assistant, Aberdeen Business School, The Robert Gordon University, Garthdee Road, Aberdeen, UK, AB10 7QE.

Nick Moore is Managing Partner, Acumen, Brompton Ralph, Taunton, UK, TA4 2RU (E-mail: nick@acumenuk.co.uk).

[Haworth co-indexing entry note]: "The Impact of New Technology on the Communication of Parliamentary Information." Marcella, Rita, Graeme Baxter, and Nick Moore. Co-published simultaneously in *Journal of Nonprofit & Public Sector Marketing* (Best Business Books, an imprint of The Haworth Press, Inc.) Vol. 14, No. 1/2, 2005, pp. 185-203; and: *Current Issues in Political Marketing* (eds: Walter W. Wymer, Jr., and Jennifer Lees-Marshment) Best Business Books, an imprint of The Haworth Press, Inc., 2005, pp. 185-203. Single or multiple copies of this article are available for a fee from The Haworth Document Delivery Service [1-800-HAWORTH, 9:00 a.m. - 5:00 p.m. (EST). E-mail address: getinfo@haworthpressinc.com].

KEYWORDS. Parliament, political marketing, technology, United Kingdom

INTRODUCTION AND BACKGROUND

This paper describes the results of a project, funded by the Economic and Social Research Council, which explored the ways in which communication between government and the public was evolving in light of the potential of new information and communication technologies (ICTs), in particular as a result of the provision of public information via the websites created to support the United Kingdom Parliament in Westminster and the new devolved legislatures–the Scottish Parliament, the National Assembly for Wales, and the Northern Ireland Assembly. The project was designed to gather data both about the services hosting such sites, their strategies and approaches, and about the response of the general public to the sites, their levels of interest in and capacity to use such resources.

The project was devised in the context of the belief, increasingly prevalent in the early 1990s, that openness and transparency were desirable features of government. The benefits associated with openness related both to public service, with an informed electorate more able to weigh arguments, make decisions and take advantages of the opportunities available to them to improve their lives, enabling citizens to become knowledgeable actors (Mansell 2002), and to encouraging public familiarity and satisfaction with the institutions of government. There was also a belief that the use of technology in support of the provision of public information and e-government initiatives would facilitate and encourage public interaction with and participation in democracy, where individuals require access to public information 'for successful . . . critical, participation in the accepted rights and responsibilities of government' (Policy Studies Institute 1995), and where citizenship is only realized when individuals are members of a socio-political community, with participation as a desired goal (Barbalet 1998; Mansbridge 1999). Such views were high on the political agenda throughout the 1990s. In late August 2001, President Bush claimed that 'it seems like to me the more accessible Washington becomes, the more likely it is people will participate in the [political] process' (Bush 2001). Alternatively, many see a growing trend in citizen empowerment as a result of the potential of new technology to enhance visibility, accountability and interaction in public administration (Kahlin 1997; La Porte, de Jong, and Demchak

1999; Welch and Wong 2001). It is also theorized that openness is increasingly a symbol of trust, modernity and global citizenship (Di Maggio and Powell 1983; Strang and Meyer 1993).

This shift in attitudes towards greater transparency is manifest in the United Kingdom, in a proliferation of official websites–at present calculated at well in excess of 1,000 distinct sites (UK Online 2003)–and in legislation, including the Code of Practice on Access to Government Information 1997 and the Freedom of Information Act 2000, due to be implemented in 2005. This move stemmed originally in Europe from the belief that greater openness and transparency would encourage consensus on the European institutions as a result of greater public understanding of and satisfaction with their activities, and in America from the Clinton administration's push for a more open Information Society, with improved communication between the government and the governed. This vision was to be achieved primarily via the use of new web technologies, underpinned by the Freedom of Information Act 'providing the underlying principles of government openness' (Clinton 1993). Similarly in the UK, Blair (1996) argued that 'the only way to restore people's trust is therefore to be completely open' where there is 'a statutory obligation on the government to make it a duty to release information to the people who elect the government.'

Recent constitutional change in the UK decentralizing certain aspects of power from Westminster to Scotland, Wales and Northern Ireland via the establishment of devolved legislatures, with for example Scotland electing its first parliament for nearly 300 years, has also been envisaged by some as an opportunity to make government more open, accountable and closer to the people (Liberal Democrat Party 1998) in 'a new sort of democracy in Scotland ... an open, accessible Parliament ... where people are encouraged to participate in the policy process which affects all our lives ... ' (Consultative Steering Group on the Scottish Parliament 1998).

There was, therefore, in the 1990s identifiable global pressure towards openness and transparency which in the UK and the United States appeared to be reinforced by the domestic context, where information and technology developments were affecting the behaviour of public administrations (in line with Welch and Wong 2001). However, despite President Bush's reported remarks, as late as August 2001, about the importance of 'making sure that information flows freely' (Bush 2001), in the aftermath of the events of September 11th, in an environment of awareness of the threat of terrorism and with the growing likelihood of war with Iraq, there has been clear evidence of a realignment of position, a backlash against the perceived dangers implicit in too great an openness. This is evident in a number of developments, such as the emergence in the United States of the concept of homeland security, which although now in common parlance is still an evolving policy concept with very clear information policy implications (Relyea 2002), and the establishment of the Office of Homeland Security and the Homeland Security Council in America (both exempt from freedom of information regulation), the US Patriot Act (2001), the UK Anti Terrorism, Crime and Security Bill (2001) and the delayed implementation of the Freedom of Information Act in the UK, which some argue indicates 'a growing sense of unease with the PM about the breadth of the Act and an uncertainty about openness and the implications of September 11th' (Birkenshaw 2002). Feinberg (2002) believes that there are very serious implications as a result of the terrorist attacks (both September 11 and the anthrax threats) for information policy in the United States, arguing that 'the parameters are rapidly changing, and there are a number of contradictory factors simultaneously restricting and expanding access to different kinds of information.' Similarly Franklin (2003), in a summary of anti-FOI measures in America, reports the emerging view that 'the administration has used a string of laws and executive orders to reverse a decades-long trend toward government openness . . . where it is impossible to say whether officials are merely protecting national security or simply expanding their power to operate without public scrutiny.' American journalists have also expressed concern at increasing secrecy in government, with the Ashcroft memorandum weighting decisions on public access against disclosure (U.S. Department of Justice, 2001).

There are also signs that e-government initiatives are in danger of failing, both at a process and ideological level. In the UK, e-government focus on use of web technologies has evolved around a strategy that emphasises the achievement of 'all dealings with government' accessible to the public by 2005, where the Office of the e-Envoy reports on a monthly basis to the Prime Minister on matters such as Internet penetration into UK households (38% in July 2002) and the progress of the UK Online initiative, aimed at ensuring that 99% of UK households will be located within five miles of an Internet access point. UK Online has been the subject of a national advertising campaign, although from informal tests carried out by the authors amongst technologically aware young people, who might be expected to be more responsive to the initiative than the majority, none were able to recall the meaning of the advert, although they did actually recall seeing it, suggesting that this high cost campaign may have been singularly ineffective. Similarly, a MORI survey (Anonymous 2000) found that more than a half of those surveyed either did not know or care what the government was doing to broaden access to the net.

Progress is evident in transformation via e-government although diminished by lack of resources, with 'true digitalized constituent services' appearing on the web, where, although the 'rhetoric is still outstripping the reality,' greater emphasis in websites on transactional convenience is making their use more relevant to people's lives (Perlman 2002). Musso, Weare, and Hale (2000) identify two dimensions of local government web use–the entrepreneurial, focusing on good service management, and the participatory, in support of democracy–with entrepreneurial more commonly encountered. Greater availability of government department and public organization websites enables citizens to monitor organizational performance more readily (Reichard 1998), although there is evidence of variability in the extent of openness (Cyberspace Policy Research Group 2001). However, the Pew Internet Report (Larsen and Rainie 2002) indicates that, post-September 11th, there are increasingly fewer opportunities on government websites to engage in policy or issue related debate.

E-government strategy is being reappraised in recognition of the lack of consistency, quality and value attached to many government websites, where the mere fact of hosting a site has been seen by managers as more important than aspirations to internal validity and the achievement of relevance to people's lives. Recent website design guidelines emphasise the importance of 'providing the information and services that users want' and evaluating the extent to which 'users' needs and expectations are being met'(Office of the e-Envoy 2002a). However, there is no evidence that such research will be carried out in a systematic, objective and holistic manner, as it must be if information and communication strategy is to develop in a way that is responsive to public need rather than reflective of governmental desire to communicate a message or to enable an activity or process. A survey of Internet users (BBC 2002) shows that 'fewer than one in 20 Internet users regularly used government websites to access public services' and that less than a third of the population has ever visited a government website. Excluded groups, amongst the heaviest users of government services, were not being reached and means of encouraging more traffic to government sites must be found.

Larsen and Rainie (2002) surveyed public use of government Internet sites in the immediate aftermath of the September 11th attacks, finding that 815 of 2,391 respondents had used government websites to locate information about terrorism and the Taliban, suggesting that in a crisis situation a significant proportion of the public will now use this means of accessing fuller or hypothetically more authoritative information about a crisis than is available in the mass media. Equally over one million electronic requests for the UK Government's Iraq Dossier were received in the first few days after its publication. The Office of the e-Envoy (2002b) interprets this as a confirmation of the Prime Minister's belief in the effectiveness of the Internet as a means of transmitting a message without the normal forms of mediation, interpretation and, potentially, criticism to which political messages are conventionally subject when disseminated via the media.

Although originally conceived in an information science research context, it has become evident that the present research has direct applicability to political marketing theory. Most research to date has focused on marketing political parties (see, for example, Mauser 1983; Kavanagh 1997; Lees-Marshment 2001; Maarek 1995; Newman 1999; and Sherman and Schiffman 2002) and politicians (such as, for example, Jackson, 2002, and 2003, on MPs' use of email and the Internet), while the marketing of parliament and communication between parliament and the general public has been little studied. Taking a pure information science approach involves the examination of the quality of the dissemination of information to the public, in terms of the information itself, the means by which it is disseminated and the value of the information to the eventual user. Political marketing theory on the contrary looks at the intentions of the information provider (i.e. the political party or parliament), the quality of the communication process and the extent to which communication with the public has assisted in the achievement of the provider's aims. In the case of parliamentary communication those aims would be to engage the electorate with parliament and its representatives and to encourage awareness of parliament and its relevance to the lives of the general public. In order to achieve such aims, parliaments may draw on marketing communication theory where models such as AIDA and DAGMAR emphasise the importance of achieving awareness and interest before a potential buyer will reach a decision and take action (AIDA). Information scientists have frequently assumed that the information user will make this leap to understanding that information has value, without pausing to examine the necessity for awareness of information value to be aroused and the means by which awareness might best be achieved.

The debate is further complicated by the political environment of legislatures, where officials, not themselves politicians, may see a need to 'inform and explain' rather than to market the political process (Winetrobe, 2002). Yet Mortimore (2002) argues that 'the need for the marketing of politics, as opposed to political marketing, is now an urgent one' in the context of diminishing political participation, as evidenced by falling voter turnout, and public disenchantment with politicians. Fox and Lees-Marshment (2002) note that Westminster is limited in terms of political marketing development, suggesting ways in which it might become more market-oriented, including the provision of greater opportunity for outsiders to interact with and influence parliament. Seaton (2002) queries the legitimacy of the Scottish Parliament expending resources on marketing itself, asking whether it is possible for this to be done without becoming embroiled in politics, arguing that while parliamentary officers can disseminate information about and promote the process, they must seek to market the process but not the politicians. This paradox lies, in the view of the authors of the present paper, at the centre of the conjunction of information science and political marketing research, where the emphasis must shift beyond the public service model to embrace marketing approaches to political communication.

AIMS AND OBJECTIVES

The aim of the project was to investigate the impact of new technology on the communication of parliamentary information from the perspectives of both those in government and of the users of that information. Project objectives, therefore, included to:

- develop a model of parliamentary information provision to the public in the UK in the context of approaches globally;
- explore, in particular, the actual benefits/drawbacks of technologically supported approaches for certain groups deemed to be in danger of exclusion; and
- develop and evaluate an interactive, electronic interview as a data collection tool delivered in a roadshow environment.

METHODOLOGICAL APPROACH

Two methodologies were adopted to gather data from informants: (i) semi-structured interviews with the managers of public information services and (ii) interactive, electronically assisted interviews with the public, during which they were given the opportunity to evaluate parliamentary websites. Eighteen face-to-face interviews were carried out with managers of the public information services–the House of Commons and House of Lords Information Offices, the Scottish Parliament Public Information Service and the National Assembly for Wales Public Information and Education Service. A telephone interview was conducted with a representative of the Northern Ireland Assembly Information Office. Although built around a semi-structured schedule, the interviews were open and conducted flexibly, in order to elicit unpredicted responses. All interviews were recorded and fully transcribed. They centred around the following areas: service objectives and strategies; information access and dissemination approaches; services' understanding and knowledge of users, from internal data collected and experience; and the role of information and communication technologies as part of the overall service strategy.

A new data collection tool was devised for interviews with the public, combining the collection of observational and attitudinal data in a single interaction, in order to explore behaviour from a phenomenological and context-based perspective. As the study involved the piloting of a new tool, the methodology has been very full described and evaluated elsewhere (Marcella, Baxter, and Moore 2003). The interview sought data about respondents' previous experience of using government information, their attitude to accessing government information via a variety of media and their response to the parliamentary and assembly websites which they were being given the opportunity to explore. Interviews were carried out in Aberdeen, Newcastle and Cardiff, at 15 roadshow events held in community centres, public libraries, academic institutions and a mosque. Over 460 people were approached and although only 79 agreed to participate–those who declined cited a lack of time and a lack of interest in politics–it was felt that this response rate (17%) was not dissimilar to that achieved in many doorstep and on-street surveys. The interviews were successful in gathering rich data illuminating respondents' search for and evaluation of public information in an electronic environment. The free-form part of the interview utilized verbal protocol analysis, where respondents were asked to think aloud as they searched, with prompts to encourage evaluation. The interviews were audio-recorded, while the online sessions were logged simultaneously.

PROJECT RESULTS

Parliamentary and Assembly Public Information Services

The interviews with representatives of the four parliamentary and assembly public information services began by discussing their mission. Each emphasized themes associated with communicating with and raising awareness, interest and participation amongst the public: to 'promote knowledge of the House of Commons amongst outside individuals and institutions' (House of Commons Library 2001); to 'promote a better understanding and knowledge of the role and work of the House' (House of Lords 2001); to ensure that 'the Parliament is as open, accessible and participative as possible. Only well-informed citizens can maximise the opportunities . . . to contribute to the democratic process' (Consultative Steering Group on the Scottish Parliament 1998); and to be 'as open, transparent, accessible and accountable as possible' (Fee 1999, of the Northern Ireland Assembly). The overarching UK Parliament website was introduced in 1996, to enable free access to parliamentary papers and legislation and to 'encourage wider public interest in, and, knowledge of, the business of the House' (House of Commons Information Committee 1996). The Scottish Parliament's public information service, heavily influenced by the Swedish model, has additionally a very clearly stated set of aims–to ensure access to *all* members of the public, to increase interest in and contribution to the work of the Parliament and to provide high quality information that meets users' needs.

Services vary markedly in size and scope, with approximately 93,000 enquiries at the House of Commons service and 25,000 at the House of Lords, while the Scottish service received only 7,400 enquiries annually: the Welsh and Northern Ireland services could not provide statistics but estimated approximately 200 enquiries each week in Wales and 120 in Northern Ireland. All services noted a very marked increase in e-mail enquiries, with around a quarter of all approaches taking this form at the time of the research: the House of Commons, for example, reported a 53% increase in e-mail enquiries and a 22% drop in telephone enquiries over the previous year. The emphasis on e-mail as a form of asking questions was considered to be potentially problematic by all services, in that staff felt that although standard responses could be developed for certain questions, these were frequently inappropriate or insufficient. In light of respondents' belief that e-mail will continue to increase, service managers were concerned about their capacity to continue to provide a meaningful and relatively speedy response without additional resources.

Major user groups for the services constituted the general public, the business community, representatives of the media, lobbyists and schools. All services noted a rise in the rate of enquiry when political topics were high on the media agenda. Otherwise the emphasis was on questions about parliamentary or assembly business, legislation, policy, membership of the body and the arrangement of visits. Highly significantly all services noted major confusion amongst inquirers as to the role of the respective body and its relationship with others, with in particular a lack of understanding of the nature of devolved and reserved matters, of the respective roles of the Commons, Lords and Government and of the nature of the membership of particular bodies. This uncertainty was manifest in the frequency of queries revealing uncertainty and misunderstanding. The services each produce a range of print and electronic publications, such as guides to the parliament or assembly, information packs, bulletins and thematic briefings. Staff of the services also receive visitors and give talks, with the Welsh Assembly's Marketing and Communications Team particularly active in organising exhibitions at major public events, such as agricultural shows and cultural festivals, and in outreach activities associated with Regional Committee meetings across Wales. Although it has a Visitor Centre, with an information desk, the Scottish Parliament service has taken a unique strategic decision not to offer talks to interested groups in order not to disadvantage remoter communities. Information service staff have, however, accompanied committee meetings held throughout Scotland, providing an opportunity for outreach. All of the services host tailored services aimed at young people, with a remit to support educational initiatives and encourage understanding of government; these include extensive visits programmes for schools.

Each service hosts a website, with the Scottish Parliament site, for example, fairly typical in aiming to provide 'a popular information service for the public, media and special interest groups' (Scottish Parliamentary Corporate Body 2000). The UK Parliament reported an erratic development pattern for their site, with disaggregated responsibility for e-content resulting in an unapproachable site for the inexperienced. The site presented navigational difficulties for those inexpert in parliamentary procedure and terminology, although a redesigned version has since been launched. A live webcasting service began in January 2002. A unique site aimed at young people, *Explore Parliament*, explains the activities of Parliament, with interactive features. The Scottish Parliament site hosts a webcasting facility broadcasting coverage of all proceedings and, in 2000-01, 6.5 million visits to website pages were made. However, this statistic indicates the number of individual pages viewed rather than the number of discrete visits made to the site. The Welsh Assembly website is regarded as a key approach in enabling openness, demonstrating commitment to inclusivity and accessibility. A variety of textual materials is available (in Welsh and English), and a pilot webcasting service is to run until April 2003. The Northern Ireland Assembly's website seeks to provide the kinds of information 'essential if the Assembly is to be an open and accountable body' (Fee 1999). It hosts Assembly documentation, information on the history and membership, as well as live video broadcasts from the Chamber. Parliamentary websites currently make no effort to contextualise their content in terms of users' lives, although UK Online, the national gateway site, does try to direct users to relevant material in terms of 14 key life events, which include having a baby, looking for a job, moving home and death and bereavement. Further development of this approach would be helpful, although it is clearly necessary for e-content designers to think beyond the fairly limited categories so far devised.

Staff of the Westminster and devolved information services seek to share good practice via an Interparliamentary Forum and reciprocal staff exchanges, although respondents reported a lack of consensus across the group. The Scottish and Welsh services have developed a systematic regional approach. In Scotland, a network of 80 public library 'Partner Libraries' has been established, acting as a focal point for information about Parliament, providing free access to the Parliament site and hosting MSPs' surgeries (Scottish Parliament Information Centre 2001). The Welsh service works with public libraries through an Information Link network, based on a formal partnership agreement, with 'free and open access' to Assembly information. There is no indication as yet that the Westminster and Northern Ireland services will adopt this approach. The Welsh service also has a publicly accessible Publications Centre.

User Information Behaviour

Respondent Demographics. 79 interviews were conducted, 24 in Newcastle, 27 in Cardiff and 28 in Aberdeen. Forty interviewees were male, 39 female. There was an even spread by age across respondents, with only those under 20 poorly represented. Ethnic minorities comprised just under 8%, a figure in line with that for the UK population as a whole. Just under a quarter (i.e. 19 of 79) of the respondents were economically active, considerably lower than the national figure, while almost 40% (30 of 79) were retired. Those respondents in employment tended to be in Socio-economic Classifications 1 and 2 (i.e., in managerial and professional occupations). Almost half (37) had completed school education only, a third (25) had completed an undergraduate or higher degree, and one-fifth had completed a further education course. Over a quarter were currently studying for a university award. Six respondents (8%) described themselves as disabled.

Parliamentary Information Need, Participation and Use of ICTs. Only 20 respondents had previously tried to find parliamentary information. Sixteen had sought information on the UK Parliament; three on the National Assembly for Wales; and six on the Scottish Parliament. Those who had sought parliamentary information had required information about: legislation (14 cases); constituencies and elected members (three); general interest (two); policy (one); parliamentary job vacancies (one); and student loans (one). Much of the material sought was required for educational reasons. Of the 69 respondents eligible to vote, 60 (87%) claimed to have voted at the 2001 General Election. This is a far higher figure than the actual national turnout of 58%, the lowest since the First World War (Gould 2001). Similarly, 59% indicated that they had voted in the 1999 European Parliament Elections: actual turnout in the UK was 23%, the lowest in the Union (BBC 1999). Either the respondents were atypically active politically or they were over-reporting. Conversely, when asked if they otherwise participated in the political process, only 19 were involved in: informal discussion (nine cases), party membership (three), pressure group membership (two), distributing political material (one), contact with local councillors (one), directorship of a political club (one), administration of the Campaign for a Welsh Parliament (one), and mock elections at school (one).

Forty-eight respondents were regular computer users and 60 (of 79) used a computer at least occasionally. Just under a quarter were first-time computer users, although fear of the technology may have deterred some potential interviewees. Eighty-five per cent of those who had used a computer found them very or quite easy to use. Forty-seven respondents had previously used the Internet, and 11 of those had previously sought parliamentary information on the Internet.

Free-form Information Seeking. Table 1 illustrates the type of search undertaken.

Just under half (39 of 79) looked for information on a specific topic, while 33 browsed generally. Seven browsed initially then began a specific search. Eighteen selected topics from a list offered by the researchers, while the other 28 chose their own topic. Information was found on the majority of topics selected, both general and very specific. They frequently looked for topics with local significance or for information about their parliamentary or Assembly Member. Thirteen participants (all aged over 45) refused to use the mouse. Of these, 11 were first-time while two were occasional computer users. The 76 online search sessions (six worked in pairs) varied considerably in length, from three to 45 minutes, with an average of 17 minutes. Factors affecting duration included: the time the respondent had to spare; level of interest in information found; and data download times.

Although the greatest proportion of online time (almost 20%) was devoted to using search engines, only 35 of the 76 searches involved any use of the search engine and those interviewees with highly specific searches spent disproportionately long on this activity. Respondents also spent significant periods (13%) on Home Pages exploring site content. Emphasising the need for navigational support, 23% of search time consisted of the interviewer providing instructions and advice, compared with only 12% of unassisted search formulation on the part of the interviewee. Experienced computer users were less reliant on advice and guidance. Of the 37 respondents whose protocols occupied 60% or more of

TABLE 1. Type of Search Undertaken

Type of search	Website			
	UK Parliament	Nat. Assembly for Wales	Scottish Parliament	Totals
Search for info on specific topic(s)	10	19	10	39
General browse leading to specific search	2	1	4	7
General browse	12	7	14	33
Total	24	27	28	79

online time, 31 were regular computer users; while of the 42 whose protocols occupied less than 60% of the time, only 17 were experienced.

A number of interesting findings emerge from the protocol analysis:

- Users frequently combined a specific search with browsing activity.
- Time spent in formulating searches ranged from just under one minute for a basic search to over 31 minutes for a highly specific search.
- Technologically experienced respondents required less interviewer support in searching.
- Search engine queries were less successful than those conducted via website menu structures.
- Users did not consult online search help facilities.
- Searches were conducted largely via keywords, with some use of limiters, such as date or type of document, often with no understanding of the significance of the latter.
- Searches tended to result in unmanageable numbers of hits, through which users began to browse but quickly became dissatisfied and discontinued the search.
- Searchers tended not to use full search functionality–only one used Boolean operators–and were unfamiliar with phrase matching.
- Inexperienced computer users required interviewer guidance on a variety of basic features.
- Much of users' online time involved reading internally and digesting information.
- The frequency of excessively large documents, with long download times, discouraged users.
- The Scottish Parliament website search engine was particularly frustrating in seeking exact phrase matches for any two keywords entered together, resulting in very low numbers of hits.
- Respondents frequently made qualitative comments about websites visited:

  a. Positive comments–on quantity and usefulness of information, ease of use of children's sections (for adults), detail available and ability to e-mail a Minister.
  b. Negative comments–website design features, text legibility, poor site structure, and broken and interrupted hypertext links.

- Users used roadshow interviews to discuss broader political issues, such as the Government, Parliament and Assembly buildings, and political participation. The roadshow approach was found to have great potential in eliciting such data.

- Many respondents also freely contributed personal information about their past use of computers, their newspaper reading habits, education, career choices and so on.

Evaluative Feedback on Parliamentary Websites. Overall, 68 of the 79 participants believed that the website they examined was a useful information source. Various themes underpinned this sense of value: depth of information coverage (15 cases); reliability of information (13); ease of access (12); that this was 'the way ahead' (eight); educational role (three); and encouraging political interaction (two). Eight participants were concerned, however, about the means and costs of access; four felt the approach more suited to younger people; and one person preferred the media as a source. Two participants felt that the information was boring; two that it was of little interest to 'ordinary people'; and six expressed dissatisfaction with search functionality. In terms of ease of use, all three sites were rated favourably (in particular the Scottish Parliament site). Of the 19 first-time computer users, 17 felt the website had been easy to use. Equally, of the 32 participants aged 55 and over, only four recorded difficulties, perhaps influenced by the help the interviewer provided. Sixty-one of the 79 participants felt that the retrieved information had been very or quite interesting (fewer for the UK Parliament site). Sixty-nine of the 79 found the retrieved information easy to understand. However, only 43 of the 79 respondents believed that the retrieved information was relevant to their lives, while 36 indicated that it was irrelevant.

If seeking more information on their chosen topics, respondents would: go back to the parliamentary website (19 cases); use a general search engine (10); consult the media (including websites) (six); approach local council or councillors (five); use libraries (five); approach other governmental websites (four); telephone experts (two); approach political party websites (one); approach interest group websites (one); approach Assembly Members or the Assembly direct (10, all Wales). Web sources were cited by 29 of the 46 participants who might search for further information, with 18 citing only online sources. Sixty-one of the 79 participants said they would use the parliamentary website again, suggesting that roadshow exposure might change behaviour: however, only 10 of the 19 first-time computer users would do so. Various reasons for possible future visits were given, including: educational (16); to expand on media reports (six); work-related (five); for a personal problem or issue (five); jobseeking (one); environmental interests (one); and local interest (one). Only three participants cited political reasons: an interest in politics (one); making voting decisions (one); and to 'harass Welsh Assembly members' (one). Participants saw advantages in electronic access as: overcoming mobility problems; keeping up with family members; materials becoming less available in print; and improved access for rural communities. For those unwilling to visit the parliamentary sites again, the following factors were influential: lack of interest in politics (seven); lack of interest in ICTs (two); lack of access to a computer (three, all retired); and an existing surfeit of information about politics (one).

CONCLUSIONS

Although the present project was a pilot and its findings should, therefore, be regarded with some caution, the results would appear to indicate that the availability of information in readily accessible electronic form is not enough alone to encourage citizen participation. Other motivators and forms of support are required in order to encourage and enable people to access, use and apply that information and to encourage them to use ICTs to interact with democracy (in line with Perlman (2002)). Those responsible for developing parliamentary ICT policy must reappraise early beliefs about the power of electronic communication to transform the democratic process. In the light of the present study and increasing levels of political disengagement and disenchantment, it is important to recognise that, while electronic communication has the power to enable and make connections with the public, the connection will presently only take place as a result of active effort on the part of a public which is not inclined to make that effort. Serious consideration must be given to ways of encouraging information use, whether via marketing and promotional efforts or through education. However, the failure of UK Online's costly television advertising campaign should serve as a reminder of the difficulties associated with marketing abstract concepts like information and communication. The issue of relevance is the single most significant factor impacting upon user information behaviour. In order to encourage participation, communication via ICTs must visibly enable meaningful and useful interaction that is relevant to citizens' everyday lives, not only process-oriented interaction but also issue debate. Despite the evidence that interactivity is highly desirable, there are also signs that debate is being downplayed on many governmental sites in the aftermath of September 11th, with very few opportunities today for visitors to express their opinions on the issues of the day in any kind of public way. Government agencies are now alert to the dangers of unmediated and uncontrolled public debate, dangers unanticipated at the height of enthusiasm for openness in public administration. As early as 2000, Coward reported that the Downing Street chatroom was attracting unwelcome and highly critical contributions which screening failed to control, suggesting naivety in original conceptions of real-time chat as a medium for open debate.

The wider availability of ICTs is changing the model of interaction between the public and government, evidenced in the significant growth of e-mail use by members of the public as a means of communicating their questions about government. However, there are also signs of concern amongst service managers about the implications of this shift and the extent to which it requires a greater frequency of personalised response than previously. The public information services of the various legislatures studied as part of this project have varying interpretations of their role, although they each emphasized notions of encouraging and promoting interest and awareness and of supporting the creation and maintenance of a well informed public. From the evidence they presented, however, it is clear that the public they presently serve is not well informed, indeed is very frequently confused and uncertain, and that–although there are certain predictable areas of information need–needs are likely to be driven by the often unpredictable political agenda of the day and to be highly influenced by media coverage of that agenda. Lack of consistency and disaggregation in service provision (both of the physical services and their corresponding websites) and lack of meaningful data about users are issues for concern. Research remains necessary to explore the extent of use (actual and potential) and its nature, going beyond the assembling of statistics normally undertaken by services, in particular in light of recent concerns about the unresponsiveness and lack of appeal demonstrated by government websites. The focus on electronic provision of services also remains a concern in light of the project's findings which suggest that particular groups, such as the elderly and those without experience of or expertise in ICTs, are likely to be unwilling or unable to take full advantage of this means of communication. However, the results of this project also suggest that supported exposure to parliamentary websites may cause individuals to change attitudes and behaviour and to develop new perspectives on the value of such information, while verifying that the roadshow concept is a valuable vehicle via which to enable such exposure while simultaneously gathering further data about user attitudes to public access to government information and ICTs.

The present research findings illustrate deficiencies in parliamentary information and communication strategies from a public service perspective, where websites are failing to engage the public with e-content: future research should broaden its scope to consider the relationship between public service and political marketing models, going beyond studies of users' needs for information about parliament and the relationship of such information to their everyday lives to consider how political marketing theories and techniques might be applied to increase awareness of political websites and retain visitor interest in their content. Studies must also reflect on the distinction between marketing politicians and marketing the political process in an apolitical way.

REFERENCES

Anonymous (2000), "Government Neglecting UK Web Interests," *Internet Magazine*, 15 (February).

Barbalet, J. M. (1998), *Citizenship, Rights, Struggle and Class Inequality*, Milton Keynes: Open University Press.

BBC (1999), "UK Turnout: Apathy or Ignorance?," http://news.bbc.co.uk/hi/english/events/euros_99/news/newsid_368000/368908.stm.

Birkenshaw, P. (2002), "Freedom of Information in the UK and Europe: Further Progress?," *Government Information Quarterly*, 19 (1), 77-86.

Blair, T. (1996), "Speech at the Campaign for Freedom of Information's Annual Awards Ceremony, 25th March 1996," http://www.cfoi.org.uk/blairawards.html.

Bush, G. W. (2001), "President's Priorities for Fall: Education, Economy, Opportunity, Security. Remarks by the President at the Launch of the White House Website," http://www.whitehouse.gov/news/releases/2001/08/20010831-3.html.

Clinton, W. (1993), "Memorandum for Heads of Departments and Agencies, Subject: The Freedom of Information Act," U.S. Department of Justice Press Release, 4 October.

Consultative Steering Group on the Scottish Parliament (1998), "Shaping Scotland's Parliament," http://www.scotland.gov.uk/library/documents-w5/rcsg-00.htm.

Coward, R. (2000), "No 10 Censors Hacked off by e-Hecklers," *The Observer*, 19 (1), http://www.guardian.co.uk/freespeech/article/0,2763,212443,00.html.

Cyberspace Policy Research Group (2001), "Home Page," http://www.cyprg.arizona.edu/index.html.

Di Maggio, P. J. and W. Powell (1983), "The Iron Cage Revisited: Institutional Isomorphism and Collective Rationality in Organizational Fields," *American Sociological Review*, 48, 147-160.

Fee, J. (1999), in Official Report (Hansard) of the Northern Ireland Assembly, 22 February, Line 300, http://www.ni-assembly.gov.uk/record/reports/990222.htm.

Feinberg, L. E. (2002), "Homeland Security: Implications for Information Policy and Practice–First Appraisal," *Government Information Quarterly*, 19 (3), 265-288.

Franklin, D. (2003), "Official Secrets," *Mother Jones*, 28 (1), 17-18.

Fox, M. and J. Lees-Marshment. (2002), "Marketing Parliament: A 19th Century Institution in a 21st Century Political Market-Place" paper presented at the Political Marketing Conference, Aberdeen, United Kingdom.

Gould, P. (2001), "A Strong Case of Election Apathy," http://news.bbc.co.uk/vote2001/hi/english/features/newsid_1371000/1371191.stm

House of Commons Information Committee (1996), *First Report on Electronic Publication of House of Commons Documents*, London: HMSO.

House of Commons Library (2001), *House of Commons Information Office Annual Report 1 April 2000-31 March 2001*, London: House of Commons Library.

House of Lords (2001), "Annual report and accounts 2000-01," http://www.publications.parliament.uk/pa/ld200001/ldbrief/2301.htm.

Jackson, N. (2003a), "MPs and Web Technologies–An Untapped Opportunity?" *Journal of Public Affairs*, 3 (3), 124-137.

Jackson, N. (2003b), "Vote Winner or a Nuisance: Email and British MPs' Relationship with their Constituents," paper presented at the PSA Conference, Leicester, United Kingdom.

Kahlin, B. (1997), "The U.S. National Information Infrastructure Initiative: The Market, the Web and the Virtual Project," in *National Information Infrastructure Initiatives*, eds. B. Kahin and E. Wilson, Cambridge, MA: MIT Press, 150-189.

Kavanagh, D. (1997), *Election Campaigning: the New Marketing of Politics*, London: Blackwell.

La Porte, T. M., M. de Jong, and C. Demchak (1999), "Public Organizations on the World Wide Web: Empirical Correlates of Administrative Openness," paper presented at the 5th National Public Management Research Conference, College Station, TX.

Larsen, E. and E. Rainie (2002), "The Rise of the e-Citizen: How People Use Government Agencies' Websites," http://www.pewinternet.org/reports/pdfs/PIP_Govt_Website_Rpt.pdf

Lees-Marshment, J. (2001), *Political Marketing and British Political Parties*, Manchester: Manchester University Press.

Liberal Democrat Party (1998), "Blair and Ashdown Launch Constitutional Declaration," press release, 11 June 1998.

Maarek, P. J. (1995), *Political Marketing and Communication*, London: John Libbey.

Mansbridge, J. (1999), "On the Idea that Participation Makes Better Citizens," in *Citizen Competence and Democratic Institutions*, eds. S. Elkin and K. Soltan, University Park, PA: Pennsylvania State University, 291-325.

Mansell, R. (2002), "From Digital Divides to Digital Entitlements in Knowledge Societies," *Current Sociology*, 50 (3), 407-426.

Marcella, R., G. Baxter and N. Moore (2003), "Data Collection Using Electronically Assisted Interviews in a Roadshow–A Methodological Evaluation," *Journal of Documentation*, 59 (2), forthcoming.

Mauser, G. (1983), *Political Marketing: An Approach to Campaign Strategy*, New York: Praeger.

Mortimore, R. (2002), "Why Politics Needs Marketing," paper presented at the Political Marketing Conference, Aberdeen, United Kingdom.

Musso, J., C. Weare and M. Hale (2000), "Designing Web Technologies for Local Government Reform," *Political Communication*, 17 (1), 1-19.

Newman, B. (1999), *The Mass Marketing of Politics: Democracy in an Age of Manufactured Images*, Thousand Oaks, CA: Sage.

Office of the e-Envoy (2002a), "Guidelines for UK Government Websites: Illustrated Handbook for Web Management Teams," http://www.e-envoy.gov.uk/oee/oee.nsf/sections/webguidelines-handbook-top/$file/handbookindex.htm.

_____ (2002b), "Report from the e-Minister and e-Envoy, 7th October 2002," http://www.e-envoy.gov.uk/oee/OeE.nsf/sections/reports-pmreports-2002/$file/rep7oct02.htm.

Perlman, E. (2002), "The People Connection," *Governing*, 15 (12), 32-34, 36, 39.

Policy Studies Institute (1995), *Information and Citizenship in the United Kingdom: A Draft Report Prepared as Part of the European Commission's Information and Citizenship in Europe Study*, London: Policy Studies Institute.

Reichard, C. (1998), "The Impact of Performance Management on Transparency and Accountability in the Public Sector," in *Ethics and Accountability in a Context of Governance and New Public Management*, Vol. 7, ed. A. Hondeghem, Amsterdam: IOS Press, 123-137.

Relyea, H. C. (2002), "Homeland Security and Information," *Government Information Quarterly*, 19 (3), 213-223.

Scottish Parliamentary Corporate Body (2000), "Annual Report of the Scottish Parliamentary Corporate Body 2000," http://www.scottish.parliament.uk/spcb/spar00-01.html.

Sherman, E. and Schiffman, L. (2002), "Trends and Issues in Political Marketing Strategies," *Journal of Political Marketing*, 1 (1), no pages.

Strang, D. and J. W. Meyer (1993), "Institutional Conditions for Diffusion," *Theory and Society*, 22 (4), 487-511.

UK Online (2003), "A-Z of Central Government," http://www.ukonline.gov.uk/Quickfind/QFCenGov/0,1588,1001~801b22~fs~en,00.html.

U.S. Department of Justice (2001), "Memorandum for Heads of all Federal Departments and Agencies, Subject: The Freedom of Information Act," http://www.usdoj.gov/o4foia/011012.htm

Winetraub, B. K. (2002) "Political but not Partisan: Marketing Parliaments and their Members," paper presented at the Political Marketing Conference, Aberdeen, United Kingdom.

Welch, E. W. and W. Wong (2001), "Global Information Technology Pressure and Government Accountability: The Mediating Effect of Domestic Context on Website Openness," *Journal of Public Administration Research and Theory*, 11 (4), 509-539.

Political Campaign Advertising: Believe It or Not

Aron O'Cass

SUMMARY. The extent that political advertising in elections is believed by voters' is an important issue for public policy, political marketing, and marketing in general. Much effort and funding is devoted to communicating with voters' during elections via advertising. This study examined political advertising believability and three potential antecedents of believability during an election. The data were gathered via a random sample of voters immediately following an election and the results indicate that believability is influenced by a voters' involvement, perceived control and satisfaction and that party preference plays a key role in believability of competing campaigns. *[Article copies available for a fee from The Haworth Document Delivery Service: 1-800-HAWORTH. E-mail address: <docdelivery@haworthpress.com> Website: <http://www.HaworthPress. com> © 2005 by The Haworth Press, Inc. All rights reserved.]*

KEYWORDS. Voter behaviour, political marketing, election campaigns

Professor Aron O'Cass is Chair of Marketing, Newcastle Business School, Social Science Building, The University of Newcastle, Callaghan, NSW 2308, Australia (E-mail: aron.ocass@newcastle.edu.au).

[Haworth co-indexing entry note]: "Political Campaign Advertising: Believe It or Not." O'Cass, Aron. Co-published simultaneously in *Journal of Nonprofit & Public Sector Marketing* (Best Business Books, an imprint of The Haworth Press, Inc.) Vol. 14, No. 1/2, 2005, pp. 205-221; and: *Current Issues in Political Marketing* (eds: Walter W. Wymer, Jr., and Jennifer Lees-Marshment) Best Business Books, an imprint of The Haworth Press, Inc., 2005, pp. 205-221. Single or multiple copies of this article are available for a fee from The Haworth Document Delivery Service [1-800-HAWORTH, 9:00 a.m. - 5:00 p.m. (EST). E-mail address: getinfo@haworthpressinc.com].

INTRODUCTION

The growth of advertising during election campaigns is a global phenomenon and is used widely to promote party policy, issues and candidate images (Dermody and Scullion 2001; Newman and Sheth 1985). There is little doubt that the use of paid advertising by political parties has grown to be a potent weapon in their campaign arsenal. In terms of dollars spent, advertising has become a major budget component in election campaigns and a dominant force in the political marketplace. At a practical level, the electoral outcomes for parties and their candidates can hinge on understanding voters' needs and wants (O'Cass 1996) and communicating with them through political advertising in an effective manner. However, political advertising has both substantial economic and social costs associated with its use.

Political parties and candidates have relied increasingly on television advertising to inform and influence voters during elections (Hayes and McAllister 1996; O'Cass 2001). This heavy reliance, has seen growing social and financial costs associated with elections, particularly in the context of influencing voters through advertising. For example, winning campaigns in 1996 in the U.S cost on average $673,000 (USD) for Congress and $4,700,000 (USD) for senate races and for local elections costs were estimated to be over $1 million (USD) per candidate (Johnson 1999). Spending in other smaller nations is also significant and increasing. For example, figures from the United Kingdom show that of the 36 parties in who by law must report spending incurred campaign expenditure £22,348,000 (GBP) in the 2001 general election (TEC 2002) and in Australia with a population of around 18 million, spending was around $34 million (AUD) on marketing, particularly advertising by parties and candidates (AEC 1999) in a recent Federal election.

The increasing election expenditure is of concern and it has been noted that the period from the 1950s through to the mid 90s election costs have been rising. According to the Centre for Responsive Politics $2.2 billion was spent on the federal in the U.S in 1996 an increase of 37% on that spent four years earlier (Wray 1999). Overall, for sometime there has been an upward spiral in electoral costs (Johnson 1999) in most countries, emphasizing the need to understand voter behavior and advertising in elections.

During the past decade or so, there has been a growing interest in the topic of political advertising, and overall, this body of work has contributed specifically to the advancement of political communications and advertising in general (e.g., Faber, Tims, and Schmitt 1993; Hill 1989; Weaver Lariscy and Tinkham 1999). However, despite the large body of research on advertising, an area that to some extent has been overlooked is the believability of political advertising. Given that advertising plays a significant role in political marketing campaigns, it seems that enhancing our understanding ad believability is needed. Therefore, understanding the advertising role and influence is only meaningfully considered against the involvement of voters in politics and elections, the perceptions of how much control they perceive they have over political outcomes, their satisfaction with politics. Also, as is often the case, the environment the individual is studied in tempers such knowledge, in that the electoral environment may have specific characteristics that make it different to the conventional marketplace in which consumer behavior takes place.

The Australian Political System: The Federal Parliament in Australia has two Houses, the Senate or Upper House and the House of Representatives or Lower House. The House of Representatives is analogous to the People's House as members are elected by the people to represent a local area or division, where in the Senate representation is for a particular State or Territory and is the legislator as opposed to the house of review. The Australian political system can most accurately be described as multiparty in form, but essentially two-partisan in function. Until the formation of the Australian Democrats, competition for government and control of the legislature was between the two major parties (Labor and Liberal). Largely, the National Party (the 3rd small major party) has, over many years aligned itself with the Liberal Party, forming a (conservative) coalition. This party system exists whether we speak of the federal parliamentary system or the state system. Historically, Labor and Liberal also dominate the electorate, consistently winning over 80 percent of the votes cast at elections. All citizens over the age of 18 years must be registered and must vote at all Federal, State and Local government elections in Australia. In Australia there are five states and two territories who operate parliamentary systems modelled on the Australian Federal system. For example, for the purposes of State government, Queensland is divided into 89 distinct areas or electoral districts (also called electorates, constituencies or seats). Each district is represented by a single Member of Parliament (MP). A Queensland general election is really 89 separate district elections. The results of these elections are added together and the majority group or party forms government. In general in a Queensland election about 25, 000 citizens caste a vote in each electoral district (ecq 2003).

Voting and Political Advertising: Political Advertising and decision making research has often sought to understand the variance in voter behavior that can be attributed to different voter characteristics, as well as voter decision criteria used to make candidate choices (see Newman and Sheth 1984) and the effect that different appeals have on voting (e.g., Faber Tims and Schmitt 1993; Hill 1989; Weaver Larscicy and Tinkham 1999). In the context of decision making and advertising, consumer involvement has been recognized as an important influence (Mittal 1989; O'Cass 2000; Putrevu and Lord 1994). Researchers have utilized voter involvement to understand electoral behavior (e.g., Burton and Netemeyer 1992; Faber Tims and Schmitt 1993; Rothschild and Houston 1979) because of its effect on information processing, attention and the like. In the context of advertising, involvement has been shown to impact on the attention paid to advertising (Andrews Durvasual and Akhter 1990; Mitchell 1981), processing central versus peripheral cues (Petty Cacioppo and Schumann 1983) and information processing (Mitchell 1981). It has also been said that within the context of marketing communications in election campaigns, that ensuring an offer is made that the electorate might find relevant, may impact involvement in the political process, even when involvement does not create relevance (Dermody and Scullion 1999). Such relevance may be found in the messages communicated during an election by the parties.

Within the context of environmental psychology, perceived dominance-control appears to have a significant influence on the behavior of individuals. This influence is also relevant in the context of the electoral environment and voters perceived control over political and electoral outcomes. Perceived control is defined as "an individual's beliefs, at a given point in time, in his or her ability to effect a change, in a desired direction, on the environment" (Greenberger Strasse, Cummings and Dunhan 1989, p. 31). In effect, it covers attributions of internal versus external control over outcomes. It has been suggested that a positive relationship is expected to exist between the degree an individual perceives some control over outcomes and their associated degree of involvement (Zaichkowsky 1985). In this context there appears to be some justification for viewing perceived control as an antecedent to voter decision involvement. In the relation to politics and voting, a voter's emotional state as identified through perceived control, appears to influence voter decision involvement. Thus,

RQ1: To what extent does the degree voters' perceive electoral environment control influence their decision involvement.

Political Satisfaction: Related to voter involvement is the issue of satisfaction and in the broader domain of consumer behavior, Richins and Bloch (1991) have argued that if a stimuli (object) is an important part of an individual's life, they have a strong motivation to avoid post-purchase dissatisfaction. Satisfaction is defined here as an overall cumulative evaluation of a set of experiences within the political context, similar to the original usage and context discussed by Evrard and Aurier (1996). In the context of involvement and satisfaction, in a related manner Day (1977) observed that satisfaction decisions are contingent on the incidence of post-purchase evaluation, and as such for stimuli of low importance, evaluations might not be triggered. Such individuals in the context of voting, have more at stake in the election situation and a greater need to make a wise choice. They have more at stake in the electoral situation and a greater need to make a wise choice, and it is argued that voters who are highly involved in politics will also seek to avoid expressing dissatisfaction. It would be expected then, that involved voters would be especially keen to experience political satisfaction because of their political involvement. Therefore, we would expect those voters, who report higher involvement in politics to also report being more satisfied with politics, politicians and their choices. Thus,

RQ2: To what extent does the level of decision involvement influence voter satisfaction.

Political Advertising Believability: An important but neglected issue in the context of elections in relation to voting is political advertising believability. The concept of advertising believability, was first proposed by Beltramini (1982), who suggested that it was the extent to which an advertisement evokes sufficient confidence in its truthfulness, so as to make it acceptable to the receiver. Whilst this notion is applicable across a wide array of domains, the examination and application of believability has been largely to social issues, through studies examining the believability of information contained in cigarettes advertising (Beltramini 1988); believability of alcohol warning labels (Andrews Netemeyer and Durvasula 1991, 1993; De Carlo Parrott Rody and Winsor 1997) and aids information sources (Raymond Tanner and Eppright 1998).

Given the nature of the existing believability research, and the definition of Beltramini (1982), believability has much in common with advertising beliefs. In a similar manner to Andrews (1989) political advertising believability is seen here as focusing on ones beliefs toward identified political ads. Importantly, beliefs associate an object with a particular attribute, and are used for information that a voter has about candidates, issues or advertising. Advertising believability (beliefs about political ads) assumes an advertising-attribute relationship in the mind of the voter. Such relationships can exist at the specific levels of particular political ads for parties, candidates or generally for political advertising. For example, political advertising believability is viewed as the extent to which an ad is capable of evoking sufficient confidence in its truthfulness to render it useful to consumers (Beltramini 1982). In the context of political advertising, it is the extent to which voters view the advertising campaign as credible and thus acceptable (O'Cass 2002).

Given that perceived control has a profound effect on behavior, it is argued that it is also related to advertising believability. This notion sees that perceived control influences the beliefs one holds about the content of messages from paid media. Focusing on the issue of perceived control, if a voter perceives themself to be dominated (i.e., lack control over events and outcomes, or are influenced) during an election campaign, they will, in all likelihood, tend to believe the advertising message. However, if they are dominant (in control), then they would have a propensity to not believe campaign communications, particularly paid advertising, thus,

> *RQ3:* To what extent does the degree of electoral environment control influence the believability of campaign advertising.

Along with the extent of control over outcomes the extent that advertising is believed, is also potentially influenced by the level of voters' satisfaction. Satisfaction potentially has an influence on advertising believability, because if a voter is satisfied with a party or politics in general, then he or she is likely to have a greater propensity to believe their advertising messages. Thus,

> *RQ4:* To what extent does voter satisfaction influence political advertising believability.

The degree to which an individual processes a particular advertising message has been argued to depend on factors, such as their ability and opportunity to process the message and their knowledge and prior experience with the object (Phelps and Thorson 1991). However, the extent that the message is believed may also depend on a consumers involvement. Laczniak and Muehling (1993) suggest that if existing beliefs are held with certainty, not only are they resistant to change, but they may be held with greater confidence after exposure to an advertising message. From a political advertising perspective, this implies that voters who believe with certainty, that the messages of parties and politicians are factually correct may not change that belief. Political communications are required by law to be communicated in a factual and truthful manner, and whilst such messages may involve the use of negative or attack themes, they are not generally misleading or factually incorrect. Individuals with higher involvement see more relevance and pay more attention to related communication on the election, believing the communicated messages. Therefore, it would be seen that those more involved in an election may believe the messages more than those who are less involved. Thus,

> *RQ5:* To what extent does the level of decision involvement influence the believability of campaign advertising.

Advertising to Voters and Message Appeals: To date, there is extensive literature that has concentrated largely on examining voting behavior, advertising appeals, and negative advertising in the U.S. (see Faber, Tims, and Schmitt

1993; Hill 1989; Sonner 1998). In Australia, however, the focus has been on the ethics of political advertising, banning political advertising, and the media's impact. Despite the differences between the two political systems (Westminster and U.S.) there are many similarities in the way electoral campaigns are undertaken and managed.

As Rothschild (1978) has commented, a growing body of work has shown a shift in communications and communications effect. Such effects require considering the potential effects on the democratic process with regard to election campaigns in regard to their general believability of the message. Focusing on the types of advertising undertaken during campaigns such as negative ads, positive ads, comparative ads and their impact on believability is important. Prior research indicates the voters' dislike negative ads and consider them unethical, deceptive and uninformative (Pinkleton 1997). Focusing on the believability and related to the type of advertising one may logically expect that more positive political advertising would be perceived more believable than negative ads, thus,

> *RQ6a:* Will positive political ads be perceived more believable than negative ads.

If political advertising is believable then the message should impact on voters' preferences for specific parties that are the identified sponsors of the messages. The connection between a voters' view that a political ad evokes sufficient confidence in its truthfulness, making it acceptable to the voter should by and large result in a preference for the sponsor of the ad, thus,

> *RQ6b:* Does advertising believability influence party preference.

RESEARCH DESIGN

The study was based on the design and administration of a self-completed questionnaire that was part of a larger study of voter behavior conducted in Australia. The survey was administered to a random sample of voters in a state election in Queensland, Australia. The data were gathered immediately following the election, and the respondents were registered, eligible to vote, and cast a vote on polling day and in total 190 surveys were returned. A drop-off and pick-up approach was utilized to administer the survey. Two electorates within the south-east region of the state were chosen, and then every third house was chosen in randomly selected streets in each of the electorates. In total 400 surveys were dropped off and 190 were collected. The respondents ranged in age from 18 to 80 years, with an average age of 28 years. Thirty-eight percent of respondents were men and 62% were women.

Political advertising believability was measured by the Beltramini (1982) television advertising believability scale, which consists of 10 semantic differential items scored on a seven-point scale, with the average of the 10 items representing a believability score, such that higher scores reflect greater believability. Items include when watching or listening to ads, would you say that they were credible to not credible, honest to dishonest and so forth. There were two banks of believability items separated by a page to tap the two campaigns that were the focus of the study. Voter decision involvement was measured via an version of Mittal's (1989) purchase decision involvement scale. The four items were adapted to suit the political context, using a seven-point scale with higher scores implying greater voter decision involvement. Voter satisfaction was measured using a four-item scale adapted from Evrard and Aurier (1996), measuring satisfaction with parties, the party voted for at the previous election, and politics in general. Voter perceived control was measured using five items, adapted from Mehrabian and Russell (1974). The items measure the extent a voter feels dominated versus in control during the election campaign, using a seven-point semantic differential scale. Party preference was measured by asking respondents to identify their preferred party.

Campaign Communications

Because the focus of the study is political advertising it is relevant to provide a brief description of the two campaigns. The Labor Party (the incumbent) used a more positive campaign in general, advertising its economic record and a leader with a positive image and high credibility, whereas the conservative coalition (the opposition) campaign used negative advertising. The conservatives highlighted a recent issue in which some Labor Party officials and politicians had been accused of electoral rorts because they had fraudulently enrolled people at addresses where they did not live to ensure they would win preselection. The conservative campaign had used the law and order issue historically, and again, this was a major issue in advertising for them, in which they attacked the government's record.

Overall, the Labor party campaign was more positive and the conservative more negative. Using the classifications provided by Pinkleton (1997) as a basis, the Labor campaign is classified as positive in that it used implied comparative advertising, direct comparative advertising, and positive advertising of itself and its record without reference to its opponents. The conservative (National Liberal) party used negative advertising, negative image advertising, and attack advertising. On examination of the content of the information presented in the political advertising during the campaign, the information was factually accurate for both parties. Even though the campaigns were very different, the content of the information was not misleading or deceptive, according to the Australian Advertising Standards.

RESULTS

All scales were initially examined for dimensionality and reliability. In the preliminary analysis, the data showed no significant skewing or kurtosis and therefore possessed acceptable normality. The scales were factor analyzed using principle components with oblique rotation, followed by reliability estimates of each scale. The factor analyses indicated that all constructs were unidimensional with factor loadings between .6 and .8, with items related to each construct explaining over 60% of the variance. The factor analysis also indicated that the believability measurement for the two campaigns loaded onto two distinct factors. The two factors explained 75.78 % of the variance, the reliability of the believability scale measuring the Labor campaign was .96 and the conservative (National Liberal) campaign was .96.

The analysis of the scales indicated that all the multi-item measures factor loadings were >.6, all loadings were found to be statistically significant at $p <$ .05, and no cross-loadings greater than .4 were identified in the factor analysis. Finally, all construct reliabilities (Cronbach's alpha) were greater than .85. Subsequently, all items within each construct were computed into composite variables to test the research questions.

Analytical Process

Given the formulation of the research questions and sample size, partial least squares (PLS) were used to analyze the data. PLS is a general technique for estimating path models involving latent constructs indirectly observed by multiple indicators (Fornell and Cha 1994). The model is formally specified by two sets of linear relationships for the outer model relationships between the latent and manifest variables and the inner model relationships between the latent variables (Chin 1998a,b; Fornell and Cha 1994; Lohmöeller 1989). The focus here is on the inner relationships because they specifically relate to the hypotheses developed for the study.

The evaluation of the relationships (hypotheses) was not made on the basis of any single, general fit index, but rather involved multiple indices are characterized by aspects such as their quality, sufficiency to explain the data, congruence with substantive expectations and precision (Lohmöeller 1989). Hence, a systematic examination of various fit indices for predictive relevance of the hypotheses was necessary (Fornell and Cha 1994), including average variance accounted (AVA), R^2, variance explained by each path, regression weights, and loadings. These indices provide evidence for the existence of the relationships rather than definitive statistical tests.

Results for Research Questions RQ1 to RQ5

Relationships between Involvement, Satisfaction, Perceived Control and Ad Believability: The results focus on examining the relationships among voter characteristics that influence political advertising believability, particularly to what extent voter involvement, satisfaction, and perceived control influence believability to assess RQ1 to RQ5. The results for the proposed theoretical relationships among voter perceived control, involvement, satisfaction, and advertising believability are presented in Table 1, which provides the inner model results.

The AVA for the endogenous variables was .13, and the individual R^2 were greater than the recommended .10 (Falk and Miller 1992) for the predicted variables, except for RQ1 and RQ2. In Table 1 all the paths exceed the 1.5% cut-off criterion (except for advertising believability-perceived control), and the bootstrap critical ratios are of the appropriate size (greater than +/- 1.96, $p < .05$). Also, the between blocks correlation coefficients of the residuals of the manifest variables were all relatively low (below .12) indicating that the blocks are distinctly defined. Therefore, the results indicate that for RQ1 perceived control in-

TABLE 1. Partial Least Squares Results for the Hypothesized Relationships

Predicted variables	Predictor variables	Hypotheses	Path	Variance due to path	R^2	Critical ratio
Voter involvement	Perceived control	Rq1	.21	.044	.044	2.48
Voter satisfaction	Voter involvement	Rq2	.24	.060	.06	3.50
Advertising believability	Perceived control	Rq3	−.12	.003		— 1.45
	Voter satisfaction	Rq4	.42	.191		6.00
	Voter involvement	Rq5	.26	.089	.28	3.32
AVA					.13	

Notes: AVA = average variance accounted for.

fluences voter involvement, RQ2 voter involvement influences satisfaction, RQ4 satisfaction influences ad believability and RQ5 that involvement influences believability. The data therefore suggest that perceived control influences voter involvement. Also that voter involvement influences satisfaction, and that involvement and satisfaction influence advertising believability. However, perceived control did not significantly influence advertising believability (RQ3), but its effect was in the direction predicted. That is those who perceive less control are more prone to believe the advertising. In relation to this it is interesting to note that perceived control did have a differing effect between the two campaigns.

Results for RQ6a

Differences in Ad Believability: To examine the difference between the rating of advertising believability across the two campaigns t-tests were conducted. The results indicate the mean score for the Labor advertising was 3.66 and conservative campaign was 3.54 (t = 1.13 not significant at any conventional level). This indicates no significant difference in the believability of the two campaigns. To further explore this examination was undertaken to assess differences taking into account part preference. To examine the differences in advertising believability between the scores of those who preferred Labor and those who preferred the Conservative party t-tests were computed. The results in Table 2 indicate significant differences existed according to preferred party and advertising believability.

The results indicate that voters indicating a preference for the Labor party rated their campaign advertising much more believable and the Conservative less believable. Those who preferred the Conservative party rated its advertising campaign more believable. However, the significance of the difference was greater for the Labor campaign over the Conservative campaign in the context of preference and believability. This analysis does not however, imply

TABLE 2. Differences in Believability According to Party Preference

	Preference	Mean	T-value	Sig
Labor party campaign	Conservative party	3.28	−4.00**	.001
	Labor Party	4.14		
Conservative party campaign	Conservative party	3.94	2.98*	.005
	Labor Party	3.32		

(**Significant @ .01, * @ .05

directionality and at this stage we do not know if preference existed prior to the campaign and is the result of the campaign messages.

Results for Proposed RQ6b

The Impact of Ad Believability on Party Preference: To test this research question a discriminant analysis was conducted to examine the predictiveness of advertising believability for party preference. The results indicated that believability of the two campaigns did predict the party preference. The results indicate that the believability of the party campaign does contribute significantly to voter preference. Preference for Labor impacted positively by Labor advertising believability and negatively by Conservative and visa versa for preference for Conservative.

In the analysis, the discriminant function was significant (Chi Square [party preference] = 23.88, df = 2; p = < .001, wilks' lambda =.81). For the tests of equality of group means, Wilks' Lambda for believability of the Labor Campaign was .86 (f-value 17.78, p < .001) and Conservative Campaign was .93 (f-value 9.00, p < .005). To assess how effectively the derived discriminant functions were able to classify cases, a confusion matrix was generated, applying the jack-knife (leave-one-out) method of classification. For party preference and advertising believability 71.3% of the grouped cases were correctly classified while 70% cross-validated cases were also correctly classified.

DISCUSSION

The results did confirm that voter decision involvement, satisfaction and perceived control do influence a voters' advertising believability. In general, the results indicate that voters perceived control influences involvement, and that involvement influences satisfaction. As such those who have higher perceived control of electoral and political events have higher involvement in voting. Also those who are more involved in voting decision making also report higher levels of satisfaction. In the context of advertising believability the findings indicate that those who are more involved, possess higher levels of satisfaction and perceived control believe the political advertising messages communicated during the election.

The results indicate that, even though one campaign was more positive in its themes and the information it provided to voters, respondents by and large believed it as much as they did the other campaign, which was more negative. The results also indicate that voters differentiated between the two campaigns, and the effects of involvement, satisfaction, and perceived control indicate differential effects across the two campaigns. Preference implies selecting a preferred party to vote for and believing that particular party's messages more than their opponents. One must remember that in the context of believability however there were no differences between campaigns. This implies that in the context of the two campaigns (one positive and the other negative) both achieved comparable levels of believability. It was only when party preference was considered that difference appeared. As such, does prior preference drive believability or can believing a message impact preference. In reality both scenarios are possible and likely in an election. The analysis of believability and party preference indicates that this issue needs further examination. What we need to explore are voters' characteristics to better understand what characteristics may impact the believability of the advertising messages and ultimately influence preference through creating messages that are believed.

This study though it makes significant contributions to our understanding of political advertising, it suffers from many of the limitations found in research of this type. A limitation of the study is the use of some scales that have not been used previously in a political context. Although the scales have been validated in commercial product contexts, further work needs to be done in the context of voter behavior and political advertising. Also, there is a need to test these scales in a broader nomological network. It would also be informative to study the constructs in a longitudinal study to plot changes in, for example, the level of involvement, confidence of voters, and information usage during a campaign. A within-subjects design, as opposed to a between-subjects design, would be a major breakthrough in political advertising.

These limitations do not render the significance of the findings any less important, but instead signal the need for more research to be conducted in this growing and important area of politics and advertising. The actual state election campaign offered an ideal situation to evaluate the effects and relationships of voter characteristics, political advertising, and voter search behavior. However, by its very nature (real life), the study's ability to identify and separate the effects of other extraneous events and issues was impaired, and therefore, we cannot conclusively establish any causation. However, this is countered by the data being gathered in the context of an actual election.

CONCLUSION

One of the principal research objectives was to examine voter psychology and its effect on advertising believability, via two specific political advertising campaigns, one communicating through negative appeals and one positive appeals and their effect on party preference. Political parties and candidates want to know how to allocate their resources during campaigns and develop better knowledge about how and why voters make the choices they do, enabling campaign strategists to target messages and mediums more effectively. Such knowledge provides insight for developing appropriate appeals to selected voter segments through media such as television and newspapers.

Understanding the principal reasons behind a voter's believability of a message can help researchers better understand advertising effects and appeals. Public policymakers can monitor the use of political advertising and various appeals and more efficiently solve problems and steer democracy in the right direction if they understand whether voters are choosing a candidate for rational or emotional reasons and to what extent voters' are influenced by party advertising. For example, if voters elect a candidate on the basis of personality, image or messages communicated during a campaign rather than substantive, meaningful issues, it may affect long-term democratic processes and trends. Candidates and their strategists might choose an information campaign rather than an image-based persuasion campaign, or they might rely on positive appeals rather than negative appeals in their advertising. This may depend on whether voters believe in the candidate because he or she is perceived to be a strong leader or because he or she advocates certain issues and policies during the course of the election campaign or has performed well previously. These issues are intertwined with the believability of the message.

Advertising in politics is a controversial issue, because of the potential influence and manipulation of voters by politicians or special interest groups through paid political advertising. However, similar to other areas of research, voter behavior studies offer the promise of a deeper understanding of voter needs and the development of improved voter communication programs. Particularly, in understanding the extent that political advertising during an election is believed by voters. In the context of advertising effects and voter behavior the nexus or linkage between voter and party through advertising is sure to continue to be a contentious issue.

REFERENCES

AEC (1999), Australian Electoral Commission http://www.aec.gov.au/pubs/reports/dosclosure/appendix2.htm

Andrews, J. Craig (1989), " The Dimensionality of Beliefs Toward Advertising in General," *Journal of Advertising*, 18 (1), 26-36.

Andrews, J. Craig, Srinivas Durvasula and Syed Akhter (1990), "A Framework for Conceptualizing and Measuring the Involvement Construct in Advertising Research," *Journal of Advertising*, 19 (4), 27-40.

Andrews, J. Craig, Netemeyer, Richard and Srinivas Durvasula (1991), "Effects of Consumption Frequency on Believability and Attitudes Towards Alcohol Warning Labels," *Journal of Consumer Affairs*, 25(2), 323-338.

Beltramini, Richard (1982), "Advertising Perceived Believability Scale," *Proceedings of the Southwestern Marketing Association*, eds. D. Corrigan, F. Kraft and R, Ross, Southwestern Marketing Association, Wichita State University, Wichita, KS, 1-3.

Beltramini, Richard (1988), "Perceived Believability of Warning Label Information Presented in Cigarettes Advertising," *Journal of Advertising*, 17 (1), 26-32.

Bloch, Peter and Marsha Richins (1983), "A Theoretical Model for the Study of Product Importance Perceptions," *Journal of Marketing*, 47, 69-81.

Burton, Scot and Richard Netemeyer (1992), "The Effect of Enduring, Situational, and Response Involvement on Preference Stability in the Context of Voting Behavior," *Psychology and Marketing*, 9 (2), 143-156.

Burton, Scot and D Lichtenstein (1988), "The Effect of Ad Claims and Ad Context on Attitude Toward the Advertisement," *Journal of Advertising*, 17(1), 3 -11.

Chin, Wynne (1998a), "Issues and Opinion on Structural Equation Modeling," *MIS Quarterly*, 22(1), vii-xvi.

Chin, Wynne (1998b), "The Partial Least Squares Approach For Structural Equation Modeling," *Modern Methods for Business Research*, ed. G. Marcoulides, Lawrence Erlbaum Associates, 295-336.

Day, Robert (1977), "Toward a Process Model of Consumer Satisfaction," in *Conceptualization and Measurement of Consumer Satisfaction and Dissatisfaction*, Ed. K, Hunt, Cambridge MA: Marketing Science Institute, 153-183.

Dermody, Janine and Scullion, Richard (2001), "Delusions of grandeur? Marketing's contribution to 'meaningful' Western political consumption," *European Journal of Marketing*, 35, 9/10, 1085-1098.

Dermody, Janine and Scullion, Richard (1999), "Perceptions of negative political advertising: meaningful or menacing? An empirical study of the 1997 British General Election campaign," *International Journal of Advertising*, 19, 2, June, 201-225.

ecq (2003) Queensland Electoral Commission, http://www.ecq.qld.gov.au

Evrard, Yves and Philippe Aurier (1996), "Identification and Validation of the Components of the Person-Object Relationship," *Journal of Business Research*, 37, 127-134.

Faber, Ronald, Albert Tims and Kay Schmitt (1993), "Negative Political Advertising and Voting Intent: The Role of Involvement and Alternative Information Sources," *Journal of Advertising*, 22 (4), 67-76.

Falk, R. Frank and Nancy. B Miller (1992), *A Primer for Soft Modeling*. Akron, OH: University of Akron Press.

Fornell, Claes and Jaesung Cha (1994), "Partial Least Squares," *Advanced Methods of Marketing Research*, ed. R. P. Bagozzi, Oxford; Basil Blackwell Ltd.

Gaski, John (1984), "The Theory of Power and Conflict in Channels of Distribution," *Journal of Marketing*, 48 (Summer), 9-29.

Gotlieb, Jerry and Dan Sarel (1991), " Comparative Advertising Effectiveness: The Role of Involvement and Source Credibility," *Journal of Advertising*, 20 (1), 38-45.

Greenberger David, Steven Strasser, Larry Cummings and Randall Dunhan (1989), "The Impact of Personal Control on Performance and Satisfaction," *Organizational Behavior and Human Processes*, 43, 29-51.

Greenwald, Anthony and Clark Leavitt (1984), " Audience Involvement in Advertising: Four Levels," *Journal of Consumer Research*, 11 (June), 581-592.

Hayes, Bernadette and Ian McAllister (1996), "Marketing Politics to Voters: late Deciders in the 1992 British election," *European Journal of Marketing*, 30 (10/11), 135-146.

Hill, Robert (1989), "An Exploration of Voter Response to Political Advertisements," *Journal of Advertising*, 18 (4), 14-22.

Johnson, Dennis (1999), "The Cyberscape Election of the Future," in *Handbook of Political Marketing* ed. Bruce Newman, Sage Publications Inc, 705-724.

Laczniak, Russell and Darrel Muehling (1993), "Toward a Better Understanding of the Role of Advertising Message Involvement in Ad Processing," *Psychology & Marketing*, 10(4), 301-319.

Lohmöeller, Jan-Bernard (1989), *Latent Variable Modeling With Partial Least Squares*, Heidelberg, Physica-Verlag.

Mehrabian, Albert and James Russell (1974), *An Approach to Environmental Psychology, Cambridge*, MA: MIT Press.

Mittal, Banwari (1989), "Measuring Purchase-Decision Involvement," *Psychology & Marketing*, 6 (2), 147-162.

Mitchell, Andrew (1981), "Dimensions of Advertising Involvement," in *Advances in Consumer Research*, Vol 8, ed. Kent Monroe, MI: Association for Consumer Research, 25-30.

Muehling, Darrel, Russell Laczniak and Craig Andrews (1993), "Defining, Operationalizing, and Using Involvement in Advertising Research: A Review," *Journal of Current Issues and Research in Advertising*, 15 (1), 21-57.

Neese, W and L Capella (1996), "An Analysis of the Independent Influences Hypothesis Across Involvement Environments: When Attitude Towards the Ad Predicts Purchase Intentions," *Journal of Promotion Management*, 4(1), 89-109.

Newman, Bruce and Jagdish Sheth (1984), "The gender Gap in Voter Attitudes and Behavior: Some Advertising Implications," *Journal of Advertising*, 13(3), 4-16.

Newman, Bruce and Jagdish Sheth (1985), "A Model of Primary Voter Behavior," *Journal of Consumer Research*, 12, 178-187.

O'Cass, Aron (1996), "Political marketing and the marketing concept," *European Journal of Marketing*,30 (10/11), 45-61.

O'Cass, Aron (2000), "An Assessment of Consumers Product, Purchase Decision, Advertising and Consumption Involvement in Fashion Clothing," *Journal of Economic Psychology*, 21, 545-576.

O'Cass, Aron (2001), "The Internal-External Marketing Orientation of a Political Party: Social Implications of Political Party Marketing Orientation," *Journal of Public Affairs*, 1 (2), 136-152.

O'Cass, Aron (2001), "Consumer Self-Monitoring, Materialism and Involvement in Fashion Clothing," *Australasian Marketing Journal*, 9, 1, 46-60.

O'Cass, Aron. (2002) Political Advertising Believability and Information Source Value During Elections, *Journal of Advertising*, XXXI (1), 63-74.

Peracchio, Laura. and David Luna (1998), "The Development of an Advertising Campaign to Discourage Smoking Initiation Among Children and Youth," *Journal of Advertising*, 27(3), 49-56.

Petty, Richard, John Cacioppo, David Schumann (1983), "Central and Peripheral Routes to Advertising Effectiveness: The Moderating Role of Involvement," *Journal of Consumer Research*, 10 (September), 135-146.

Phelps, Joseph. and Ester Thorson (1991), "Brand Familiarity and Product Involvement Effects on the Attitude Toward an Ad–Brand Attitude Relationship," *Advances in Consumer Research*, 18, 202-209.

Pinkleton, Bruce (1997), "The Effects of Negative Comparative Political Advertising on Candidate Evaluations and Advertising Evaluations: An Exploration," *Journal of Advertising*, 26 (1), 20-29.

Pinkleton, Bruce (1998), "Effects of Print Comparative Political Advertising on Political Decision-Making and Participation," *Journal of Communication*, Autumn, 24-36.

Putrevu, Sanjay and Kenneth Lord (1994), "Comparative and Noncomparative Advertising: Attitudinal Effects Under Cognitive and Affective Involvement Conditions," *Journal of Advertising*, 23(2),77-90.

Raymond M, J Tanner and D Eppright (1998), "The Aids Pandemic: Changes in the Believability and Use of Information Sources," Health Marketing Quarterly, 15 (4), 1-24.

Richins, Marsha and Peter Bloch (1991), "Post-Purchase Product Satisfaction: Incorporating the Effects of Involvement and Time," *Journal of Business Research*, 23, 145-158.

Rothschild, Michael (1978), "Political Advertising: A Neglected Policy Issue in Marketing," *Journal of Marketing Research*, 15, 58-71.

Rothschild, Michael and Michael Houston (1979), "Individual Differences in Voting Behavior: Further Investigations of Involvement," in *Advances in Consumer Research*, Vol 7, ed J Olson, Ann Arbour, MI: Association for Consumer Research, 655-658.

Sonner, Brenda (1998), "The Effectiveness of Negative Political Advertising: A Case Study," *Journal of Advertising Research*, (November-December), 37-42.

TEC (2002) The Electoral Commission: Executive Summary, www.electoralcommission.gov.uk.

Weaver Lariscy, Ruth and Spencer Tinkham (1999), "The Sleeper Effect and Negative Political Advertising," *Journal of Advertising*, 28 (4), 13-30.

Wolburg, Joyce (2001), "The Risky Business of Binge Drinking Among College Students: Using Risk Models for PSAs and Anti-Drinking Campaigns," *Journal of Advertising*, XXX (4), 23-39.

Wray, Harry. J (1999), "Money and Politics," in *Handbook of Political Marketing* (ed) Bruce Newman, Sage Publications, Inc, 741-758.

Zaichkowsky, Judith (1985), "Measuring the Involvement Construct," *Journal of Consumer Research*, 12 (3), 341-352.

An Exploratory Assessment of Voter and Governmental Interface on Pertinent Issues Facing American Children and Youth

Tanuja Singh
Elisa Fredericks

SUMMARY. The strength of the social fabric of a country is determined, to a large extent, by the quality and potential of its children. While parents are expected to bear the primary responsibility for the well-being of their children, various other institutions including the government exist in a society to provide the support structure through which the quality of life for its children can be enhanced. In recent years, considerable attention has been drawn to the problems that children and young adults face in the U.S. However, more than ever, Americans view government-sponsored programs and their ability to help troubled youth of the country with skepticism. Using an open systems paradigm within the context of the resource exchange theory, this research empirically investigates the attitudes of the voting public towards the problems facing children and youth in a sample population of the U.S. It also evaluates

Tanuja Singh, DBA (E-mail: Tanuja@niu.edu), is Associate Professor, and Elisa Fredericks, PhD (E-mail: elisa@niu.edu), is Assistant Professor, Department of Marketing, College of Business, Northern Illinois University, DeKalb, IL 60115-2897.

[Haworth co-indexing entry note]: "An Exploratory Assessment of Voter and Governmental Interface on Pertinent Issues Facing American Children and Youth." Singh, Tanuja, and Elisa Fredericks. Co-published simultaneously in *Journal of Nonprofit & Public Sector Marketing* (Best Business Books, an imprint of The Haworth Press, Inc.) Vol. 14, No. 1/2, 2005, pp. 223-245; and: *Current Issues in Political Marketing* (eds: Walter W. Wymer, Jr., and Jennifer Lees-Marshment) Best Business Books, an imprint of The Haworth Press, Inc., 2005, pp. 223-245. Single or multiple copies of this article are available for a fee from The Haworth Document Delivery Service [1-800-HAWORTH, 9:00 a.m. - 5:00 p.m. (EST). E-mail address: getinfo@haworthpressinc.com].

the perceptions of the respondents regarding the efficacy of government-sponsored programs targeted at children as well as public-policy and social marketing implications of these findings. *[Article copies available for a fee from The Haworth Document Delivery Service: 1-800-HAWORTH. E-mail address: <docdelivery@haworthpress.com> Website: <http://www.HaworthPress. com> © 2005 by The Haworth Press, Inc. All rights reserved.]*

KEYWORDS. Children and youth, government and social programs, voter attitude, open systems, resource exchange theory, public-policy marketing

INTRODUCTION

Children are one of the most important resources a society has, since its future is governed to a large extent by the quality and potential of its children. There can be little disagreement that children's issues such as health-care, education, alcohol and drug abuse, and teenage pregnancy are issues critical to the well-being of the American economy. To achieve a better quality of life for children, the government spends considerable sums of money to provide a variety of services needed to offer the desired quality of life and improve their potential of becoming productive citizens in the future.

However, research suggests that the future of the American youth is hindered by a plethora of problems today. For example, almost 50% of America's children and youth (aged 10-17 years) engage in problematic behaviors such as abusing alcohol, drugs, and other controlled substances, dropping out of school, committing crimes, and engaging in early unprotected sexual intercourse (Dryfoos 1990a, 1990b). Teenage birth rates in the U.S. are more than double that of other developed countries such as Canada (Moore 2003) and teenage childbearing alone costs the U.S. society $8.9 billion every year (Passell 1996). Numerous studies have investigated these problems and costs to society caused by alcohol abuse, unwanted teenage pregnancy, inadequate and poor education, and crime. In a recent report (Moore 2003) concluded that, ". . . we have to acknowledge that all is not well with all of America's children . . . data show that drug use and violence rates remain high. In addition, the proportion of children living in deep poverty remains as high as it was a quarter century ago." However, public investment in child and youth-centered prevention programs remains minimal relative to other developed nations.

While several studies have investigated the issues facing children and youth in America, to date, no study has investigated the attitude of the voting public towards public-policy programs targeted towards the children and youth. Furthermore, no study has used attitude data to develop voter profiles within this context or proposed marketing strategies to educate and motivate the voting public to fund public-policy programs. This research addresses some of these issues. The objectives of this study are:

- To understand the nature of the problems facing children and youth as perceived by the voters in a sample county.
- To understand the perceived severity of the problems.
- To test the perceived relevance and usefulness of the identified solutions developed to address these problems.
- To test the willingness of voters to provide additional funding for the identified solutions.
- To evaluate the public-policy implications of these findings that can be used to assist in the development of effective public-policy campaigns.

BACKGROUND

The Nature of Problems Facing American Children and Youth

According to recent statistics, problems facing children and youth in America are quite serious and will have serious long-term consequences for the country unless they are addressed in a timely manner (Children's Defense Fund 2002). According to the most recent statistics, one in five American children is born poor and one in six babies is born to a mother who did not receive prenatal child care. Further, one in seven youths drops out of high-school and one in eight is unemployed. In the year 2000, more than 1.7 million youths were arrested in the United States for a variety of crimes. Yet, on average, states spend three times more per prisoner than per public school pupil (Children's Defense Fund 2002).

Drug and alcohol abuse among American youth are at problematically high levels and have been correlated with 50% of teenage deaths, physical and sexual aggression, and anxiety and depression. This is a serious issue since research suggests that drug and alcohol abuse among youth are primers for continuous drug use later in life. The instances of marijuana, cocaine, hallucinogens, inhalants, and heroin use are significantly higher for youths that abused alcohol and drugs earlier in their lives (American Academy of Child and Adolescent Psychiatry 2001). The Center for Disease Control reports the prevention of tobacco use among adolescent and teenagers as one of America's most important health challenges. The U.S. Department of Health and Human Services (2001) estimates that each day 3000 young people are converted to regular tobacco use and one third of them will die from smoking related diseases. In the face of these individual and societal challenges, public investment in prevention still remains minimal.

Public-policy concerns reflect both intangible and tangible costs associated with problematic behaviors among children and youth. While monetary costs associated with corrective measures such as health-care, law enforcement, remedial education, welfare, and rehabilitation programs are significant, intangible costs due to lost potential, hopelessness, desperation, and resignation are no less important (Bogenschneider 1996; Hawkins, Catalano, and Miller 1992).

Most of the challenges facing American children and youth are highly inter-linked. For example, higher school enrollment rates are generally associated with strong family and community bonding. However, the combined effects of poorly educated parents, the absence of parents, and inner city residence continue to be contributors to teenage drop-out rates (Hirschman 2001). There is considerable evidence that rebirths among teenagers are associated with other outcomes such as a propensity to drop out of school, living in poverty, or receiving welfare. These outcomes are even more pronounced for those teenagers who are parenting one child (Guttmacher Report 2000). Studies clearly suggest that these behaviors share common antecedents such as sexual risk taking and sexual intercourse which often result in unwanted teenage pregnancies (Coleman 2002; Burnett 2002). Many of the problems facing youths can be traced back to their childhood. For example, unstable family life, lack of social programs, poor performance at schools, and lack of role models during childhood, may subsequently contribute to a troubled adolescent life as well (Dembo and Schmeidler 2003).

Research has consistently shown a connection between early intervention through social programs and a reduction in later outcomes such as crime, welfare-dependence, teenage pregnancy, and school dropout rates (Schorr 1989). Prevention scholars have proposed several recommendations for building community-based preventive programs that work and the need to support them through legislative and other means (e.g., Bogenschneider 1996; Weissberg and Elias 1993).

However, more than ever, Americans view government-sponsored programs and their ability to help troubled youth of the country with skepticism (Bogenschneider 1996; Schorr 1988). Researchers suggest that ecological risk processes that affect the American youth range from individual and family factors such as poor parental monitoring to community factors such as media influences. Social scientists conclude that "promoting positive youth development is . . . more than just taking steps to help children avoid problems" (Bogenschneider 1996, p. 129). While public funding for community-based organizations is not the only answer to the problem, there is enough empirical evidence to show that community-based organizations play an important role in alleviating problems that plague our children and youth (Bogenschneider 1996; Comer 1993; Gilchrist and Schinke 1983; Lerner 1995; McKnight and Kretzman 1992; Plotnick 1993; Rhode 1993-94).

Further compounding the problems is the fact that funding available for government-sponsored services has decreased in recent years. For example, Children's Defense Fund (2002) reports that in 2002, the current administration cut $3.1 billion dollars in 14 children's programs including programs that addressed child abuse, and maternal and child health. Further, twenty-nine other programs that target the well-being of children and youth saw budget freezes. These included child-care and after- school programs, child health, education for homeless children, and services to train youths for jobs and prevent juvenile delinquency. The report concludes that as children's needs have grown considerably due to the widening gap between society's haves and have-nots, overall services and governmental funding for these services have declined (Children's Defense Fund 2002).

In summary, empirical evidence clearly suggests that issues pertaining to early childhood education, health-care, teenage pregnancy, substance abuse, and others are paramount to the well-being of children and youth in any society. However, as described earlier in this paper, recent decline in governmental funding for some of the critical programs raises important societal concerns. The future of these programs as well as the responsibility for funding them need to be addressed to ensure that problems facing children and youth in America are not ignored. Furthermore, in light of the budgetary constraints facing these programs, public-policy advocates need to identify the most important issues facing children and youth as well as the most promising solutions that could address these challenges. Further, public policy advocates need to develop the most effective social marketing strategies to engage their audience, particularly the voting public, to ensure that the magnitude of issues facing American children and youth is clearly understood.

Organizing Framework

The open systems (Katz and Kahn 1966) and resource exchange theories (Thibaut and Kelly 1959; Emerson 1962) are two complementary frameworks used to describe the interactions between government and the public. An open system includes individuals, groups, organizations and other living entities that interact and exchange things of value on a regular basis. Such systems receive inputs from their environment, transform those inputs into outputs, and thereby send new outputs into the environment (Katz and Kahn 1966). All social systems have at least two important characteristics: (1) behavior among the members of the social system is motivated by both individual and collective interests, and (2) interdependence processes emerge because of specialization and division of labor.

The economic structures of contemporary societies can be viewed as consisting of four types of open systems or institutions, which engage in receiving, transforming and distributing resources to society: households, private firms, public enterprise, and government. Households sell labor to and buy goods from private firms and public enterprises through market exchanges. Likewise, government institutions engage in market exchanges when purchasing services and goods from households, firms and other institutions (Pandya and Dholakia 1991).

In the context of this research, we narrow our focus to the perceptions of one open system namely the voting public of a large county in the United States, and determine its willingness to engage in exchanges with the government. Because of the vast number of issues confronting government and the public, and the complexity, technicality, time, and financial resources needed to address each, specialization and division of labor have emerged between the two as coping mechanisms for dealing with paramount issues. This is particularly evident in areas affecting the welfare of children.

In the area of specialization, one of government's functions is to effectively develop and maintain programs, which are self-initiated or mandated by its citizens. The public in turns pays for these programs through appropriated tax dollars. The public, more specifically parents or guardians, are responsible for the day-to-day care of children, while government-initiated programs such as public schools and day-care programs aid parents in the rearing of children. Therefore, both governments and the public are developing specific expertise (specialization) and work interdependently to achieve societal goals.

The resource exchange theory, originally developed by Thibaut and Kelly (1959) and Emerson (1962), further explains how government and the public engage in market exchanges or trades to achieve mutually beneficial goals. A market exchange takes place when there is simultaneous transaction of valued goods, services and ideas between two entities. Marketing has been described as an exchange process (Kotler 1969, 1972) between two or more social systems in which money, information, goods, and services are a few of the resources which are exchanged between them (Donnenworth and Foa 1974). A trade takes place when both parties have the ability to accept or reject the values offered, when each one considers dealing with the other as appropriate and proper, and when both are capable of communicating and delivering the goods and services in question. A critical element of this equation is the trust in each other's ability to deliver the promised goods to ensure a continuation of this exchange.

This paper investigates the willingness of one open system, the voting public, to engage in resource exchange with government to address and alleviate some of the problems facing children and youth today. It also addresses the importance of social marketing for achieving public policy goals within the current context.

RESEARCH METHOD

Sample Selection

Three simultaneous data collection methods were employed for this research: (a) telephone survey of a random sample of registered voters in a large south eastern county of the U.S.; names of respondents were randomly selected from a list of registered voters to avoid sampling bias; (2) mall intercept at a major shopping mall in a large South Eastern City; and (3) direct mail addressed to employees of large public and private-sector corporations (registered voters only) in the county since many of these organizations have gift-matching programs for charitable donations. The telephone surveys were conducted during random hours of the day including weekends to ensure the likelihood of finding a diverse range of respondent categories. The mall intercept was conducted on a Saturday between 12:00 noon and 5:00 p.m. A personal letter from the researchers accompanied the direct mail survey explaining the non-commercial nature of the research along with standard privacy and confidentiality of information disclosure.

The main sampling frame was derived from the total population in a county of the southeast region of the United States with a total population of 398,989 persons listed in 27 zip codes. Telephone survey and direct mail data were collected from all zip codes in the sample county to ensure a proportional and representative sample. Therefore, the sampling technique is a combination of random sampling (for the telephone and direct mail surveys) and convenience sampling (for the mall intercept surveys).

Of the 1,500 people contacted via telephone, 420 agreed to respond to the survey resulting in a response rate of 28%. An additional 1,500 surveys were mailed directly to employees of public and private organizations; 315 usable surveys were returned from this group resulting in a response rate of 21%. An additional 93 usable surveys were collected from the mall intercept. Therefore, the total sample size is 828. Table 1 provides information obtained from the U.S.

TABLE 1. U.S. Demographics

Gender	%	Marital Status	%
Male	49.10	Married	59.5
Female	50.9	Single	23.8
		Divorced/separated	16.6
Age		Income	
Under 5	6.8	Less than $10K	9.2
5-19	21.8	10K-14,999K	7.3
20-34	20.9	15K-24,999	14.1
35-44	16.0	25K-34,999	12.7
45-54	13.4	35K-49,999	15.8
55-64	8.6	50K-74,999	18.4
Above 64	12.4	Above 75K	22.6
Race			
Caucasian	80.9		
African-American	13.3		
Other	5.9		

Source: U.S. Bureau of the Census, Statistical Abstracts of the U.S. 2001 Census.

Census Bureau about the demographic makeup of the U.S. population. Table 2 provides demographic information for the sample used in this study. While not all categories can be directly compared due to the differences in category labels, categories such as race and marital status for the sample are comparable with the U.S. Census Bureau data on U.S. population. The one difference is in the respondents' gender distribution; for the overall U.S. population, the distribution of males and females is 49% versus 51% whereas the current sample is 61% female. However, many of the issues identified in the survey relate to child rearing, an area which still remains the primary responsibility of females in the U.S. society. Thus, it is plausible that more females responded to the survey because they are more knowledgeable about the issues raised.

Questionnaire Design

A preliminary survey was developed after reviewing several articles from the academic literature, which dealt with the issues raised in this study. This survey was independently evaluated for face and content validity by two researchers

TABLE 2. Sample Demographics

Gender	%	Political Affiliation	%
Male	39	Democrats	42
Female	61	Republicans	36
		Independents	21
		Other	1
Age		**Voting Frequency**	
18-25	5	Every election	36
26-35	27	Nearly every election	35
36-45	31	Some elections	7
46-55	24	Rarely or never	12
56-65	10		
Above 65	5		
Race		**Income**	
Caucasian	82	Less than $10K	5
African-Americans	11	$11-$20K	15
Hispanic	3	$21-$30K	20 .
Asians	2	$31-40K	16
Others	2	$41-50K	15
		$51-60K	9
		Above 60K	20
		Children at Home	53

(not otherwise associated with this study), whose primary areas of interest included children and adolescent behaviors, particularly risky behaviors among American youth. After suggested modifications, the final survey was deemed acceptable by the independent researchers and finalized for the study. The survey consisted of the following distinct sections that addressed issues raised in the study: (a) general statements addressing the nature of perceived problems facing American children and youth; (b) questions dealing with specific problems facing American children and youth as perceived by sample respondents; (c) tangible solutions to the problems that were perceived to be the most effective by the respondents, opinions about the roles of various stakeholders in developing and funding these solutions; and (d) standard demographic data. Questions also asked respondents about their voting behaviors.

Analysis and Results

General Statements Concerning Issues Facing Children and Youth

The first part of the survey consisted of seven questions in an agree/disagree format, and was designed to assess voters' general perceptions of the problems facing children and the youth in the county. It was also meant to assess whether there was general agreement among the voters regarding problems facing children and youth before problem-specific questions could be asked. Table III lists these statements which include, "we need to pay more attention to problems facing children and teenagers," and "children should be the responsibility of their parents and no one else." Overall, the data suggested that a large majority of the respondents agreed that children's issues were important to the overall well-being of the country.

As shown in Table 3, almost the entire sample is in agreement with the statement that more attention needs to be paid to issues involving children. It is pertinent to mention that irrespective of their political affiliation and economic status, a majority of respondents agree that issues that affect children also affect the future of a society and must be addressed. The strongest agreement is in favor of education where an overwhelming majority (98%) agreed that irrespective of their parents' financial status, children should be able to get some education. The second highest level of agreement (96%) was on the issue of health-care for children where the respondents feel that health-care should not be denied to any child.

It appears that women feel more strongly about some issues than men. For example, agreement among women for the statement "children should be able to get healthcare even if their parents cannot afford it," is 97% whereas 93% of the men agree with the statement and the difference between the genders is statistically significant at .05. There is some difference in perception along racial lines as well. For example, more Caucasians are in agreement with providing education and health-care services for children irrespective of their parents' financial status relative to African-Americans.

However, due to the fact that the level of agreement with the six statements listed in Table 3 is above 85%, difference of a few percentage points is not relevant from an operational viewpoint since an agreement of more than eighty-five percent clearly demonstrates a sample-wide consensus on these important issues.

There also seems to be no systematic association between income levels and agreement or disagreement with the issues. In general, all income groups agree that the issues outlined are very important for the well-being of the country. Only one statement, which assigns responsibility for children, namely,

TABLE 3. General Statements Regarding Problems Facing Children and Youth

Problem Statement	Agreement with Statement %	Demo. Vs. Repub. Chi-Square (Sig.) N = 628	AA Vs. CSN Chi-Square (Sig.) N = 780	Women Vs. Men Chi-Square (Sig.) N = 818
Need to pay more attention to children's issues.	93	2.008 (.157)	1.404 (.236)	7.134 (.008)**
Paying more attention to children's problems will ensure a better future for the country.	91.	7.910 (.005)**	1.500 (.221)	1.567 (.211)
Lack of attention to children today is one reason why there has been an increase in crime.	88	.812 (.367)	.002 (.960)	.404 (.525)
Children should have access to health services even if their parents cannot afford it.	96	.239 (.625)	3.565 (.059)	7.694 (.006)**
Children should be able to get some education even if their parents cannot afford it.	98	.016 (.901)	9.458 (.002)	1.015 (.314)
If poor families could have access to health and educational facilities, if would be beneficial for the entire country.	92	2.980 (.084)	.296 (.586)	1.778 (.182)
Children should be the responsibility of their parents and no one else.	39	.222 (.638)	.857 (.355)	3.197 (.077)

Note: AA = African-Americans, CSN = Caucasians
** Scores are significantly different at .05.

"children should be the responsibility of their parents and non-one else," evokes somewhat different reactions. While only 39% of the overall sample agreed with this proposition, a somewhat higher number of men than women (45% versus 36%) believe that children should indeed be the responsibility of their parents alone. Political affiliation and race seem to have no statistically significant relationship with the response.

Analyzing Respondents' Perceptions of Problems Facing Children and Youth

Next, the survey addressed respondent perceptions about the sources of problems facing children and the youth. Nine statements in a Likert-type format anchored from strongly agree (1) to strongly disagree (5) were presented to respondents. The statements ranged from "lack of parental involvement in their children's lives is a serious problem," to "children have no safe place to go to after school." Parental involvement is defined as efforts that empower and encourage parents to become involved in children's education, and partnering with schools and community at large regarding issues pertaining to children and youth (National Education Association 2003). Table 4 provides a comparative look at the perception of the problems as a function of political ideology, race, and gender.

Respondents were also given an opportunity to voice their own opinions about what they believed the problem sources were as opposed to the ones listed in the survey. A content analysis of these responses revealed that the responses varied considerably and that they were not systematically associated with any particular respondent characteristic. Nevertheless, it is relevant to note that these responses included such things as "lack of religious principles"

TABLE 4. Respondent Perceptions of Specific Problems Facing Children and Youth

Problem Statement	Agreement with Statement (%)	Don't know or Unsure (%)	Mean Values Demo. Vs. Repub. (Sig.) N = 628	Mean Values AA vs. CSN (Sig.) N = 780	Mean Values Women Vs. Men (Sig.) N = 818
Lack of parental involvement	88	9	1.68 vs. 1.75 (.656)	1.54 vs. 1.71 (.084)	1.69 vs. 1.72 (.655)
Children in abusive homes	62	34	2.16 vs. 2.24 (.258)	2.18 vs. 2.13 (.564)	2.14 vs. 2.30 (.011) **
Children using drugs and alcohol	82	16	1.73 vs. 1.84 (.061)	1.59 vs. 1.80 (.015) **	1.69 vs. 1.95 (.000) **
Children born to single mothers	57	28	2.30 vs. 2.36 (.475)	2.34 vs. 2.29 (649)	2.35 vs. 2.41 (.472)
Teenage pregnancy	61	34	2.11 vs. 2.16 (.455)	1.94 vs. 2.18 (.019) **	2.10 vs. 2.30 (.001)
Children dropping out of school	70	26	2.02 vs. 2.09 (.309)	1.94 vs. 2.18 (.142)	2.04 vs. 2.12 (.156)
Lack of quality of healthcare for children born to single mothers	36	36	2.79 vs. 2.85 (.498)	2.63 vs. 2.87 (.047) **	2.85 vs. 2.87 (.779)
Lack of preventive programs for children	61	38	2.25 vs. 2.53 (.000)**	2.16 vs. 2.44 (.008) **	2.35 vs. 2.55 (.004)**
Lack of safe after-school options for children	49	30	2.46 vs. 2.74 (.001)**	2.40 vs. 2.92 (.008) **	2.69 vs. 3.07 (.000) **

Note: AA = African-Americans, CSN = Caucasians
Numbers represent mean scores reported on Likert-type Scale where 1 = Strongly agree and 5 = Strongly disagree
** Scores are significantly different at .05.

and "breakdown of social structure." Unfortunately, respondents' comments were not detailed enough to gauge their intent from these comments.

Responses indicate that respondents view the lack of parental involvement in their children's lives and drug and alcohol abuse as the two most serious problems facing children. These responses indicated the highest levels of agreements with the problem statements although other problems such as children in abusive homes, children born to single mothers, teenage pregnancies, increasing high school drop-out rates, among others, are also viewed as important.

Overall, 88% of respondents either agree or strongly agree with the statement that lack of parental involvement in their children's lives is a serious problem facing children. T-tests revealed no significant differences between Democrats and Republics, between the two primary racial groups, and between men and women in terms of how they responded to this statement.

Respondents also believed that drug and alcohol abuse by children were major problems with 82% of the sample in agreement with the statement. It is pertinent to note that there are no statistically significant differences between how Democrats and Republicans view this problem (84% of the former and 85% of the latter are in agreement with the problem statement). On the other hand, there are differences between how African-Americans and Caucasians (86% versus 82%) view this problem. The mean values for the statement, "drug and alcohol abuse are major problems facing children and youth today" were different for African-Americans versus Caucasians (1.59 vs. 1.80; sig. < .015). Furthermore, significantly higher number of women than men (86% versus 76% respectively) believes that drug and alcohol abuse are major problems facing children and youth. The mean values for women and men also differ for this statement (1.69 vs. 1.95; sig. < .000).

As shown in Table 4, there are few differences in the sample as a function of political ideologies. The only areas where Democrats and Republicans differ relate to the statements dealing with lack of preventive programs for children (mean values 2.25 vs. 2.53; sig. < .000) and lack of safe after-school programs (mean values 2.46 vs. 2.74; sig. < .001).

On the other hand, there are several areas where African-Americans and Caucasians differ in their level of agreement with problem statements dealing with teenage pregnancy (mean values 1.94 vs. 2.18; sig. < .019), lack of quality healthcare for single mothers (mean values 2.63 vs. 2.87; sig. < 047), lack of preventive programs for children (mean values 2.16 vs. 2.44; sig. < 008) and lack of safe after-school options (mean values 2.40 vs. 2.92; sig. < .008)

Women and men also differ in their level of agreement with problems dealing with children in abusive homes (2.14 vs. 2.30; sig. < .011), teenage pregnancy (2.10 vs. 2.30 (.001), lack of preventive programs for children (2.35 vs.

2.55; sig. < .004) and lack of safe after-school options (2.69 vs. 3.07, sig. < .000).

It is important to note that a large number of respondents are unaware or unsure about the following issues/problems facing children: availability of preventive programs for children (38% unsure), availability (or lack thereof) of good healthcare for children born to single mothers (36% unsure), children in abusive homes (34% unsure) and teenage pregnancies (34% unsure).

A recent report on the State of America's children (Children's Defense Fund 2002) details the magnitude of these problems facing American children and youth. However, it appears that the voting public is not aware of the extent of these problems. Therefore, for any public-policy initiative to succeed, it would be important to develop communication strategies that educate the voting public about the seriousness of these issues facing American children and youth. Additional implications of these findings are discussed later in this paper.

Analyzing Respondents' Perceptions Regarding the Solutions

Table 5 lists the perceptions of the respondents in terms of the best solutions that they believe would address the identified problems. Respondents were specifically asked to suggest solutions based upon what *they* believed were the most critical problems facing children. Seven statements in a Likert-type format anchored from strongly agree (1) to strongly disagree (5) were presented to the respondents. Respondents were also encouraged to "write in" what they considered to be the best solutions if they did not think that the options given were adequate or appropriate to address the problems.

As shown in Table 5, all of the solutions offered generated positive response from the sample. In particular, two solutions generated over 90% approval from the respondents–vocational and other programs to reduce high-school drop out rates and drug and alcohol abuse prevention programs. Respondents also overwhelmingly agreed with offering educational and parenting programs for better parenting, day-care and after-school programs, pre- and postnatal care for teenage mothers and integrating child-care programs as part of other community-based programs.

The support for vocational and educational programs is very high in the sample. There are no statistically significant differences between Democrats and Republicans and both African-Americans and Caucasians agree with this solution despite differences in the level of agreement with the statement (mean values 1.47 vs. 1.66; sig. < .037).

Finally, while there are differences in the percentage of women and men that agree with this solution (93% vs. 87%) as well as the level of agreement

TABLE 5. Respondent Perceptions Regarding Solutions to the Problems

Solution Statement	Agreement with Statement (%)	Don't know or Unsure (%)	Mean Values Demo. Vs. Repub. (Sig.) N = 619	Mean Values AA vs. CSN (Sig.) N = 780	Mean Values Women Vs. Men (Sig.) N = 818
Educational and training programs for better parenting	85	8	1.85 vs. 1.85 (.982)	1.59 vs. 1.88 (.003)**	1.80 vs. 1.98 (.005)**
Day-care and after school programs	87	6	1.69 vs. 1.98 (.000) ***	1.53 vs. 1.84 (.002)**	1.70 vs. 2.01 (.000)**
Drug and alcohol prevention programs	91	4	1.39 vs. 1.49 (.064)	1.45 vs. 1.46 (.858)	1.46 vs. 1.47 (.830)
Pre and post natal care for teenage mothers	85	7	1.77 vs. 1.92 (.044)**	.1.75 vs. 1.84 (.368)	1.74 vs. 2.02 (.000)**
Vocational and other programs to reduce dropout rate	91	4	1.60 vs. 1.67 (.253)	1.47 vs. 1.66 (.037)**	1.56 vs. 1.78 (.000)**
Rewards for students for staying in school	62	21	2.32 vs. 2.34 (.839)	2.07 vs. 2.38 (.024)	2.28 vs. 2.48 (.022)
Making child-care programs an integral part of community-based programs	79	9	1.81 vs. 2.09 (.001)**	1.70 vs. 1.96 (.028)**	1.84 vs. 2.11 (.000)**

Note: AA = African-Americans, CSN = Caucasians
Numbers represent mean scores reported on Likert-type Scale where 1 = Strongly agree and 5 = Strongly disagree
** Scores are significantly different at .05.

with the statement that vocational programs should be offered to mitigate the problems facing the American youth (mean values 1.56 versus 1.78; sig. < .000), it is important to note that both men and women overwhelmingly agree with the solution.

The support for drug and alcohol abuse prevention programs is also 91% in the sample with 88% of the men and 92% of the women in agreement. As shown in Table 5, there are no statistically significant differences Democrats and Republicans, between African-Americans and Caucasians, or between men and women.

Other solutions which elicited highly positive responses from the sample included support for providing day-care and after-school programs for children (overall support 87%), providing educational and training programs for better parenting (overall support level 85%), pre- and post-natal programs for teenage mothers (overall support 85%) and making child-care programs an integral part of community-based programs (overall support 79%). The differences in mean values for the statements that address each of these issues (between Democrats and Republicans, between men and women, and between African-Americans and Caucasians) are listed in Table 5.

Surprisingly, relatively fewer respondents supported offering rewards for staying in school (62%) and a large percentage of the respondents disagreed with this solution (20%). However, there are differences in how men and women view this solution. The mean values for the statement that children and youth should be rewarded for staying in school differ for women and men (2.28 vs. 2.48; sig. < .022). The difference between African-Americans and Caucasians is also significant for this solution (mean values 2.07 vs. 2.38; sig. < .024).

Respondents' Views of the Best Solutions

The survey also asked respondents to identify what they believed were the best solutions given resource and other constraints. Thirty-three percent of the respondents suggested that teaching better parenting skills was the best solution; twenty-two percent supported developing vocational and other programs to reduce drop-out rates; drug and alcohol prevention programs were believed to be the best solution by 12% of the respondents and an equal number supported day-care and after-school programs for children as the best alternative. There are some differences in the perception of best solutions as well. For example, more Republicans than Democrats are in favor of teaching better parenting skills (43% versus 30%) whereas more Democrats favor day-care and after-school programs (16% versus 9%). However, agreement between the two groups is similar for providing vocational programs to decrease drop-out rates (23% Democrats versus 21% Republicans) and for providing drug and alcohol abuse prevention programs (13% versus 12%).

Analyzing the Willingness to Fund Programs and Perceptions of Program Responsibility

Seventy-nine percent of the respondents are willing to pay additional taxes to support these programs with 43% willing to pay $5 per month. However, neither income nor ethnic background seems to systematically affect the amount of money respondents are willing to pay to fund these programs. On the other hand, those with children at home are significantly more willing to fund the programs than those with no children at home (82% versus 74%).

The respondents were also queried about who should be responsible for providing these services that they believed would help alleviate the problems. As before, the statements were listed in a Likert-type format and anchored from strongly (1) agree to strongly disagree (5). Table 6 shows the detailed responses.

TABLE 6. Respondent Perceptions Regarding Responsibility for the Programs

Responsibility Statement	Agreement with Statement (%)	Don't know or Unsure (%)	Mean Values Demo. Vs. Repub. (Sig.) N = 628	Mean Values AA vs. CSN (Sig.) N = 780	Mean Values Women Vs. Men (Sig.) N = 818
It is the responsibility of the Government to provide these programs	65	17	2.18 vs. 2.56 (.000)**	1.74 vs. 2.41 (.000)**	2.30 vs. 2.41 (.145)
All citizens should pay for these services	56	17	2.41 vs. 2.78 (.000)**	2.44 vs. 2.71 (.096)	2.61 vs. 2.79 (.061)
Only Parents with children at home should pay for these services	16	15	3.87 vs. 3.66 (.018)	3.92 vs. 3.85 (.624)	3.72 vs. 3.90 (.039)**

Note: AA = African-Americans, CSN = Caucasians
Numbers represent mean scores reported on Likert-type Scale where 1 = Strongly agree and 5 = Strongly disagree
Scores are significantly different at .05.

Should the government pay for these services?　.

Overall, 65% of the respondents believe that providing the solutions and the appropriate programs should be the responsibility of the government. However, 17% disagree that government should be responsible for providing these programs. A significantly higher number of Democrats than Republicans (72% versus 57%) agrees that the responsibility to provide these programs should lie with the state/county government (Chi-square = 25.576 and 2-tailed significance < 001). The mean values for the statement that providing these programs should be the responsibility of the government are also significantly different for the two groups (2.18 versus 2.56; sig. < .000).

Among the two primary racial groups, the distribution is 63% Caucasians in agreement with the statement versus 87% African-Americans and the difference is statistically significant (Chi-square = 19.957; 2-tailed significance < .001). The difference in the mean value for the statement that providing these programs should be the responsibility of the government is also significant between African-Americans and Caucasians (1.74 vs. 2.41; sig. < .000).

While slightly higher numbers of women agree that it should be the responsibility of the government to provide these programs (67% women versus 63% men), the difference is not significant. Further, mean values for the statement that it should be the responsibility of the government to fund these programs are not different as a function of gender (2.30 vs. 2.41; sig. < 145).

Should all citizens pay for these services?

Fifty-six percent of the respondents agree that all citizens should pay for these services while 26% disagree with that proposition. The difference between Democrats and Republicans is significant, with a higher percentage of Democrats (66%) agreeing with the statement that all citizens should pay for these services as opposed to 48% Republicans (Chi-square = 24.820; 2-tailed significance < .002). Not surprisingly, mean value for the statement that all citizens should pay for these services also differs as function of political ideology (2.41 vs. 2.78; sig. < .000).

There are no differences between the two predominant racial groups–an equal percentage, 57% agrees with the proposition and mean values for the statement that all citizens should pay for these services do not differ (2.44 vs. 2.71; sig. < .096).

A larger number of men than women agree with the proposition (58% versus 54% women). The mean values for the statement that all citizens should pay for these services are 2.61 vs. 2.79 for men and women but the difference is not significant (sig. < .061). Men and women respond differently in that a significantly higher number of men disagree with the statement as well (31% versus 24% women). While this may sound confusing, it becomes clear when we analyze the "unsure" responses–more women are unsure about whether all citizens should pay for these services (22% versus 11%).

Should only those with children at home pay for these services?

Overall, 69% of the sample disagrees that only those citizens who have children living at home should pay for these services while 16% agree with that proposition. The difference is significant between Democrats and Republicans. A much larger percentage of Republicans (18%) agrees that only parents with children at home should pay for these services whereas only 12% Democrats think this is appropriate. Seventy-seven percent of Democrats disagree with the proposition versus 64% Whites (Chi-square = 11.002; 2-tailed significance < .004). Mean values for the statement that only those citizens that have children living at home should pay for these services are also different for Democrats versus Republicans (3.87 vs. 3.66; sig. < .018).

There is no difference between African-Americans and Caucasians; 70% of the Caucasian respondents and 74% of the African-American respondents disagree that only parents with children at home should pay for these services. Mean values for the statement that only those citizens that have children living at home should pay for these services are also not significantly different for the two groups (3.92 vs. 3.85; sig. < .624).

Seventy-one percent of the men versus 69% of the women disagree with the statement. Mean values for the statement that only those citizens that have children living at home are also different for women versus men (3.72 vs. 3.90; sig. < .039).

Perhaps not surprisingly, whether the respondents have children at home influences their opinion about who they think should be responsible for administering and funding these programs. Sixty-eight percent of the respondents who have children at home feel that the county/state governments should provide these programs as opposed to only 62% who do not have children at home. Twenty-three percent of those respondents who do not have children living at home think that the responsibility to fund these programs should lie with those parents who have children that live with them.

CONCLUSION

The findings of the study indicate that Americans feel strongly about many issues facing children and youth in the country. They recognize that there are numerous problems facing children and youth in the society and that these concerns should be addressed adequately to ensure a better future for children as well as the country, and help minimize future problems.

It is encouraging to note that respondents strongly believe that lack of financial means on the part of his/her parents should not inhibit any child from getting education and health-care services. Furthermore, a vast majority is willing to pay additional moneys in taxes to fund appropriate programs that would help mitigate the problems facing American children and youth. While there are a few noticeable differences along gender, racial and political dimensions, in general, the agreement to fund appropriate solutions is quite high among the sample.

Not surprisingly, while Democrats and Republicans agree on providing vocational programs and drugs and alcohol abuse prevention programs, they differ in terms of how they view the other solutions that address the problems facing children and youth. For example, more Republicans than Democrats view providing training on better parenting skills as a top priority. Democrats on the other hand, are more favorable towards community-based programs and child-care programs. Interestingly, child care advocacy groups such as the Children's Defense Fund (2002) and National Education Organization (2003) have found that programs do not work in isolation but have to be developed coherently in conjunction with other programs that address related problems. To illustrate, a program on drug and alcohol abuse prevention would be much less effective unless it can be combined with a program that teaches life skills to help the children and young adults later in life.

The differences between men and women are quite pronounced in how they view some of the problems and their solutions. In general, women felt much more strongly about the problems and were more supportive of a wider variety of solutions offered. It is quite possible that since women are often the primary caregivers for their children, they are more attuned to the issues that face children and youth in America. They might also be more aware of the inter-connectivity between the problems and their solutions.

It is also important to recognize that a higher percentage of African-American respondents agree with wide-ranging solutions to address the problems. For example, more African-Americans than Caucasians agree that providing day-care and after-school programs would be beneficial. While this study did not address this issue specifically, it is plausible to hypothesize that a lack of adequate day-care and after-school programs is more pronounced for the African American community. The Children's Defense Fund (2002) also notes that some of the problems facing American children and youth, such as lack of pre-natal care, lack of adequate health-care, poverty and infant mortality are more severe among African American and Latino children as compared to the rest of the population.

It is somewhat troubling to note that a large number of respondents are unaware or unsure about the problems facing children and youth. Since people are less likely to support funding for programs if they are not aware that a problem exists, it is critical to recognize that a deliberate educational campaign would be required to educate citizens about the nature and severity of problems facing children.

It is also intriguing that overall approval for the proposed solutions is quite high but respondents differ in terms of who they believe should provide these solutions or how these programs should be funded. These issues are very important in that they might reflect: (a) a general distrust in the ability of the government to adequately develop and implement the programs; (b) lack of information about the efficacy of government-initiated or government-sponsored programs which have a proven track record of success; and (c) lack of knowledge about the magnitude of the problems facing children and youth.

Since there is enough empirical evidence to demonstrate that programs such as the one espoused by this research do indeed help alleviate problems facing children and youth (Bogenschneider 1996; Comer 1993; Children's Defense Fund 2002; Gilchrist and Schinke 1983; Lerner 1995), it is indeed a social marketing challenge to enlist the support of the voting public that ultimately decides whether this exchange between the government or related agencies, and the public would be successful.

IMPLICATIONS FOR PUBLIC POLICY

Issues surrounding the problems facing children and youth and their resultant remedies are inherently controversial. While there is considerable agreement among the voting populace regarding the problems that face American children as reflected in the attitudes gleaned from this research, the degree of convergence declines significantly in so far as the solutions to these problems are concerned. It is evident that years of research continue to present government, parents, and scholars with sometimes conflicting and challenging findings and viewpoints on how best to serve this young populace. Despite the fact that a vast majority of programs discussed earlier have actually been implemented in many parts of the country with tangible, positive outcomes (Children's Defense Fund 2002), the overall perception of government-sponsored programs appears to be negative.

As noted by Andreasen (2002), one of the problems facing social change issues is that often successes associated with the change are not publicized. He suggests that social change can only gain favor if it can document the effectiveness of the change and establish its superiority over other alternatives. Thus, marketing of programs targeting children and youth, or "marketing of social marketing" is also important to ensure that the general populace is aware of the success stories associated with social change programs. Andreasen (2002) further suggests that social marketing should not be geared only towards promoting ideas but changing behaviors, an issue of particular importance within the context of this study.

To overcome the resistance or the apathy of the voting public, there must be a deliberate public-policy campaign to educate the voting public about these issues. Thus, government-sponsored programs developed to serve the children could be coupled with educational programs targeted at the voting public. Further, the efficacy of these programs and their outcomes would have to be substantiated through documented outcomes and through targeted public-policy campaigns. In other words, public support for public policy may have to be "marketed "to the voting populace with documented evidence of past success stories.

Furthermore, expertise of organizations such as the Children's Defense Fund, Save the Children, Children's Campaign, and others, that have an excellent track record of being children's advocates, could be used to partner with community-based organizations to enhance the credibility of government-initiated programs. These organizations have a clearer understanding of the problems facing children and youth as well as of the solutions that work well.

One tenet of marketing is that both government and the public are open systems and in order to coexist, mutually-beneficial exchanges must exist through which mutually-beneficial outcomes are derived. As an open system, each contributes to the maintenance, survival and growth of the other, as well as that of the country as a whole. While engaging in resource exchanges in the form of services and tax dollars, government and parents or caregivers attain their respective objectives. An absence of information about the success of this exchange may also explain why current exchanges between government and parents are not perceived to be mutually beneficial. This can only be corrected by using social marketing tools such as the ones discussed above.

Future research might investigate whether perceptions regarding sources of children and youth's problems are parental, societal, or both. It would also be informative to investigate how people view the relative importance of parents versus society in so far as the role of each is concerned in ensuring a better future for society.

REFERENCES

American Academy of Child and Adolescent Psychiatry (2001), *Alcohol and Drug Abuse-Glossary of Symptoms and Mental Illnesses Affecting Teenagers*, available at http://www.aacap.org/.
Andreasen, A. R. (2002), "Marketing Social Marketing in the Social Change Marketplace," *Journal of Public Policy and Marketing*, 21(1), Spring, 3-13.
Bogenschneider, K. (1996), "An Ecological Risk/Protective Theory for Building Prevention Programs, Policies, and Community Capacity to Support Youth," *Family Relations*, 45, 127-138.
Burnett, G. (2002), "Unwed Teenage Mothers: An Ounce of Prevention is Worth a Ton of Cure," *American Journal of Family Therapy*, 30(1), 57-61.
Children's Defense Fund (2002), "The State of Children in America's Union 2002," report available at http://www.childrensdefense.org/data.php.
Coleman (2002), "New Opportunities for Reducing the Risk from Teenage Pregnancy–What is the Evidence Base for Tacking Risk Behaviours in Combination?" *Health, Risk, and Society*, 4(1), 77-93.
Comer, J. P. (1993), "The Potential Effects of Community Organizations on the Future of our Youth," *Teachers College Record*, 94 (3), 658-6.
Dembo R. and J. Schmeidler (2003), "A classification of High-Risk Youths," *Crime and Delinquency*, 49(2), 201-230.
Donnenworth, G. V. and U.G. Foa (1974). "Effects of Resource Class on Retaliation to Injustice in Interpersonal Exchange," *Journal of Personality and Social Psychology*, 29 (6), 785-93.
Dryfoos, J.G. (1990a), *Adolescents at Risk: Prevalence and Prevention*, New York: Oxford University Press.
Dryfoos, J.G. (1990b), "Community Schools: New Institutional Arrangements for Preventing High-Risk Behavior," *Family Life Educator*, 8 (4), 4-9.
Emerson, R. M. (1962), "Power Dependence Relationships," *American Sociological Review*, 27, 31-41.

Gilchrist, L. D. and S. P. Schinke (1983), "Teenage Pregnancy and Public Policy," *Social Service Review*, June, 307-322.

Hawkins, J.D., R.F. Catalano, and J.Y. Miller (1992). "Risk and Other Protective Factors for Alcohol and Other Drug Problems in Adolescence and Early Adulthood: Implications for Substance Abuse Prevention," *Psychological Bulletin*, 112, 64-105.

Hirschman, C. (2001), "The Educational Enrollment of Immigrant Youth: A Test of the Segmented Assimilation Hypothesis," *Demography*, 38(2), 317-336.

Katz, D. and R. L. Kahn (1966), *The Social Psychology of Organizations*, New York: Wiley.

Kotler, P. and S. J. Levy (1969), "Broadening the Concept of Marketing," *Journal of Marketing*, 33, 10-15.

Kotler, P. (1972), "The Generic Concept of Marketing Science," *Journal of Marketing*, 36, 46-54.

Lerner, R.M. (1995), *America's Youth in Crisis: Challenges and Choices for Programs and Policies*, Thousand Oaks, Calif.: Sage.

McKnight, J.L., and J. Kretzman (1992), "Mapping Community Capacity," *New Designs for Youth Development*, 10 (1), 9-15.

Moore, K. A. (2003), "The State of America's Children 2003: The Good News . . . . and the Bad," presented at the State of Society Panel: The National Press Club (January 13): Washington, D.C., available at http://www.childtrends.org/PDF/CommunitarianTalk.pdf.

National Education Association (2003), available at http://www.nea.org/parents/.

Passell, P. (1996), Economic Scene, *The New York Times*, June 20.

Pandya, A. N. Dholakia (1992), "An Institutional Theory of Exchange in Marketing," *European Journal of Marketing*, 26 (12),14-41.

Plotnick, R. D. (1993), "The Effect of Social Policies on Teenage Pregnancy and Childbearing," *Families in Society*, 74(6), 325-328.

Rhode, D. L. (1993-94), "Adolescent Pregnancy and Public Policy," *Political Science Quarterly*, 108 (4), 635.

Schorr, L. B. (1989), "Early Intervention to Reduce Intergenerational Disadvantage: The New Policy Context," *Teachers College Record*, 90 (3),362-374.

The Guttmacher Report of Public Policy (2000). Teenagers Need Programs to Help Prevent Rebirths, July 13, available at http://www.agi-usa.org.

Thibaut, J.W. and H. H. Kelley (1959), *The Social Psychology of Groups*, New York: John Wiley & Sons.

U.S. Department of Health and Human Services (2001), HHS Fact Sheet, Preventing Disease and Death from Tobacco Use, January 8, available at www.hhs.gov/news/press 2001pres/01 fstbco.htm.

US Bureau of the Census (2001), Statistical Abstract of the U.S. 2001, Vital Statistics Available at http://www.census.gov/prod/2002pubs/01statab/vitstat.pdf.

Weissberg, R.P., and M.J. Elias (1993), "Enhancing Young People's Social Competence and Health Behavior: An Important Challenge for Educators, Scientists, Policymakers, and Funders," *Applied and Preventive Psychology*, 2, 179-190.

Marketing Military Service: Benefits Segmentation Based on Generalized and Restricted Exchange

Kimball P. Marshall

Caroline Fisher

SUMMARY. Willingness to engage in exchange is based on desired benefits. In typical commercial transactions, restricted exchange benefits dominate. However, public policy, social marketing situations might require consideration of both restricted and generalized exchange benefits. Applying factor analysis, cluster analysis and cross-tabulation, this paper reports research that has successfully segmented a young adult target mar-

Kimball P. Marshall, PhD, is Professor of Marketing, College of Business Administration, Loyola University New Orleans, 6363 St. Charles Avenue, New Orleans, LA 70118 (E-mail: kimball.p.marshall@netzero.net). His research and teaching include broad areas of government programs, not-for-profit marketing, technology commercialization and new product development.

Caroline Fisher, PhD, is Bank One/Francis Doyle Distinguished Professor of Marketing, College of Business Administration, Loyola University New Orleans, 6363 St. Charles Avenue, New Orleans, LA 70118 (E-mail: fisher@loyno.edu), specializing in consumer analysis and research.

Address correspondence to: Kimball P. Marshall, PhD, at the above address.

Office of Navy Research Funded Project Number N00014-01-1-0363.

[Haworth co-indexing entry note]: "Marketing Military Service: Benefits Segmentation Based on Generalized and Restricted Exchange." Marshall, Kimball P., and Caroline Fisher. Co-published simultaneously in *Journal of Nonprofit & Public Sector Marketing* (Best Business Books, an imprint of The Haworth Press, Inc.) Vol. 14, No. 1/2, 2005, pp. 247-267; and: *Current Issues in Political Marketing* (eds: Walter W. Wymer, Jr., and Jennifer Lees-Marshment) Best Business Books, an imprint of The Haworth Press, Inc., 2005, pp. 247-267. Single or multiple copies of this article are available for a fee from The Haworth Document Delivery Service [1-800-HAWORTH, 9:00 a.m. - 5:00 p.m. (EST). E-mail address: getinfo@haworthpressinc. com].

doi:10.1300/J054v14n01_14   *247*

ket regarding interest in military service based on considerations of generalized and restricted exchange motivations. This research contributes to a growing body of literature on generalized exchange as a key conceptual element for social marketing. Results demonstrate the utility of the generalized exchange concept in identifying a market segment distinguished by strong interest in military service and positive perceptions on several key generalized exchange factors. *[Article copies available for a fee from The Haworth Document Delivery Service: 1-800-HAWORTH. E-mail address: <docdelivery@haworthpress.com> Website: <http://www.HaworthPress. com>* © *2005 by The Haworth Press, Inc. All rights reserved.]*

KEYWORDS. Social marketing, military recruitment, non-profit, generalized exchange, restricted exchange, cluster analysis, government marketing

INTRODUCTION

In recent years, a growing body of literature has begun to emerge regarding the concept of generalized exchange and generalized exchange benefits as useful tools in public policy and social marketing. Social marketing involves influencing voluntary behavior of people towards a broad social end by offering or demonstrating benefits to be received as a result of desired behaviors (Bagozzi 1975, Kotler and Andreasen 1991). Social marketing presents a dilemma to marketers in that marketers typically focus on an exchange model that emphasizes self-interest, whereas social marketing programs often address situations in which individuals are asked to act in the interest of others or the broader social group (Bendapudi, Singh and Bendapudi 1996). Altruism and the needs of others are common themes, but these may be seen as lacking an exchange orientation, a fundamental principle of marketing. Generalized exchange, as a social marketing concept, offers an alternative to appeals based on altruism and other's need. Generalized exchange firmly roots social marketing efforts in a marketing exchange context by emphasizing indirect exchange benefits desired by target markets rather than altruistic orientations or direct reciprocal exchange benefits. In so doing, generalized exchange ties individual self-interest to the interest of the social group. Previous examples of applications of generalized exchange to social marketing include tax support for public education and social welfare systems (Bagozzi 1975, Marshall 1998). These are discussed further below. While cognizant of Hutton's (2001) concerns over the expansion of the field of marketing, the current research follows a long tradition in which a marketing exchange perspective is applied to encouraging voluntary behaviors in which two or more entities transfer values to mutual benefit (Houston and Gassenheimer 1987, Bagozzi 1975).

The current project applies the social marketing concept of "generalized exchange" to the recruitment of personnel into the all-volunteer military. Although to many, pure volunteerism would not involve pay or other restricted exchange benefits, we follow social convention here by referring to today's military in the United States as "all-volunteer." Given the commitment and sacrifices involved in modern military service, it would be unrealistic to expect the military to depend only on persons who would serve without pay or related benefits. Still, such pay and benefits clearly separate today's United States military personnel from the theoretical "ideal type" of unpaid volunteer helping behavior such as discussed by Bendapudi, Singh and Bendapudi (1996). Moreover, in this paper we explore the extent to which interest in joining a military service is associated with a community service orientation in comparison to financial and other types of restricted exchange benefits. However, we do not depend on altruism as a motivator as might the pure volunteerism concept. Instead, we consider the possibility of a linkage of community interest and self-interest as a motivator for military service.

We have set as our objective the determination of whether perceptions of generalized exchange and restricted exchange benefits can be useful dimensions for segmenting the target market of young adults into clusters with clearly different levels of interest in military service. Military recruitment as social marketing (Kotler and Andreasen 1991) is a particularly useful test of the generalized exchange concept because military service requires an extensive time commitment and demanding, often dangerous, service to society. The current research is based on data from 600 respondents to a national telephone survey carried out in the Summer of 2001 among young adults eighteen to twenty-four years of age who were non-institutionalized, unmarried and without their own children living in their home. In this paper, we first review prior research into interest in military service among young people and research into the field of public service motivations. We then review research and theoretical foundations of the concept of generalized exchange and distinguish it from restricted exchange. Last, factor analysis, cluster analysis and cross-tabulations are applied to assess the utility of joint consideration of generalized and restricted exchange factors for identifying and targeting market segments for military recruitment.

PRIOR RESEARCH

Three substantive avenues of prior research relate to this project: propensity of youth for military service, public service motivations, and generalized exchange. The first, the field of propensity of youth to serve in the military, is largely demographic in nature and reports on trends among high school students regarding interest in serving in the military, and the demographic characteristics of military enlistees following high school. This work has largely developed from the "Monitoring the Future" (MtF) project (Segal et al. 1999; Segal et al., 1998, Segal, 1986; Bachman et al., 1998) and the "High School and Beyond" (HSB) studies (Teachman and Call 1993) sponsored by the United States Department of Defense. These studies have involved frequent surveys of high school students since 1975 regarding interest in military service. Findings indicate substantial variation across major demographic groups and over time, but such factors as parents' lower socioeconomic background and education, lower student grade point averages, rural versus urban locations, Southern United States origin, and lack of college education aspirations tend to be associated with propensity for military service. While the demographic patterns associated with interest in and actual military service are interesting and might imply underlying socioeconomic motivations, this largely demographic research does not document underlying motivations for military service that might aid development of recruitment programs to help recruiters target potentially highly motivated candidates. The current project addresses this gap.

The *second* line of research, public service motivations (PSM), has not explicitly addressed military service. However, its emphasis on citizenship and the relationship between the individual and contributions to the larger society can be informative as to potential motivations and attitudes that might underlie propensity toward military service and commitment to completion of terms of duty. This work is represented by Perry (Perry and Wise 1990, Perry 1996, 1997), Houston (2000), Crewson (1997), Wittmer (1991), Frederickson and Hart (1985), Kelman (1987), Buchanan (1975), and Rainey (1982). In general, these researchers have demonstrated differences in motivations of public service employees and managers as compared to private, for-profit organizations' employees and managers. In large part, public service employees are reported to be more motivated by contributing to the common social good and by a sense of duty, than are private, for-profit sector employees. Public sector employees are reported to place higher values on intrinsic job rewards, helping others, and performing work worthwhile to society, while being less money, prestige and status oriented. However, this line of research also recognizes that both intrinsic and extrinsic rewards (including financial rewards) must be present and balanced to provide an effective motivational system. This holds an important implication for application of the concept of generalized exchange, as it suggests that effective social marketing programs may need to promote a wide range of benefits that go beyond immediate utilitarian self-interest.

The *third* line of research, generalized exchange, has been addressed by sociological, anthropological, and marketing researchers (Bearman 1997; Marshall 1998, 1999; Takahashi 2000). Generalized exchange was first introduced into the sociology and anthropology literature by Levi-Strauss (1969) and subsequently reviewed as an element of sociological exchange theory by Ekeh (1974). In 1975, the generalized exchange concept was introduced into the marketing literature by Bagozzi who offered it as a central social marketing concept and illustrated it with a theoretical analysis of taxpayer support for a social welfare system for the needy. In the nineties, Marshall (1998, 1999) elaborated the concept of generalized exchange and applied it to voter support for taxation and volunteerism in support of public schools.

Bagozzi (1975) contrasted generalized exchange with two other types of exchange, restricted exchange and complex exchange. Restricted exchange involves the direct reciprocal transfer of values between two parties. The partners in restricted exchange receive desired benefits directly, although actual receipt of the benefit (e.g., retirement benefits) may be delayed to a future delivery date. Restricted exchange is the usual form of exchange studied by marketers. An example would be a typical sales situation in which, for example, a person provides money in exchange for a house, a car or groceries. Complex exchange involves a sequence of restricted exchanges such as characterize sales distribution channels involving a manufacturer, a retailer and a final customer. The baker sells a loaf of bread to a storeowner for a dollar, and the storeowner then sells the bread to a customer for two dollars. This chain may be extended to include any number of transfers, but each is a direct, reciprocal transfer characteristic of restricted exchange.

Generalized exchange is fundamentally different from restricted and complex exchange in that the exchange process, as described by Bagozzi in 1975 and Marshall in 1998, involves a system of indirect, univocal exchanges. In generalized exchange, an individual contributes a value to a social system without the expectation of a direct, reciprocal return benefit, but with the expectation of an overall improvement in the state of the system that will eventually yield an indirect benefit to the contributing individual as a member of the system. Through generalized exchange, the individual ties his own self-interest to the interest of the larger society.

As presented by both Bagozzi (1975) and Marshall (1998), the concept of generalized exchange suggests that, within a social marketing context, individuals may be motivated to desired behavior as a result of awareness of the broad community benefits of their behavior, and awareness that they will benefit personally (including benefits to loved ones) should the broad community benefits occur. The concept of generalized exchange is distinguished from altruistic appeals. Altruism refers to a situation in which an individual acts without expectation of a benefit to himself or herself. In contrast, in the case of generalized exchange, the individual recognizes that he or she will benefit as a member of the society from the community benefits that result from his or her behavior.

Generalized exchange and restricted exchange rewards may be complementary. In Bagozzi's view (1975), restricted and generalized exchange may involve utilitarian rewards (monetary or barter goods, or even overt behavior or labor may be provided in the current author's view) and symbolic rewards. Symbolic rewards are psychological and social intangibles that carry meaning, such as status or prestige, and may be independent of or attached to tangible goods (Levy 1959). While both utilitarian and symbolic rewards may result from either generalized or restricted exchange, symbolic rewards such as social prestige, identity with community, and pride in conformity to social norms might be more frequently characteristic of generalized exchange. Generalized exchange benefits are linked to community well being. Restricted exchange rewards are received directly from the specific exchange partner and do not depend on the broad social impact of the individual's exchange behavior. However, utilitarian and symbolic rewards may derive from either type of exchange.

GENERALIZED EXCHANGE AND MILITARY RECRUITMENT

Social exchange theory essentially posits that successful exchanges involve transfers of values among two or more parties, such that each party feels that he or she has obtained something of equal or greater value than that which was given up, and that the exchange was entered into voluntarily (Houston and Gassenheimer 1987). Values that are transferred may be monetary, objects with utilitarian functions, services, or symbolic values (Bagozzi 1975, Levy 1959). Voluntary willingness to enter into exchange requires that each party see the exchange as beneficial in terms of self-interest. These criteria fit the case of recruitment and retention of enlistees into the all-volunteer military. Potential recruits are asked to provide extensive time and dedication to the military mission, and are asked to voluntarily give up extensive personal freedom. In return, the military organization offers a variety of rewards including monetary benefits, job training, medical care, team membership, close friendships and contributions to the larger society.

The concept of "generalized exchange" is particularly appropriate as a social and marketing concept applicable to military recruitment. A society's military organizations exist to benefit the society by providing protection and security. Presumably, the security that results from adequate military protection allows other transactions and activities occurring within the social system to be carried out with greater confidence, thus improving the state of the system and the quality of life of its members. As government-based organizations, military services might be well positioned by appealing to "generalized exchange" perceptions and values that tie the individual's well being to the state of the social system (i.e., the contributions the organization makes to society).

The current study provides an opportunity to assess generalized and restricted exchange motivations for enlistment in the United States military. The United States military recruits some 55,000 Americans per year to join its active duty ranks (United States Navy 1998). However, for the past decade, some military recruiters have struggled to meet their annual recruitment goals (Ryan 2001). Researchers have attributed these difficulties to ambiguity about military missions (Segal et al. 1999), less job security provided by the military, as evidenced by the 1980's military downsizing (Barley 1998; Segal 1986), a lack of patriotism (Faris 1995), and disingenuous military advertising (Shyles and Hocking 1990). Moreover, the current military situation in the Middle East might either stimulate patriotic movements, and so facilitate recruitment, or produce an anti-military backlash that would impede recruitment. In addition, the broader implications of research into generalized exchange for social marketing programs must not be overlooked. By linking the individual to the broader society through univocal exchange benefits rather than altruism, generalized exchange, if viable, ties self-interest to community interest and so can broaden the appeal of social marketing programs to audiences whose immediate and reciprocal benefit interests might not be adequate motivations. In so doing, generalized exchange can, potentially, enhance social cohesion.

The present research proposes that an individual's propensity for military service can be explained within a combined generalized exchange and restricted exchange paradigm. In this paradigm, young adults' interest in joining the military will be influenced by their perceptions of benefits that derive from military service both for themselves and for the larger community. As the society seeks labor (behavior) and long-term psychological and social commitment from the individual, a social marketing challenge is presented. When a strong military is perceived to benefit society in a way that enhances the quality of life of all members of the society, the potential for generalized exchange is present. To the extent that military service may offer direct benefits to the individual in the form of money, prestige, lifestyle or job training (as examples), potential restricted exchange benefits are present. The question then becomes whether market segments related to interest in military service could be defined on the basis of perceptions related to generalized and restricted exchange benefits.

GENERALIZED AND RESTRICTED EXCHANGE MOTIVATORS

The current project investigates whether the concepts of generalized and restricted exchange can be used to segment young adults in the United States into distinguishable clusters that are related to interest in military service. This research has importance to social marketing theory in that the generalized exchange concept is a potentially powerful social marketing tool that (1) ties the interests of the individual to the larger society, (2) is independent of the more elusive notion of altruism that does not incorporate transference of values, and (3) may complement restricted exchange benefit appeals. As such, it is appropriate to attempt to define clusters based on configurations of generalized exchange and restricted exchange factors. This work is rooted in marketing (Gundlach et al. 1995; Houston and Gassenheimer 1987; Bagozzi 1975), sociology and social-psychology exchange theory (Blau 1994, 1964; Ekeh 1974; Homans 1974), and theories of public service motivations (Raadschelders 1995; Crewson 1997; Houston 2000). Should "interest in military service" clusters be identified that incorporate high levels of both generalized and restricted exchange motivators, the argument that restricted and generalized exchange factors are potentially complementary would be supported. If this is the case, recommendations could be made to incorporate appeals to both types of motivators together in social marketing programs. By the same token, clusters might be discovered that emphasize one or the other of these factors. Should this be the case, this too would be an opportunity to provide recommendations to enhance social marketing campaigns.

The Marshall generalized exchange model (1998, 1999), developed and applied in regard to the generation of support for public schools, incorporates four factors related to willingness to engage in generalized exchange: (1) perceptions of broad community benefits; (2) perceptions of the effectiveness of the organization's performance; (3) perceptions of a social responsibility ethic; and (4) perceptions of equity in the sense of equal participation by all members of society. Perceptions of community benefits as generalized exchange motivators are stressed in the Marshall model because they represent indirect benefits that the individual desires and believes can result from his or her contribution to improving the state of the community or society. Performance perceptions are included based on expectancy theory. Perceptions that the organization performs effectively reflect the expectation that the organization is able to succeed in its mission and therefore that the desired improvements in the state of society will result.

The original Marshall model also included perceptions of a social responsibility ethic because group norms may exist that encourage or mandate behavior in support of the organization (Takahashi 2000). Alternatively, group norms might not exist to support the organization or might operate to actively discourage participation in the organization. The issue of group norms addresses in part what Takahashi (2000) refers to as the risk of "unilateral resource giving," "an invitation to exploitation," and the "free rider problem" (p. 1107). Takahashi addresses this issue on theoretical grounds by postulating the possibility of a collective norm of reciprocity–the universal reciprocity principle. This principle is represented by perceptions of a social responsibility ethic calling for military service by all qualified citizens, although law does not require such service. This potential factor is incorporated by inclusion of "perceptions of a social responsibility ethic" as a group norm as noted above.

Perceptions of equity were also included in the original Marshall model and are included in the current model because resistance to participation may result if an individual feels that more is demanded of him or her than of others. Takahashi addresses this in the context of "fairness-based selective giving in pure generalized exchange" (2000, p. 1113). This also addresses the "free-rider" problem in that including equity perceptions in the model allows assessment of the degree to which subjects perceive that inequitable situations exist in regard to military service. To the extent to which equity is perceived, individuals may be more willing to engage in generalized exchange out of a sense of fairness because perceptions of equity may reinforce perceptions of a social responsibility ethic. However, if military service is seen as inequitably distributed through the society, such perceptions may undermine the social responsibility ethic and reduce interest in serving.

METHODOLOGY

The data for this project were gathered through a national telephone interview survey of 300 male and 300 female young adults between 18 and 24 years of age who were not married, did not have children living at home, lived in the continental United States, and had not enlisted in or been rejected by the military. Data were collected in June and July of 2001. Initially efforts were made to limit the study to persons age 18 to 20 who not enrolled in a four-year college. However, because locating such respondents was found to be too expensive, after approximately 150 respondents were interviewed, the sample frame was expanded to include persons through age 24 and persons enrolled in four-year colleges. Fixed list calling was carried out with a sample of 24,000 names and phone numbers from throughout the continental United States. Fact-Finders, Inc. of St. Louis carried out the telephone interviews and recorded the data in SPSS system files. Calls were placed in random order. The purchased list was to provide names and phone numbers of young adults up to age 24. A total of 25,025 call attempts were made and 6,983 individuals were contacted. The overall response rate was 63.7% (persons contacted who agreed to be interviewed), the overall disqualification rate was 93.1% (interviewed but disqualified due to screening criteria–primarily age and, during the preliminary stage, four-year college attendance), and the completion rate for qualified respondents was 93.2%. These approaches to assessing response rates correspond to American Association for Public Opinion Research (2000) recommendations.

OPERATIONALIZATION OF KEY CONCEPTS

Three categories of variables were used in this study: interest in military service, restricted exchange motivators drawn from current military recruitment campaigns, and the components of generalized exchange drawn from the Marshall model (1998, 1999). All respondents provided data for all variables used in this report.

Interest in Military Service. One item was used in this study to indicate the main outcome variable–Interest in Military Service. The fourth question asked "At this time, how interested are you in enlisting in the United States Military? Would you be ____?" Options read included "not at all interested" coded "1," "somewhat disinterested" coded "2," "neither interested nor disinterested' coded 3," "somewhat interested," coded "4," and "very interested," coded "5." Volunteered "don't know" responses were coded as "3" as these were deemed to reflect a neutral orientation. For purposes of this study, responses were recoded into "no interest" (codes 1, 2 and 3) and "some or very much interest" (codes 4 and 5).

Potential Restricted Exchange Benefits. During the exploratory phase of the research and in the process of developing the questionnaire, the members of the study team visited recruiting offices, reviewed recruiting materials, and informally spoke with recruiters in person and via telephone, in order to identify key restricted exchange benefits of military enlistment that were stressed in recruitment campaigns and appeals. The intention was to identify benefits of military service that were promoted in then-current recruitment campaigns so that the appropriateness of these to target markets of young adults could be assessed. Such benefits are, in effect, promises held out by the military to young adults with the intention of motivating potential recruits.

Because the intention was to assess the relevance of currently promoted benefits, the list is not offered as inclusive of all possible benefits that might be of interest to young adults. Many important restricted exchange motivators may be overlooked by United States military campaigns and would not, therefore, have been considered in this research project. This is an important limitation of this study. Nonetheless, based on the research team's reviews of recruitment materials, visits to recruitment offices, and discussions with military recruiters, the benefits considered here substantially reflect the range of restricted exchange benefits promoted by the United States Military.

While many themes emerged in the exploratory phase of the research, the themes identified were reduced to thirteen key benefits that fit the situation of restricted exchange. These benefits are reported in Table 1. Further validation of the range of items was obtained from an open-ended question that asked respondents who expressed that they were "somewhat" or "very" interested in enlistment to give reasons underlying their interest. These responses were compared with the restricted exchange benefits listed and considerable overlap was observed, particularly in regard to the most frequently mentioned open-ended items that relate to discipline, travel, career training, pay, life experience (a possible reference to adventure), military image (a possible reference to social respect and prestige), and health benefits. However, the open-ended responses also revealed some potentially important restricted exchange benefits not explicitly included in this study such as pay for schooling, physical fitness, life experience, and a friend in the military.

The thirteen restricted exchange benefits items were incorporated as structured, importance ratings questions in the twenty-minute telephone interview. During the telephone interview, the respondent was asked, "Now I'm going to read a few reasons people might give for enlisting. For each, tell me if that reason would be very important, somewhat important, neither important nor unimportant, somewhat unimportant, or not at all important if you were to enlist in the U.S. military?" The benefits were then read with random rotation to prevent order bias. In the current analyses, responses were coded "1" for "not important," "2" "somewhat unimportant," "3" "neither" (interpreted in these analysis as a neutral response, "4" "somewhat important," and "5" for "very important."

Generalized Exchange Items. The four components of the Marshall generalized exchange model were represented in the interview by 15 items (Table 1). "Perceptions of Community Benefits" was represented by six items. "Perceptions of a Social Responsibility Ethic," "Perceptions of Performance," and "Perceptions of Social Equity" were each represented by three items. Each of the items in these scales were coded on a five point Likert scale with 1 for strongly disagree, 2 for disagree, 3 for don't know or neutral, 4 for agree, and 5 for strongly agree. These items are presented in Table 1.

TABLE 1. Item Labels and Rotated Factor Loadings for Restricted and Generalized Exchange Factors[1]

Scale	Items[2]	Community Benefits	Social Resp.Ethic	Military Perform.	Social Equity	Social Rewards	Financial Security
Community Benefits	Military protects freedom of Americans	.69670					
	America is safer because of the US military	.72257					
	US is more stable society because of the US military	.66222					
	Americans have a better life because of the US military	.73979					
	We should be proud of the contribution the US military makes to our society	.64443					
	National defense is important to the well being of American citizens	.74601					
Social Responsibility	Although not required by law, it is the civic duty of all citizens to serve in the military		.79153				
	Military service is an important way of paying society back		.68234				
	Military service is an important obligation of citizenship		.72093				
Military Performance	Our military forces do their job very well			.66941			
	The United States Military is well run			.73203			
	The United States Navy is a well run organization			.75223			
Social Equity	Americans from all walks of life contribute to the US Military				.71486		
	The burdens of military defense are carried out fairly by all Americans				.62546		
	Military service is appropriately shared by all groups in America				.75579		

258

Scale	Items[2]	Community Benefits	Social Resp.Ethic	Military Perform.	Social Equity	Social Rewards	Financial Security
Social Rewards	Importance of job training					.62305	
	Importance of belonging to team					.70852	
	Importance of adventure					.69940	
	Importance of life-long friendships					.62181	
	Importance of social respect-prestige					.63962	
	Importance of a disciplined lifestyle					.52797	
	Importance of travel					.60946	
Financial Rewards	Importance of pay						.68834
	Importance of twenty year retirement						.73200
	Importance of VA home loans						.60327
	Importance of guaranteed medical care						.61449
Alpha		.8325	.7721	.7562	.6034	.7958	.6804
Excluded Items	Importance of duty station	.51603				.45187	.44900
	The United States Military is an effective fighting force			.45327			
	Importance of combat/firearms training						
	Factor Eigenvalues	6.77819	1.39556	1.18329	1.09352	3.64377	1.60178
	Percent of Variance	23.4	4.8	4.1	3.8	12.6	5.5

[1]Only rotated factor loadings above .4 are reported. Principal Components Extraction and Varimax Rotation were used. Generalized exchange (community benefits, military performance, social equity and social responsibility) scales' items coded as 1 = strongly disagree, 2 = disagree, 3 = don't know/neutral, 4 = agree, 5 = strongly agree. Restricted exchange (social rewards and financial rewards) scales' items importance items coded "1" for "not important," "2" "somewhat unimportant," "3" "neither" (interpreted in these analysis as a neutral response, "4" "somewhat important," and "5" for "very important."

STATISTICAL ANALYSES AND FINDINGS

The analyses reported here proceeded through four phases: factor analysis, cluster analysis, analysis of variance, and cross-tabulation. In the first phase, factor analysis of twenty-nine restricted and generalized exchange items was carried out to select items for specific generalized and restricted exchange scales (see Table 1). Varimax and Principal Components methods were used. Based on the factor analyses, three items were excluded either because they loaded 0.4 or above on more than one factor, or because they did not load .4 or above on any factor. These items are noted in Table 1. As indicated in Table 1, the remaining twenty-six items were assigned to scales based on the factor on which each item loaded 0.4 or higher. All factors had eigenvalues greater than 1.0 (Hair 1998). The generalized exchange items loaded as anticipated for the four dimensions of the Marshall generalized exchange model, and the restricted exchange items generated two factors reflecting social rewards and financial rewards. Scale scores were computed by summing respondents' raw scores for the selected items. These scales were then assessed using Cronbach's Alpha reliability coefficients (Nunnally 1978, Peterson 1994). The Alpha coefficients ranged from .6034 to .8325 (Table 1), within the ranges for exploratory (.6 to .7) and basic (.7 to .9) research suggested by Nunnally (1978).

In the second phase, two-stage cluster analysis (Punj and Stewart 1983) was used to develop groups of respondents distinguished by their generalized and restricted exchange scales' scores (see Table 2). In the two-stage procedure, the Ward's method was first used to identify the number of clusters and initial cluster centroids. Solutions using from two to nine clusters were examined and a five-cluster solution was chosen as best because it provided the largest number of clusters without producing any cluster with fewer than thirty respondents. The SPSS K-means Cluster procedure was then applied, specifying five clusters and using the scale centroids from the Ward's five-cluster solution as input to the K-means Cluster procedure. The resulting five-cluster solution was used to assign respondents to clusters. Table 2 shows the numbers of respondents assigned to each of the final clusters and the scale centroids for the final clusters.

In the third phase, analysis of variance was used to assess differences in centroids (means of the six generalized and restricted exchange scales) among the final clusters (see Table 3), and labels were assigned to clusters to describe their overall patterns on the generalized and restricted exchange scales (Tables 4 and 5). Each cluster differed from every other cluster on at least two of the scales. Cluster 1 differed significantly from all clusters on the four generalized exchange scales and all but Cluster 3 on the two restricted exchange scales.

TABLE 2. Cluster Analysis–Cluster Labels, N's and Scale Centroids

Cluster	Scale Centroids for Final Clusters[1]						N (%)
	Community Benefits	Military Performance	Social Equity	Social Responsibility Ethic	Social Rewards	Financial Rewards	
1	25.75	12.10	11.30	10.20	31.38	18.10	233 (38.8)
2	23.78	10.67	10.22	8.02	14.72	10.98	54 (9.00)
3	18.58	9.78	9.19	7.85	31.31	17.26	78 (13.0)
4	24.78	11.07	10.26	8.63	24.78	15.40	167 (27.8)
5	17.56	9.21	8.72	5.85	20.87	14.34	68 (11.3)
Overall Means and N	23.44	11.06	10.35	8.77	26.98	16.17	600 (100)
Number of Items in Scale	6	3	3	3	7	4	

[1]Scales created by summing the raw scores of the items selected by the factor analyses results reported in Table 1.

TABLE 3. Significant Cluster Centroid Differences[1]

Scale Centroid	Clusters				
	1	2	3	4	5
Community Benefits	2,3,4,5	1,3,5	1,2,4	1,3,5	1,2,4
Military Performance	2,3,4,5	1,3,5	1,2,4	1,3,5	1,2,4
Social Equity	2,3,4,5	1,3,5	1,2,4	1,3,5	1,2,4
Social Responsibility Ethic	2,3,4,5	1,5	1,5	1,5	1,2,3,4
Social Rewards	2,4,5	1,3,4,5	2,4,5	1,2,3,5	1,2,3,4
Financial Rewards	2,4,5	1,3,4,5	2,4,5	1,2,3	1,2,3

[1]ANOVA revealed significant differences across clusters for all five scales. Numbers in cells represent clusters for which centroids for the corresponding scale were statistically significantly different from the cluster corresponding to the column based on the Tukey true difference multiple comparisons test, $P < .05$.

Cluster 2 differed significantly from Clusters 1 and 5 on the generalized exchange scales and from all clusters on the restricted exchange scales. Cluster 3 differed significantly from Cluster 1 on the generalized exchange scales and from clusters 2, 4, and 5 on the restricted exchange scales. Cluster 4 differed significantly from Clusters 1 and 5 on the generalized exchange scales and

TABLE 4. Cluster Centroid Ranks[1]

	Centroid Ranks and Comparisons (1 = Lowest, 5 = Highest)					
Cluster Number	Community Benefits	Military Performance	Social Equity	Social Responsibility Ethic	Social Rewards	Financial Rewards
1	5 High	5 High	5 High	5 High	5 High	5 High
2	3 Medium	3 Medium	3 Medium	3 Medium	1 Low	1 Low
3	2 Low	2 Low	2 Low	2 Medium	4 High	4 High
4	4 Medium	4 Medium	4 Medium	4 Medium	3 Medium	3 Low Medium
5	1 Low	1 Low	1 Low	1 Low	2 Low Medium	2 Low Medium

[1]Where centroid values for adjacent ranks were not statistically significantly different (Table 3), ranks were considered to be tied and were assigned the same labels.

TABLE 5. Cluster Labels and Descriptions

Cluster Number	Rank on Interest in Military Service[1]	% Interest in Military Service	Generalized Exchange	Restricted Exchange
1	5	26.6	High	High
2	1	5.6	Medium	Low
3	4	15.4	Low	High
4	3	6.0	Medium	Medium
5	2	5.9	Low	Low

[1]Interest in military service ranks are arranged with 1= low and 5 =high. Percentages are based on respondents reporting somewhat or very interested in military service. Chi square analysis indicates statistically significant differences among clusters in proportions indicating interest in military service with interest. Chi-square = 43.08205, P < .0001.

from Clusters 1, 2, and 3 on the restricted exchange scales. Cluster 5 differed significantly from Clusters 1, 2, and 4 on the generalized exchange scales and from Clusters 1, 2, and 3 on the restricted exchange scales.

Using the final cluster centroids, the clusters were ranked and identified as being high, medium, or low on each scale (see Table 4). Where centroid values for adjacent ranks were not statistically significantly different (based on analysis of variance results in Table 3), ranks were considered to be tied and were assigned the same labels. Based on these rankings, clusters were assigned labels indicating their overall standings on generalized and restricted exchange (see Table 5). Cluster 1 was labeled as high on both generalized and restricted exchange. Cluster 2 was labeled as low on restricted exchange and medium on generalized exchange. Cluster 3 was distinguished as high on restricted exchange but low on generalized exchange. Cluster 4 was labeled as medium on both generalized and restricted exchange. Cluster 5 was distinguished as low on all generalized exchange scales and low medium on both restricted exchange scales.

In the fourth phase, cluster membership was cross-tabulated with "interest in military service" (using two levels of interest, "no interest" and "some or very much interest" as described previously) to assess whether the final clusters are distinguished by substantial differences in interest in military service (see Table 5). Results of this cross-tabulation determine whether the generalized and restricted exchange concepts developed here are useful for identifying benefit segments for military recruitment campaigns, and, by extension, social marketing campaigns. Chi square analysis indicated that the clusters differed significantly in the proportion indicating interest in military service (Chi-square = 43.08, p < .0001). The social marketing utility of the generalized exchange model is supported in that the highest degree of interest in military service was indicated by members of Cluster 1, which was distinguished by the highest levels of both generalized and restricted exchange. The percentage of Cluster 1 with interest in military service was 26.5%, ten points higher than Cluster 3 (15.4%), which was characterized by high scores on both restricted exchange scales but low scores on three generalized exchanges scales (perceptions of Community Benefits, Military Performance, and Social Equity) and a medium rank for the generalized exchange scale Perceptions of a Social Responsibility Ethic. The clusters that showed the least interest in military service with 6% or fewer members indicating interest (Clusters 2, 4, and 5), rated at most medium on either type of exchange.

STUDY LIMITATIONS

The primary limitation of this study is that the final sample under-represented racial and ethnic minorities. This is not unusual in telephone interview projects (Adams-Esquivel and Lang 1987, Keeter 1995, Marin, Vanoss and Perez-Stable 1990, Smith 1990), but it is unfortunate in regard to African-Americans, given this group's historical patterns of high propensity for and actual service in the United States Military. African-Americans represented only 6.2 percent of the final sample.

A second limitation is the small proportion of persons who expressed high interest in military service. However, since these estimates are in line with data from the HSB and MtM studies, this may be less of a limitation and more of a reflection of the representativeness of the sample. A third possible limitation is the limited range of restricted exchange benefits considered. While the open-ended item discussed earlier helps to validate the items that were used, other potentially important items may have been excluded. Future studies might expand the range of benefits presented.

DISCUSSION AND RECOMMENDATIONS

The present research proposed that an individual's propensity for military service could be explained within a combined generalized exchange and restricted exchange paradigm. The results support this proposal. First, factor analysis supported the four dimensions of generalized exchange, and the two dimensions of restricted exchange reflecting social rewards and financial rewards directly received by the individual. Second, cluster analysis determined five distinct market segments that were statistically significantly different based upon the dimensions of generalized and restricted exchange considered. Third, these segments differed regarding interest in military service with strong substantive and statistical significance and in directions consistent with the generalized exchange model.

The segment that exhibited the highest percentage of interest in military service had high scores on both the generalized exchange and the restricted exchange dimensions. The segment with the second highest percentage of interest in military service was high on the restricted exchange dimension, but low on the generalized exchange dimension. The other three segments were not high on either dimension and did not show a high percent of interest in military service. These results support the argument that restricted and generalized exchange factors are potentially complementary.

The findings of this report support the utility of the concept of generalized exchange as social marketing tool, particularly in light of the fact that this research has applied the generalized exchange concept to a very different social marketing issue than has been considered previously. While the current study is not definitive, promising target market segments have been identified and distinguished using components of the Marshall generalized exchange model and generalized exchange benefits. In addition, the proposition that social marketing programs may benefit from joint consideration of both generalized and restricted exchange factors has also been supported in that the segment with the highest interest in military service exhibited high scores on generalized exchange factors and on restricted exchange financial and social rewards.

On practical grounds, it is recommended that military recruitment campaigns give greater emphasis to the contributions that enlistees make to the larger society, while continuing to make clear the restricted exchange benefits that the enlistee obtains. Linking community interest and self-interest may yield highly effective social marketing programs. Current efforts to recruit young people into the military have stressed only the restricted exchange benefits. These efforts are likely to have attracted the members of the cluster with the second highest level of interest in the military, but are less likely to have attracted the members of the cluster that is most interested in such service. The former cluster represented only 13.0 percent of the sample, compared to 38.8 percent in the latter cluster. Thus, the efforts of the military to attract recruits may have been falling far short of the potential by ignoring the concepts of generalized exchange.

The broad utility of the concept of generalized exchange must also be acknowledged. At this point, generalized exchange has been applied with some success to both public education and to military recruitment. Thus, evidence mounts that the utility of the concept as a social marketing tool can be extended to many different social issues. While further work is needed regarding operationalization of core concepts and to demonstrate external validity, it does not seem too early to suggest that new research projects explore the application of this concept to such diverse social marketing fields as ecology, charitable giving, volunteerism, and public heath and safety.

REFERENCES

Adams-Esquivel, H., and Lang, D. A. (1987). The reliability of telephone penetration estimates in specialized target groups: The Hispanic case. *Journal of Data Collection*, 27 (1), 35-39.

American Association for Public Opinion Research (2000). *Standard Definitions: Final Dispositions of Case Codes and Outcome Rates for Surveys.* (http://www.aapor. org/ethics/stddef.html).

Bachman, J. G., Segal, D. R., Freedman-Doan, P., and O'Malley, P. M. (1998). Does enlistment propensity predict accession? High school senior's plans and subsequent behavior. *Armed Forces and Society*, 25 (1), 59-81.

Bagozzi, R. P. (1975). Marketing as exchange. *Journal of Marketing*, 39 (October), 32-39.

Barley, S. R. (1998). Military downsizing and the career prospects of youths. Annals of the *American Academy of Political and Social Science*, 559 (September), 141-158.

Bearman, P. (1997). Generalized exchange. *American Journal of Sociology*, 102 (5), 1383-1415.

Bendapudi, Neeli, Singh, Surendra N., and Bendapudi, Venkat (1996), "Enhancing Helping Behavior: An Integrative Framework for Promotion Planning," *Journal of Marketing*, 60 (July), 33-49.

Blau, P. M. (1964) *Exchange and power in social life.* New York, NY: John Wiley and Sons.

Blau, P. M. (1994). *Social exchange. Structural context of opportunities* (pp. 144-172). Chicago, IL: The University of Chicago Press.

Buchanan, B., II, (1975). Red tape and the service ethic. *Administration and Society*, 6 (4), 423-444.

Crewson, P. E. (1997). Public service motivation: Building empirical evidence of incidence and effect. *Journal of Public Administration Research and Theory*, 7 (4), 499-519.

Ekeh, P. P. (1974). *Social exchange theory: The two traditions*. Cambridge, MA: Harvard University Press.

Faris, J. H. (1995). The looking-glass army: Patriotism in the post-cold war era. *Armed Forces and Society*, 21 (3), 411-435.

Frederickson, H. G. and Hart, D. K. (1985), The public service and patriotism of benevolence, *Public Administration Review*, 45 (September/October), 309-331.

Gundlach, G. T., Achrol, R. S., and Mentzer, J. T. (1995). The structure of commitment in exchange. *Journal of Marketing*, 59 (January), 78-92.

Hair, J. F., Jr., Anderson, R. E., Tatham, R. L., and Black, W. C. (1998). *Multivariate Data Analysis (5th Ed.)*. Upper Saddle River, NJ: Prentice Hall.

Homans, George C. (1974), *Social behavior: Its elementary forms*, New York: Harcourt Brace Jovanovich.

Houston, D. J. (2000). Public-service motivation: A multivariate test. *Journal of Public Administration Research and Theory*, 10 (4), 713-728.

Houston, F. S., and Gassenheimer, J. B. (1987). Marketing and exchange. *Journal of Marketing*, 51 (October), 3-18.

Hutton, James G. (2001), "Narrowing the concept of marketing," *Journal of Nonprofit and Public Sector Marketing*, 9 (4), 2-24.

Keeter, S. (1995). Estimating telephone non-coverage bias with a telephone survey. *Public Opinion Quarterly*, 59 (2), 196-217.

Kelman, Steven (1987). Public choice and public spirit, *Public Interest*, 87 (Spring), 80-94.

Kotler, P. and A. Andreasen (1991). *Strategic marketing for nonprofit organizations*. Englewood Cliffs, NJ: Prentice-Hall.

Levi-Strauss, Claude (1969). *The Elementary Structure of Kinship*. Boston, MA: Beacon Press.

Levy, S. J. (1959). Symbols for sale. *Harvard Business Review*, 37 (July-August), 117-119.

Marin, G., Vanoss, B., and Perez-Stable, E. J. (1990). Feasibility of a telephone survey to study a minority community: Hispanics in San Francisco. *American Journal of Public Health*, 80 (3), 323-326.

Marshall, K. P. (1998). Generalized exchange and public policy: An illustration of support for public schools. *Journal of Public Policy*, 17 (2), 274-286.

Marshall, K. P. (1999), Volunteerism among non-clients as marketing exchange, *Journal of Nonprofit and Public Sector Marketing*, 6 (2,3), 95-106.

Nunnally, Jum C. (1978), *Psychometric Theory, 2nd Ed.* New York, NY: McGraw-Hill.

Perry, J. I. (1996). Measuring public service motivation: An assessment of construct reliability and validity. *Journal of Public Administration Research and Theory*, 6 (1), 5-23.

Perry, J. L. (1997). Antecedents of public service motivation. *Journal of Public Administration Research and Theory*, 7 (2), 181-198.

Perry, J. I., and Wise, L. R. (1990). The motivational bases of public service. *Public Administration Review*, 50 (3), 367-373.

Peterson, Robert A. (1994), "A meta-analysis of Cronbach's Coefficient Alpha," *Journal of Consumer Research*, 21 (September), 381-391.

Punj, Girish and Stewart, David W. (1983), "Cluster analysis in marketing research: Review and suggestions for application," *Journal of Marketing Research*, 20 (May), 134-48.

Raadschelders, J. C. N. (1995). Rediscovering citizenship: Historical and contemporary reflections. *Public Administration*, 73 (Winter), 611-625.

Rainey, H. G. (1982), "Reward preferences among public and private managers: In search of the service ethic," *American Review of Public Administration*, 16 (Winter), 288-302.

Ryan, N. R. (2001), Military recruiting and retention. *FDCH Congressional Testimony*, Chief of Naval Personnel, April 24th Testimony.

Segal, D. R. (1986), Personnel. in J. Kryzel, Ed., *American Defense Annual*, Lexington, KY: D.C. Heath, 139-152.

Segal, D. R., Bachman, J. G., Freedman-Doan, P., and O'Malley, P. M. (1999). Propensity to serve in the U.S. military: Temporal trends and subgroup differences. *Armed Forces and Society*, 25 (3), 407-427.

Segal, M. W., Segal, D. R., and Bachman, J. G. (1998). Gender and the propensity to enlist in the U.S. military. *Gender Issues*, 98 (3), 65-88.

Shyles, L., and Hocking, J. E. (1990), The Army's 'Be All You Can Be' campaign. *Armed Forces and Society*, 16 (2), 369-383.

Smith, T. W. (1990). Phone home? An analysis of household telephone ownership. *International Journal of Public Opinion Research*, 2, 369-390.

Takahashi, N. (2000). The emergence of generalized exchange. *American Journal of Sociology*, 105 (4), 1105-113.

Teachman, J. D., and Call, V. R. A. (1993). Family, work, and school influences on the decision to enter the military. *Journal of Family Issues*, 14 (2), 291-314.

United States Navy (1998), *Sailor 21: A Research Vision to Attract, Retain, and Utilize the 21st Century Sailor*, Navy Personnel Research Studies and Technology, Washington, D.C.

Wittmer, Dennis (1991). Serving the people or serving for pay: Reward preference among government, hybrid sector, and business managers. *Public Productivity and Management Review*, 14 (Summer), 369-83.

Political Issue Promotion
in the Age of 9-11

Cynthia R. Morton
Jorge Villegas

SUMMARY. This study presents an exploratory investigation of the effect of political frames applied in advertising communication on audience evaluations of source credibility. Framing is the filtering of reality by any message that leads the audience to a certain conclusion of what and how to think about an issue. However, this process is not automatic since variables like communication source and the credibility attributed to that source can influence the communicator's ability to transfer the salience of issue frames to the audience. The results of this study show that societal issues, such as terrorism, might be more productively sponsored by governmental offices or not-for-profits than by for-profit organizations. *[Article copies available for a fee from The Haworth Document Delivery Service: 1-800-HAWORTH. E-mail address: <docdelivery@haworthpress.com> Website: <http://www.HaworthPress.com> © 2005 by The Haworth Press, Inc. All rights reserved.]*

KEYWORDS. Political frames, agenda setting, source credibility, persuasion

Cynthia R. Morton, PhD (E-mail: cmorton@jou.ufl.edu), and Jorge Villegas, PhD (E-mail: jvillegas@jou.ufl.edu), are affiliated with the Department of Advertising, College of Journalism and Communications, University of Florida, P.O. Box 118400, Gainesville, FL 32611-8400.

[Haworth co-indexing entry note]: "Political Issue Promotion in the Age of 9-11." Morton, Cynthia R., and Jorge Villegas. Co-published simultaneously in *Journal of Nonprofit & Public Sector Marketing* (Best Business Books, an imprint of The Haworth Press, Inc.) Vol. 14, No. 1/2, 2005, pp. 269-284; and: *Current Issues in Political Marketing* (eds: Walter W. Wymer, Jr., and Jennifer Lees-Marshment) Best Business Books, an imprint of The Haworth Press, Inc., 2005, pp. 269-284. Single or multiple copies of this article are available for a fee from The Haworth Document Delivery Service [1-800-HAWORTH, 9:00 a.m. - 5:00 p.m. (EST). E-mail address: getinfo@haworthpressinc.com].

INTRODUCTION

The traditional agenda-setting paradigm is based on an idea that the salience of any issue can be transferred from the media agenda to the public agenda. Regardless of the communication context, this salience transfer is accomplished as a result of "the emphases [placed on an issue by] the news media and the perceived importance of these topics to the news audience" (Protess and McCombs 1991). The packaging of mass media messages ensures that the villains are discernable from the victims (Protess, Cook, Curtin, Gordon, Leff, McCombs, and Milles 1987) and an issue's priority relative to competing issues is understood. Tankard (2001, p. 97) notes that news framing "can eliminate voices, weaken arguments . . . and define the terms of a debate without the audience realizing that it is taking place."

However, the nature of an issue may necessitate that the role of mass communication agents evolve beyond the agenda transfer function. In the wake of the catastrophic series of terrorist attacks that occurred in the United States on September 11, 2001, there was less of an onus on the news media to set the public agenda as there was to frame the issues surrounding the events. That is, media gatekeepers' role in the context of 9-11 was to facilitate the process of how the public should think about the events rather than to prioritize the events on the public's agenda. The media accomplished this through the framing news content in such a way that emphasized the elements of the 9-11 events that would be most important in interpreting and evaluating the issue overall (Entman 1993).

The significance of the 9-11 attacks, combined with the quantity and duration of news media coverage since September 2001, has ensured a sustained a level of attention on a subset of issues–specifically terrorism, war, and homeland security–over a time period atypical of other issues on the public agenda (e.g., taxes, employment, education, etc.). Although the news media has played a pivotal role in disseminating framed perspectives crafted by official government officials and independent newsmakers that have weighed in on these issues, it has not been the sole channel used to deliver message frames. In the period post-September 11 (9-11), government agencies and politically-motivated organizations have utilized traditional marketing communication tools (i.e., advertising and public relations) to create and control their own message frames, which may, in turn, reinforce the salience of the frame to the media gatekeepers. A web site sponsored by the United States Department for Homeland Security, an office established following the 9-11 attacks to monitor terrorist threat in the U.S., is an example of how political frames are applied. The frame of *calm preparedness* is a prevalent component of the site, reinforced by a succinct advertising copy line that states, "Terrorism forces us to make a choice. Don't be afraid . . . be ready." The tone of self-empowerment and nature of the information provided (i.e., what to stock and for what purpose) also reinforced the frame applied to the web site. Following the federal government's lead, the national and local news media were instrumental not only in echoing the preparedness message, but also in providing further details, many of which were featured on the web site, about steps the public should take to get prepared.

Furthermore, broad societal issues as these tend to be enough in breadth and depth to invite a range of frames from sponsors operating independently from the news or government organizations. Corporations have also been noted participants in perpetuating issue frames with advertising messages that assert the sponsors' concerns about, and interests in, these issues. This phenomenon of for-profit participation in sociopolitical realms traditionally reserved for government and not-for-profit organizations can work to either contribute to the effort to promote the latter's mainstream agenda or distract from it. Yet, limited research has been conducted to investigate the effectiveness of varying message sources when they are evaluated in context of sociopolitical message frames.

Though effectiveness can be measured based on a number of outcome criteria (e.g., increased visibility of the message, enhanced believability of the message content, or through an increased intent to change one's behavior as a result of message sponsor), this paper will focus on the means by which the issue communication affects evaluations of an organization's credibility. What is the effect of issue frame and source identity on the audience's perception of source credibility? Further, does source credibility, in turn, influence the issue message's persuasiveness?

The paper begins with a discussion of agenda setting and the means by which issues attributes become more salient through framing. Then, source is discussed as a framing criterion, with particular emphasis given to the dimensions associated with evaluating source credibility. Following an explanation of the research method, findings from an experimental design are reported. The discussion concludes with implications of source effects on issue frames and recommendations for future research.

AGENDA SETTING AND THE MASS MEDIA

The area of agenda setting was first introduced in the late 1960s when McCombs and Shaw (1972) conducted research to detect the existence of a relationship between the mass media's agenda and the public's perception of the "most important problems" the country faced. The researchers polled a community of North Carolina voters prior to the 1968 presidential election and examined the issues identified as important to individuals with the issues that dominated the news media during the time period prior to the election. Their research found a positive correlation between the mass media agenda and those issues that the public perceived to be most important.

Consistent with the origins of agenda setting, the majority of early research exploring the behavioral outcomes of issue salience has looked at voting intent as a result of exposure to media agendas during political campaigns. Ghorpade (1986) examined the salience of political advertising issues on the public agenda and also found a strong positive correlation between the focus of media messages and subsequent voting intent. Faber, Tims and Schmitt's (1990) research on the impact of negative political appeals of voting intent replicated Ghorpade's conclusion while also suggesting that individual partisanship may have some effect on voting behavior.

Roberts (1992) examined contingent conditions important in predicting voting outcome. In a series of studies, Roberts analyzed characteristics of the voting population such as voter orientation, gender, or involvement to determine what role, if any, these elements played in influencing behavioral outcome. The findings from the study suggest that the media's persuasiveness on the public does not operate in a vacuum; rather, media's agenda setting influence is limited in part by characteristics the individual brings to the voting process. The implication of Roberts' research is that the media's ability to set and sustain the public agenda may be as much a function of the demographic, sociographic, and psychographic characteristics of the public as of the agenda of issues advanced in media.

The impact of media agenda salience on public policy is probably the best example of macro-level agenda setting. Under such circumstances an issue becomes salient to an elite group of policymakers who have the power and authority to alter conditions for the masses, which may or may not play a role in elevating the issue to prominence. Protess et al. (1987) illustrated the means by which policy change could occur with public involvement. The researchers conducted a series of studies that analyzed the use of investigative reporting practices to catapult otherwise unobtrusive public issues to the top of a policymaker's agenda. Similarly, Nelson's (1984) historical analysis of the emergence of child abuse from obscurity to an issue of general public concern provided a poignant example of how the media's agenda helped generate behavioral change on a socially enduring level.

Research that links media agenda setting with behavioral outcomes is not limited to the political arena. Bloj (1975) examined the relationship between media coverage on air transportation and subsequent consumer demand for air travel. Media coverage on airline accidents and fatalities was correlated with two consumer behavior indicators: (1) fluctuations in ticket sale volume and (2) the amount of air travel insurance purchased. Bloj concluded that when news coverage on air transportation was negative and product salience was high, consumers were more likely to engage in preventative measures, such as choosing other modes of transportation or buying more passenger insurance, in an attempt to control negative outcomes.

The latter study illustrates the means by which the media's characterization of the issue could influence an audience's evaluation of the issue and subsequent behaviors are a result of those evaluations. McCombs, Llamas, Lopez-Escobar, and Rey (1997) referred to this second level of agenda setting as framing, in which attributes of the issue become the central elements of salience transfer. The following section discusses the concept of framing further and source as a framing criterion.

SOURCE CREDIBILITY AND ISSUE FRAMING

Entman's (1993, p. 52) definition of framing involves "[selecting] some aspects of a perceived reality and [making] them more salient in a communicating text, in such a way as to promote a particular problem definition, causal interpretation, moral evaluation, and/or treatment recommendation for the item described." Similar to the way a well-chosen picture frame evokes a mood to complement the image it encases, communication frames give readers a perspective for interpreting message information. Depending on the tone (positive, negative, or neutral), voice (first- versus third person), or lens (individual, community, or societal) imposed in telling the story, audience opinions about an issue and its merits can vary dramatically. One example of this phenomenon was reported in Gamson and Modigliani's (1989) study of the shifts in public opinion on the issue of nuclear power over an extended time period. The researchers found that support in favor or against the issue closely replicated the way it was packaged in the news media.

External cues that imply an issue's importance relative to other issues on the media agenda are also part of the framing process. The visibility given to an issue in media venues, the time and/or space dedicated to an issue, as well as the number and caliber of references called on to analyze the issue can also add to the salience of issue frames in the minds of the audience. A communication source and the credibility attributed to that source is also a variable that may influence the communicator's ability to transfer the salience of issue frames to the audience. In the context of the news media, source not only refers to the credibility associated with the journalist who writes or reports a news story, but also the reputation of the media organization that employs the journalist. Conversely, evaluations of source credibility in advertising communications are directed toward the brand or company credited for sponsoring the message.

Early research on audience evaluations of a source's effectiveness defined credibility in terms of the degree of trustworthiness and expertise associated with that source (Dholakia and Sternthal, 1977; Hovland and Weiss 1952; Hovland, Janis, and Kelley 1953; Kelly 1967). More recent researchers have a tendency to include objectivity with expertise and trustworthiness when referring to factors of a source's credibility (Solomon 1994). Later, attractiveness, operationalized by physical attributes, image, or reputation, was added as the third measurement variable for evaluating the credibility associated with an advertising persona, such as a celebrity endorser or in-ad spokesperson (Goldsmith, Lafferty, and Newell 2000; Joseph 1982; Ohanian 1990). Solomon (1996) defines source attractiveness as a source's perceived social value, which emanates from the person's physical appearance, personality, or social status, or from his or her similarity to the receiver. Perceptions of credibility are bolstered if the source's attributes are relevant to the product endorsed (Joseph 1982; Ohanian 1990; Solomon 1996). Criteria traditionally used to evaluate physical attractiveness in humans may be inappropriate for inanimate sources. Recent research has modified the attractiveness dimension to include criteria more appropriate for evaluating brands or corporations (Davis 1994; Goldsmith et al. 2000).

Source credibility literature suggests that the ability to effectively transfer an agenda to an audience through persuasive communication can be as much a function of the source's intent as of the message content itself. Eagly, Wood and Chaiken (1978) have noted that the persuasive impact of the message can be diminished when the audience perceives that the source to be biased in his or her presentation. Nonetheless, research also supports the idea that message receivers spend less time creating message counterarguments and are more easily influenced by the message itself when a source's credibility is perceived to be high (Grewal, Gotlieb and Marmorstein 1994).

Regardless of the combination of variables measured, the underlying implication of credibility appears to be that a source's credibility merits can not be separated from the context in which it is evaluated. Indeed, the message and the means by which it is delivered seem to play as great a role in establishing credibility as the source attributed to delivering the information (Bochner and Insko 1966; Wanzenreid and Powell 1993; Wu and Shaffer 1987). Kelly (1967) suggested that when presented with a message, audiences evaluate whether the message itself is an accurate presentation of the source messenger and whether the source itself lacks credibility. In keeping with this, political advertisements that frame issues such as terrorism will be scrutinized as much based on *who* frames the issue as for *how* the issue is framed.

In examining the influence of issue frames and source attribution on audience evaluation, the objectives of the present research is twofold. First, the study seeks to extend the research on framing from its traditional foundation as a news media domain to issue-based political advertising, an under-investigated area in agenda setting and framing research that has proved instrumental in shaping public opinions about the merits of various general welfare issues. Second, no research to date has examinèd the relationship between the issue frames and source attribution, particularly when the identity of the latter challenges audience expectations about a source's appropriateness as issue messenger. The present study explores the effect of issue frames applied in advertising messages about terrorism on audience evaluations of advertising sponsor's credibility.

METHOD

Exploratory research was conducted to investigate the effects of issue frame and source on source credibility, as well as to examine the relationship between credibility and message persuasion. The study was conducted in two stages. The purpose and contribution of each stage to the overall design is discussed in the sections below.

Content Analysis

In order to examine the influence issue frames and source attribution have on audience evaluations of source credibility, it was necessary to identify an issue that would resonate with the intended audience. The issue framed in advertising was identified by means of a content analysis of the daily student newspaper distributed on a large southeastern university campus. The rationale for selecting the student newspaper was to identify the subset of issues most salient to the audience from which the research sample would be drawn. Average daily circulation for the student newspaper is 35,000, with readership estimated to include 94% of the student population, according to publication data. Therefore, this vehicle was particularly appropriate for identifying and gauging the salience of issues to the subject pool.

The content of 51 newspaper editions, issued over an eight-week time period between September and November 2001, was analyzed for recurring issues. Two graduate students were hired as independent coders following six hours of training. Inter-coder discrepancies during the coding process were reconciled between the researchers and coders. Coders were instructed to identify the issues covered in news articles featured on the front page and in the business/community sections of the newspaper. Inter-coder reliability was calculated at a chi square of .60, above the acceptable level of .40 established by Landis and Koch (1977).

The content analysis identified a total of 13 issues. The most frequently recurring issues identified were then measured for relevance among a pretest sample of university students (N = 78). A total of nine issues were evaluated from the original pool of 13. The results confirmed that terrorism was the most salient issue to the audience relative to other issues on the media agenda. Therefore, it was selected as focus for developing the test stimulus.

Experimental Design

A 3 × 2 factorial design was developed around the terrorism issue identified in the content analysis. The independent variables consisted of (1) source, and (2) the frame applied to the ad message. Source represented the type of organization identified as the advertising sponsor and was manipulated at three levels: for-profit, not-for-profit, and government. Message frame was manipulated at two levels according to the intensity of threat (high versus low) associated with the ad message. The dependent variables measured were (1) the credibility attributed to the message source, and (2) the evaluations of message persuasion.

Independent Variable: Source

Three organizations were identified to serve as stimuli for the message source. Each organization selected represented one of three industry sectors–for-profit, not-for-profit, and government–to which a threat message could be attributed. In choosing organizations to represent the not-for-profit and government sectors, the researchers used Internet search engines and current events sources to identify organizations that would be perceived as appropriate sponsors for ad messages about terrorism. The researchers were confident in their ability to satisfactorily choose the sources without additional evaluation by a larger review panel. The not-for-profit source selected was the Information Technology Association of America, an organization dedicated to information security in an age of cyber-terror. The U.S. Department of Homeland Security, the agency in charge of disseminating information regarding the risk of terrorist acts to the American people, was selected as the government source.

The for-profit source organization was selected by cross referencing *Fortune* magazine's 2001 rankings of the "Global Most Admired" companies with *Advertising Age's* "100 Leading National Advertisers." Companies that appeared on the "Global Most Admired" list were ranked on nine attributes ranging from the quality of their products, financial soundness, and ability to retain and cultivate employee talent to community responsibility, innovativeness, and global business acumen (Stein, 2000). The "100 Leading National Advertisers" list, an annual ranking of companies based on yearly advertising expenditures, was used as a supplement for identifying additional company names that would be more recognizable as a result of their visibility in the media.

A total of 24 companies representing various industries comprised the final selection pool, and a pretest was conducted in order to measure the sample's familiarity with each company name. The researchers believed that familiarity with the company name would provide a stronger context for evaluating its credibility as an issue advertiser. A student sample[1] (N = 78) was asked to evaluate each corporation on a five-point scale anchored by "unfamiliar/familiar." The results from mean analyses indicated that a majority of companies (n = 22) were familiar to the pretest sample. However, two corporations were dropped from the list for low familiarity.

The remaining sample of 22 corporations was then evaluated in a second pretest (N = 39) that examined the perceived appropriateness of each corporation as an advertising sponsor of terrorism threat messages. The objective of the research was to optimize the match between the company sponsor and the terrorism issue. The results from the second pretest selected Southwest Airlines as the corporate source for the for-profit condition.

Independent Variable: Frame

The first step in developing test stimuli was to create advertising messages that framed the issue in a way that would resonate with the target audience. An ideation session comprised of ten graduate students was conducted to brainstorm potential advertising tag lines that would frame the terrorism issue as a high threat or low threat to the audience. The group was instructed to generate potential advertising tag lines around words and ideas associated with the topic of terrorism. A total of 79 tag lines were generated over a one and a half hour ideation session.

From these, the researchers selected a subset of 17 tag lines from the composite list on the basis of their potential to stimulate some degree of threat in a message audience. Then, an independent review panel of four independent faculty judges was asked to evaluate the tag lines according to the level of fear each was likely to elicit from the public. Judges recorded their ratings on a five-point scale anchored by "weak fear/strong fear."

Means by tag line were calculated and analyzed relative to others in the issue category, and the two tag lines from each category of weak and strong fear, respectively, were pretested on a student sample (N = 78). The winning advertising tag lines according to pretest responses were then included in the experimental design. The advertising tag line tested for the high threat condition was, "Terrorism. The beginning of the end?" The tag line tested for the low threat condition was, "Terrorism is contagious."

Dependent Variable Measurement

Source credibility was measured based on four dimensions–business expertise, competency, character and trustworthiness–adapted from several established credibility measurement scales (Jones 1994; McCroskey 1966; Ohanian 1990). Each dimension consisted of between four and seven items and was measured on a seven-point semantic differential scale. The composite instrument used to measure source credibility included a total of 22 items. The reliability for the composite credibility score of $\alpha = .88$ suggested that the items adequately represented the construct.

The second dependent variable, message persuasion, was evaluated using two scale items adopted from Dillard et al.'s (1996) research. The scales were anchored by "not at all persuasive/very persuasive" and "not at all convincing/very convincing." Subjects evaluated each item on a seven-point semantic differential scale.

RESULTS

The subject pool was recruited from several lecture classes in mass communications at a large southeastern university, the same campus on which the content analysis was conducted. The lecture classes used were different from those used in pretest. Subjects were randomly assigned to one of the six test conditions according to the version of questionnaire instrument they received during experiment implementation. They were exposed to a single message stimulus and asked to complete a questionnaire comprised of 59 items that measured emotional response, perceptions of source credibility, and message persuasiveness. All questionnaires were completed independently and took approximately 15 minutes to finish.

A total of 416 college students participated in the study. An analysis on the demographic profile of subjects indicated that 80 percent (n = 322) reported their academic classification as junior or senior. The average age of the sample was 22 years, and the majority (73%) of subjects were female (n = 302). Seventy-eight percent (n = 319) of the sample reported their race as Caucasian/White, 12 percent (n = 51) as Hispanic/Latino, and less than eight percent (n = 33) of the sample reported race as African American/Black, Asian American/Asian, or Native American.

An analysis of variance (ANOVA) was run to investigate the effect of the independent variables on credibility. A composite mean score for credibility was calculated for each message frame to facilitate between group comparisons by issue frame (high threat v. low threat). The main effect of issue frame on credibility was statistically significant ($F(1, 399) = 7.99$, $p = .005$). The composite mean score for credibility was greater for the low threat condition than for the high threat condition ($M = 4.77$ v. 4.50, respectively). This finding suggested that issue frame was an influence on audience evaluations of the message source. Similarly, composite credibility means were calculated for each source in order to facilitate between-group comparisons by source. The main effect for source credibility was also statistically significant ($F(2, 398) = 5.62$, $p = .004$). However, the interaction between the frame and source was not found to be significant. Table 1 presents the outcome of this analysis.

Post hoc analyses[2] were conducted on the source organizations to identify the origin of significant difference between groups. The findings indicated that the mean credibility score for Southwest Airlines was perceived as significantly lower from the U.S. Department of Homeland Security on credibility ($M_{SW} = 4.47$, $M_{US} = 4.81$, $p < .005$), but from the not-for-profit ITA. The composite mean for credibility was greater for the government agency than for Southwest Airlines.

In order to better understand the nature the credibility evaluations, post hoc tests were also conducted on the individual credibility components to confirm which of the four component variables motivated the difference in source evaluations. Coefficient alpha reliability tests run for each dimension of source credibility satisfied Nunally's (1978) criterion of .70 or higher as a standard for basic research (business expertise $\alpha = 0.84$, competency $\alpha = 0.93$, character $\alpha = 0.69$ and trustworthiness $\alpha = 0.87$). The results from the post hoc analysis confirmed that two components differentiated Southwest Airlines from the U.S. Department of Homeland Security as an advertising source for terrorism awareness messages. These components were business expertise (Scheffe's $p = .000$) and competency (Scheffe's $p = .000$), two dimensions that represent an organization's proficiency in a given context.

The effect of source credibility on message persuasion was investigated. A correlation analysis determined the two items that measured persuasion were highly correlated (Pearson's $r = 0.86$, $p < 0.01$). Source credibility was dichotomized using a median split that resulted in two equal groups of 199

TABLE 1. Source Credibility ANOVA Results

Source	n =	M	Type III Sum of Squares	df	Mean Square	F	p
Corrected Model	--	--	18.22	5	3.64	3.873	.002*
Intercept			8607.57	1	8607.57	9145.09	.000*
Source			10.58	2	5.29	5.621	.004*
ITA	137	4.68					
SWA	132	4.42					
USDHS	132	4.81					
Frame			7.52	1	7.52	7.993	0.005
High Threat	198	4.50					
Low Threat	203	4.77					
Source x Frame	--	--	0.19	2	0.098	0.104	0.901
Error	--	--	371.78	395	0.941		
Total	--	--	9010.59	401			
Corrected Total	--	--	390.01	400			

R Squared = .047 (Adjusted R Squared = .035)

Note: Asterisk indicates statistical significance at $p \leq .05$.

subjects. The comparison of persuasion means between groups was statistically significant ($F(1,396) = 88.27$, $p = .002$). In keeping with prior research findings (Kelly 1967; Eagly, Wood and Chaiken 1978), higher levels of source credibility contribute greater message persuasiveness than low source credibility ($M_{HC} = 4.61$ v. $M_{LC} = 3.22$).

DISCUSSION

The purpose of the study was to investigate the means by which issue frame and source influence evaluations of the source credibility and message persuasiveness. This study explored the issue of terrorism as the frame for issue communication and found that the audience's assessments of the source do indeed vary according to the sponsor associated with the message. The United States Department of Homeland Security was clearly determined to be the most credible source on the issue of terrorism, due to the audience's perceptions of its business expertise and competency on the topic. This finding is not surprising given that issues of national interest are the domain of government responsibility. However, Southwest Airlines, the for-profit source, was rated low in credibility due to its ratings on the components of business expertise and competency, two dimensions that represent an organization's proficiency. The implication of this finding for companies sponsoring issue messages that appear unrelated to their corporate mission is that there may be a limit to what the public will tolerate in terms it appropriateness as a message source. Such actions may compromise a for-profit organization's objectives with negative outcomes such as low credibility evaluations or ineffective attempts to persuade all due to either the issue addressed or the frame applied.

One major limitation of the study is the use of a student sample. The debate of the appropriateness of the recruitment of this type of subjects is the topic of much debate (i.e., Peterson 2002). However, the exploratory nature of the study made the use of a student sample appropriate for testing internal validity and investigating relationships between the research variables. The findings generated were meant to directional rather than projectable to the general population.

The fact that the study analyzed the university's newspaper as a source for finding the issue may also be perceived as a limitation. However, the use of this vehicle was minimized the obstacles that may have been create from this age group's lack of exposure to, or low readership of, mainstream media. Efforts taken to pretest the issue's relevance among a subset of the sample frame also helped to ensure that the issue used as a framing stimulus was relevant to the subjects of the study.

Although the model for source credibility found significant main effects for issue frame and source, the model's explanatory power ($R^2 = .035$) is weakly explained by the variables tested. This suggests that other variables can be identified to increase the strength of the model. Future research should investigate additional variables that may mediate the relationship and increase the effect size.

An interesting question that goes beyond the scope of this study is the effect of cognitive processing levels (i.e., Peracchio and Meyers-Levy 1997) on subjects' appraisal of credibility and persuasion. For example, does the motivation to process terrorism-related media content influence evaluations of the source or message? The combination of communication and consumer behavior theories is an intriguing idea for future research.

It is evident that a research agenda that includes other frames (i.e., unemployment, health issues) that might be more appropriate for a corporation than for the government would be fruitful. Also, another extension of this initial exploration is to develop full advertisements that induce more specific frames and agendas on the audience.

The exploration of agenda setting and frames allows for the integration of a fuller understanding of audiences and message. For example, McCombs and Ghanem (2001) mention cognitive and affective attributes as important elements of second level agenda setting. Similar emphasis on cognitive and affective responses can be found in other studies of persuasion (i.e., Dillard et al. 1996).

NOTES

1. The pretest sample used to rate issue relevance is the same as that used to evaluate familiarity of company names.
2. The Scheffe test was applied to all post hoc analyses discussed in the Results section.

REFERENCES

Bloj, A.G. 1975. Into the Wild Blue Yonder: Behavioral Implications of Agenda Setting for Air Travel. Unpublished manuscript in *Studies in Agenda Setting*, eds. M.E. McCombs and G. Stone. Syracuse, NY: Syracuse University, Newhouse Communications Research Center.

Bochner, Stephen and Chester Insko. 1966. Communicator Discrepancy, Source Credibility and Opinion Change. *Journal of Personality and Social Psychology*, 4: 614-621.

Davis, Joel J. 1994. Consumer Response to Corporate Environmental Advertising. *Journal of Consumer Marketing*, 11(2): 25-37.

Dillard, James Price, Courtney A. Plotnick, Linda C. Godbold, Vicki S. Feimuth, and Timothy Edgar. 1996. The Multiple Affective Outcomes of AIDS PSAs: Fear Appeals Do More than Scare People. *Communication Research*, 23(1): 44-72.

Dholakia, Ruby R. and Brian Sternthal. 1977. Highly Credible Sources: Persuasive Facilitators or Persuasive Liabilities? *Journal of Consumer Research*, 3(4): 223-233.

Eagly, Alice H., Wendy Wood, and Shelly Chaiken. 1978. Causal Inferences about Communicators and their Effect on Opinion Change. *Journal of Personality & Social Psychology*, 36(4): 424-435

Entman, Robert M.1993. Framing: Toward Clarification of a Fractured Paradigm. *Journal of Communication*, 43(4): 51-59.

Faber, Ronald J., Albert R. Tims, and Kay G. Schmitt. 1990. Accentuate the Negative?: The Impact of Negative Political Appeals on Voting Intent. In *Proceedings of the 1990 Conference of the American Academy of Advertising*, ed. Patricia A. Stout, 10-16. Austin, TX: American Academy of Advertising.

Gamson, William and Andre Modigliani. 1989. Media Discourse and Public Opinion on Nuclear Power: A Constructionist Approach. *American Journal of Sociology*, 95 (1): 1-37.

Ghorpade, Shailendra. 1986. Agenda Setting: A Test of Advertising's Neglected Function. *Journal of Advertising*, 26(4): 23-28.

Goldsmith, Ronald E., Barbara A. Lafferty, and Stephen J. Newell. 2000. The Impact of Corporate Credibility and Celebrity Credibility on Consumer Reaction to Advertisements and Brands. *Journal of Advertising*, 29(3): 43-54.

Grewal, Dhruv, Jerry Gotlieb, and Howard Marmorstein. 1994. The Moderating Effects of Message Framing and Source Credibility on the Price-Perceived Risk Relationship. *Journal of Consumer Research*, 21(1): 145-153.

Hovland, Carl I., Irving L. Janis, and Harold H. Kelley. 1953. *Communication and Persuasion*. New Haven: Yale University Press.

Hovland, Carl I. and Walter Weiss. 1951. The Influence of Source Credibility on Communication Effectiveness. *Public Opinion Quarterly*, 15(4): 635-650.

Jones, J. 1994. *Development of a Scale to Measure Advertisement Credibility*. Unpublished Master Thesis, University of Florida, Gainesville, FL.

Joseph, W. Benoy. 1982. The Credibility of Physically Attractive Communicators: A Review. *Journal of Advertising*, 11(3): 15-24.

Kelly, Harold H. 1967. Attribution Theory in Social Psychology. In *Nebraska Symposium of Motivation*, ed. D. Levine, 192-238. Lincoln: University of Nebraska Press.

Landis R.J. and G.G. Koch. 1977. The Measurement of Observer Agreement for Categorical Data. *Biometrics*, 33: 159-174.

Maher, T. Michael. 2001. Framing: an Emerging Paradigm or a Phase of Agenda Setting? In *Framing Public Life: Perspectives on Media and Our Understanding of the Social World*, eds. Stephen D. Reese, Oscar H. Gandy and August E. Grant, 83-94. Mahwah, NJ: Lawrence Erlbaum Associates.

McCroskey, James C. 1966. Scales for the Measurement of Ethos. *Speech Monographs*, 33, 65-72.

McCombs, Maxwell E. and Donald Shaw (1972), "The Agenda-Setting Function of Mass Media," *Public Opinion Quarterly*, 36: 178-185.

McCombs, Maxwell E., Juan Pablo Llamas, Estaban Lopez-Escobar, and Federico. Rey Lennon (1997). Candidate Images in Spanish elections: Second-level agenda-setting effects. *Journalism & Mass Communication Quarterly*, 73(4): 703-717.

McCombs, Maxwell E. and Salma I. Ghanem. 2001. The Convergence of Agenda Setting and Framing. In *Framing Public Life: Perspectives on Media and Our Understanding of the Social World*, eds. Stephen D. Reese, Oscar H. Gandy and August E. Grant, 67-81. Mahwah, NJ: Lawrence Erlbaum Associates.

Nelson, Barbara. 1984. Making an Issue of Child Abuse. Reprinted in *Agenda Setting. Readings on Media, Public Opinion, and Policymaking*, eds. D. Protess and M. McCombs, 161-170. Hillsdale, NJ: Lawrence Erlbaum Associates.

Nunnally, Jum C. 1978. *Psychometric Theory*. New York: McGraw-Hill.

Ohanian, Roobina. 1990. Construction and Validation of Scale to Measure Celebrity Endorsers' Perceived Expertise, Trustworthiness, and Attractiveness. *Journal of Advertising*, 19(3): 39-52.

Peracchio, Laura A. and Joan Meyers-Levy. 1997. Evaluating Persuasion-Enhancing Techniques from a Resource-Matching Perspective. *Journal of Consumer Research*, 24 (2), 178-191.

Peterson, Robert A. 2001. On the use of College Students in Social Science Research: Insights from a Second-Order Meta-Analysis. *Journal of Consumer Research*, 28 (3), 450-461.

Protess, David L., Fay Lomax Cook, Thomas R. Curtin, Margaret T. Gordon, Donna R. Leff, Maxwel E. McCombs and Peter Milles. 1987. The Impact of Investigative Reporting on Public Opinion and Policymaking: Targeting Toxic Waste. *Public Opinion Quarterly*, 51: 166-185.

Protess, David L. and Maxwell E. McCombs. 1991. *Agenda Setting. Readings on Media, Public Opinion, and Policymaking*. Hillsdale, NJ: Lawrence Erlbaum Associates.

Roberts, Marilyn S. 1992. Predicting Voting Behavior Via the Agenda-Setting Tradition. *Journalism Quarterly*, 69(4): 878-892.

Solomon, Michael R. 1994. *Consumer Behavior: Buying, Having, and Being* (2nd Edition). Englewood Cliffs, NJ: Prentice Hall.

_____ 1996. *Consumer Behavior: Buying, Having, and Being* (3rd Edition). Englewood Cliffs, NJ: Prentice Hall.

Stein, Nicholas. 2000. The World's Most Admired Companies. Fortune.com (October 2). Time Inc.

Tankard Jr., James W. 2001. The Empirical Approach to the Study of Media Framing. In *Framing Public Life: Perspectives on Media and Our Understanding of the Social World*, eds. Stephen D. Reese, Oscar H. Gandy and August E. Grant, 95-106. Mahwah, NJ: Lawrence Erlbaum Associates.

Wanzenried, J.W. and F.C. Powell. 1993. Source Credibility And Dimensional Stability: A Test Of The Leathers Personal Credibility Scale. *Perceptual & Motor Skills*, 77 (2): 403-407.

Wu, Chenghuan and David R. Shaffer. 1987. Susceptibility to Persuasive Appeals as a Function of Source Credibility and Prior Experience with the Attitude Object. *Journal of Personality and Social Psychology*, 52(4): 677-688.

Political Opinion Leadership
and Electoral Behavior

Aron O'Cass
Anthony Pecotich

SUMMARY. A micro-model that focuses on political opinion leadership within an extended nomological network is developed and tested. Data were gathered from a sample of voters in an election. The results indicate that political opinion leadership played a central role in the voting behavior. Key antecedents to opinion leadership were voter involvement, subjective knowledge, and indirectly, information seeking behavior. Important consequences were voting stability, perceived risk and political satisfaction. *[Article copies available for a fee from The Haworth Document Delivery Service: 1-800-HAWORTH. E-mail address: <docdelivery@ haworthpress.com> Website: <http://www.HaworthPress.com> © 2005 by The Haworth Press, Inc. All rights reserved.]*

KEYWORDS. Political opinion leadership, election

Professor Aron O'Cass is Chair of Marketing, Newcastle Business School, Social Science Building, The University of Newcastle, Callaghan, NSW 2308, Australia (E-mail: aron.ocass@newcastle.edu.au).

Dr. Anthony Pecotich is affiliated with The University of Western Australia, Department of Information Management and Marketing, Nedlands, Perth, Western Australia 6009 (E-mail: tpecotich@ecel.uwa.au).

[Haworth co-indexing entry note]: "Political Opinion Leadership and Electoral Behavior." O'Cass, Aron, and Anthony Pecotich. Co-published simultaneously in *Journal of Nonprofit & Public Sector Marketing* (Best Business Books, an imprint of The Haworth Press, Inc.) Vol. 14, No. 1/2, 2005, pp. 285-307; and: *Current Issues in Political Marketing* (eds: Walter W. Wymer, Jr., and Jennifer Lees-Marshment) Best Business Books, an imprint of The Haworth Press, Inc., 2005, pp. 285-307. Single or multiple copies of this article are available for a fee from The Haworth Document Delivery Service [1-800-HAWORTH, 9:00 a.m. - 5:00 p.m. (EST). E-mail address: getinfo@haworthpressinc.com].

Available online at http://www.haworthpress.com/web/JNPSM
© 2005 by The Haworth Press, Inc. All rights reserved.
doi:10.1300/J054v14n01_16

INTRODUCTION

Modern marketing concepts and practices have been applied to virtually all areas of human endeavor from commerce and education to religion and healthcare. It is somewhat surprising, that despite the impetus given by such writers as Jamieson (1984) and some work in marketing by Rothschild (1978), Newman and Sheth (1985), Burton and Netemeyer (1992), O'Cass (2002a,b) and others, that little empirical research has been conducted in the political arena from the marketing perspective, particularly voter behavior. Yet, from a consumer behavior point of view marketing has much to contribute to politics and the proper functioning of the democratic process. Such contributions may be seen in investigations of central topics in consumer behavior such as, involvement, information search and opinion leadership. For example, involvement and information search are a vital part of virtually all treatments of human decision making in marketing and consumer behavior and it is an equally important element in the decision making of mass electorates (Converse 2000).

Given the nature of the extant consumer research related to the purchase and consumption of a wide range of products and services, it appears relevant to ponder the translation of this body of knowledge across into the voter behavior domain to study electoral markets. This is important, as politics in effect has a significant impact on all citizens, whether they vote or not. Just as it is important to understand consumer behavior in the commercial domain, it is important to understand consumer behavior in the electoral domain. Importantly, the effect of electoral activity by parties during political campaigns must be tied significantly to understanding voter behavior, just as the marketing of consumer goods and services is tied to an understanding of consumer behavior. As is often the case, the environment the individual is studied in tempers such knowledge, and in this context, the electoral environment may have specific characteristics that make it different to and/or similar to the conventional marketplace in which consumer behavior takes place. It is our purpose to bring marketing concepts and ideas to the study voter behavior and so to take a step towards an integrated research perspective while providing new evidence concerning political processes and voter behavior.

Consumer Behavior Theory and Voter Choice

One of the primary objectives facing marketers is to present consumers with information for use in decision-making. The presentation of marketplace information for decision-making presents an interesting dilemma. One the one-hand marketers are charged with developing and transmitting much of the information available in the marketplace, however, much information is also interpersonal (i.e., between marketplace actors or consumers). It is this type of information and those who are primarily seen as being responsible for it transmission that are the often assigned a position of influence in decision-making. However, what is not clear is how those who see themselves as possessing such an influential role (opinion leaders-OLs) make their own decisions and behave in the marketplace. That is not who or how they influence others and promote the diffusion of innovations, but what characteristics of themselves that influence their own OL and what is consequences are for their own decisions. Opinion leadership is founded within two overlapping, but identical phenomena; opinion leaders and word-of-mouth according to Leonard-Barton (1985). On this point, it has been argued that not all WOM originates from OLs, nor do they necessarily influence through WOM alone (Leonard-Barton 1985). Apart from the influence process and WOM, it is possible that much of the variance in decision-making may be attributed to characteristics of consumers, such as their level of OL.

Voter decision-making related to electoral choice has been an area of interest to political scientists and consumer researchers (e.g., Rothschild 1978; Newman and Sheth 1985; O'Cass 2002a). Such research has often sought to understand the variance in voter behavior that can be attributed to different voter characteristics such as education and involvement (O'Cass 2002b), as well as the decision-making criteria used to make candidate choices (see, Newman and Sheth 1984). In general the study of politics and voter behavior as a non-traditional area of marketing has been of sporadic interest over the past two and a half decades (e.g., Rothschild 1978; Rothschild and Houston, 1979; Swinyard and Coney, 1978; Burton and Netemeyer, 1992 and Newman, 1999), and although opinion leadership has been of interest in the conventional commercial areas of consumer research, very little has focused on the non-traditional (political-voter behavior) contexts in more recent times. This is interesting, as the original introduction of opinion leadership is derived largely from the political context by Lazerfeld, Berelson and Caudet (1948) with studies of elections in the early 1940s. In the political milieu Converse (2000, p. 332) bemoaned: "the extreme variance in political information from the top to the bottom of the public. This is not controversial either. But the degree of this heterogeneity is widely underestimated, and the implications of this heterogeneity for research seems even less well understood." It is this statement that provided the impetus for our study. In consumer behavior it has long been recognized that consumers vary in the amount of information and knowledge they may possess and the role they see themselves playing in information movements in the marketplace. To quantify and conceptualize this variation, the idea of opinion leadership has been proposed, where the opinion leader is the interested and involved consumer (Gilly, Graham, Wolfinbarger and Yale 1998) with the potential to exert influence over the attitude's and behaviors of others. The role of the opinion leader in the voting process appears to have been overlooked in more recent times. To address this we propose a model where opinion leadership is a primary focus and examine its relationships with the antecedents of voter education, involvement, subjective knowledge and information seeking, and the consequents of stability, perceived risk, satisfaction and confidence (see Figure 1).

The following discussion revolves around developing an understanding of political opinion leadership that is hypothesized to be an important element to the voter decision-making process (see Figure 1). The discussion covers the theoretical issues related to these constructs and how they may enhance our understanding of voter behavior. This discussion is based on a similar premise to that of Newman (1985) who argued that inherent in the extension of marketing techniques to politics is the assumption that the characteristics of voters and consumers are similar enough to justify the application of consumer behavior models to voting behavior.

Voter Opinion Leadership

The value of interpersonal communication in consumer decision-making has been documented extensively in consumer research (Gilly et al. 1998; Richins and Root-Shaffer, 1988). Models or frameworks of opinion leadership often outline its effects on recipients, and resulting new product success or failure (Leonard-Barton 1985). Opinion leadership is the central construct in our model (Figure 1) and the justification for this positioning emanates not only from consumer behavior research, but also from some of the classical works in economics and politics (Lazarsfeld et al. 1944; Converse, 2000; Downs, 1957). In justifying his position for the rational utilization of scarce resource to obtain data for decision-making, Downs (1957, p. 207) stated that "traditional economic theory assumes that unlimited amounts of free information are available to decision makers. In contrast, we seek to discover what political decision making is like when uncertainty exists and information is obtainable only at a cost." Further, he goes on to suggest that "the incentive of most citizens to acquire information before voting is very small 'and' the large percentage of citizen do not become informed to any significant degree on the issues involved in elections." This differential information seeking suggests that some well-informed citizens may play the role of opinion leaders and influence voting patterns. This is consistent with the value placed on interpersonal communication in consumer decision-making that has been documented extensively in consumer research (Richins and Root-Shaffer, 1988). Models

FIGURE 1. The Antecedents and Consequents of Political Opinion Leadership: Model A

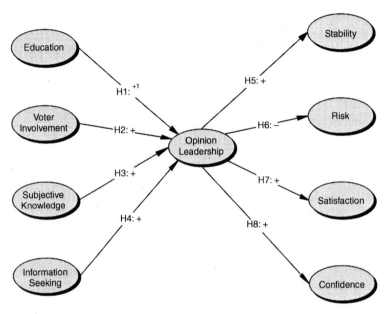

Note:[1] This indicates the hypothesis number and the direction of the relationship.

or frameworks of opinion leadership often outline its effects on recipients, and resulting new product success or failure. However, little interest has been shown in understanding the dynamics of opinion leadership in a broader array of consumer behavior variables. Opinion leaders are credited with a large amount of interpersonal communication and studies have examined selected demographic and social characteristics of opinion leaders. Opinion leadership has been identified as having a strong influence in many social situations, where for example, Flynn and Goldsmith (1994) found that opinion leaders are more likely to write to politicians and influence others to perform certain behaviors. Much less effort has been directed at understanding the drivers of opinion leadership and even less in the context of voter behavior. The role of opinion leadership in the political process is an important one, as Omura and Talarzyk (1983) argue that the potential for opinion leaders to shape public opinion is great.

    In discussing the maldistribution of information within an electorate Converse (2000, p. 334) identifies "a small fraction of the electorate claims a large fraction of the total political information accessible in memory to anyone," and by implication he emphasizes the central role of opinion leadership. Taking this as a point of departure our model in Figure 1 identifies opinion leadership as being a function of education, voter involvement, subjective knowledge, and information seeking. Essentially opinion leaders are influential because of their knowledge, involvement, expertise and experience in a product category, and knowledge and expertise, are enhanced and facilitated by formal education (Myers and Robertson, 1972). The variable that has often been postulated as the clearest differentiator of opinion leadership has been formal education and this has even been found in the political context (Converse 2000). Robertson and Myers (1969) in fact showed that education was positively correlated with opinion leadership in politics. However, this relationship has not always been found. For example, Chaney (2001) found a non-significant relationship between education and OL for the product category wine. Despite this the general consensus is that OL and education are positively related and we also concur with this view. Thus,

H1:   Formal education will have a positive effect voter opinion leadership.

Along with opinion leadership the concept of involvement has been of significant interest to both conventional consumer researchers and non-traditional researchers. Over the last decade or so there have been many theoretical propositions regarding involvement and a wide variety of involvement types and effects (Muehling, Laczniak and Andrews 1993; Mittal 1988; 1989; 1995; O'Cass 2000; Rothschild and Houston 1979). Political researchers have recognized the value of understanding voter involvement in decisions involving elections, parties and politicians (Rothschild and Houston 1979; Burton and Netemeyer 1992).

Continuing on with the involvement stream in consumer behavior recently, O'Cass (2000) proposed that the content of involvement does not vary; only its context varies. The view adopted here is that involvement refers to the extent to which the consumer views the focal object as a central part of their life, a meaningful and engaging object in their life and important to them (O'Cass, 2000). Such propositions allow for a unified approach to involvement and thus make it a more theoretically useful construct in a wider array of contexts, voter behavior. As such we see a major role for involvement in determining voter choice, focusing on the involvement-OL connection. Some of the more important contributions to this debate are works by Dichter (1966), Richins and Root-Shaffer (1988) and Venkatraman (1990). These studies proposed and investigated the relationship between involvement, opinion leadership traits and behaviors. Dichter (1966) argued that involvement with a product class is an important determinant of word-of-mouth. The proposition raised here is that involvement in politics should be a strong determinant to political opinion leadership and that political opinion leaders are motivated to discuss politics or offer advice because of their personal involvement in it. Similar to the arguments by Feick and Price (1987) and Gilly et al. (1998) involvement appears to be the predominant explanation for opinion leaders' conversations about politics. Our theoretical formulation (Figure 1) takes the perspective of placing opinion leadership as a consequent, where voter involvement is directly related to opinion leadership. Thus,

H2: Voter involvement will have a significant direct positive effect on perceived political opinion leadership.

A prominent issue for political parties, politicians and voters is the extent of political knowledge that exists in the electorate. How much a voter believes they know about parties, politicians and elections is vital in the sense that it will influence information acquisition and decision-making. Strangely, even though both involvement and knowledge are used as descriptors in the definition of the opinion leadership, no research appears to have placed them as antecedents to the construct (opinion leadership). However, in this area, a synthesis of the consumer behavior and voter behavior literature indicates that voter involvement has the potential to influence a voters perception of how much they think they know regarding elections, political parties and politicians. This also extends to the enhanced (stronger) beliefs that opinion leaders may hold about their knowledge of a focal object (e.g., politics). As indicated by Corey (1971) opinion leaders involvement in a specific product class distinguishes them from non-opinion leaders. Also as discussed by Gilly et al. (1998) and Chaney (2001) opinion leadership has a relationship with consumers' levels of subjective knowledge. Their results indicated that opinion leadership did influence perceived knowledge. The argument is advanced here that it is ones level of knowledge that causes the development of expertise that characterizes the OL. Our initial position suggests that subjective political knowledge is a necessary antecedent to OL, because knowledge must be developed or perceived to be held prior to being seen as an OL. Thus,

H3: Voter subjective political knowledge has a significant positive effect on political opinion leadership

Information search or seeking in the context of electoral choice is defined, as the information seeking process which voters engage in to facilitate decision making in an election and the value placed on various sources of information (including newspapers, television, paid advertising, and word of mouth) to aid in their decision making (O'Cass 2002a). Although not specifically defined in the literature, we may view extent of information search as a desire to be informed and keep up to date. This is particularly relevant in the political choice context if we consider the varied information sources available for voters to access information during campaigns and the significant volume of communications that occurs during an election. Search for information related to choice is a major element of consumer behavior theory. There have been indicators that consumers, in general, seek little pre-purchase information (Beatty and Smith 1987). Historically however, increased search activity has been associated with involvement in the stimulus and also increased involvement with opinion leadership (O'Cass 2002a,b). In their discussion Gilly et al. (1998) have also indicated that there are indications that increased exposure or receiving more information is a characteristic of opinion leaders. This has also been found by Coulter et al. (2002) with OL's seeking more information than non OL's. Therefore, we contend that opinion leaders are active information seekers from a variety of sources (Bayus Carroll and Rao 1985; Gilly et al. 1998). As such, information seeking will be related to opinion leadership. Thus,

H4: Voter information seeking behavior will have a positive effect on voter opinion leadership.

Having specified the critical antecedent variables to opinion leadership in an election context we now specify the relationships with important outcome variables. The stability of voter behavior is a primary concern to many parties. We use the term voting stability to refer to the extent that a voter consistently votes for the same candidate or party overtime. This behavior may be because of strongly held preferences or as a means of reducing decision-making effort. This issue is not the focus here, but the extent this activity occurs is our focus. In another context Kuusela, Spence and Kanto (1998) argued that experts (OLs) are more consistent (stable) in their decisions. If the electoral market is comparable to the commercial market then such behavioural aspects should be consistent between the two. What we argue is, that in the context of electoral behavior, voters who are identified as opinion leaders will exhibit more stable voting behavior than non-leaders. Thus,

H5: Voter opinion leadership will have a positive effect on stability in voting choices.

Bauer (1960) in one of his earliest statements concerning perceived risk suggested that consumer behavior involved uncertainties and risks. Childers

(1986) for example, suggested that opinion leadership should be positively correlated with perceived risk. However, while many have offered theoretical arguments, few have substantiated them with empirical work. For example, Dowling and Staelin (1994) while attempting to specify a process model of perceived risk including information search and product involvement did not attempt to test the relationships. In the proposed model (figure 1) opinion leadership is placed centrally within the process with perceived risk a critical outcome variable. Following Bauer's (1960) in initial formulation we postulate that in situations of uncertainty opinion leaders will perceive less risk. This is indirectly driven by the influence of information search and perceived higher knowledge they hold. Therefore, the OL will in the context of decisions they will make in an elections not see as much risk associated with them as the non-OL. Thus,

H6: Voter opinion leadership will have a negative effect on perceived risk.

Consumer satisfaction is widely recognized as an important outcome variable in marketing and is a fundamental concept in marketing (Mittal and Lassar 1998). While consumer satisfaction has been defined in many different ways (Oliver 1997), at its most fundamental level it is a positive or negative feeling about the consequences or the results of the consumption process. Traditionally, it is viewed as an outcome of a series of consumption and post purchase events, and comparison processes. In general and at a very broad level one would anticipate a positive relationship with positive outcomes of the process. So for example, if fulfillment of expectation is achieved then a consumer would be satisfied and/or if their expectations are disconfirmed then the consumer would be dissatisfied (Oliver 1997). In the situation of opinion leadership in the voting context, we assert that given differential information possessed by the voters that whatever the outcome of the election the OL voter will be more satisfied. Such a consumer has made an effort to make an informed and confident voting decision and is, therefore, more likely to use the argument "I did the best I could and am therefore happier whatever the outcome of the election." Thus,

H7: Voter opinion leadership will have a positive effect on satisfaction.

Relatedly, the confidence with which one holds their beliefs is an important contributor to consumer behavior. Consumer confidence has been argued to consist of fundamentally two types; knowledge confidence and choice confidence (Nataraajan and Madhukar 1997; Urbany, Dickson and Wilkie 1989).

Confidence is argued to represent a consumers' certainty regarding what is known about the stimuli under consideration, including attributes and the importance of attributes and their performance. Choice confidence however, represents a consumer's certainty about which brand to choose or making the right choice (Nataraarjan and Madhukar 1997). Given the identified characteristics of opinion leaders it is argued here they will hold stronger confidence in their political choices as indicated in Figure 1. Thus,

H8: Opinion leadership will have a significant positive effect on voter confidence.

RESEARCH DESIGN

The study was based on the development of a self-administered questionnaire that was administered as part of a larger study of elections and voting. The survey was administered to a sample of voters in a Federal Australian by-election. A by-election occurs when ever a vacancy occurs in the House of Representatives because of the death, resignation, absence without leave, expulsion, disqualification or ineligibility of a Member, a writ may be issued by the Speaker for the election of a new Member. A writ may also be issued when the Court of Disputed Returns declares an election void (AEC 2003).

The survey was administered on the day of the by-election using a drop off and pick up approach yielding 238 useable surveys out of 500 dropped off. Cluster sampling was used to identify households randomly, within three randomly chosen suburbs of the electorate. A survey was left with the potential respondents and a field worker later returned to collect the survey (up to two call-backs were attempted). The sample was evenly split between male and females, with an average age of 51, with 8% between 18 and 25, 15% between 26 and 35, 22% between 36 and 45, 10% between 46 and 55 and 45% aged 56 years and over. Education was measured across four specific education levels, with 40% of respondents possessing a junior high school certificate, 42% possessing a senior high school certificate, 11% possessing an undergraduate university degree and 7% holding a postgraduate university degree. The sample makeup compares well with the profiles of Australian averages gender, age and education.

The scales used were based on instruments that have been used previously and validated in other contexts as well as some in electoral studies. Voters' involvement was measured using a seven-item scale adopted from O'Cass (2002b). The scale is oriented toward assessing the position (centrality) that politics occupies in an individual's life. Voters' subjective knowledge of politics was measured via a four-item scale based on the work of Flynn and Gold-smith (1999). Information seeking was measured according to the propensity to seek information during the election via three items. Political opinion leadership was measured via a six-item scale adapted from the work of Reynolds and Darden (1971). The opinion leadership scale was oriented toward politics and as such all items were reworded to the context of politics and voting. Perceived risk was measured via five items adapted from Evrard and Aurier (1996), as was voters' satisfaction via four-item satisfaction measure. The measure was adapted to measure satisfaction with political parties, the party the respondent voted for at the previous election, and satisfaction with politics in general. Voters' decision confidence was measured by three-items focusing on choosing the right party, politician and confidence in making the right choice of whom to vote for adapted from O'Cass (2000). Respondents provided ratings on seven point scales for these measures. Voting stability was measured via a three pole (yes, no, most of the time) single item asking the voter if they vote for the same party at elections.

RESULTS

Despite all scales being used successfully in previous studies, it was considered necessary to examine their psychometric properties in this research context. Table 1 shows the results of scale evaluation, indicating that the loadings for constructs ranged from .45 to .98, and the average variance extracted ranged from .75 to .90 and Cronbach alphas for measures was between .73 and .95. These were all above established standards and it was, therefore concluded that the unidimensionality and reliability of the measures used were satisfactory in this research context.

To test for common method variance we used Harmon's one factor test where all items, measuring the different constructs, were subjected to a single factor analysis (Igbaria et al. 1997). Using this approach and after entering all items into a factor analysis, seven factors were extracted with eigenvalues greater than 1, that accounted for 69.3% of the variance. As there was not one factor (or a common factor underlying the data) and as the majority of the variance was not accounted for by one general factor, common method variance was not evident.

Following assessment of common method variance convergent and discriminant validity were examined. As argued by Fornell and Larcker (1981), convergent validity is achieved if the average variance explained (AVE) in items by their respective constructs is greater than the variance unexplained (i.e., AVE > .05). Therefore, in order to assess the constructs (factors) for conver-

TABLE 1. Construct Loadings and Weights

Components and manifest variables	Loading[a, b, c]	
Voter Involvement		
Means a lot to me	.87	
Significant to me	.90	
Relevant part of my life	.93	
Personally important to me	.93	
Interested in	.90	
How involved are you	.92	
I am involved in	.82	
AVE[d]		.90
Coeficient Alpha		.95
Subjective Knowledge		
I know a lot about	.90	
Classify myself as an expert	.86	
Compared to most people I know more	.93	
I am knowledgeable about	.86	
AVE		.89
Coeficient Alpha		.91
Political Opinion Leadership		
My friends and neighbours ask	.88	
I sometimes influence	.88	
Come to me for information	.90	
Regarded as a good source of information	.91	
Think of two people who I spoke to	.64	
I spend a lot of time talking	.85	
AVE		.84
Coeficient Alpha		.91
Information seeking		
You have to seek out information	.86	
I tried to keep up to date during the election	.45	
Use your instincts during the election	.95	
AVE		.75
Coeficient Alpha		.73
Voter Perceived Personal Risk		
Making a poor choice would be troubling	.80	
If wrong candidate gets elected a lot to lose	.91	
If wrong party gets elected a lot to lose	.88	
There is a lot hinging on election	.80	
Voting has a high degree of risk	.66	
AVE		.81
Coeficient Alpha		.87

Components and manifest variables	Loading[a, b, c]	
Satisfaction		
I am satisfied with the party I voted for in the last election	.83	
I am satisfied with the politician I voted for in the last election	.78	
I am satisfied with politics in general	.83	
I am satisfied with political parties in general	.83	
AVE		.82
Coeficient Alpha		.84
Decision making confidence		
I am confident I chose the right party/politician	.71	
I have confidence in my ability to make a good decision	.98	
Confidence in ability in deciding who to vote for	.81	
AVE		.83
Coeficient Alpha		.82
Stability (Formative categorical variable)		
I generally vote for the same party at elections		
No	0.00	
Maybe	0.27	
Yes	1.12	

[a] Bootstrap critical ratios(t-values) are not shown but they were all significant at p < .05.
[b] All figures are loadings with the exception of stability where weights are shown.
[c] As no changes were made for the analysis the results are identical and are not shown
[d] Average variance extracted

gent validity, the squared multiple correlations from the confirmatory factor analysis were used to calculate the average variance explained. All factors average variance explained (AVE) was greater than .50.

To assess the discriminant validity the arguments of Gaski (1984) were followed, which suggests that if the correlation between two composite constructs is not higher than their respective reliability estimate, then discriminant validity exists. Following assessment of convergent validity all items within each construct were computed into composite variables. The results indicate all reliability estimates (Cronbach's alpha) were greater than the correlations between constructs, such that all reliabilities were greater than .73 and correlations ranged between .66 and .31.

Results for the Measurement and Structural Models

Partial Least Squares (PLS) was used to evaluate the theoretical hypotheses using PLSgraph 3.0 (Chin, 1998). PLS is a variance based SEM technique for estimating path models using latent constructs. Evaluation of the PLS results are not to be judged on the basis of any single fit index, but through indices which are characterized by aspects such as their sufficiency to explain the data, congruence with substantive expectations and precision (Lohmöller 1989). These indices provide evidence of the relationships, rather than definitive statistical tests which may be contrary to the philosophy of soft modeling (Falk and Miller 1992). Using the available criteria the results indicated all the reflective latent variables had acceptable bootstrap critical ratios (all greater than 1.96) and the Average Variance Extracted (AVE) for the measurement models was uniformally high (range from .75 to .90). The between blocks correlation coefficients of the residuals of the manifest variables were all relatively low (below .11) indicating that the blocks are distinctly defined. The loadings were virtually identical for Models A and B and no measurement improvement was necessary. The formative measurement model was used for the categorical 'voting stability' variable. The regression weights rather than the loadings are used in evaluating the relationships for the hypotheses. These are shown in Table 1 and the weights are virtually identical and significant (p < .05) for models A and B. Evaluation of the theoretical Model A (Figure 1) is shown in Table 2. The mean proportion of variance accounted (AVA) for the endogenous variables was .18 and the individual R^2 were greater than or close to the recommended .10 (Falk and Miller 1992) for all of the predicted variables (opinion leadership = .47, stability = .09, risk = .20, satisfaction = .07 and confidence = .09).

The bootstrap critical ratios are of the appropriate size (greater than 1.96) so supporting hypotheses two, three and five were significant, but contrary to expectation the direction of the results for hypothesis six was in the opposite direction to the hypothesis, but was still significant. The data, therefore suggests that opinion leadership is positively predicted by voter involvement and subjective knowledge. It is also a positive predictor of voter stability and satisfaction. Surprisingly it is associated with higher risk, but is not associated with confidence, and not predicted by education and nor directly by information seeking.

As a further step in the evaluation of the theoretical model the non-significant measurement paths were trimmed, the correlations between the latent variables were examined and the large ones were considered for inclusion in the new model given a theoretical rationale. The model was then re-estimated. The results of this process are shown in Table 2 as "Model B" and in Figure 2. The average variance explained increased to .31, a significant improvement from Model A. For the retained paths the results are virtually identical with very small changes in R^2's (see Figure 2 and Table 2 model B) and critical ratios. This suggests that compared to Model A little was lost by eliminating the non-significant paths. However, we also discovered seven significant unhypothesized (UH) relationships. Voter involvement was found to be directly

TABLE 2. PLS Results for Hypotheses

			Model A			
Equation	Predicted variables	Predictor variables	Hypothesis	Path	R^2	Critical ratio[a]
1	Opinion Leadership	Education	H1	0.05	0.47	0.89
		Voter involvement	H2	0.27		2.78
		Subjective knowledge	H3	0.47		5.98
		Information seeking	H4	−0.05		0.76
2	Stability	Opinion leadership	H5	0.29	0.09	4.44
3	Risk	Opinion leadership	H6	0.44	0.20	8.01
4	Satisfaction	Opinion leadership	H7	0.26	0.07	3.79
5	Confidence	Opinion leadership	H8	−0.12	0.09	−1.69
	AVA[c]				0.18	
			Model B			
Equation	Predicted variables	Predictor variables	Hypothesis	Path	R^2	Critical ratio[a]
1	Opinion Leadership	Education	H1		0.45	
		Voter involvement	H2	0.26		2.91
		Subjective knowledge	H3	0.47		6.72
		Information seeking	H4			
2	Stability	Opinion leadership	H5	0.29	0.09	4.84
3	Risk	Opinion leadership	H6	0.20	0.44	3.23
		Voter involvement	UH1b	0.19		2.78
		Information seeking	UH5	0.44		
4	Satisfaction	Opinion leadership	H7	0.26	0.07	4.28
5	Confidence	Opinion leadership	H8			
6	Confidence	Subjective knowledge	UH6	0.44	0.38	9.34
		Information seeking	UH7	0.28		4.42
7	Subjective knowledge	Voter involvement	UH2	0.61	0.50	14.31
		Information seeking	UH4	0.17		3.12
8	Information seeking	Voter involvement	UH3	0.48	0.23	9.20
	AVA[c]				0.31	

[a] Bootstrap estimate divided by bootstrap standard error (critical ratio = 1.96, p < .05, and critical ratio = 2.58, p < .01).
[b] Unhypothesized discovered effects.
[c] Average Variance Accounted for.

FIGURE 2. The Revised Model of the Antecedents and Consequents of Political Opinion Leadership: Model B

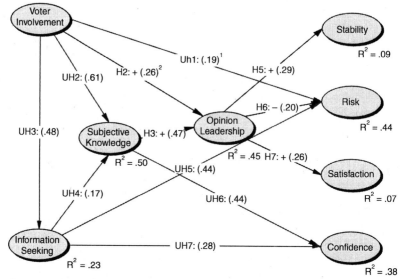

Note: [1] UH1 indicates that the relationship was unhypothesised and the figures in parentheses are regression coefficients all of which were significant at p < .01.
[2] H1 indicates that the relationship was hypothesised, the + or − indicate the direction of the postulated relationship and the figures in parentheses are regression coefficients all of which were significant at p < .01.

and positively related to risk (UH1), subjective knowledge (UH2) and information seeking (UH3). Information seeking was directly related to subjective knowledge (UH4) and confidence (UH7). The data also suggested that the greater the subjective knowledge the greater the confidence UH6. Given the significant improvement in AVA and the high proportion of variance explained for some of the new individual equations, it may be concluded that the alternate model may form useful basis for further research. These possibilities are examined more thoroughly in the discussion below.

DISCUSSION

In this study, we sought to apply theoretical insights from consumer behavior to the political context of voter decision-making in an election. Specifically we placed opinion leadership central to the process of electoral behavior and sought to investigate its antecedents and consequents. The results suggest that, although opinion leadership is central to the process, some of the relationships were not as expected. We found that opinion leadership is, as expected, directly influenced by voter involvement and subjective knowledge, but, unexpectedly, only indirectly affected by information seeking, and that it is not at all influenced by education. The elimination of education from the model is surprising giving the strong findings of previous research (see: Converse 2000). Our findings, therefore, seem to suggest that education may not be an important variable in electoral OL. It is important to emphasize that these findings may only hold within the context of political opinion leadership and may not discount the effect that education may have on other voter behavior characteristics and behaviors. For example, O'Cass (2002b) has shown that education does have a significant effect on voter involvement. However, other research by Chaney (2001) has shown no effect for education.

Still focusing on OL and its consequences we found that opinion leadership was also found to be a significant antecedent of voting stability and satisfaction as expected but no relationship was found with voter decision confidence. So the findings here do not concur with other work in this area (Coulter et al. 2002). Also, the relationship with perceived risk was in the opposite direction to that predicted. It appears that contrary to hypothesis 6 opinion leadership increases perceived risk. The contrary and unhypothesized relationships with regard to risk and confidence are of particular interest as they suggest a possible new direction for research. Risk was found to have positive relationships with voter involvement and information seeking (unhypothesized) and also a positive relationship with opinion leadership. While these finding are different from some of the previous research, it is also consistent with other work (see: Beatty and Smith 1987; Chadhuri 1998) and by implication suggest that the processes involved in voter behavior may be different from those previously proposed in commercial goods and services marketplace behavior. As originally formulated by Bauer (1960) consumers seek ways of reducing risk by searching for information, and therefore, may be viewed as both the motivator of the search process and a consequent, outcome variable. We have formulated it as a consequent, where the processes of opinion leadership should lead to a reduction in risk. This formulation although consistent with the classic position on risk, involvement and information search has not been strongly demonstrated even in consumer behavior (Blackwell et al. 2001). Our finding suggests a more complex process in which voter involvement directly affects information seeking and risk, and information seeking itself positively affects risk. These findings are difficult to explain within the classic consumer behavior framework where the purpose of, for example, information seeking is to reduce risk (Bauer 1960; Dowling and Staelin 1994). However, in the political context where the issues are highly complex and emotionally charged the knowledgeable opinion leader perceives greater risks in the political process. Interestingly, the absence of a relationship between opinion leadership and confidence completes the picture of the opinion leader as complex individual who although stable and satisfied with the political process, nonetheless, perceives higher levels of risk and is less confident in decisions. This is somewhat contrary to Chan and Misra (1990) who found that risk perceptions and opinion leadership were not related, but we argue our findings and justification make sense in relation to the voter in the electoral marketplace.

Unhypothesized direct effects were also found between voter involvement, risk and information seeking. This indicates that the more voters' become involved in politics the greater their desire or propensity to seek out electoral related information. There appears to also be, unique aspects of the domain of voter choice that are directly the result of the interaction between voters (consumers of politics) and the context of the marketplace they operate in (elections/politics). It is interesting to note that political opinion leadership is affected by voter involvement, and that subjective knowledge strongly affects opinion leadership. Further, subjective knowledge was shown to have a strong effect on a voter's confidence in their political choices. This study is one of the first to test these relationships, in the context of voter choice. Whilst other research has been conducted to investigate the constructs studied here they have not studied the same combination of variables nor looked at them in relation to voter choice in the political marketplace.

This study makes several important contributions to research on voter choice and by exploring voters' involvement and its effect on voter opinion leadership the study has tested a relationship that, whilst expressed in the literature in consumer behavior, has not been given the attention it deserves in voter behavior. Overall it appears that political involvement gives rise to voter opinion leadership and also that involvement moderates the relationship between opinion leadership and subjective voter knowledge, and information seeking. Additionally the finding that subjective knowledge gives rise to higher voter confidence in decisions related to choice is a new finding that enhances our understanding of political choice behavior.

Limitations and Future Research

This study, while making significant contributions to our understanding of voter choice, has some limitations. For example, the study was conducted in a single by-election and used some scales that have not been extensively used in a political context. Whilst the scales have been validated in the goods context, further work needs to be done in the context of political voter behavior. The study is also limited to a single political system (Australia). It would also be important to study the constructs in a longitudinal study to examine changes, for example, in the level of opinion leadership, involvement and knowledge of voters, in a within subjects design as opposed to a between subjects design.

CONCLUSION

It is believed this study contributes to furthering our knowledge of voter behavior. It appears that opinion leadership may play an important role in voter decision-making. If the results are generalizable to other populations and electoral contexts the results may have important implications for political marketers, parties, public policy advocates and academics. Ultimately, the variables examined here all impact on voters' ultimate choices of candidates and parties in an election. Voter behavior is analyzed during elections to provide interested groups a better understanding of voters and their choices and to be able to explain and to predict voting behavior. Parties and political candidates want to know how to allocate their resources during campaigns and knowledge about how and why voters make the choice they do enables campaign strategists to target their marketing efforts better. Such knowledge also provides insight for developing appropriate appeals to selected voter segments via media such as Television, radio or print and in this era of market segmentation, targeting, and extensive promotion.

The strategies that are developed and implemented in a campaign by a party would be seen to differ significantly according to the extent of opinion leadership. Also of importance is the finding that involvement influences opinion leadership (and its consequences) which subsequently affects the level of knowledge a voter believes they have and their ultimate satisfaction with their decision-making capacity. Also involvement influences information seeking and risk. As such, one would see different types of information being targeted at voters with high versus low involvement. This is so because low involvement is related to lower knowledge and confidence and less information seeking and sharing (a tendency of non-opinion leaders), whereas high involvement is related to greater opinion leadership tendencies (information sharing) and greater knowledge and confidence and also greater satisfaction. One may see such strategies used in targeting the low involvement voter. However, the outcome of targeting less involved voters has always been a heated point from the public policy advocates point of view. Such voters are the most susceptible and least concerned with voting and political outcomes (least involved). By understanding the nature or characteristics of the voters in the marketplace parties and politicians will be better able to develop and target them with appropriately designed campaigns. This fact is not new, but it is our growing understanding of the of voter psychology that is. This is the progress we make, now and into the future about what makes voters behave as they do.

Despite continued technological and scientific progress we live in a period of great political and social turbulence and uncertainty. At a time when it should be possible for all citizens to live peacefully and in happiness and participate in democratic processes the world is wracked with problems. Given this situation humanity everywhere is beset by helplessness and despair, and an apparent universal loss of faith in political institutions and political processes to improve their condition. And yet it is clear that there is no other hope for the future but through open and democratic political processes in which people participate freely.

REFERENCES

Arnould, H. (1982), "Moderator Variables: A Clarification of Conceptual, Analytical and Psychometric Issues," *Organization Behavior and Human Performance*, 29, 143-174.

Australian Electoral Commission (2003) "by-elections" http://www.aec.gov.au/_content/when/by_elections/overview.htm

Barber, Mary and Meera Venkatraman, (1986) "The Determinants of Satisfaction for a High Involvement Product: Three Rival Hypotheses and Their Implications in the Health Care Context," in *Advances in Consumer Research*, 13, 316-320.

Bauer, Raymond. A (1960), "Consumer Behavior as Risk-Taking," in *Dynamic Marketing for a Changing World*, ed. R. S. Hancock, Chicago: American Marketing Association, 389-398.

Bayus, V, V Carroll, A and Rao, (1986) "Harnessing the Power of Word of Mouth," in *Innovation Diffusion Models of New Product Acceptance*, eds. V Mahajan, and Y Wind, Cambridge, MA: Ballinger, 61-83.

Beatty, Sharron, Lyne, Kahle and Patricia, Homer (1988), "The Involvement-Commitment Model: Theory and Implications," *Journal of Business Research*, 16(2), 149-167.

Beatty, Sharon and Scot Smith (1987), "External Search Effort: An Investigation Across Several Product Categories," *Journal of Consumer Research*, 14, 83-95.

Blackwell, Roger. D, Paul W Miniard and James F Engel (2001), *Consumer Behaviour* (9 ed.) New York: Harcourt College Publishers.

Burton, Scot and Richard, Netemeyer (1992), "The effect of Enduring, Situational, and Response Involvement on Preference Stability in the Context of Voting Behavior," *Psychology and Marketing*, 9(2), 143-156.

Chadhuri, Arjun (1998), "Product class effects on perceived risk: The role of emotion," *International Journal of Research in Marketing*, 15, 157-168.

Chaney, Isabella (2002) "Opinion Leaders as a segment for Marketing Communications," *Marketing Intelligence and Planning* 19(5), 302-308.

Childers, Terry (1986), "Assessment of the Psychometric Properties of an Opinion Leadership Scale," *Journal of Marketing Research*, 23 (May), 184-187.

Chin, Wynne., and T A Fry (2000), *Pls-Graph 3.0 Build 176* Houston: Department of Decision and Information Science, University of Houston.

Chin, Wynne (1998a), " Issues and Opinion on Structural Equation Modeling," *MIS Quarterly*, 22(1), 7-16.

Chin, Wynne (1998b), "The Partial Least Squares Approach for Structural Equation Modeling," in *Modern Methods for Business Research*, Ed. G. A. Marcoulides CA: Lawrence Erlbaum Associates, 295-336.

Converse, Paul. E (2000), "Assessing the Capacity of Mass Electorates," *Annual Review of Political Science*, 3, 331-353.

Corey, Lawrence (1971), "People Who Claim to be Opinion Leaders: Identifying Their Characteristics by Self-report," *Journal of Marketing*, 35 (October), 48-53.

Coulter, Robin, Feick, Lawrence and Price, Linda (2002), "Changing Faces: Cosmetics Opinion Leadership Among Women in the New Hungary," *European Journal of Marketing*, 36(11/12), 1287-1308.

Day, R (1977), "Toward a Process Model of Consumer satisfaction," in *Conceptualization and Measurement of Consumer Satisfaction and Dissatisfaction*, ed. Hunt, K, Cambridge MA: Marketing Science Institute, 153-183.

Dichter, Ernest (1966), "How Word of Mouth Advertising Works," *Harvard Business Review*, 44 (November), 147-166.

Dowling, G. R., and Staelin, R (1994), "A Model of Perceived a Risk and Risk-Handling Activity," *Journal of Consumer Research*, 21(June), 119-134.

Downs, A (1957), "An Economic Theory of Democracy," New York: Harper Row Publishers Evrard, Yves and Philippe Aurier (1996), "Identification and Validation of the Components of the Person-Object Relationship," *Journal of Business Research*, 37, 127-134.

Falk, R. F., and N Miller (1992), *A Primer for Soft Modeling*, Akron: University of Akron University.

Fazio, R and M Zanna (1981), "Direct Experience and Attitude-Behavior Consistency, in *Advances in Experimental Social Psychology*, Vol 4, ed. L Berkowitz, New York: Academic Press, 161-202.

Feick, Lawrence and Linda Price (1987), "The Market Maven: A Diffuser of Marketplace Information," *Journal of Marketing*, 51 (January), 83-98.

Flynn, Leisa.R and Ronald E Goldsmith (1994), "Opinion Leadership in Green Consumption: An Exploratory Study," *Journal of Social Behavior and Personality*, 9(3), 543-553.

Flynn, Leisa.R and Ronald E Goldsmith (1999), "A Short, Reliable Measure of Subjective Knowledge," *Journal of Business Research*, 46, 57-66.

Fornell, Claes, and J Cha (1994), "Partial Least Squares," in ed. R. P. Bagozzi, *Advanced Methods of Marketing Research*, Oxford: Basil Blackwell Ltd.

Fornell, Claes., and David P Larcker (1981), "Structural Equation Models with Unobservable Variables and Measurement Errors," *Journal of Marketing Research*, 18(2), 39-50.

Gilly, M, J Graham, M Wolfinbarger and L Yale (1998), "A Dyadic Study of Interpersonal Information Search," *Journal of the Academy of Marketing Science*, 26(2), 83-100.

Igbaria, M, N Zinatelli, P Cragg and A Cavaye (1997), "Personal Computing Acceptance Factors in Small Firms: A Structural Equation Model," *MIS Quarterly* (September), 279-302.

Klugman J (1999), "Social and Economic Policiesto Prevent Complex Humanitarian Emergencies: Lessons from Experience," A Policy Brief, *United Nations University World Institute for Development Economics Research* (UNU/WIDER), A Research and Training Centre of the United Nations University, Katajanokanlaituri 6 B,00I60 Helsinki, Finland.

Kotler, Philip and Neil, Kotler (1981), "Business marketing for political candidates," *Campaigns and Elections* (Summer), 24-33.

Kuusela, H, M Spence and A Kanto (1998), "Expertise Effects on Pre-choice Decision Processes and Final Outcomes A Protocol Analysis," *European Journal of Marketing*, 3/2(5/6), 559-576.

Laroche, M, C Kim and L Zhou (1996), "Brand Familiarity and Confidence as Determinants of Purchase Intention: An Empirical Test in a Multiple Brand Context," *Journal of Business Research*, 37, 115-120.

Lazarfeld, P, B Berelson and H Gaudet (1948), *The People's Choice*, New York: Columbia University Press.

Leonard-Barton, Dorothy (1985), "Experts as negative Opinion Leaders in the Diffusion of Technological Innovation," *Journal of Consumer Research*, 11 (March), 914-926.

Lohmoeller, Jan-Bernard (1989), *Latent Variable Modelling with Partial Least Square*, Heidelberg: Physica-Verlag.

Mittal, Banwari (1988),."Measuring purchase decision involvement," *Psychology and Marketing*, 6, 157-162.

Mittal, Banwari (1989), "Must consumer involvement always imply more information search?" in *Advances in Consumer Research*, 16, 167-172.

Mittal, B (1995), "A comparative analysis of four scales of consumer involvement," *Psychology and Marketing*, 12(7) (October), 663-682.

Mittal, Banwari and W Lassar (1998), "Why do customers switch? The dynamics of satisfaction versus loyalty," *Journal of Services Marketing*, 12(3), 177-194.

Mittal, Banwari and Myung-Soo Lee (1989), "A causal model of consumer involvement," *Journal of Economic Psychology*, 10, 363-389.

Myers, James H and Thomas S Robertson (1972), "Dimensions of Opinion Leadership," *Journal of Marketing Research*, 9 (February), 41-46.

Nataraajan, Rajan and A Madhukar (1997), "Perceived Control in Consumer Choice: A Closer Look," in *European Advances in Consumer Research*, 3, 288-292.

Newman, Bruce (1999), "A Predictive Model of Voter Behavior: The Repositioning of Bill Clinton," in *Handbook of Political Marketing*, ed. Bruce Newman, Sage Publications, 259-282.

Newman, Bruce (1985), "An Historical Review of the Voter as a Consumer," in *Proceedings of the Association For Consumer Research International meeting*, Singapore, eds. Tan, C and J Sheth, 257-261.

Newman, Bruce and J Sheth (1984), "The gender Gap in Voter Attitudes and Behavior: Some Advertising Implications," *Journal of Advertising*, 13(3), 4-16.

Newman, Bruce and Jagdish, Sheth (1985), "A Model of Primary Voter Behavior," *Journal of Consumer Research*, 12, 178-187.

O'Cass, Aron (2000), "An assessment of consumers product, purchase decision, advertising and consumption involvement in fashion clothing," *Journal of Economic Psychology*, 21, 545-576.

O'Cass, Aron (2002a), "Political Advertising Believability and Information Source Value During Elections," *Journal of Advertising*, XXXI (1), 63-74.

O'Cass, Aron (2002b), "A Micro-Model of Voter choice: Understanding the Dynamics of Australian Voter Characteristics in a Federal By-Election," *Psychology and Marketing*, 19(12), 1025-1046.

Oliver, Richard. L (1997), *Satisfaction: A Behavioral Prospective on the Consumer*, Boston: The McGraw-Hill Companies Inc.

Omura, G and W Talarzyk (1983), "Shaping Public Opinion: Personal Sources of Information on a Major Political Issue," in *Advances in Consumer Research*, 10, 484-489.

Park, C and P Lessig (1981), "Familiarity and Its Impact on Consumer Decision Biases and heuristics," *Journal of Consumer Research*, 8 (September), 223-230.

Park, C, D Mothersbaugh and L Feick (1994), Consumer Knowledge Assessment. *Journal of Consumer Research*, 21 (June), 71-82.

Reynolds, Fred and William Darden (1971), "Mutually Adaptive Effects of Interpersonal Influence," *Journal of Marketing Research*, 8 (November), 449-454.

Richins, Marsha and Peter Bloch (1991), "Post-Purchase Product satisfaction: Incorporating the Effects of Involvement and Time," *Journal of Business Research*, 23, 145-158.

Richins, Marsha and Teri Root-Shaffer (1988), "The Role of Involvement and Opinion Leadership in Consumer Word-of-Mouth: An Implicit Model Made Explicit," in *Advances in Consumer Research*, 15, 32-36.

Robertson, T and J Myers (1969), "Personality Correlates of Opinion Leadership and Innovative Buying behavior," *Journal of Marketing Research*, 6 (May), 164-168.

Rothschild, Michael (1978), "Political Advertising: A Neglected Policy Issue in Marketing," *Journal of Marketing Research*, 15, 58-71.

Rothschild, Michael and Michael Houston, (1980), "Individual Differences in Voting Behavior: Further Investigations of Involvement," in *Advances in Consumer Research*, Vol. 7, ed. J Olson, 655-658.

Shama, A (1973), "Applications of marketing concepts to candidate marketing," Proceedings of the fourth Conference of the Association for Consumer Research, 793-801.

Smith, M and M Carsky, (1996), "Grocery Shopping Behavior," *Journal of Retailing and Consumer Services*, 3(2), 73-80.

Swinyard, William and Kenneth Coney (1978), "Promotional effects on a High Versus Low Involvement Electorate," *Journal of Consumer Research*, 5, 41-48.

Venkatraman, M (1990), "Opinion Leadership, Enduring Involvement and Characteristics of Opinion Leaders: A Moderating or Mediating Relationship?" in *Advances in Consumer Research*, 17, 60-67.

Zinkhan, George and A Muderrisoglu (1985), "Involvement, Familiarity, Cognitive Differentiation, and Advertising Recall: A Test of Convergent and Discriminant Validity," in *Advances in Consumer Research*, 12, 356-361.

Index

Order a copy of this book with this form or online at:
http://www.haworthpress.com/store/product.asp?sku=5442

Current Issues in Political Marketing

____ in softbound at $34.95 ISBN-13: 978-0-7890-2438-1 / ISBN-10: 0-7890-2438-1.
____ in hardbound at $59.95 ISBN-13: 978-0-7890-2437-4 / ISBN-10: 0-7890-2437-3.

COST OF BOOKS _____

POSTAGE & HANDLING _____
US: $4.00 for first book & $1.50
for each additional book
Outside US: $5.00 for first book
& $2.00 for each additional book.

SUBTOTAL _____

In Canada: add 7% GST. _____

STATE TAX _____
CA, IL, IN, MN, NJ, NY, OH, PA & SD residents
please add appropriate local sales tax.

FINAL TOTAL _____
If paying in Canadian funds, convert
using the current exchange rate,
UNESCO coupons welcome.

BILL ME LATER:
Bill-me option is good on US/Canada/
Mexico orders only; not good to jobbers,
wholesalers, or subscription agencies.

Signature _____

Payment Enclosed: $ _____

PLEASE CHARGE TO MY CREDIT CARD:

Visa   MasterCard   AmEx   Discover
Diner's Club   Eurocard   JCB

Account # _____

Exp Date _____

Signature _____
(Prices in US dollars and subject to change without notice.)

Name		
Address		
City	State/Province	Zip/Postal Code
Country		
Tel	Fax	
E-Mail		

May we use your e-mail address for confirmations and other types of information? Yes   No We appreciate receiving
your e-mail address. Haworth would like to e-mail special discount offers to you, as a preferred customer.
We will never share, rent, or exchange your e-mail address.   We regard such actions as an invasion of your privacy.

Order from your local bookstore   or directly from
The Haworth Press, Inc.   10 Alice Street, Binghamton, New York 13904-1580 • USA
Call our toll-free number (1-800-429-6784) / Outside US/Canada: (607) 722-5857
Fax: 1-800-895-0582 / Outside US/Canada: (607) 771-0012
E-mail your order to us: orders@haworthpress.com

For orders outside US and Canada,   you may wish to order through your local
sales representative, distributor, or bookseller.
For information, see http://haworthpress.com/distributors

(Discounts are available for individual orders in US and Canada only, not booksellers/distributors.)

Please photocopy this form for your personal use.
www.HaworthPress.com

BOF05